MW01156481

Terror and Its Discontents

Terror and Its Discontents

Suspect Words in Revolutionary France

Caroline Weber

University of Minnesota Press
Minneapolis
London

Copyright 2003 by the Regents of the University of Minnesota

All rights reserved. No part of this publication may be reproduced, stored in
a retrieval system, or transmitted, in any form or by any means, electronic,
mechanical, photocopying, recording, or otherwise, without the prior written
permission of the publisher.

Published by the University of Minnesota Press
111 Third Avenue South, Suite 290
Minneapolis, MN 55401-2520
http://www.upress.umn.edu

Library of Congress Cataloging-in-Publication Data

Weber, Caroline, 1969–
    Terror and its discontents : suspect words in revolutionary
France / Caroline Weber.
        p.   cm.
    Includes bibliographical references and index.
    ISBN 0-8166-3886-1 (alk. paper) — ISBN 0-8166-3887-X (pbk. :
alk. paper)
    1. France—History—Reign of Terror, 1793–1794.   2. French
language—18th century—Political aspects—France.   3. France—
History—Revolution, 1789–1799—Language.   4. Revolutionaries—
France—Language.   I. Title.
DC183.5.W43 2003
944.04'4—dc21   2002011940

Printed in the United States of America on acid-free paper

The University of Minnesota is an equal-opportunity educator and employer.

12 11 10 09 08 07 06 05 04 03   10 9 8 7 6 5 4 3 2 1

Les mots, comme les choses, ont été des monstruosités.

—Jean-François Laharpe,
Du Fanatisme dans la langue révolutionnaire

Autre chose... ce me semble que l'épars frémissement d'une page ne veuille sinon surseoir ou palpite d'impatience, à la possibilité d'autre chose.

—Stéphane Mallarmé, "La Musique et les lettres"

Contents

Acknowledgments

At its best, the republican ideal envisioned by Jean-Jacques Rousseau and the leaders of the French Revolution involved a blissfully collective view of human interaction: the small-minded and selfish *I* giving way, in the name of national interest, to a transcendent, harmoniously functioning *we*. Without wishing to ascribe to my own book any of the tyrannical possibilities this model often implied, I must nevertheless emphasize that *Terror and Its Discontents* has been the work of many, and I owe a great debt of gratitude to the numerous interlocutors who helped me bring it to completion. In attempting to articulate this debt, I find myself face to face with another hallmark Terrorist concern, which is the inadequacy of language, a medium whose notoriously fragmentary and difference-ridden character makes all-inclusive expression more or less impossible. Apologies in advance, then, to those friends, colleagues, and mentors whose names appear here as merely partial, regrettably imperfect testimonies to their generous contributions.

First, I would like to thank the people and institutions that nurtured this project at its inception. To my inspiring early-stage advisers, Peter Brooks and Denis Hollier, and incisive first readers, Christopher Miller and Debarati Sanyal, I am particularly grateful; as a fledgling scholar I could not have asked for more knowledgeable and rigorous guidance. This I received as well in a classroom capacity from Claudine Kahan, who first introduced me to much of the material examined herein and whose pedagogical brilliance encouraged me to study the Terror in greater depth, and more informally from Philippe Roger, who kindly agreed to sponsor me during my study in France. I am thankful to the French-American Foundation and the École normale supérieure for providing me, respectively, with the financial and academic means to conduct critical research in Paris in 1997–98, and to the Yale University Department of French for awarding me a modest but helpful book prize in 1999.

In more recent years, I have benefited enormously from exchanges with my colleagues at the University of Pennsylvania. Joan DeJean, Jean-Michel Rabaté, and Maurie Samuels were kind enough to read and comment on various iterations of the manuscript, thereby enabling me to refine it in significant ways, and Kevin Brownlee made some astute observations at an oral presentation I gave on Rousseau in the spring of 2000. It is no exaggeration to say that without the sage counsel of Liliane Weissberg and Jerry Singerman, I might not have found such a welcoming home for my book as the University of Minnesota Press has proven to be. I am extremely appreciative of Doug Armato's willingness to take on the project, his infinite editorial wisdom, and his indefatigable good humor. The contributions of Robin Whitaker, my copy editor, were truly invaluable. Thanks also to Gretchen Asmussen and Eric Lundgren at the Press for their patience and hard work and to the two outside readers who reviewed my work on Minnesota's behalf. One of these reviewers, Marie-Hélène Huet, has long been one of my idols in the field of French eighteenth-century studies, and I feel fortunate to have received her expert feedback (and her vote of confidence) before revising my manuscript for publication. One of my primary goals for this book is that it not fall too short of what she magnanimously deemed to be its promise. Although originally wary of my attempt to combine historical and literary analysis, I hope that my second, anonymous reader will note the changes, in the pages to follow, reflective of my engagement with his or her many incisive suggestions.

A few more people remain to be acknowledged, no less important, though several of these individuals are not connected to my scholarship in direct institutional ways. Karl Britto, Elaine Freedgood, Noah Guynn, and Susan Weiner offered me helpful insights derived from their own academic pursuits, while other friends, Anne Farrar, Eve Herzog, Sheryl Sandberg, Valerie Schweitzer, Tayibe Gulek, and Stephen Kenneally, provided me with unflagging emotional support even at times when I probably didn't deserve it. The same holds true in spades for my parents and brother, whose love has sustained me in scholarly and extracurricular struggles alike, and in whom I am exceedingly blessed. It is to them and to Tom Stegeman, my fiancé, my best friend, and all-around favorite person, that this book is dedicated.

PROLOGUE

The Revolution Is Frozen

> The Revolution is frozen. . . . That which brings about the general good is always terrible.
> —Louis-Antoine Saint-Just, *Fragments d'institutions républicaines*

> Only the writer was supposed to be executed, but it is the man whose head has been cut off.
> —Jean Paulhan, *Les Fleurs de Tarbes ou la Terreur dans les lettres*

What does it mean to be frozen with terror? Camille Desmoulins, a journalist writing under the Montagnard regime of 1793–94, once remarked that France's new order had replaced "the language of democracy" with "the cold poison of fear, which paralyze[d] thought in the bottom of people's souls, and prevent[ed] it from pouring forth at the tribunal, or in writing."[1] This formulation is a suggestive one, in that it links the constrictive policies of the Montagnard government, collectively known as the Reign of Terror, to a paralysis of thought and language. Desmoulins knew what he was talking about: under the leadership of his one-time friend Maximilien Robespierre, the grand ideals of the Revolution had transmuted into a rigid and unforgiving "despotism of liberty."[2] At the dawn of the French republic, when formidable destabilizing forces threatened the nation from within and without, the politicians who governed the country were concerned above all with rallying their constituents uniformly around the revolutionary cause. In this context, individual liberties, including the freedom of expression, were construed as subordinate to and even at odds with the all-important general will.[3]

This unifying principle, drawn from the pages of Rousseau's *Social Contract*, held that all intersubjective differences, all personal opinions and desires, had to be sacrificed on the altar of the common interest: freedom in such a schema meant the equal and selfless devotion of all citizens to the revolutionary cause. That which brings about the greater good is therefore terrible, as the epigraph from Robespierre's right-hand man Saint-Just indicates, because it necessarily freezes or stultifies anything that fails to operate, like Kant's categorical imperative, in the same way for all people at all times.[4] But writing and self-expression, to return to Desmoulins's chief area of concern, tend by their very nature to resist such radical generality—a fact that may now appear little more than a bland poststructuralist truism, but that provoked the utmost anxiety among the founders of the first French republic. Consistently urging their countrymen not to become "the dupes of words" or let their patriotism be "degraded in discourse,"[5] Robespierre and Saint-Just were painfully aware of the capacity of language to mean something other than what it appeared to say, to signify differently to different people, to mutate over time and space, to undo rather than to secure a fusion between word and referent.[6] Whereas Desmoulins's ideal "language of democracy" fostered the proliferation of all points of view, even those not readily assimilated into the common good, Montagnard ideology demanded a strict embargo on discursive difference, for "any alternative meaning would imply the annihilation of the Revolution" itself.[7] And so, Laurent Jenny writes of the Robespierrists' predicament, "hostile to [their] own words, [they] entered into the age of violence and fury."[8]

Indeed, it is well known that Robespierre and his henchmen relied far too heavily on the guillotine to protect and solidify what they termed their "republic one and indivisible"—whence Desmoulins's allusion to the overwhelming fear with which they incapacitated their compatriots in the process.[9] Subsequent commentators on the Reign of Terror have accordingly, and appropriately, placed considerable emphasis on the suffering and destruction it perpetrated upon citizens' bodies. Less frequently discussed, however, are the serious infringements it imposed upon citizens' expressive faculties—the speech and writing Desmoulins so perceptively qualified as frozen under Robespierrist rule. It is this often overlooked but significant aspect of the Terrorist phenomenon that Jean Paulhan highlights when, analyzing a range of later French avant-garde authors and critics united in their marked ambivalence toward

language, he describes his subjects' collective attitude as "Terror in literature" *(la Terreur dans les lettres)*.[10] Although neither Paulhan's study nor
Laurent Jenny's response to it, *La Terreur et les signes,* discusses the historical Terror at length, both works identify a paradoxical brand of anti-
poetics in which "every word becomes suspect" for its potential to out-
strip authorial intention and control.[11] Not coincidentally, Robespierre
and his colleagues effected in their own texts something of this very
kind as they labored to solidify the new state in word as in deed. To the
extent that politics, as Keith Michael Baker has convincingly argued, is
by definition a discursive affair,[12] the Montagnards could hardly content
themselves with deploring the slippery properties of written and spoken
media; they had to develop an idiom in which to formulate goals and
communicate policies. The pressure to do so was heightened by the overthrow of France's thirteen-hundred-year-old monarchy in August 1792
and by the attendant demise of Catholicism; these changes left the revolutionaries little choice but to create a new set of signifiers through
which the people might thenceforth filter all social, political, and moral
experience.[13] The challenge faced by the Montagnard revolutionaries
was thus to devise a language that would promote unifying doctrine
and abstract patriotism while keeping expressions of divisive heterogeneity at bay. In drafting the countless speeches, tracts, and legislative
proposals that constituted their daily labor, Robespierre and his associates endeavored to proceed, as Paulhan remarks of "his" Terrorist writers, as if they were not writers at all.[14]

As it so happens, the Robespierrists' effort to formulate a political
program without opening the Pandora's box of discursive difference finds
a close approximation in the theories of the sublime that dominated
European aesthetics at the end of the eighteenth century. Longinus's
classical treatise on the subject, newly influential in continental circles
thanks to Boileau's recent and lively French translation, presented the
sublime as a form of artistic expression that disguised or undermined its
own artistry. Immanuel Kant took this idea and, with characteristic
rigor, made it his own, postulating a complex, self-effacing aesthetic
that subsequent scholars came to qualify as "negative presentation" because of its radical abandonment of conventional linguistic properties.[15]
As Marie-Hélène Huet has demonstrated in her groundbreaking investigation of Terrorist politics and poetics, the paradoxically antidiscursive
discourse of the Kantian sublime was in many ways the guiding light of

the Terror itself[16]—"a torch blazing in a tomb," in Saint-Just's memorable parlance.[17] The deathly connotations of this metaphor are not in the least bit incidental to Huet's analysis, or to my own. Locating analogues for the Robespierrists' antirepresentational bias not just in Kant's aesthetics but in Rousseau's political philosophy, Huet shows how the "revolutionary sublime" called for the violent eradication of anything short of pure, generalizable abstraction.[18] Rousseau himself was of course famously averse to the mediating "obstacles" that language's polyvalent possibilities interposed between himself and his interlocutors and readers, not to mention between one voice in his head ("Rousseau") and another ("Jean-Jacques").[19] For the political party that emerged around Robespierre—in his own estimation the *philosophe*'s greatest admirer—mediation and particularity achieved the status of sworn enemies of the republic. Even if they manifested themselves "only" in speech, elements like these stood to engender division in a state struggling above all to maintain its indivisibility against a host of internal and external foes. Because they enacted or gestured toward deeper political and philosophical discord, the differential aspects of language were put to death in the ruthlessly universalizing pronouncements of the Terror.

If, however, Saint-Just's figure of a lamp in a tomb is of relevance here, this is not simply because it calls attention to the brutal, often deadly treatment to which he and his colleagues subjected difference and dissent. To be sure, my analysis of Robespierrist political discourse, like Huet's, aims to highlight the severe restrictions that the group placed on any utterance held to disrupt the government's universalizing, homogenizing agenda. At the same time, though, my work expands upon Huet's findings by emphasizing that the language so virulently suppressed by the Terror did not remain definitively silenced. A glow lingered in the tomb where the Montagnards labored to inter discursive particularity and variety—and that glow signaled these repressed elements' refusal to accept defeat. From Antigone's brother to Hamlet's father to Michael Kohlhaas's horses, the great corpses of the Western literary canon have given voice to profound discontent, calling attention to and railing against the injustices that drove them to the grave. Similarly, expressions of difference found their way into language notwithstanding the vigilant censorship that Robespierre and his cohorts exercised on the new state's speaking subjects. At times, such expressions even returned to haunt the Terrorists' own sublimely general assertions about the will of the people, the good of the republic, the universal verities of the Revolution, and the like. When read in its full context, Saint-Just's above-cited simile itself attests to this phenomenon. "The truth," he declared axiomatically, "burns in silence in the hearts of men, like a torch blazing in a tomb." Although this proclamation has patently gnomic pretensions, identifying an abstract property (truth) of a universal category (men), the figure of speech with which it concludes conveys a message of another sort entirely. To state that the truth is like a torch is in effect to concede that it is not "like" itself, that it can function as something other than what it presumably is. As such, it ceases to stand as a transcendental value that everyone can reliably be expected to construe in the same way.[20] Instead, to use one of Desmoulins's favorite terms, it turns into a "relative truth"[21]—inevitably prone to comparisons, interpretations, and other mediating filters capable of engendering substantial intersubjective differences in a community. Similarly, the very word *Terror*, with which the Montagnards labeled their vigorous efforts to unify and homogenize republican discourse, is inhabited by an underlying split or discrepancy. Technically speaking, *Terror* is after all a catachresis: an expression founded in a metaphor (the program known as Terror is "like" psychological terror in that both phenomena, as Desmoulins suggests, have something to do with fear) but lacking a "literal" counterpart (there is no alternative word for the Robespierrists' enterprise).[22] In its rhetorical essence, the term *Terror* thus attests to the impossibility of maintaining strict boundaries between figurative and literal reference, between otherness and sameness, between multiplicity (the Terror is comparable to something else) and unity (the Terror is equivalent only to itself and brooks no difference). In this sense, "Terror" joins Saint-Just's figuratively rendered idea of truth in contravening the Robespierrist project of eradicating differential speech in the polity. Although Robespierre himself dismissed linguistic mutations of this kind as "perversity aim[ed] at confounding contrary meanings,"[23] it is my hope that a close examination of language's divisive qualities and destabilizing possibilities will shed new light in the seemingly monolithic tomb of Terrorist rhetoric, by revealing how its meanings became confounded in their very articulation. Inadvertently pointing in this very direction, Saint-Just proffered another vexed truism: "All stones are cut to build the structure of freedom; you can build a palace or a tomb out of the same stones."[24]

Perhaps the most ambiguous and two-faced term in the Terrorist lexicon, as deployed in the political writings of Rousseau and the Montagnards, is *totality,* oneness, the "all." As I argue in the first two chapters of
this book, although the social contract envisioned by the Swiss *philosophe*
and his revolutionary admirers was supposed to be an arena in which
"all voices [were] counted,"[25] this concept of discursive totality depended
on some very significant exclusions. In its pretensions to protosublime
transcendence, such a social pact militated strongly, as I have just noted,
against linguistic and interpretive discrepancies among its constitutive
members. But discrepancies of this kind were not the only casualties of
Terrorist wholeness. Rousseau, Robespierre, and Saint-Just all conceived
of discursive and hermeneutic variation as homologous, related, and/or
conducive to other forms of unacceptable difference, which they also
militantly condemned. Meditating on the philosophical import of the
Terror, Maurice Blanchot describes it as a phenomenon that ensured
homogeneity and totality in the republic by stifling in its citizens every
private store of resistance, reserve, and feeling. In a Terrorist society,
Blanchot observes, "virtue" means the repression or elimination of the
individual's "obliqueness" and "intimacy"[26]—his or her subjective desires and nongeneralizable penchants—in the interests of the state's
collectivist enterprise. (A passion for one specific lover, for example,
must be renounced insofar as it detracts from the abstract "fraternal"
love with which a citizen should embrace all his or her compatriots.)
The vocabulary of the eighteenth century rendered Blanchot's "obliqueness" and "intimacy" as "passions" and "sensitivity" *(sensibilité),* which
were identified principally with women in the era's sociopolitical and
literary imaginary.[27] Largely as a result of this association, though the
Terrorist "whole" suppressed individual biases and attachments across
the board, it construed women as prime harbingers of such sentiments
and so attacked them with particular vehemence. In Rousseau's ideal
polity and in the Robespierrists' republic, the "right to say everything,"
as Sade ironically dubbed it, was drastically curtailed for those speaking
subjects perceived to harbor "effeminate" (because anticommunitarian)
inclinations and interests.

Confronting this series of exclusions, my goal in this book is thus to
examine the multiple discursive structures to which the Terror's rhetoric
of oneness gave rise and in which the stated objective of unilateral freedom was, at the level of language as in other critical respects, not infre-

quently undercut. As compelling an insight as I believe this to be, I can nonetheless hardly claim to be alone in detecting such substantial internal contradictions in the articulation of Terrorist ideology. On perhaps the most obvious level, I am referring here to authors like Jacques André, Keith Michael Baker, Antoine de Baecque, Marc-Éli Blanchard, Albert Camus, and Lynn Hunt: scholars who have explored a host of textual and visual material to reveal the limitations and mystifications inherent in the Robespierrist project. On another level, however, I am alluding to two individuals who participated directly in Montagnard politics in the early 1790s, but who retreated from revolutionary orthodoxy once it transformed liberty, equality, and fraternity into the despotism of liberty, equality before the guillotine's blade, and—to cite that chillingly revelatory Terrorist motto—"fraternity or death." These individuals are Camille Desmoulins, the dissident journalist to whom I have already alluded, and the Marquis de Sade, who doubtless requires no introduction. Desmoulins, to my knowledge, has received virtually no attention from literary critics, whereas Sade has perhaps been the subject of overly much academic debate in recent years. Nevertheless, the two writers found substantial common ground in the sophisticated, well-informed, and daring criticisms they leveled against the Terror's restrictions on free speech. Desmoulins challenged Robespierrist dogma by envisioning a polity in which clemency and sentiment, a tolerance for human diversity, and truly unfettered self-expression, with all its antagonistic and disruptive potential, would flourish. For his part, Sade imagined a parodically inverted republic of debauchery, where words such as *freedom* and *virtue* (the building blocks of Saint-Just's proverbial palace) blatantly transmute into *oppression* and *crime* (the stones of the countervailing tomb) and where feminine sentimentality is annihilated for the sake of libertine unity. Like the renowned pair of Sadean sisters, good-hearted Justine and ruthless Juliette, the political alternatives posed by Desmoulins and Sade supplement one another in subversively reconfiguring the era's dominant political doctrine and exposing its most significant flaws. Additionally, they represent an important addendum to the analysis of Terrorist discourse provided in the first half of this book; for they give ample and eloquent voice to the discontents that Rousseauist and Robespierrist political thought tends only to acknowledge under erasure or under duress.

In devoting more or less equal attention to the Terror's most influential spokesmen and its most astute critics, my book as a whole thus endeavors to give a balanced (if not totalizing) account of how this discursive phenomenon operates in what Freud would call both its manifest and its latent dimensions. Although my approach is not a psychoanalytic one, my coterminous reading of the "Terror *and* its discontents" does rest on the fundamental insight that "the repressed is, by definition, always in the process of returning,"[28] that what the Terror confines to unspeakable darkness may well figure forth its most illuminating truths. To suppress difference or to revel in it, to institute a universalizing discourse or to explode it: the very use of language to which all of the authors studied here—not to mention all of us—are condemned involves a constant oscillation between these polarized extremes. At bottom, it is in its own structural openness to interpretation, division, and deformation that the rhetoric of the Terror, in spite of its practitioners, enables the critiques that expose, enact, and reconfigure its apparent suppressions. In this regard, I hope to substantiate my hypothesis that what Roland Barthes has dubbed "the absolutely Terrorist character of language,"[29] along with Jürgen Habermas's model of a community founded on universal, transparent, "unbroken" communication,[30] are themselves variations on a persistent Terrorist fiction. "Absolutely Terrorist" discourse and "unbroken" communication designate, in short, a fantasy of a world where political and semiotic theory coincides perfectly with its practice, where discursive totality is thought to be achieved because no difference is tolerated in the interrelated arenas of self-expression and "reality." One does not have to entertain particularly cynical notions about past or contemporary political experience to conclude that such a fantasy is woefully utopian. But then again, after a fashion, so was the Reign of Terror. Therefore, instead of dismissing with the relative clarity of hindsight our Terrorist authors' flawed attempts to "say everything," I strive rather to give these efforts their due as illustrative both of the seemingly "Terrorist character of language" and of its sometimes salutary transformation into its opposite.

Finally, one caveat about method. Despite the clearly historical nature of its subject matter, this book does not purport to be a work of or about history properly speaking. As the foregoing pages have in all likelihood already revealed, my training is that of a literary scholar, and my principal concern is the functioning of language. In broaching this notoriously slippery subject, I avail myself of the relatively heterodox combination of discourses—philosophy, psychoanalysis, and poststructural theory as well as "history" and "literature"—that have made my profession the bane of some readers and (speaking for myself, at least) the pleasure of others. However, my intention in submitting the rhetoric of the Terror to such a treatment is by no means to deemphasize its historical import. On the contrary, my objective in marshaling all these approaches is to show how language constituted itself as such a formidable, but also such a vexed, political force in the revolutionary period. "Terror," conceded none other than Saint-Just, in one of his more self-consciously nuanced generalizations, "is a double-edged sword, used by some to serve the people and by others to serve tyranny."[31] By turns liberating and tyrannical, the double-edged strategies of the Terror are certainly a fact of history. But they are also a fact of language—which, like the love evoked at the end of W. H. Auden's poem "Law Like Love," seldom keeps its promises, even to the most admirable and sacrosanct of abstract principles.

CHAPTER ONE

Rousseau's "Contradiction of Words"

Sublime Totality and the Social Pact

> If there were no differing interests, common interest would scarcely make itself felt, because it would never encounter any obstacles: everything would proceed directly from itself, and politics would cease to be an art.
>
> —Jean-Jacques Rousseau, *The Social Contract*

> Not everything is presented.
>
> —Philippe Lacoue-Labarthe, "Sublime Truth"

At the core of *The Social Contract* lies the tenet that civic virtue derives from categorical obedience to the general will. The constitution of a truly egalitarian society, Jean-Jacques Rousseau maintains throughout his 1762 treatise, requires each citizen to submit willingly and utterly to the dictates of communal harmony. Such conformity often demands the suppression of personal interests and instincts that could undermine the greater good—interests and instincts that Immanuel Kant, envisioning a categorical imperative of his own some twenty years after the publication of Rousseau's tract, would term, provocatively linking non-generalizable pathos with moral sickness, "pathological." Similarly, Rousseau equates the elimination of private penchants with the triumph of sound, collectively determined moral principles—principles from which the ideal state should spring: "Do you want the general will to be accomplished? If so, make sure that all the particular wills conform to it; and since virtue is nothing other than this conformity of the particular to the general will, to put it another way, let virtue reign."[1]

Despite the sacrifices that such virtue demands (for Rousseau, we shall soon observe, makes no secret of the vexed position individual desires occupy in his polity), the author of *The Social Contract* stresses the radical plenitude that the ethic of self-restricting citizenship makes possible. Describing the process of self-abnegation that occurs as men give up their potentially disruptive, selfish impulses for the sake of political harmony, he concludes on a note of triumph: "The alienation is without reserve [sans réserve], the union is as perfect as it can be, and no individual associate has anything left to demand [nul associé n'a plus rien à réclamer]."[2] The vocabulary of union and perfection—the latter etymologically suggesting thoroughness or wholeness—works here to emphasize the annihilation of difference evoked by phrases like "without reserve" and "[no]thing left to demand" (the negative language of the expression is much stronger in the French original: "*nul* associé *n'a plus rien* à réclamer"). Although it is founded on an originary alienation, on the negation of private reservations and demands, the Rousseauist polity is presented here as a world without difference.

This conception of the state is significant in several ways. On the most general level, it bespeaks an elimination of heterogeneity under the social contract. Having given himself over entirely to the community, no citizen withholds a private store of individual resistance ("reserve") that could detract from the perfect universality of the general will. More specifically, this statement has profound implications for the position of language in Rousseau's republic. For as it has become a commonplace of contemporary literary theory to observe, and as the *philosophe* himself demonstrates quite clearly in his theoretical writings on language (of which more later), heterogeneity and difference are constitutive features of linguistic expression.[3] By dint of its homogenizing or totalizing nature, then, the discourse of civic goodness would logically appear to eradicate the need for language as such.[4] Rousseau postulates that once alienated from his anterior mode of being, the citizen has nothing left to ask for, nothing left to protest (these being the two slightly different senses of Rousseau's original term *réclamer*). The converse implication would seem to be that, without the intervention of the social pact, the individual remains bogged down in the experience of need and a disposition toward dissidence. As a paradoxical consequence of this state of affairs, the social contract—itself a form of alienation or mediation—serves to do away with constructs of a structurally antiso-cial, patently linguistic variety.

This paradox opens up three principal lines of questioning. First, why does a certain kind of discursive difference prove inadmissible in Rousseau's republic of virtue, and how does the author effect its elimi-nation? Second, how does Rousseau distinguish between mediations that stand to unify the polity and those that threaten to disintegrate it? Why and how does the passage from brute nature to socialized culture also bring about a transition from a "bad" representation (the acknowl-edgment of lack or imperfection inherent in any avowal of need or dis-sent) to a "good" one (the artificial construction of an alienating gen-eral will)? And what, finally, is at stake in Rousseau's attempt to stage such a shift? Politically, philosophically, and aesthetically speaking, what are the implications of the idea that the Rousseauist polity cannot or will not accommodate certain forms of alterity? In the pages that fol-low, I pursue this vein of inquiry through a fine-grained examination of Rousseau's political musings and especially of *The Social Contract*, which constitutes his most sustained and, in the eighteenth century as in the twenty-first, best-known meditation on the problem of ideal commu-nity formation.[5] My approach highlights the reliance of Rousseauist po-litical virtue upon *(a)* the systematic suppression of discourses of polit-ical, ontological, and linguistic difference; *(b)* the privileging, and the equation, of political generality and linguistic transparency; and *(c)* the self-conscious dissimulation of the opaque, fictitious, and mediated un-derpinnings of his own formulations of the general will. Taken together, these three aspects of the *philosophe*'s social contract theory constitute what I describe throughout this chapter and this book as a politics and a poetics of Terror. By a Terrorist program, I mean one that, on the civic and the linguistic level alike and often with oppressive consequences, seeks to efface all difference for the sake of absolute stability and con-trol. As we shall also see, though, because of the unavoidable instabili-ties of his written medium, the textual implementation of such a pro-gram proves for the author to be a far cry from its theoretical exposition. Toward the end of the chapter, I therefore shift my focus from Rousseau's general notion of what a polity should be to the tensions that exist be-tween Terrorist theory and writerly practice in his own texts. I will con-clude by showing how, despite his own sensitivity to these tensions, he attempts to negate them when he transposes his theoretical musings into the realm of fiction in *Le Lévite d'Éphraïm*, a short piece of prose narrative that he wrote shortly after the publication of *The Social Contract*. With the fictional text, the totalizing and repressive aspects of Rousseau's political theory assume an explicitly gendered dimension. Coding as feminine those impulses (personal, political, linguistic) that threaten the homogeneity of the body politic, and narrating the triumph of virile communitarianism over womanly particularity, *Le Lévite d'Éphraïm* paves the way for the gender-based suppressions performed in earnest under the Reign of Terror and with graphic, ironic gusto by the Marquis de Sade.

The Silence of the Passions

Written eight years before *The Social Contract, The Discourse on the Origin and the Foundations of Inequality among Men* elaborates an opposition that structures virtually all Rousseauist political thought: the antinomy between natural and civil man. Also known as *The Second Discourse*, the study on inequality was composed as a sort of follow-up to *The Discourse on the Sciences and the Arts*, which launched its author to fame and fortune in 1750 by expressing the view—practically unheard of in the Age of Enlightenment—that the arts and sciences did more to impoverish than to improve man's lot.[6] *The Second Discourse* continues in this vein by juxtaposing accounts of natural and unnatural human conditions and privileging the former in no uncertain terms. In a state of nature, Rousseau argues in this text, man subsists as best he can, preoccupied solely with his own survival and concerning himself not at all with his fellows. As a result, apart from the natural differences (in size, strength, gender) with which each individual is endowed from birth, all men in this state enjoy what Rousseau considers to be a "rigorous equality":[7] they know neither rich nor poor, *I* nor *thou*, just nor unjust, good nor evil. Only when their inborn differences lead them to fraternize with one another—a small man's self-interest leads him to cultivate the protection of a large man, and so on—does inequality arise. Once they band together and begin to "attach importance to the rest of the world" instead of "living within [themselves]" (*Second* 136), individuals come to institutionalize the characteristics that distinguish them. The strong, the clever, the beautiful—all socially constructed and relative qualities—soon take inexorable precedence over their negative counterparts. Significantly, and we shall return to this point later on in the chapter, Rousseau highlights the linguistically mediated nature of this shift: "Those relationships which we express by the words 'large,' 'small,' 'strong,' 'weak,' 'fast,' 'slow,' . . . and other similar ideas, compared when necessary and almost unthinkingly, eventually produce in [men] some kind of reflection" leading to the entrenchment of oppositional or differential principles (*Second* 110). Classes form, prejudices develop, and perfectly "natural" sentiments such as empathy for one's fellow man or the basic wish to survive give way to corrupt, egotistical desires: the passion for gain, for power, for recognition, for self-advancement.[8] And because the latter passions engender competition, envy, and discord, the result is universal alienation and the perpetual subjugation of losers to winners. At the end of his study, the author remarks that in the most extreme case, that of despotism,

> all individuals become equal again because they are nothing, . . . [they] have no longer any law but the will of the master, nor the master any other rule but that of his passions. . . . Here everything is restored to the sole law of the strongest, and consequently to a new state of nature different from the one which we began, only that that one was the state of nature in its pure form and this one is the fruit of an excess of corruption. (*Second* 135)

Through the corrupting mechanisms of systemic social iniquity, the valences that Rousseau has attached to the civil/natural antithesis throughout the rest of his text here undergo a notable inversion. The "natural" state over which an oppressive master presides no longer displays the utopian qualities of its antecedent; rather, it resembles Hobbes's horrifying scenario wherein all are pitted against all and only the strongest can hope to come out ahead.[9] Like their savage forebears, subjects of despotic rule—those who have lost in the proto-Hobbesian struggle for domination—possess no individuality as such. But unlike the inhabitants of a "pure" state of nature, they place stock in an egocentric and oppositionally defined sense of self.[10] As a result, these people are condemned, as subjects in less exaggeratedly unjust societies are to a lesser degree, to suffer alienation, dissatisfaction, and strife under the unnatural system that their own perverted habits and practices have come to naturalize.

It is fairly easy to deduce from this grim schema, so vividly realized in mid-eighteenth-century European political culture, the reasons for Rousseau's attraction to social contract theory. In a note to *The Second Discourse,* he concedes wistfully but humorously that civilized man can hardly, at this late stage in his evolution, be expected to revert to a state of peaceable and selfless savagery, to "destroy societies, annihilate *meum* and *teum* and return to live in the forests with the bears" (*Second* 153). Because alienation, artifice, and "violent passions" (*Second* 149) have to a large extent come to constitute humankind's second nature, the task Rousseau sets himself in *The Social Contract* is that of deploying society's own harmful qualities against it. This classic Rousseauist strategy, which Jean Starobinski has identified as finding "the remedy in the ailment,"[11] and which we will consider in more detail later, involves the neutralization of civilized men's warring desires by subordinating them all in equal measure to a "salutary" alienating principle: the general will. Because it is aimed at nurturing the equitable well-being of all citizens, this principle cannot by definition reflect each and every interest harbored by its constituent members. Rather, the general will derives its efficacy from the fact that all people can agree, in theory, to its categorical validity and value: no matter how rich or poor, how weak or strong, everyone has a say in defining the code that regulates collective conduct.[12] "For the will to be general," Rousseau explains in a footnote to his 1762 opus, "it does not always have to be unanimous, but all the voices must be counted [il est nécessaire que toutes les voix soient comptées]. Any formal exclusion destroys its universality" (*Contract* 70n). What is noteworthy about this assertion, from the perspective of the discursive analysis that I aim to undertake in this chapter, is that it implies a dominant sociopolitical discourse constituted through the participation of *all* voices— even those that might prevent outright "unanimity" from carrying the day. True generality would thus be understood to depend less on widespread agreement than on the unfettered proliferation of all citizens' opinions, however divergent or mutually contradictory these may be. In this sense, Rousseau's social pact would appear to offer a civil version of the "state of nature in its pure form." Under the all-inclusive auspices of the general will, every individual is free to express his or her viewpoint in all its irreducible specificity, without risk of censure from a political apparatus that holds some perspectives to be more valid than others. Rather than being "equal because they are nothing," as in a despotic regime, the citizens entering together into a social contract would seem to be equal because they are *something*—because they all achieve equal positivization in the discourse of the general will.[13]

In the broader context of *The Social Contract*, however, this mention of the general will's universally comprehensive nature stands less as an unqualified affirmation of free speech in the ideal polity than as an exception that proves a very different rule. In contradistinction to the textually or organizationally "repressed" (consigned to a footnote) postulation of discursive unanimity examined above, the bulk of the treatise alleges on the contrary that the best political system is one in which all voices are *not* heard, or rather in which some voices take definite priority. Insofar as Rousseau continues, often despite his best intentions, to duplicate the logic of hierarchical exclusion perpetrated by "despotic" orders, echoes of the inequality, oppression, and discontent decried in *The Second Discourse* resurface in the discourse of contractual communitarianism articulated in the philosopher's later text. The symptoms of the malady, as Starobinski or Rousseau himself might say, linger on in the so-called remedy, as for instance when *The Social Contract* first describes the transformation that men must undergo in order to become citizens under an egalitarian social pact:

> The passage from the state of nature to civil society produces a remarkable change in man; it puts justice as a rule of conduct in the place of instinct, and gives his actions the moral quality they previously lacked. It is only then, when the voice of duty has succeeded [succéder à] physical impulse, and right that of desire, that man, who has hitherto thought only of himself, finds himself compelled to act on other principles, and to consult his reason before listening to [avant d'écouter] his inclinations. (*Contract* 64)

As an example of what Paul Hoffmann has termed the Swiss thinker's Manichaean "all-or-nothing logic,"[14] this statement is, it should be admitted, far from unique. Published shortly before *The Social Contract*, Rousseau's great novel *Julie* (1761) likewise posits the moral and social development of its protagonists as a function of suppressing personal inclinations—those "violent passions" fostered by corrupt civilizations—in favor of abstract virtue and community-oriented duty.[15] And in the *Émile*, written and published contemporaneously with the 1762 political work, the author also presents the opposition between (self-interested) man and (disinterested) citizen as an irreducible one: "One must choose between making a man or a citizen: for one cannot make both at once."[16] This particular citation from *The Social Contract*, however, is significant in that it assigns a *voice* to civic virtue in the struggle against private passion and asserts the relative importance of this voice by positing it as that which the citizen must obey first and foremost.[17] By delineating a chronological order in which self-interest and public obligation must be heard (the citizen heeds the latter before listening to the former; the one succeeds the other), Rousseau does not in theory ban personal appetite from society altogether. He acknowledges its existence but makes it temporally secondary to the all-powerful "voice of duty"—and discursively secondary as well, insofar it is not, in contrast to the force that opposes it, endowed with a voice.[18] Thus, although the footnote examined above evinces a social pact predicated on universal freedom of expression, in this instance (and the same will hold true for the rest of the text) some voices are distinctly more equal than others. The vocalization of private inclinations must, Rousseau suggests, be kept to a minimum, ceding the floor to the favored discourse of social morality and duty.

Paradoxically, this discursive bracketing of personal desires seems for Rousseau to represent a means of minimizing the pain that the "normal" civilized man—one who does not enjoy the equality offered by a general will—consistently endures in a society that both inspires *and* negates pronounced egotistical drives. The author describes this more typical case in a fragmentary essay from the spring of 1762:

> What makes humans miserable is the contradiction that exists between
> our state and our desires, between our duties and our penchants,
> between nature and social institutions, between man and the citizen;
> make a person one or the other, and you will make him as happy as he is
> capable of being. Give him over entirely to the state or leave him entirely
> to himself, but if you divide his heart, you will tear him apart.[19]

In a nonegalitarian regime, a contradiction exists between the state and our desires, because the latter are violently, if problematically, engendered by the former. Following the logic of *The Second Discourse*, the reader might imagine, by way of example, the following scenarios. If I am a courtier, the king may not approve of my wish for personal advancement, but the very fact of a court hierarchy sets me to dissatisfied dreaming, to craving the glitter and glory that I never could have coveted as a lone savage dwelling among the bears. Even a despot who reduces me to nothing cannot entirely stamp out the visions of grandeur that an envious identification with him—which I conjure up in secret, from the depths of my abjection—is bound to inspire.[20] Under these conditions, man's heart is, for Rousseau, tragically divided and can be healed (from the point of view of social reform) only if he is "given over entirely to the state." This is why "the alienation is without reserve," *must* be without reserve, under the social contract. If man is stripped as completely as possible of his subjective inclinations and is left with nothing but the generalized "voice of duty" ringing in his ears, then he has no choice but to identify wholly with that voice. The alienating rift between self and state is overcome through a more thorough "alienation" of private in public discourse, and the broken hearts nursed by folks in other societies are nowhere to be found in Rousseau's hypothetical polity. As he maintains, likewise, in the *Émile:* "The best social institutions are those which know best how to denature man, how to take from him his absolute existence in order to give him a relative one...; such that each particular person only has a sense of himself as part of the whole" (249).

The ultimate objective behind this arrangement, which would be the end of social inequality and the needless suffering it engenders, sounds appealing enough, but the eradication of all individual, nongeneralizable passions cannot possibly be easy, as Rousseau's very reference to a "denaturing" process reveals. As an author whose nontheoretical texts focus largely on the vicissitudes of private desire in his own life,[21] Rousseau himself is perfectly conscious of this difficulty. The manner in which he proposes to resolve it, though, again bears unmistakable traces of the repressive political culture he is attempting to overcome, for he suggests nothing less than a recourse to compulsion as a means of making new citizens conform to an ethos of pure "generality." We have already encountered this dynamic, in fact, in the quotation narrating the individual's transformation into a social contractant: "man, who has hitherto thought only of himself, finds himself compelled to act on other principles." This allusion to force suggests a strange type of freedom, one that Rousseau associates even more explicitly with coercion in the following account of the social pact's operations: "It tacitly asserts... that whoever refuses to obey the general will shall be constrained to do so by the whole body, which means nothing other than that one shall force him to be free [on le forcera d'être libre]" (*Contract* 64). In what is perhaps the most paradoxical of all *The Social Contract*'s maxims, external pressure is posited as the very precondition of civil liberty: the individual is forced to be free. What is more, the constrictive power that impels the citizen to freedom derives from two curious sources. On the one hand, the arbiter of civic virtue is collective: "the whole body" monitors the lone citizen; the societal "one"—a collective and implicitly plural pronoun in French—militates against any potentially deviant activities on the part of the individual ("one shall force him . . ."). On the other hand, this force is merely "tacit." As such, it does not necessarily exist anywhere in concrete form: as Rousseau remarks elsewhere in the text, "the clauses of this contract, . . . although they may never have been formally enunciated, are everywhere the same, everywhere tacitly admitted and recognized" (*Contract* 60). Although working on behalf of the "voice of duty," the clauses that constitute the social pact do not find overt expression and thus compose a type of silence or erasure. As with the voice of reason, which makes itself heard at the expense of the passions, something has *not* to be said in order for the general will to prevail. In both cases, the vox populi derives its incontrovertible strength from the fact that it emanates from beyond or outside language. "Silence gives the presumption of tacit consent" (*Contract* 135), Rousseau declares in one passage. And in another: "[From] the silence of the people, one must assume [on doit présumer] their agreement" (*Contract* 70), the implication in both of these assertions being that the collective engagement that binds all citizens to the polity does not even have to be articulated to enter into effect. But the second statement, in particular, identifies a subtle agent at work to guarantee the "correct" interpretation of the people's silence: and that agent, which we have already encountered, is the normative "one," a metonym for the general will itself. As long as this "one" stays on the scene, advocating duty (implied by the French verb *devoir,* in the locution "on doit") and presuming universal agreement, there is no risk of silence being interpreted as anything other than what it ought to be—the abolition of individual difference for the sake of social unity.

In a twentieth-century philosophical context, the communal and implicit nature of Rousseau's normative "one" calls to mind Martin Heidegger's claims, in *Being and Time,* about the inevitable and irrefutable character of man's preexisting social conditions, collectively dubbed *das Man*—the German equivalent of the pluralistic French pronoun *on.* Simultaneously opposing and conflating the sphere of private existence ("the . . . world nearest to us," "one's own *Da-sein*") and the broader realm of public or social experience ("being-with-one-another," "everyday-ness"), Heidegger states:

> The public "surrounding world" is always already at hand and taken care of in the surrounding world nearest to us. . . . This being-with-one-another dissolves one's own *Da-sein* completely into the kind of being of "the others" in such a way, that the others, as distinguishable and explicit, disappear more and more. In this inconspicuousness and unascertain-ability, the they [das Man] unfolds its true dictatorship. We enjoy ourselves . . . the way *they* enjoy themselves. We read, see, and judge . . . the way *they* see and judge. . . . The they, which is nothing definite and which all are, . . . prescribes the kind of being of everydayness.[22]

In qualifying the pervasive influence of *das Man* as a "dictatorship," Heidegger underscores the political dangers that a set of incontestable public prescriptions may entail. Although such dangers in fact materialize with a vengeance during the Reign of Terror, Rousseau himself does not—true in this way to the optimistic Enlightenment context in which he wrote—dwell on the tyrannical possibilities of his theory. Nevertheless, he adamantly advances the belief that true political freedom requires the outright eradication of certain elements, coded inadmissible. "For to be governed by appetite alone is slavery," he declares, "while obedience to a law one prescribes to oneself is freedom" (*Contract* 65). In this formulation, the "one" emerges yet again as the agent of a prescriptive, self-constraining civic morality, while the self-interested impulse of "appetite alone" is relegated to the politically undesirable status of slavery. And effectively, slaves have no rights in Rousseau's political system, if for no other reason than because he prevents the very term, anathema to a proclaimed enemy of social injustice, from signifying in his text. "The right of the slave is void," he argues, "not only because it is illegitimate, but also because it is nonsensical, because it has no meaning. The words 'slavery' and 'right' are contradictory, they cancel each other out" (*Contract* 58). By extension of this logic, though, personal inclination, qua "slave," itself has no rights ("the right is void") and no meaning in Rousseau's discursive framework.[23] The dictatorship of *das Man*, of the controlling, civic-minded "one," nullifies it in the name of freedom.

If, however, the societal "one" necessarily prevails in *The Social Contract*, why must this victory come specifically at the expense of subjective desire? If alienation—that dastardly feature of man's "second" nature—can be recuperated and beneficially deployed in the construction of a more egalitarian society, then why cannot personal sentiment too be allowed to exist under the new order? On the most obvious level, in discounting the passions so harshly in his text, Rousseau adheres to a binary principle that is as old as Western philosophy itself: namely, the opposition between mind/spirit and matter/body. When Plato introduces the opposition in his work, he privileges the former pole, as does virtually all of Christian theology from the Middle Ages onward, and in the seventeenth century, René Descartes reinscribes the polarity in his groundbreaking formulation of the cogito. In the Enlightenment, the debate comes to include and indeed to turn on the issue of freedom: how can man ever be free if he lets himself be whipsawed by his own passions and those of others? Finding its expression in the early part of the century in Locke and Montesquieu, as well as in Rousseau's own *Second Discourse,* this strain of the argument reaches its apogee in the *philosophe*'s best-known German contemporary and admirer, Immanuel Kant, for whom moral behavior consists in subjugating the contingent forces of sensual experience to a dispassionate, purely rational will.[24] The Swiss thinker himself anticipates Kantian philosophy when he writes in the *Émile:* "The inner voice . . . cries out in a tone that is difficult not to recognize, but my will is independent of my senses. I consent to my passions or I resist them, I succumb to my passions or I conquer them. I always have the power to determine my actions according to my will" (585). Most interesting for our purposes is the fact that Rousseau here again couches the conflict between reason and the passions in terms of warring verbal forces. Once more, it is a question of silencing one voice, "the inner voice," in favor of another, "the will"—the purely rational, community-minded element that can be aligned with the voice of duty. "My will is independent of my senses": the individual's freedom, as defined or conferred by the communitarian general will, depends, as we have seen before, upon constraint of an explicitly discursive nature. It requires that the citizen, submitting to a higher, antisensual, and impersonal power, censor the voices of contingent inclination. "The voice of reason," Kant asserts, in turn echoing Rousseau, "demands totality," and totality thus conceived requires not the articulation but the annihilation of anything that cannot be absorbed into the homogenizing discourse of universal law.

This observation leads us to the point that in *The Social Contract*'s devalorization of "my passions," the other element to come under attack is the highly personal nature of these forces. In contrast to "one," an impersonal grammatical function simultaneously designating both everyone and no one, the "I" of the passions can refer to only one particular being at a time, a being who by definition distinguishes himself from an anonymous collectivity. To utter "I" is, as Émile Benveniste has shown, to bring an ego into being.[25] And an ego, Rousseau knows better than anyone else, is invariably replete with inclinations of the most selfish, antisocial variety.[26] In short, the "inner voice" of the passions is a discourse of particularity, and the very structure of the social contract, like that of Kantian totality, necessitates its suppression. A good political system is one, as the *philosophe* puts it, that "transports the *ego* into the common unity" (*Émile* 249; Rousseau's emphasis). "For indeed," he warns, "every individual as a man may have a private will contrary to, or different from, the general will that he has as a citizen. *His private interest may speak with a very different voice from that of public interest*" (*Contract* 63; my emphasis). Any private interest stands to threaten the depersonalized universality of the general will.[27] And given that "either the will is general, or it does not exist [la volonté est générale, ou elle n'est pas]" (*Contract* 70), the individual ego has no place in Rousseau's depersonalized polity. The discourse of personal difference, which "may speak with a very different voice," must defer to the discourse of public interest implied by the collective "one." So if, returning to Rousseau's formulations of the absolute plenitude provided by his political system, the "individual . . . has [no]thing left to demand" once he has entered into society, if he is no longer torn between "desires and [the] state," we can now say that this is because the individual, as such, no longer exists. At the very least, the individual no longer exists *in language*. Incapable of saying (and thus becoming) "ego," the person-turned-citizen is forbidden from speaking "with a different voice." Consequently, the citizen's difference can no longer be verbalized: the individual has nothing left to demand. To demand the fulfillment of one's personal desires is, after all, to be a slave, and, as Rousseau has already pointed out, "the right of the slave is void."

So what kind of right is the right to self-negation? Maurice Blanchot, following Hegel's famous analysis of the Reign of Terror as the radical assimilation of personal to public identity, proposes the following:

People cease to be individuals . . . : each person is universal freedom. No
one has a right to a private life any longer, everything is public, and the
guiltiest person of all is the suspect—the person who has a secret, who
keeps a thought, an intimacy to himself. And in the end no one has a
right to his life any longer, to his actually separate and physically distinct
existence. This is the meaning of the Reign of Terror. Every citizen has a
right to death, so to speak: . . . he needs death so that he can proclaim
himself a citizen.[28]

For Blanchot, when the citizen kills off all traces of a private life for the
sake of the polity, he exercises his "right to death."[29] Rousseau concurs
and likewise uses death as a metaphor for the fate with which an individual's passions and preferences must meet when he enters society:
"The nearer men's natural powers are to extinction or annihilation, the
stronger and more lasting [are] their acquired powers, the stronger and
more perfect is the social institution" (*Contract* 85). The one notable
difference between Rousseau's point of view and Blanchot's is the former's insistence on what the citizen gains in return for his sacrifice. In
contrast to Blanchot—who writes his essay from the sobering perspective of someone looking back on the historical Terror (not to mention
the political upheavals of the first half of the twentieth century)—the
author of *The Social Contract* is wont at least to underscore the political
development that accompanies the individual's annihilation. The citizen must die, as a pathologically desiring individual, but unlike the subject of Blanchot's Terror or even the victim of despotism whose subjective abasement Rousseau decries in *The Second Discourse,* he dies so
that the nation can live. This is why the *philosophe,* without the irony
betrayed by Blanchot, refers to the citizen's position in this zero-sum
game between himself and society as a "right to life and death." Recuperated as a "right," this position is thus presented as a positive contribution to society: one example of the civil rights and benefits that the citizen derives from affiliation with a larger, legally regulated whole.

   This relatively sunny conception of the "right to death" notwithstanding, Rousseau does not stop at an account of the metaphorical
death to which individuals entering society must subject their more unruly instincts. In the chapter that he calls, precisely, "The Right to Life
and Death," he briefly abandons the figurative vein to reflect on the actual death that will be visited upon those members of the body politic
who deviate from society's established norms. Rousseau's chief example

of such a deviation is the murder of one citizen by another. Arguing
that capital punishment represents the best response to this unforgivable wrong against the common good, he explains that "it is in order to
avoid becoming the victim of a murderer that one consents to die if one
becomes a murderer oneself" (*Contract* 79). But that is not all. Reintroducing a metaphorical conception of the "right to death" alongside his
apologia of capital punishment, Rousseau goes on to assert that when a
person has seriously violated the social pact, he must be excluded from
the community both literally *and* figuratively:

> Since every wrongdoer attacks the society's law, he becomes by his deed
> a rebel and a traitor to the nation; he ceases to be a member of it. . . . And
> in this case, the preservation of the state is incompatible with his preser-
> vation; one or the other must perish. . . . He is no longer a member of the
> state . . . and he must either be banished into exile as a violator of the
> social pact or be put to death as a public enemy; such an enemy is not a
> moral person [une personne morale], but a man, and therefore the right
> of war makes it legitimate to kill him. (*Contract* 79)

As in the proposition according to which the citizen's private interests
must be killed off if the republic is to live, this passage is predicated on a
mutually exclusive relationship between the insurgent and the state: one
or the other must perish. And in this case, the death that Rousseau prescribes can be physical, symbolic, or both. On the physical level, the
rebel may be exiled or executed. But he is eliminated on a symbolic
level no matter what the ultimate fate of his body, for as soon as he attacks the social pact, he loses his symbolic status as citizen and is recat-
egorized as enemy. He is, as Rousseau says later in the same chapter, an
outlaw *(hors la loi)*, meaning he is ontologically as well as practically excluded from the realm of citizenry, and therefore enjoys none of the
privileges belonging to a "moral person." His death or exclusion from
the public sphere thus only concretizes or underscores the radical, irre-
mediable loss of civil rights that results from his infraction. As we shall
have ample occasion to observe in chapter 2, when the French revolutionaries apply the same logic to Louis XVI during their epic trial of the
deposed king, this loss constitutes yet another one of the key discursive
suppressions upon which the republic of virtue is founded.

Despite the "fury for destruction,"[30] as Hegel calls it, that such death-
bearing logic is prone to unleash in the polity, Rousseau's implementation of Terrorist virtue does posit the eradication of particularity as a

salutary dialectical movement in which the citizen's loss becomes the state's gain. More precisely, the institution of a polity involves an exchange of personal sentiment for communitarian reason: where the passions are silenced, the voice of duty will speak in their place.[31] Presumably, this shift confers some benefit, not just upon the state as a whole, but also upon each private citizen, who through it secures representation in and by the general will. In leaving the state of nature and becoming a citizen, the individual forsakes the ability to indulge his every antisocial desire and caprice but in return receives security, freedom, and equality under the law. Having agreed to keep his own egotistical impulses in check, the citizen no longer risks being subjected to the potential tyranny of other people's particular interests.[32] It is this sort of liberty that allows, under the social contract, for the creation and maintenance of a "stronger and more perfect" polity, to refer back to Rousseau's account of how and why the citizen's "natural forces" must be sacrificed on the altar of the state. Because it excludes any biases of a purely individual nature, the social pact ostensibly provides representation by, for, and of the people as a whole.

Nevertheless, the question remains as to how representation can be possible in a society designed to be lasting, strong, and perfect. For the first two adjectives, when cast in a political register, imply stability, a regime from which the potentially destabilizing vagaries of individual passions have been expelled ("near . . . to extinction and annihilation"). And from an etymological point of view, *perfection* suggests, as we remarked earlier apropos of the "perfect" Rousseauist union, accuracy, completion, and plenitude. Yet in his writings on language, Rousseau himself explicitly addresses the difficulties and even impossibilities of attaining such perfection in the realm of symbolic representation, riddled as it is with gaps and differences. In this, he followed a current that had begun to shape academic discussions of language earlier in the century— prompted by works such as Du Marsais's *Des Tropes ou des différents sens dans lesquels on peut prendre un même mot dans une même langue* (1730) (Of Tropes or Different Meanings in Which One Can Take a Single Word in a Single Language)—but he redirected it toward his own broader philosophical concerns. *The Second Discourse,* as mentioned already, links the inequalities that develop among men to the differential properties of the language that they develop in emerging from a state of nature. "Those relationships which we express by the words 'large,' 'small,' 'strong,' 'weak,'... and other similar ideas, [are] compared almost un-thinkingly" (*Second* 110): the relational quality of linguistic reference in-stantiates and propagates a sense of distinctions among speaking beings. Worse still, as he shows in *The Essay on the Origin of Languages* (1754–1763), because man's tendency to compare himself with his fellows is in-evitably influenced or inflected by his passions, the process leads to error and, on a linguistic level, to figurative speech. To give Rousseau's most fa-mous example: A frightened individual dubs a passerby a giant, only to realize later that this creature was merely another human like himself; but "he retain[s] the word 'giant' for the fictitious object that impressed him during his delusion."[33] While the term *giant* correctly reflects its orig-inator's subjective state (fear), it does not accurately reflect the objective condition of its referent; in Rousseau's own parlance: "The first idea that it conveys to us is not that of the truth" (*Essay* 13). The result, as Paul de Man notes in his gloss on the *Essay*, is a metaphor, which "is error because it believes... in its own referential meaning"[34]—and which "naturalizes" an artificial, irregular correspondence between subjective experience and objective condition. The key point is that Rousseau posits linguistic ex-pression as an error-fraught medium based on personal sentiments and nonobjective figures:[35] "Because man's first motives for speaking were passions, his first expressions were Tropes, ... consist[ing] of a transfer-ence of meaning" (*Essay* 12). In this light, his consistent definition of re-publican virtue as the silencing of discursive as well as subjective "voices" makes eminent sense. Because they etymologically and effectively consti-tute a "transference" away from empirical truth and toward subjectively mediated fiction, tropes stand invariably, like the passions, to subvert the hard-won homogeneity and universality of the social pact; as Du Marsais's title indicates, they can create multiplicity within "one single word [and] one single language." This is the reason for the patently anti-linguistic bias that betrays itself time and again in *The Social Contract*, as for instance in the strange footnote where the author exclaims: "Shall we never see behind the precepts of books and the crude self-interest which prompts the authors to speak?" (*Contract* 130n). According to this for-mulation, private feeling, already established as the enemy of true social harmony, is inextricably bound up with textual activity itself; both rep-resent dangerous deviations from a homogeneous, universalizing norm.

The solution that Rousseau devises to solve the political conundrums posed by linguistic deviance is radical to say the least. If the new polity is to keep the slings and arrows of difference at bay, if it is to protect itself and its citizens from unwanted deviations, then it must at the limit do away with the logic of representation altogether. The social collectivity must not be mediated through or by anything; a theory also surfaces in Rousseau's *Lettre à d'Alembert,* which deems "nothing, if you please," to be the optimal subject of a public spectacle aimed at preserving social harmony.[36] Reintroducing this idea of representational transparency in *The Social Contract,* Rousseau assigns to it a more narrowly political application: "My argument, then, is that sovereignty, being nothing other than the exercise of the general will, can never be alienated, and that the sovereign, which is simply a collective being, cannot be represented by anyone but itself—power may be transmitted [peut se transmettre], but the will cannot be" (*Contract* 69). The *philosophe* could hardly express himself more clearly on this point: the general will cannot be "alienated" in something other than itself; it cannot be "transmitted" in language or in any other representational system. "The general will," he states later in the text, in a chapter repudiating the idea that elected officials can properly stand in for the people, "cannot be represented; it is the same, or it is other [elle est la même, ou elle est autre], there is no intermediate possibility" (*Contract* 141).[37] When it comes to establishing and protecting the common good, no difference whatsoever must intervene between the signified ("a collective being") and its signifier ("itself"). They somehow have to become one and the same.

Sublimity and Dissimulation: The Legislator's Language

Now the conflation of word and thing is a tall order, and Rousseau does not recommend it to the average mortal. "Gods would be needed," he hypothesizes, "to give laws to men" (*Contract* 84). The author's recourse to a conditional verb here reveals the profound implausibility of his proposition—a point to which I will return later on in this chapter, in discussing both the legislator's and Rousseau's own efforts to reconcile theoretical language and practical action. For now, suffice it to say that Rousseau's hypothetical prescription sidesteps the obviously problematic idea of traditional political "representation" by elected deputies, and sets the stage, however provisorily, for a sort of god incarnate, someone who will manage to transcend the frustrating divisions and differences inherent in earthly representation. Enter the legislator to purge the polity once and for all of such destabilizing elements.

Consistent with Rousseau's primary concern throughout his social and political writings, the principal difference that the legislator must undertake to abolish is the one that separates the natural man from the citizen. In his opening characterization of the lawmaker, Rousseau stresses the importance of this task:

> Whoever [celui qui] ventures on the enterprise of setting up a people must be ready, shall we say, to change human nature, to transform each individual . . . into part of a much greater whole. . . . The founder of nations must weaken the structure of man in order to fortify it, to replace the physical and independent existence we have all received from nature with a moral and communal existence. . . . So much so, that if each citizen is nothing [chaque citoyen n'est rien] except through cooperation with others, . . . then one can say [on peut dire] that law-making has reached the highest point of perfection. (*Contract* 84–85)

As we now know, the negation of the individual and the natural ("physical and independent existence") under the social contract is a commonplace in Rousseau's text. What is new in this passage is the fact that this nullification occurs no longer through the agency of the impersonal "one" but through the machinations of the legislator: "If each citizen is nothing . . . then . . . law-making has reached the highest point of perfection." Although the pronoun *one* still figures as a voice of broad, societal approval ("one can say that law-making"), in this case it functions principally to endorse the actions of one particular person, "whoever" *(celui)*, whose referent appears in Rousseau's chapter heading, "The Lawgiver." And yet, this individual's very discourse, that of legislation, is presented as an indeterminate abstraction in Rousseau's text—an invisible mediating structure, like the social pact itself, held to lie outside the realm of representational particularity. Located by Rousseau outside the bounds of ordinary, subjective speech, the legislator emerges as the transformer of human nature, the author of civic virtue ("moral and communal" values), the eliminator of difference and the source of plenitude ("perfection") for society as "a much greater whole."

With the legislator, Rousseau thus paradoxically transfers the task of enforcing anti-individualistic norms from the collective "one" to a single individual. This apparent contradiction, however, is in fact constitutive of the lawgiver's mandate, which is to resolve or reconcile the conflict between the general and the particular. In the above-cited instance, the individual legislator assumes the role of the impersonal "one." He is, "in every respect, an extraordinary man in the state" (*Contract* 85) precisely because he exists solely to serve the interests of the collectivity and so effectively embodies a merging of the personal and the political. If, in other words, Rousseau sees the legislator as a god, this is because he figures the ability to transcend discourses of human individuality and deviance while still remaining an identifiable agent of broad-based, normative control. Although personally singled out to "change human nature," the legislator himself is a being whose nature is already impersonal, inhuman—his is "a special and superior function which has nothing to do with the human condition" (*Contract* 85). Unlike humanity, which is subject to divisive, self-interested appetites, the legislator "understand[s] the passions of men without feeling any of them, [and has] no affinity with our nature but kn[ows] it to the full" (*Contract* 84). In this way, he remains free from the forces of particularity that could, unchecked, tear the polity asunder. "Otherwise," Rousseau warns, echoing *The Second Discourse,* "the laws, being offspring of the legislator's passions, would often merely perpetuate . . . injustice" (*Contract* 85). More important still, the lawgiver functions to expunge from those around him those passionate impulses that breed iniquity and discord.

This exemption from human particularity has far-reaching consequences for the legislator's relationship to language. Although Rousseau, for reasons that will become clear shortly, reveals a marked ambivalence toward the use of examples in *The Social Contract,* he does provide one (albeit elliptical) instance of the *type* of discourse that a mouthpiece for pure generality might adopt. Toward the end of his chapter on the legislator, Rousseau points to "the Law of the Hebrews, which still lives," as a prime example of "that great and powerful genius which lies behind all lasting things" (*Contract* 87–88).[38] Given the fact that Rousseau sees the elimination of discursive difference as the necessary precondition of a stable and lasting polity, it seems safe to assume that Judaic law promises such a result—and indeed it does, in at least two ways. First and most obvious, the founding laws of the Jewish people, the Ten Commandments, contain an interdiction against graven images.[39] Contrasting "the Law of the Hebrews" to activity of a purely mimetic nature, Rousseau scoffs at the latter: "Any man can carve tablets of stone" (*Contract* 87); his own ideal is a universal political principle "engraved in [people's] hearts, not inscribed on marble or brass" (*Contract* 99). For Rousseau, the early Hebrews adhere to this ideal, insofar as their political and moral community is based on the repudiation of all mimetic activity. This repudiation is apparent in what Rousseau takes to be the second exemplary aspect of the Jewish people: for in preparing to hand down his (antirepresentational) commandments to Moses, God appears to his mortal delegate in the form of a burning bush and proclaims: "I AM THAT I AM."[40] This pronouncement in fact foreshadows and enacts the interdiction against graven images. It constitutes a dramatic reformulation of representation as such, not only because it is heralded by a sign that destroys itself in its very appearance (the burning bush), but also because the sentence's main clause and its subordinate clause completely coincide. In the tautological preamble to the "Law of the Hebrews," there is no room for the glaring sort of gap, say, that separates the figure of speech *giant* from its nongigantic referent. In keeping with the Hebrew tradition, and in service of a collective "sovereign that . . . can only be represented by itself," the Rousseauist lawgiver should therefore ideally implement a form of *representation without difference*. Therein, according to the *philosophe*, lies the key to maintaining a "great and lasting" social pact.

As these last quotations suggest, Rousseau's concern with the suppression of representational difference also betrays a desire to protect the polity from alterations occurring along a temporal axis. For time—along with subjective desire, error, and metaphor—represents another central ingredient in Rousseau's wary speculations about how language works. We have already noted that he locates the origins of verbal expression in the passions ("man's first motives for speaking were passions"), and these forces are bound to subvert a structure of absolute generality insofar as they tend to vary over time. Love turns into hate, excitement yields to indifference, and so on; it is the very mutability of "pathological" feeling that disqualifies it, in Kant's philosophical system, as a categorically legitimate base of moral behavior. To Rousseau's mind, linguistic activity specifically and temporal activity generally are in this respect analogous to the passions. "Imagine someone in a painful situation that is fully known," he speculates: "When you look at the afflicted person, you are not likely to weep. But give him time to tell you what he feels and soon you will burst into tears" (*Essay* 8). In this scenario, a narrative movement—from the beginning to the end of a tale of woe—produces a shift in the listener's passions: crucially, both the discursive and the affective changes unfold in time. Just as surely as the vicissitudes of passion and language, time itself appears as a force for change par excellence that threatens to introduce alterity into any given status quo.[41] This is why the *philosophe* characterizes the legislator as "a superior intelligence . . . who would be content to wait in the unfolding of time [le progrès des temps] for a distant glory, and to labor in one age to enjoy the fruits in another [travailler dans un siècle et jouir dans un autre]" (*Contract* 84). By deferring his own need for earthly reward and even eroticized enjoyment (*jouissance*), the legislator effectively removes himself from the "unfolding of time" to which mere mortals are subject.[42] His supposed superiority thus consists in his imperviousness not just to the conventional demands of desire and of representation but also to those of time itself. Because all three of these influences are wont to make states and men differ from themselves and from one other, the legislator must figure, on behalf of his constituency, a capacity to overcome them altogether.

According to the same transcendental logic, the legislator's utterances should function to collapse the boundaries not only between subject and object, particular and general, but also between now and later. It is precisely this sort of immediacy that Rousseau extols when describing the radical performativity of divine speech in a fragmentary essay called "De la puissance infinie de Dieu": "What! Creating light is such a simple operation, that it suffices calmly to tell light to be, for light instantaneously to be! . . . The same simplicity of speech and of execution. So what is this unknown order of knowledge, whose slightest operations are beyond human comprehension?"[43] In this passage, Rousseau is of course referring to Genesis, where God creates the world by means of the command "fiat lux." While Rousseau remarks that this operation impresses him above all because of its simplicity, the simplicity that he identifies is of a fairly complex or at least an uncommon nature; for it is a simplicity that eliminates the usual delay between a speech and its execution, that is to say its consequences in the material world.[44] It can indeed be said that God's call for light *simplifies* the relationship between speech and action by making them one and the same: they occur simultaneously, instantaneously. Like the Judaic interdiction against graven images, this divine utterance transcends or abolishes the divisions and differences inherent in traditional representation. According to Rousseau, it falls to the legislator to put such discourse into effect in the republic of virtue.

Before examining precisely how the legislator is supposed to go about such a task, however, it would perhaps be useful to make a brief excursus into some philosophical and aesthetic material with which Rousseau's allusions to otherworldly utterances resonate. I propose this detour because interestingly enough, the *philosophe*'s two prime examples of ideal, nondifferential language—"the Law of the Hebrews" and "fiat lux"— also form the basis of two extremely influential theories of the aesthetic "sublime": one put forth by an author commonly known as Longinus in the third century A.D.; and the other developed by Kant in *The Critique of Judgment* (1794). In her illuminating study of the "revolutionary sublime," Marie-Hélène Huet uses the latter thinker as a lens through which to understand the poetics of immediacy that Rousseau's thought inspired the architects of the Reign of Terror both to preach and to practice in their political dealings.[45] For her, Kant's conception of the sublime—which as we shall see turns on a special example of divine discourse—frames in a particularly illuminating way the radical (anti)-discursive strategies that inform Rousseauist and Robespierrist political theory. While I am entirely in agreement with Huet's findings, my aim here is both to expand upon some of her points about Kantian aesthetics and to supplement them by introducing another figure, Longinus, to the mix. The juxtaposition of the two theoreticians of the sublime is intended to emphasize the simultaneously representational *and* moral aspects of the condition or phenomenon that both philosophers dub sublime. Because for Longinus, as for Kant, a superior sort of virtue accompanies or entails a transcendental form of discourse, a short discussion of their musings on the sublime should enrich our understanding of Rousseau's own version of linguistic and social sublimity, as exemplified by the legislator.

The writer generally identified as Longinus, whose unfinished tract *Peri Hypsous (Of the Sublime)* was "rediscovered" by French academicians in the late seventeenth century—and who became central to European aesthetics thereafter—focuses primarily on the sublime as a rhetorical device.[46] In a departure from his own predecessors and contemporaries, who largely understood sublime language as either an object of contemplation or a means of persuasion, the author of *Peri Hypsous* conceives of the sublime as a form of expression that transports the senses above or beyond these conventional realms.[47] Longinus opens his treatise wondering whether "there is an art of the sublime" (*Hypsous* 101) and, answering the question in the affirmative, consecrates the remainder of the text to identifying the characteristics of this "art . . . [that] scatters everything before it like a thunderbolt" (*Hypsous* 100) in the works of Homer, Demosthenes, and Plato. And yet, although he appears willing to offer positive definitions of the sublime (an "art"; or, as he writes elsewhere, "a command of language" [*Hypsous* 108]), his use of the lightning metaphor betrays an understanding of the sublime as a fundamentally destructive force—a rhetorical device that destroys rhetoric. This notion surfaces throughout Longinus's text when he consistently deems sublime those figures of speech that work to disguise or undo their own figurality. For instance: "A rhetorical figure [is] most effective when the fact that it is a figure is not apparent" (*Hypsous* 127), and: "Art is perfect only when it looks like nature, and again, nature hits the mark only when she conceals the art that is within her" (*Hypsous* 131). Similarly, when pressed to provide concrete examples of sublime speech, Longinus offers up two cases of language working to undermine its own properly linguistic status. First, he praises the sublime "nobility of soul" *(hypsous)* inspired by Homer's decision to leave Ajax speechless during his visit to the underworld in *The Odyssey,* because this "silence is grand, more sublime than any words" (*Hypsous* 109).[48] Secondly, Longinus identifies as sublime Rousseau's favorite quotation from the Book of Genesis, the command that collapses the difference between speech and action: "So too the law-giver of the Jews, no ordinary person, having formed a high conception of the power of the Divine Being, gave expression to it when at the very beginning of his Laws he wrote: 'God said'—what? 'Let there be light, and there was light; let there be land, and there was land'" (*Hypsous* 111). Both of these examples demonstrate the degree to which Longinus's idea of the sublime relies upon a conception of language that hovers on the brink of nonlanguage: silence in the case of *The Odyssey;* radically performative, immediately self-materializing speech in the case of Genesis. It bears noting that in the latter instance, sublime speech is moreover the exclusive property of Moses, "no ordinary person"—a figure strongly reminiscent of Rousseau's lawgiver, "an extraordinary man in the state" who takes his cue from the Mosaic prohibition of graven images.

In this way, Longinus foreshadows Rousseau's valorization of forms of representation that negate or undermine representation as such: both philosophers postulate a language that would bring about the elimination of linguistic difference. As Philippe Lacoue-Labarthe comments in his reading of Longinus: "The paradox of the effacement of *technè* [resides in the fact that] . . . the more *technè* accomplishes itself, the more it effaces itself. The height of *mimèsis* is in its veiling and its dissimulation."[49] In accentuating the paradoxically self-dissimulating or repressed figurality of the sublime, Lacoue-Labarthe's description of this aesthetic figure could also be said to describe the linguistic and political Terror that the Rousseauist suppression of particularity implies. Indeed, as my examination of the surprisingly duplicitous machinations and "secret" fictions of the lawgiver will soon reveal, the "veiling and dissimulation" proper to the sublime constitute the very essence of Rousseau's supposedly transparent rhetoric of virtue. In short, manifestations of the Longinian sublime, like the general will and the legislator charged with enforcing it, call for the superficial disavowal of the very logic that underpins them: the logic of representation.

Roughly the same paradox subtends the definition of the sublime put forth by Immanuel Kant, according to whom it "can never be anything more than a negative presentation" (*Judgment* 127). Like Longinus and Rousseau, the German philosopher proffers a biblical citation to support his argument:

> Perhaps there is no more sublime passage in the Jewish Law than the commandment: Thou shalt not make unto thee any graven image, or any likeness of any thing that is in heaven or on earth, or under the earth, &c. This commandment alone can explain the enthusiasm which the Jewish people, in their moral period, felt for their religion, when comparing themselves to others. . . . (*Judgment* 127)

At this point, it almost goes without saying that Kant's reference to the interdiction against representation implies the same (anti)linguistic stance sketched out by his Greek and Swiss predecessors.[50] What is interesting about Kant's formulation, however, is that he immediately links his exemplary "negative presentation" to the *moral* superiority of some men over others: the sublimity of the commandment against graven images derives at least in part from its enabling the Jewish people to "compar[e] themselves" favorably with others. To emphasize the moral underpinnings of his model, Kant prefaces his discussion of Mosaic law with the assertion that "a feeling for the sublime is hardly thinkable unless in association with an attitude of mind resembling the moral" (*Judgment* 120).[51] Of course, the paradox here resides in the simultaneous emergence of a differential principle (that of men comparing themselves with others) and the invocation of a language that is intended to do away with heterogeneity. Morality, even or perhaps especially that of a "sublime" nature, thus requires difference even as it seeks to eliminate it.

Albeit to a lesser extent, Longinus too imbues his conception of sublimity with a moral cast,[52] and so winds up reinstating difference, specifically of a representational variety, in the very process of dispensing with it. The moral aspect of the Longinian sublime emerges principally in his frequent evocations of the lofty status that sublime utterances enable the soul to attain—a phenomenon that we have already come across in the author's allusion to the "nobility of soul" inspired by Homer's silent Ajax. He also, when alluding to the performative command of the Judeo-Christian God, lauds it as a testimony to "the power of the Divine Being" (*Hypsous* 111), further associating sublimity with a universal spiritual code. These intimations of moral transcendence notwithstanding, however, Longinus ultimately defines sublimity as a profoundly mediated and fictitious achievement: "For by some innate power the true sublime uplifts our souls; we are filled with a proud exaltation and a sense of vaunting joy, just as though we had ourselves produced what we had heard" (*Hypsous* 107). In this assertion, Longinus credits the experience of the sublime with the ability to improve the very condition of the human spirit, which, in being pushed beyond the limits of ordinary thought or aesthetic experience, becomes infused with "proud exaltation." To encounter the sublime is thus, for Longinus as for Kant, to achieve some degree of superiority in the moral sphere. This superiority, moreover, stems from the spirit's ability to overcome traditional boundaries between language and reality, between speech and the world: the sublime enables us to feel "as though we had ourselves produced what we had heard." Like the interdiction against graven images referenced by Kant, the experience Longinus describes here implies the transcendence of ontological difference. Nevertheless, his qualification of this achievement as a purely hypothetical occurrence, signaled by the phrase "as if," indicates that even the sublime relies upon the very representational difference it aims to eradicate. A mediating fiction (a belief that one has produced a sound that in fact comes from elsewhere) turns out to be the very precondition for doing away with mediation.

It is above all in this manner that the Longinian and Kantian notions of the sublime rejoin and explicate the constitutive paradox of Rousseau's legislator. The legislator's mandate, we recall, is to "change, we might say, human nature." On the one hand, this mission involves the moral transformation of mankind, a virtually godlike task ("gods would be needed...") best effected through the overcoming of all-too-human linguistic difference. On the other hand, despite its stated aim of suppressing the particularity and divisiveness inherent in conventional discourse, the task of changing, "we might say, human nature" itself cannot do without a differential principle. In the most basic sense, Rousseau's recourse to a figure of speech ("we might say"; in the French original: "pour ainsi dire") when outlining this enterprise implies, like Longinus's use of "as if," that figurality inheres even in the project of transporting mankind to a world beyond figures. And, perhaps more obviously, the very presence of the verb *to change*, like Kant's allusion to men "comparing themselves to others," reveals the degree to which difference is necessary to its own supposed transcendence. That such a bias informs Rousseau's ideas on moral improvement becomes even more evident if we reexamine a quotation from *The Social Contract* cited earlier:

> The passage from the state of nature to civil society produces a remarkable *change* in man; it puts justice as a rule of conduct *in the place* of instinct, and gives his actions the moral quality they *previously* lacked. It is only then, when the voice of duty has *succeeded* [succéder à] physical impulse, and right that of desire, that man, who has *hitherto* thought only of himself.... (*Contract* 64; my emphasis)

Inscriptions of spatial and temporal heterogeneity manifest themselves not only in the word *change* (closely linked to the legislator's duty to change human nature) but also in the other words emphasized in this passage. As Rousseau himself observes in the *Essay on the Origin of Languages*, anticipating Roman Jakobson's analysis of metonymy and metaphor, the very act of figuration involves a series of substitutions: of signs for things and of one sign for another.[53] This notion surfaces in a quotation that we already examined in part in our earlier discussion of the *Essay*: "The figure consists only of a transference of meaning. It is necessary to substitute the idea that the passion presents to us for the word that we transpose. For one does not only transpose words; one also transposes ideas" (12). More succinctly, following Rousseau and Jakobson, Paul de Man asserts that "from the moment we begin to deal with substitutive systems, we are governed by linguistic rather than by natural or psychological models: one can always substitute one word for

another."[54] So much, then, for the exclusion of representational difference from the ideal polity: Rousseau's effort to substitute certain terms
for other, different ones (*justice* for *instinct* and *right* for *desire*) reveals
the fundamentally linguistic underpinnings of his project. What is
more, his use of chronologically inflected terms such as *previously, hitherto,* and *succeed* suggests a transition or a difference between one temporal dimension (the reign of brute instinct/appetite) and another ("the
moral quality they previously lacked"). This intimation of temporal
change further underscores the degree to which Rousseau's republic of
virtue is structured like a language, for as we have already noted, following countless critics, symbolic activity inevitably unfolds in time.[55] Indeed, although he insists largely on a polity "without reserve" (*Contract*
51), in the above-cited passage Rousseau in fact subscribes to the logic
of representational aporia by accentuating the spatially and temporally
differential nature of his proposed change. Thus, discursive difference
emerges at the very point where we would expect to see it eliminated—
along with instinct, physical impulse, and desire—once and for all.

And so it is that the legislator himself winds up drawing his power
from the very linguistic mediation that it supposedly aims to transcend.
More specifically, Rousseau reveals that the lawgiver—himself modeled
on "gods"—can gain the people's trust only by cultivating the fiction
that his wisdom comes directly from a divine being:

> There are thousands of ideas which cannot be translated into the
> language of the people [la langue du peuple] . . . ; it is difficult for the
> individual, who has no taste for any scheme of government but that
> which serves his private interest, to appreciate the advantages to be
> derived from the lasting privations which good laws impose. . . . It is this
> which has obliged the founders of nations throughout history to appeal
> to divine intervention and to attribute their own wisdom to the gods; for
> then the people, feeling subject to the laws of state as they are to those of
> nature, and detecting the same hand in the creation of both man and the
> nation, obey freely and bear with docility the yoke of the public welfare.
> (*Contract* 86–87)

To a student of political philosophy, there is perhaps nothing remarkable in Rousseau's suggestion that rulers use religion to legitimate their
earthly machinations. At the time of *The Social Contract*'s publication,
this idea enjoyed fairly common currency among European intellectu-
als: the "appeal to High Heaven" as a political strategy,[56] to use John

Locke's term, had been a well-known concept ever since the extensive treatment it received from Machiavelli in *The Prince*, which Rousseau himself describes as a "handbook for republicans" (*Contract* 118). In this sense, we might be tempted to conclude that Rousseau's recommended recourse to the gods is merely a variation on one of Enlightenment political philosophy's more tired themes. Rousseau, however, puts a new and, for literary purposes, more interesting spin on the subject by insisting on the centrality of language to the task of lawgiving. To be sure, this notion is implicit in the conditional verb of his remark, "gods would be needed to give laws to men" (*Contract* 84), in that his choice of verb tense underscores the hypothetical and, at the limit, fictitious nature of the "divine" intervention citizens can expect under the social contract. It is more apparent still in his allusion to a "language of the people," which he characterizes as a language of particularity, of divisive personal interests. "Divine intervention," for Rousseau, will function above all to introduce a discourse of depersonalized abstraction that overrides or erases such unruly, individualistic elements. In requiring citizens to submit "to the laws of the state . . . and bear with docility the yoke of the public welfare," this discourse, like the impersonal "one" discussed earlier, effectively forces them to be free ("one will force him to be free"). Significantly, unlike the perfect conflation of the two clauses implied by "I AM THAT I AM" or the absolute immediacy of "fiat lux," the discourse of the legislator is patently one of mediation and figuration. Insofar as he derives his political legitimacy from the fiction of divine right, the legislator's ability to enforce the freedom of his people resides in a source outside himself.

Like the process by which rational civic virtue replaces the passions and which we have determined to be fundamentally linguistic in nature, the lawgiver's reliance on gods is informed by a logic of metonymic substitution. Asserting that the legislator's prime duty is to "make gods speak," Rousseau elaborates: "This sublime reasoning, which soars above the heads of the common people, is used by the law-giver when he puts his own decisions into the mouth of the immortals, thus compelling by divine authority persons who cannot be moved by human prudence" (*Contract* 87). This passage recalls Longinus and Kant to the extent that it posits moral superiority, implicit in terms like *sublime* and *soaring* (in French, Rousseau uses the term *élever*, which is the closest French approximation of Longinus's *hypsous*), as the by-product of linguistic mediation. Only in "put[ting] his own decisions into the mouth of the immortals," in substituting different pronouncements for his own, does the legislator appear to enjoy an irrefutable divine authority. Similar to Longinus's and Kant's figures of sublimity (the thunderbolt, the burning bush), which destroy representational logic as it is commonly understood, the fiction of the legislator's divine authority serves to overwrite the differential "language of the people." Ironically enough, then, dissent on the part of the common people becomes impossible through the legislator's own recourse to fiction.

The lawgiver's derivation of power from structures of particularity and mediation becomes even more apparent when we note that he ascribes his decisions to multiple immortals—an inscription of pluralism that also appears in the line that we discussed earlier, by means of which Rousseau introduces the lawgiver: "gods would be needed to give laws to men." Up until this point, we have been reading the legislator's reliance upon divine discourse as an attempt to position his own dictates beyond the realm of differential human speech. However, the claims to absolute univocality that such a project implies are compromised not only by its metonymic underpinnings but also, and perhaps more surprisingly, by the intimation of pantheism inherent in Rousseau's qualification of godlike speech as emanating from a variety of origins. Indeed, the appeal to a plurality of gods runs against the very grain of the monotheistic "Law of the Hebrews" that the lawgiver is charged with emulating: for rather than consolidating all authority in a single, indivisible being, it allows for a proliferation of differing opinions. If the transcendental subject of "I AM THAT I AM" becomes dispersed in a host of different entities or sources ("immortals," "gods"), nothing remains, on a structural level, to distinguish his commands from those "private interests" that the legislator is supposed to silence for the sake of political stability.

Perhaps it is because of this inherent danger in the legislator's strategic mediations that he must, according to Rousseau, keep them well concealed from his subjects. Like Longinus's figure, which achieves sublime status by hiding its own figural nature, the legislator's authority becomes sublimely incontestable when it dissimulates its mediated underpinnings. In the interest of protecting the absolute, nondifferential generality upon which his idea of the social pact is founded, Rousseau winds up encouraging the legislator to keep his fictitious machinations under wraps. This problem surfaces most visibly in his brief comment on the formation and control of social mores, worth citing here more or less in full. Deeming public morality and opinion "the most important of all [laws]," Rousseau continues:

> [This law] which is inscribed [gravé] neither on marble nor on brass, but in the hearts of citizens, a law which forms the true constitution of the state; . . . which, when other laws age or wither away, reanimates or replaces them; . . . which imperceptibly substitutes the force of habit for the force of authority. I refer to morals, customs, and above all, [public] opinion: this feature, unknown to our political theorists, is the one on which the success of all the other laws depends; it is the feature on which the great law-giver bestows his *secret* care, for though he *seems* to confine himself to detailed legal enactments, which are really only the arching of the vault, he knows that morals, which develop more slowly, ultimately become its immovable keystone. (*Contract* 99–100; my emphasis)

With this invocation of a fundamental law that cannot be represented as such, we find ourselves back in the familiar territory of the "tacit" social contract and the universal consent that the silence of the people necessarily implies. Morals join these other forms of transparent communication in ostensibly evading the pitfalls of linguistic difference and adhering to the Judaic interdiction against graven images invoked by Kant. Nevertheless, like other purportedly transparent discourses mentioned in conjunction with the sublime, morals succeed in shaping republican law and virtue only insofar as they inscribe themselves in a network of embellishments and substitutions: the law of public morality "replaces" other laws and "substitutes" habit for authority. And yet, what is perhaps most striking here is not the paradox that we have already encountered at numerous points in *The Social Contract*—namely, the degree to which mediation inheres in the very effort to eliminate it. Rather, the most extraordinary aspect of Rousseau's comment on mores is his provision for the outright deception of one class of speaking subjects by another. As the adverb *imperceptibly* suggests, the metonymic shift from authority to habit is to take the citizens unawares, while the legislator acts as the hidden hand behind their transformation. He manipulates and controls their behavior in secret, without revealing to them the project of conversion that he has undertaken on their behalf. What is more, the lawgiver must cultivate the *appearance* of spending his time on "legal enactments" other than those that truly occupy him.

Thus, while it might have seemed to us up until now that perfectly trans-parent, nonmediated discourse is a social force desirable for all citizens but attainable by none, we can now come to quite a different conclu-sion. It appears that in Rousseau's ideal polity, the inevitable opacity of language is less a phenomenon of which everyone is cognizant than a quality that one person understands and deploys in the name of a largely ignorant majority. At the limit, Rousseau appears to be making the culturally undemocratic suggestion that linguistic difference itself is one of the "thousands of ideas which cannot be translated into the lan-guage of the people." At the very least, he indicates that social order and unity can be maintained only if the people as a whole remain unaware of the impossible and fictional nature of totalizing, nondifferential speech. Such knowledge becomes the exclusive property of the legislator.

Endowed with this unique awareness, Rousseau's lawgiver functions within the polity not only as a god but also as an artist—a conscious, active manipulator of signs and half-truths ("he *seems* to confine him-self"; "his *secret* care") designed to maintain the widespread illusion that the polity is a space of pure, unmediated generality. In addition to numerous references to the "great art of the legislator," which he makes throughout *The Social Contract,* Rousseau goes so far as to describe the populace as a "blind multitude" and the lawgiver himself as the only one capable of enabling this ignorant body "to see things as they are, and sometimes as they should be seen; it must be shown the good path which it is seeking, and secured against seduction by the desires of indi-viduals" (*Contract* 380). Not content merely to orchestrate public per-ceptions in accordance with "things as they are," the legislator pushes his people into conformity with some indeterminate, normative public policy (things "as they should be seen"), itself established to suppress the underlying fact of their individual differences.[57] In other words, Rousseau's political leader engages in an outright reconstruction of re-ality—one that guides citizens firmly along "the good path" toward the general will and preserves them from the "seduction" of individual in-terests and desires. Implicit in such an effort is the conviction that, left to its own devices, the so-called blind multitude is incapable of viewing social conditions as it "should": in accordance with a rule of hypotheti-cal, disinterested generality.

Given the people's presumed need for a fiction and for someone to construct and enforce it on their behalf, artistic intervention would seem to be a necessary evil in Rousseau's republic of virtue—a "remedy in the ailment" much like the mediating structure of the social contract itself. The author concedes as much in a preliminary version of *The Social Contract*, when he speaks of mediation as both a threat to political unity and a cure for political discord: "Let us endeavor to draw from the evil itself the remedy that should cure it.... Let us show,... through perfected artistry [dans l'art perfectionné], the reparation of the evils that art, from the beginning, wrought upon nature."[58] While maintaining an underlying belief in the morally dangerous nature of fictions (the "evils that art ... wrought upon nature"), these statements point to the possibility of a "perfected artistry" that would eradicate the "bad" consequences of representation (e.g., private interests) while establishing the "good" fiction of an undisrupted, genuinely universal general will. In this framework, the artful machinations of the legislator would ideally feed into and fortify the "more perfect social institution" that Rousseau holds up as his foremost political desideratum.

Significantly enough, however, this glimpse of a utopia achieved through art is itself suppressed in Rousseau's final version of *The Social Contract*. If, in the latter, Rousseau does admit that the legislator ultimately needs fictions to make the polity work, he nevertheless insists that such tactics fall far short of his ideal.[59] As a matter of fact, Rousseau follows his theoretical discussion of the perfect lawgiver, whose fidelity to the principle of Mosaic law places him beyond representation, with an allusion to one specific political leader, Peter the Great, whose dependence on mimetic strategies excludes him from the category of the sublime. The European-oriented Russian emperor fails to measure up to the likes of Judaism's Yahweh, according to Rousseau, because "Peter the Great had the talent of a copyist; he had no true genius, which is creative and makes everything from nothing" (*Contract* 90). Whereas creation ex nihilo involves the complete performative conflation of word and thing ("fiat lux"), imitation means marking a spatial, temporal, and ontological difference from an origin.[60] And as Rousseau comments in an unfinished essay on taste: "Man only creates beauty through imitation, but the more we move away from the original, the more our representations are disfigured."[61] If the legislator's task is to prevent the disfigurement or distortion of a unitary general will, then any copyist he may deploy to this end invariably threatens to undermine the goal it sets out to accomplish.[62]

Insofar as Peter the Great relies upon mimesis as a political strategy, the state entrusted to his care therefore remains flawed, unstable, and doomed to failure. Rousseau makes this point clear by predicting dire things for the Russian Empire:

> Peter... wanted to turn [his subjects] into Germans or Englishmen instead of making them Russians. He urged [them] to be what they were not and so prevented them from becoming what they might have been. This is just how a French tutor trains his pupil to shine for a brief moment in his childhood and then grow up into a nonentity, into nothing [rien]. The Russian Empire would like to subjugate Europe and will find itself subjugated. Such a revolution seems to me inevitable. (*Contract* 386)

It is remarkable, and paradoxical, that in his condemnation of Peter the Great's politics, Rousseau faults the Russian emperor for causing his people to be something other than what they are—even though the author himself defines the ideal legislator as one who is able to change human nature. Similarly, although he insists elsewhere that "if each citizen is nothing [n'est rien] except through" the work of the lawgiver, Rousseau reproaches Peter's nullification of the Russian people by comparing him to a tutor whose training fates the student to be a nonentity, to be nothing. Peter fails as a legislator, according to the logic of Rousseau's own argument, because he engages in the mimetic and mediating activities that sublime discourse is supposed to transcend.

This contradiction indicates that as soon as Rousseau's legislator ceases to be a pure abstraction (a figure whose only identifying characteristic is a philosophical kinship with the makers of "the Law of the Hebrews") and assumes a specific identity (Peter the Great), he can no longer perform the godlike duties that his position theoretically requires. His very being entails particularity; his most essential function, that of changing human nature, requires a fundamentally artistic transformation of reality. And while Rousseau's earlier draft of *The Social Contract* may openly acknowledge the need for aesthetic mediation in the realm of lawgiving, his ultimate conclusions on the subject suggest otherwise. At best, the legislator should hide his debt to fiction and artifice from the people whom he, precisely, represents. At worst, in allowing for the uncensored expression of mimetic tendencies and differential impulses, the legislator lays himself and his polity open to dissent, to discord, and even, as Rousseau presages for the Russian Empire, to "revolution." As we shall see in chapter 2, the link between linguistic polyvalence and political upheaval becomes an issue of the utmost importance for the thinkers of the Revolution and the Terror.

The Writer's Admission: A Call for Grace

What does this pessimistic view of the legislator's recourse to difference mean for the writer—for Rousseau himself as a writer of political texts? Perhaps even more explicitly than in his conceptualizations of the ideal lawgiver, Rousseau displays a deep-seated ambivalence to the role of representation when commenting on his own status as author. Yet he emphasizes from the opening paragraph of *The Social Contract* that the writer and the legislator are two irreducibly distinct categories, with very different types of self-expression at their disposal: "I may be asked whether I am a prince or a legislator that I should be writing about politics. I answer no: and indeed that is my reason for doing so. If I were a prince or a legislator, I should not waste my time saying what ought to be done; I should do it, or I should keep silent [je le ferais, ou je me tairais]" (*Contract* 49). With this disclaimer, Rousseau introduces an opposition that structures much of the treatise to follow and that raises repeated questions about the nature of literary, as distinct from political, discourse.[63] From the outset, the political leader (prince or legislator) is presented with a pair of extreme options: action (*faire*) or silence (*se taire*). The common ground shared by these two is an immediacy that we might, in view of our earlier observations about the legislator, term sublime. For the legislator is portrayed here as someone who would "not waste [his] time saying what ought to be done," who would always choose action or silence over linguistic mediation. Neither action nor silence is subject to the delays, slippages, and differences—between now and later, presence and absence, word and thing—that characterize such mediation. Neither gets bogged down in the waste or loss of time that Rousseau here identifies with writing. By definition, however, the same cannot be said of the author, who distinguishes himself from the legislator precisely through his ability and inclination to *say* "what ought to be done." Rousseau makes the great divide between writer and lawgiver still more apparent by placing his authorial "I" in a strange temporal and ontological position: "If I were a prince or a legislator...I would not waste my time.... I should do it or I should keep silent." As the conditional structure of this statement indicates, the writer's only access to the allegedly unmediated efficacy of politics is through fiction:

the transformation of writer to legislator is purely hypothetical, occurring in a time zone that will never coincide with the present tense. This noncoincidence of author and lawgiver attests to the tremendous difference between the type of discourse that each one's position requires him to adopt.[64] In short, writerly theory is explicitly constituted by the very temporal disjunctions and mediated relationships that political praxis is supposed to transcend.

Indeed, upon examining the language employed by Rousseau himself in the composition of *The Social Contract*, we realize that like the "copyist" tendencies of Peter the Great, it fails to meet the requirements of sublime Terror delineated in his description of the lawgiver. For instance, the Russian emperor's political reforms derive from a logic of exemplarity that is inherently differential in nature—and that therefore disqualifies him from the category of the true Rousseauist legislator.[65] Nevertheless, in writing *The Social Contract*, the author himself engages in a constant struggle between articulating general political principles on the one hand and, on the other hand, corroborating these statements with specific examples that make them meaningful to his readers.[66] The following passage illustrates this tension nicely: "Grotius denies that all human government is established for the benefit of the governed, and he cites the example of slavery. His characteristic method of reasoning is always to offer fact as a proof of right. It is possible to imagine a more logical method, but not one more favorable to tyrants" (*Contract* 51). Rousseau dismisses examples as subject to abuse by authorities and authors because they always reflect a single instance of a phenomenon ("fact") rather than a universal principle ("right") that holds true for all people at all times. Although his political theory valorizes the universal at the expense of the particular, in this instance the *philosophe*'s general qualification of the rhetoric of exemplarity as favorable to tyrants derives from his own recourse to the case of Grotius. The writer relies upon particular examples even as the political theorist questions their validity.[67]

Inconsistent though it may be with Rousseau's theoretical assertions, the example of Grotius immediately engenders another. Seeking additional validation for his proposition about the dangers of reasoning by example, the author goes on to relate how Caligula, one of history's most infamous "tyrants," put this method to use: "Just as a shepherd possesses a nature superior to that of his flock, so do those shepherds of men, their rulers, have a nature superior to that of their people. Or so, we are told, the Emperor Caligula argued, concluding, reasonably enough with this same analogy, that kings were gods or alternatively that the people were animals" (*Contract* 51). Here Rousseau condemns Caligula for purporting to derive a universal truth from the particular model of the shepherd and his flock. Like Peter the Great's imitation of Europe, with its patently nonsublime dependence on ordinary mimesis, the Roman emperor's logic, with its mediated and highly particular nature, draws Rousseau disapproval. As a writer, however, Rousseau once again finds himself in the same predicament as the lawgivers who fail to meas- ure up to his theoretical ideal. For in this case, as in the allusion to Grotius, Rousseau corroborates his gnomic diatribe about the tyranny of exam- ples by alluding to a single figure from world history. More interesting still, he condemns Caligula for invoking a particular god, a single "su- perior nature," to justify his imperial reign. We know, however, from our earlier examination of the legislator that the author resorts to sim- ilar examples ("gods would be needed"; "a special and superior func- tion which has nothing to do with the human condition") to elaborate his own theory of legitimate political authority.

As Rousseau proceeds with his discussion of leadership styles, his re- liance upon examples becomes more complicated but no less pronounced. Wrapping up his comments on Caligula, he notes: "I have said nothing of the King Adam or of the Emperor Noah, father of the three great monarchs who shared the universe between them, like children of Sat- urn, with whom some authors have identified them. I hope my readers will be grateful for this moderation..." (*Contract* 52). This passage is re- markable above all for its assemblage of negative examples (much more apparent, as usual, in the original French: "Je n'ai rien dit ni du roi Adam, ni de l'empereur Noé, etc."). By claiming not to need Adam, Noah, the three great monarchs, and the children of Saturn for his argument, Rousseau seemingly dispenses with the logic of exemplarity, which his praeteritio ("I have said nothing") nevertheless maintains. Like the re- course to examples, this technique of revealing and concealing some- thing at the same time runs counter to the poetics of totality and trans- parency that the Rousseauist lawgiver is supposed to espouse. Unlike the legislator, the author traffics in partiality, particularity, and differ- ence—a fact that he himself highlights when he refers to "this modera- tion" in his style. To be moderate, Rousseau's praeteritio indicates, is precisely to abstain from saying everything, in direct contrast to the extreme, totalizing pretensions of the legislator.

Rousseau also deviates from the sublime discourse of the legislator by introducing the writer's subjectivity into *The Social Contract*. This occurs when the author professes his hopes that people will appreciate his textual strategies: "I hope my readers will be grateful. . . ." While the legislator is meant to be a wholly impersonal entity, who exists beyond time and human nature, the writer, in this statement, bears the pronominal markings of particularity, the "I," and the subjective inclinations to go with it. When the author admits, "I hope," he makes way, at least semantically, for personal being and personal desire in one fell swoop. In fact, a similar inscription of the writer as a desiring individual occurs in the text's opening line, where Rousseau proclaims: "I want to consider [je veux chercher] if, in political society, there can be any legitimate and sure principle of government, taking men as they are and laws as they might be" (*Contract* 49). The first two words of this sentence merit considerable attention. For with the pronouncement "I want," Rousseau is quite literally asserting a particular will—his own—by way of an introduction to a work that argues for the suppression of individual interests in the name of collective unity. He follows this insertion of himself into the text with a more abstract overview of the concerns that will preoccupy him in the pages to follow: questions of democracy, political stability ("any legitimate and sure principle of government"), and the relationship between actual human nature and hypothetical legislative perfection ("men as they are and laws as they might be"). Still, the fact remains that from the outset, these issues—geared toward instituting a polity where universal principles will prevail over the vagaries of contingent subjectivity—coexist and commingle with Rousseau's particular will.

In many cases, Rousseau's acknowledgment of a subjective authorial involvement does more than simply attest to the presence of writerly desire in *The Social Contract*. More frequently still, he introduces the "I" of the writer to discuss the difficulty of eradicating interpretive difference from the text. For instance, Rousseau tends to abandon an impersonal narrative voice and adopt a first-person pronoun whenever he is confronted with terminology that he finds singularly difficult to define. Thus, in an attempt to elucidate a classic principle of political philosophy, "the right of the strongest," he exclaims: "But shall we never have this phrase explained? Force is a physical power; I do not see how its effects could produce morality. . . . In what sense can it be a moral duty?" (*Contract* 52). Following as it does on the heels of a long and highly abstract discussion of the relationship between force and law, this sudden emergence of a "we" and an "I" is jarring indeed. It signals that, far from a set of transcendental truths, the ideas under discussion are being mediated through an explicitly subjective lens. The "we" is also provocative in that it presupposes or conjures up some kind of community of readers, in which the writing subject himself has a place. In marked contrast to the legislator, who rises above his fellow man's conditions ("*our* nature," Rousseau specifies), the author implies here that he and his readers are in the same hermeneutic boat. Which is to say, they—"we"—are all subject to linguistic undecidability. Rousseau wonders whether he and his readers will ever figure out how to interpret "the right of the strongest," and the negative syntax of his query anticipates a negative reply, as if to discourage his readers from expecting any interpretive certainty in the matter. To drive the point home, he concludes with a question instead of an answer: "In what sense can it be a moral duty?" Left in the hands of a group of subjective readers, meaning becomes an open-ended proposition. In this way, the writer again takes his distance from the legislator, who maneuvers disingenuously to make his ideas (e.g., the fiction of godly legitimation) appear like transcendental, impersonal truths in his subjects' eyes.

The author establishes a similar link between subjective hermeneutics and terminological instability when he takes on Grotius's supposition that "a whole people [may] alienate its freedom and become the subject of a king." Refuting this claim, Rousseau writes: "In this remark there are several ambiguous words which would require [auraient besoin de] explanation, but let us confine ourselves to one—to 'alienate'" (*Contract* 54). Such equivocal semantics are a far cry from the sublime discourse that Rousseau attributes to the legislator. Rather than offering an ostensible coalescence of word and thing, as offered by Mosaic law, the writer presents his readers with "several ambiguous words." Furthermore, he situates any effort to hit upon a definitive definition for these terms in the realm of pure hypothesis: the words "would require explanation," but nothing in Rousseau's conditional phrasing guarantees that such clarification is forthcoming. Finally, as we saw him do earlier, here again Rousseau enlists a clearly subjectivized audience to join him in an attempt to limit, rather than expand, the scope of his language. "Let us confine ourselves to one—to 'alienate,'" he urges, narrowing the range of dubiously defined words to a single term. The pronoun *we* underscores the complicity or parity between the author and his readers, but its explicitly personal status prevents the resultant interpretive community from turning into an abstract, anonymous "one" like the one figured by the social pact itself.

Not limited to designating or accompanying instances of potential interpretive difference, first-person pronouns also appear at places in *The Social Contract* where Rousseau is struggling with the explicitly temporal nature of his enterprise. We have already examined the passage where the writing subject surfaces in the text to distinguish himself from a "prince or a legislator" and to explain that his own work involves the very loss of time that political leaders must necessarily avoid. But this is by no means the only case of such an editorial intervention. For example, in the middle of Rousseau's articulation of the "right to life and death," a frustrated authorial "I" interrupts to complain about the temporal constraints of his medium: "Since every wrongdoer attacks the society's law, he becomes by his deed a rebel and a traitor to the nation; he ceases to be a member of it. . . . And in this case, the preservation of the state is incompatible with his preservation; one or the other must perish. . . . All my ideas hold together, but I would not know how [je ne saurais] to elaborate them all at once" (*Contract* 79). Indeed, however cohesive the writer's postulations about enemies of the state may be, however much his "ideas hold together," the nature of the language he employs makes it impossible for them all to be expressed simultaneously. Rousseau further emphasizes this impasse by concluding that even hypothetically, he would not be able ("I *would not know how*") to put forth all his thoughts at once. The fact, moreover, that he makes these comments in the middle of an extreme Terrorist political statement ("one or the other must perish") only serves to undermine its message. The writer, in short, remains ensnared in difference even when he is giving voice to the demands of pure generality. In contrast to the supposedly transcendental lawgiver, the writing subject fails to construct an argument that transcends himself or his being in time.

In a footnote appended to a highly convoluted definition of the term *sovereignty,* the authorial "I" likewise appears in conjunction with a request for more time: "I beg of you [je vous prie], attentive readers, do not hasten to accuse me of contradictions. I cannot avoid a contradiction of words, because of the poverty of language; but wait" (*Contract* 74n). This combination of direct pleading ("I beg of you") and imperative verb forms ("do not hasten"; "wait") underscores Rousseau's anxiety about the inability of his medium—"words," "language"—to achieve immediacy and completeness, given the time pressures that inhere in it. At the beginning of the footnote, he begs his readers not to hurry through his text, and at the end, he urges them to wait for the pieces of his argument to fall into place, since these ideas cannot, structurally, all be "elaborate[d] . . . at once." "Because," as he says, "of the poverty of language," his readers will have to be "attentive"—willing to wait (the French adjective *attentif* being etymologically linked to the verb *attendre*) and to tolerate the impingements of time on his text.

Rousseau solicits his readers' patience in a similar fashion at the beginning of Book Three of his treatise, where he cautions: "I must warn the reader that this chapter should be read with care, for I have not the art to make myself clear [l'art d'être clair] to those who do not wish to be attentive" (*Contract* 101). Again making use of the adjective *attentive* and joining it to the qualification *with care*, Rousseau reiterates his preference that his work be read slowly. Here, as in the address to his "attentive readers," he asserts that meaning cannot materialize all at once, like God's instantaneously performative call for light, but rather that it has to unfold in time. In this way, his poetics diverge significantly from the transparent immediacy that supposedly characterizes the Longinian and Kantian notion of God as well as Rousseau's own legislator. Their sublime utterances purport to repudiate the delays and deformations proper to "the unfolding of time." The author's "art" of clarification, on the other hand, consists in these very phenomena and strives to engender a tolerant attitude toward them.

It is in this light that we can begin to understand Rousseau's interjections about desire, time, and language as designating, albeit elliptically, a need for *grace*, by which I mean tolerance of the differential elements that his own theoretical postulates try to ban but that his actual textual practice cannot avoid.[68] Reviled and negated by sublime discourse, the tendency to "speak differently"—ascribed by Rousseau to the antisocial passions—pervades the *philosophe*'s political thought and impels him to seek forgiveness for his own unavoidable engagement of difference in numerous forms. Nowhere does the author reveal this attitude more vividly than when he is describing how the Greek and Roman empires maintained public order by categorically refusing to pardon any and all criminals. In the midst of a statement about the efficacy of this strategy, Rousseau's "I" intervenes and admits that the policy nevertheless gives him pause: "Frequent pardons signal that crimes will soon need no pardon; and anyone can see what that must lead to. However, I can feel my heart whispering and restraining my pen; let us leave the discussion of these questions to the just man who has never erred and has therefore had no need of pardon" (*Contract* 80). While this commentary begins with a gnomic generalization about the importance of taking a hard line on social agitators, it develops quickly into an overtly personal praeteritio suggestive of the writer's own imperfections and need of pardon. Rousseau alleges that his heart, the site of desire and individual difference, prevents him from pursuing a Terrorist line of reasoning any further. He then proceeds to inscribe this unruly, sentimental "I" in a first-person community of readers ("*let us*"), this time to share with them in speechless sympathy for unavoidable human error. Against the lawgiver's transcendental work of Terror, Rousseau thus opposes the author's inclusive call for grace. In the process, the poles of the opposition that we encountered at the beginning of *The Social Contract*—between unmediated political practice (*faire, se taire*) and detached authorial commentary ("saying what ought to be done")—are reversed. Now, the theoretical evaluation of Terror is shown to be the domain of the legislator ("*the discussion* of these questions [belongs] to the just man who has never erred"), where the practical imperative of silence falls to the writer. This imperative falls also to the extended community of "us" individuals who, like Rousseau, know what it is to err and, thus, to be human.

Now error, clearly, has a lot in common with linguistic figuration and invention,[69] a fact that Rousseau's own account of the genesis of the term *giant* makes plain. In his reading of *The Social Contract*, Louis Althusser highlights the vexed nature of the philosopher's attempt to combine political theory and authorial practice and identifies literary language itself as the escape hatch through which Rousseau attempts to avoid the problems raised by this unholy mix. When all else fails, Althusser writes of the Rousseauist political project, "only one single road remains open: a transference of the impossible theoretical solution onto the other of theory, namely literature."[70] According to this formulation, the recourse to "pure" fiction, like the recourse to God advocated in Rousseau's treatise, would seem to represent a way out of the divisions that structure ordinary human experience and the contradictions that attend any theoretical project of transcendence. At least as far as *The Social Contract* is concerned, though, Althusser's understanding of how "the other of theory" functions in Rousseau's work misses the critical fact that its Terrorist suppressions persist, in the face of all glaring contradictions, when the *philosophe* transposes his political musings into the realm of fiction. As an amendment or supplement to this oversight, I would therefore like to offer a short analysis of the widely neglected narrative "prose poem" that Rousseau drafted immediately after the controversial publication of *The Social Contract* and the *Émile*.[71] Not only does this text, *Le Lévite d'Éphraïm*, reinscribe the limiting logic of totality on which Rousseau's political philosophy is predicated, and not only does it entirely suppress the brief evocation of mercy that surfaces in *The Social Contract,* but more dramatically still, it also adds a new, specifically gendered twist to the Terrorist exclusions that operate throughout Rousseau's political work. To the political, ontological, and linguistic differences that must be eradicated from the ideal polity, this short story adds feminine sexual difference as an equivalent, and equally intolerable, counterdiscourse. Because femininity meets with virulent repression under Robespierre and Saint-Just—as well as in Sade's republican dystopia—we would do well to take a brief look at *Le Lévite d'Éphraïm* before moving away from Rousseau and toward those for whom his intimations of Terror prove so important.

The Sexual Contract: Feminine Dismemberment and Virile Membership in *Le Lévite d'Éphraïm*

Although it has been virtually ignored by readers of Rousseau's writing—literary, philosophical, or otherwise—his retelling of the biblical tale of the Levite of Ephraim, taken from the Book of Judges, was described by the author himself as the only work worthy of being mentioned on his epitaph.[72] Written during the firestorm generated by the publication of *The Social Contract* and the *Émile* in the summer of 1762, the story most likely earned such exaggerated praise from its author, at least in part, because of the condemnations that his more publicly visible texts had just garnered. For students of Rousseau's political philosophy, however, *Le Lévite d'Éphraïm* merits no small portion of the importance

that Rousseau accorded to it insofar as it economically and explicitly re-
formulates many of *The Social Contract*'s principal tenets. More precisely, the text depicts the successful creation of a citizen (the eponymous Levite, who, perhaps not incidentally, hails from the Israelites'
law-administering caste)[73] and of a state (ancient Israel) as resulting
from the numerous suppressions already prescribed by *The Social Contract*. The imperative of absolute unity, the stifling of individual passions and private interests, the valorization of sublime, nondifferential
"legislator's" discourse: all of these features are combined, in *Le Lévite
d'Éphraïm*, with an overt and sustained abolition of feminine sexuality
that is likewise posited as anathema to political stability. To Carole Pateman's convincing arguments about the male-oriented "sexual contract"
that underpins social life in Rousseau's writings, a close reading of *Le
Lévite d'Éphraïm* adds the insight that his Terror, too, is sexual as well as
political. The unified state, Rousseau's biblical rewriting tells us, depends just as much on the destruction of femininity as it does on the
extirpation of subjective, political, and linguistic difference.[74]

The close intertwining of questions of gender, politics, and language
in Rousseau's reworking of the biblical tale is apparent as early as his
Essay on the Origin of Languages, in which he provides a short summary of the Levite's drama. The background of the story's key episode
is the gang rape and collective murder of a Levite's concubine by a ma-
rauding group of Benjamites. The wronged Levite, Rousseau suggests in
the *Essay,* responds with maximum efficacy to this heinous deed by eschewing writing altogether when he calls upon his Israelite cousins to
help him avenge it:

> When the Levite of Ephraim wanted to avenge the death of his wife, he
> wrote nothing to the tribes of Israel, but divided her body into twelve
> sections, which he sent to them. At this horrible sight they rushed to
> arms, crying with one voice: *Never has such a thing happened in Israel,
> from the time of our fathers' going out of Egypt, down to the present day!*
> And the tribe of Benjamin was exterminated. In our day, however, this
> affair, recounted in court pleadings and discussions, perhaps in jest,
> would be dragged out until this most horrible of crimes would in the
> end have remained unpunished. (*Essay* 7; Rousseau's emphasis)

This passage prefigures *The Social Contract*'s emphasis on instantaneous,
unmediated communication ("he wrote nothing") and the unified po-

litical front ("they rushed to arms, crying with one voice") that results directly therefrom. Instead of dismissing as primitive or condemning as gory the Levite's decision to cut up his lover's corpse, Rousseau presents it as a preferable alternative to more conventional legal measures, with their potential for undesirable temporal delay ("dragg[ing] out") and interpretive difference ("jest"). In an elliptical way, the Levite's cold-blooded treatment of his beloved's cadaver also anticipates the violence to one's "natural" passions or instincts that Rousseauist socialization requires—and indeed, Rousseau's more thorough retelling of the story will make this apparent. In *The Social Contract,* the body that one must submit to brutal constraints is one's own (we recall the "extinction or annihilation" to which the citizen's private attachments are condemned), whereas in this case, that brutality is *displaced* from the Levite's own body onto that of his female companion. While the death and dismemberment of this woman ultimately spur her lover on to a campaign for justice and his fellow Israelites on to military valor, the female figure herself has no further role once her body has been destroyed. For this reason, we might say of the female body what Rousseau says of the outlaw in *The Social Contract:* "The preservation of the state is incompatible with [her] preservation; one or the other must perish" (*Contract* 79).

Even more explicitly than its kindred passage in his essay on language, Rousseau's *Lévite d'Éphraïm* strongly establishes the mutual incompatibility of feminine/individual and political/collective survival. The explicitness of this message manifests itself above all in the story's structure: the text is organized into three separate movements, each of which features the sacrifice of a feminine body and the resultant fortification of the body politic. The first of these three episodes is evoked proleptically in the story's opening lines, when the *philosophe* conjures up the image of the Levite's dead concubine, before going back to relate how it all happened:

> O you men of meekness, enemies of all inhumanity; you who, for fear of facing up to your brothers' crimes, would rather let them go unpunished; what tableau do I come to put before you? The body of a woman cut into pieces, her limbs torn apart and sent, palpitating, to the twelve Tribes [of Israel]; the whole people, seized with horror, raising up to the Heavens a unanimous clamor, and crying out with one voice: *No, never has such a thing happened in Israel from the time of our fathers' going out*

of Egypt until the present day. Holy people, gather together, utter a verdict on this horrible act. In the face of such offenses, whoever averts his eyes is a coward and a traitor to justice; real humanity confronts [offenses] head-on in order to know them, to judge them, to detest them.[75] (*Lévite* 1208; Rousseau's emphasis)

Like the paragraph in the *Essay on the Origin of Languages,* Rousseau's intimation here is that justice is better served by the cutting up of the woman's body than by a more timorous response to her gang rape and murder at the hands of the Benjamites. Whereas the "men of meekness" who are ostensibly the prose poem's readers would, according to Rousseau, be more likely to avoid than embrace punishing the Benjamites' crime, the Levite who chopped up his loved one brooked no such hesitation. Like the sublime language of the lawgiver in *The Social Contract,* the Levite's butchery occurs instantaneously, outside time. And like the legislator's dictates, the bereaved lover's prompt, unmediated activity brings about radical unity in the state as a whole. As in the *Essay,* the Israelites' response to their cousin's bloody offering is universal and homogeneous: the "whole people" kick up a "unanimous clamor, . . . crying out with one voice." That univocal cry, meanwhile, thematizes the discursive and political unification that it simultaneously performs, for it constitutes a command that the people of Israel "gather together" to pass judgment on the Benjamites' act. It also expresses unflinching intolerance for anyone who would hesitate to mete out justice to the wrongdoers. Interestingly enough, this intolerance seems directed not only at any potential "traitor[s] to justice" within the Israelite camp but also at the extradiegetic "men of meekness" to whom Rousseau's own text is addressed. This slippage between intradiegetic and extradiegetic frames of reference surfaces in the rhetoric of "real humanity"—which paradoxically teaches people to treat offenses with hatred—that the Israelites demand of themselves and each other, in contrast to the erroneous aversion to "inhumanity" that characterizes the meek. The political function of the dismembered feminine corpse is thus twofold; it is designed to inspire both a love of justice through a defeat of pathological cowardice and a shared sense of purpose in the men within and without the story.

Having established the broader community-building purpose of this gruesome tableau, as he calls it, Rousseau backtracks to explain exactly how the Levite's mistress wound up getting raped by the Benjamites, dismembered by her lover, and avenged by the Israelites. Hers is the first of the three movements, which initially looks like a fairly conventional boy-meets-girl scenario: a young Levite from the town of Ephraim spies a beautiful maiden in Bethlehem; is immediately smitten; showers her with gifts; and takes her away to live with him.[76] Although Rousseau chronicles in some detail the couple's subsequent domestic bliss, their happily-ever-after narrative eventually takes a turn for the worse and ends in tragedy. One day, the young beauty gets bored with her Levite lover, "perhaps because he left nothing for her to desire" (*Lévite* 1211). This phrase resonates strangely with the "[no]thing left to demand" promised by Rousseau's social pact, but in fact it has the opposite meaning. Whereas the social contract leaves its members no room for desire by quashing all their individual attachments, the Levite has been too assiduous in catering to his concubine's every whim, to the point where he becomes unattractive and even effeminate in her eyes. The woman leaves him and resumes residence with her father, a stern, law-abiding man who has little patience for his daughter's love-struck beau. But the Levite, pathologically amorous, follows her and, defying her father's request to leave the girl be, takes her away again, "like a mother bringing her child back from the nurse's, and worrying that the slightest breath of air could do the child harm" (*Lévite* 1212). This metaphor speaks volumes about the character of our Levite. It casts him in the grotesque role of an excessively solicitous maternal figure from whose clutches the wife had wanted to individuate, and who himself never fully adapted to the demands of sociability symbolized by the bride's father's house and commandments.[77]

The logic of the story requires that this primordial, socially unassimilable bond with the ersatz maternal body be severed—and severed it is, in the bloodiest way imaginable. After a long day's journey away from his lady's paternal home, the Levite finds lodgings for them in the town of Gibeah, where he feels sure they will meet with decent treatment, because it is populated by "our brothers... from the tribe of Benjamin" (*Lévite* 1212). However, instead of extending a warm welcome to the newcomers, the local Benjamite men surround the inn where the couple are staying and demand that the aging innkeeper turn over the young man to them at once:

> "The men of [Gibeah] came and surrounded the house, knocking loudly on the door and screaming to the old man in menacing tones: "Hand over to us this foreign young man that you have received within our

walls; let his beauty be the price we collect in return for his asylum. . . ."
(*Lévite* 1213)

Picking up on the erotic overtones of this demand, the sympathetic innkeeper endeavors to protect his guest by offering the mob his own virgin daughter to placate them: the duties of hospitality and honorable social conduct, he declares, take precedence over even those of familial love. But the Levite—this time feminized by the male Benjamites' sexual interest in his "beauty"—will hear of no such sacrifice. Warming to the requirements of gentlemanly honor, the Levite shows his gratitude to the innkeeper by handing over his own young mistress instead. The Benjamites promptly rape and kill her, and in so doing, they enable the Levite, freed at last from his emasculating and antisocial romantic attachment, to become a citizen, manly and militant.

How does he do it? By gazing, as the tribes of Israel will soon be doing, on the tableau of his girlfriend's violated corpse.

> What a sight for his shattered heart! He raises a plaintive cry up to the Heavens, avenger of all crime. . . . The young woman does not answer him; he grows anxious, he looks, he touches her, she is no more. "O maiden too lovable, and too loved [o fille trop aimable, et trop aimée], was it for this that I removed you from your father's house? Was this the fate that my love was preparing for you?" He finished these words ready to follow her, and only stayed alive so that he could avenge her. (*Lévite* 1215)

Significantly, it is when he is faced with the spectacle of the broken female body—for him the erstwhile repository of his sentimental weakness and the cause of his social ineptitude—that the Levite at last manages to turn his attention to weightier issues like crime and punishment. Recognizing too late the unhealthy and excessive nature of his love for his mistress ("trop aimable, et trop aimée"), he realizes that he was wrong to violate her father's request that he temper his improper feelings. Although he himself wishes to die, he suppresses his grief, which is pathological in proportion to his love, and assumes the virile task of revenge through military retaliation.

As my reference to the military should indicate, the revenge that the Levite has in mind is, unlike love, a social impulse, an affair between tribes and not individuals. His enemies are, after all, a band of brothers who asserted their own esprit de corps by cooperating in the young woman's destruction. (Rousseau underscores the communal nature of their brutality by likening them to a "pack of wolves falling upon a feeble heifer" [*Lévite* 1214].)[78] So, to gain the force and backing necessary to avenge his wife's death, the Levite responds in kind by appealing to his, and the Benjamites', broad network of family members. In an effort to galvanize the Israelites and rally them to his side, he decides to create a spectacle even more galling than the one that he beheld after her rape. "From this moment on," Rousseau recounts,

> preoccupied with the one plan that filled his heart, he was deaf to any other sentiment: love, regret, pity. The very sight of that body, which should have made him burst into tears, no longer wrenches from him either protests or tears [ni les plaintes ni les pleurs]: he no longer sees in it anything but an object of rage.... Without hesitating, without trembling, [he] dares to cut this body into twelve pieces, with a firm and steady hand he strikes without fear, he cuts the flesh and the bones, he separates the head and the limbs, and after having sent these dreadful packages to the Tribes, he goes ahead of them to Mizpeh, ... flings himself on the ground when they arrive, and with great shouts demands justice from the God of Israel. (*Lévite* 1215–16)

This paragraph describes with considerable economy the Levite's metamorphosis from a softhearted lover into a pitiless fighter. His retributive plan alone occupies his soul, to the exclusion of all the tender mercies that he used to have for his mistress. Even when he contemplates her mutilated remains, the voice of the passions falls on deaf ears. The Levite has grown impervious to effeminate feelings like love, regret, and pity, and his lover's cadaver itself incites in him nothing more than "rage," that is, a desire for revenge against the men who offended him. Armed with this anger, the man is capable of unflinchingly dismembering his beloved's body for distribution to the tribes of Israel. And when he arrives in Mizpeh to prepare the Israelites for what he has sent them, it is not anguished bereavement but a desire for justice that motivates his "great shouts," addressed to the ultimate tribal patriarch, "the God of Israel." The private discourse of sentiment has given way to the public discourse of morality and honor.

The first movement of *Le Lévite d'Éphraïm* does not, however, stop with its eponymous hero's transformation from an effete lover into a militant citizen of the law. As Rousseau's opening focus on the Israelites'

unification suggests, the Levite's story is also, and perhaps more important, that of a nation consolidating itself in the name of disinterested
· fairness. This aspect of the text again comes to the fore when the Levite
delivers a rousing speech before the assembled Israelite population. Revising his proleptic prologue, which focused on the outrage of the Israelite
people at the sight of the twelve "packages" of feminine flesh, Rousseau
writes: "There arose in Israel one single cry, explosive, unanimous: 'Let
the blood of this young woman fall back on her murderers. . . . Not a
single one of us will return to his hearth until Gibeah has been laid to
waste'" (*Lévite* 1216). Once he sees the mass of his kinsmen so thoroughly aligned on his side, uttering "one single, [unanimous] cry," the
Levite's own job is done, and he falls dead on the spot, provoking further consensus about, and shared commitment to, the retribution he
was seeking. "His corpse was honored in a public funeral ceremony.
The young woman's limbs were gathered together and placed in the
same sepulchre with his, and all of Israel mourned them" (*Lévite* 1216).
The public nature of the Levite's funeral and the symbolic gathering
together of the couple's mortal remains both reflect and catalyze the
unity that now characterizes "all of Israel." Furthermore, now that the
catalytic corpses are dead and buried, the exclusion upon which the Israelites base their social identity persists in a different form: in the interdiction against returning home ("not a single one of us will return to
his hearth") that accompanies the nation's pledge of vengeance. Like
the socially irresponsible or paternally unacceptable domestic bliss originally prized by the Levite, the preference of the hearth to the battlefield
cannot be allowed to persist in the newly fortified Israelite alliance. As
long as a patent wrong remains to be righted, the space of the home
must be forsaken for the space of warfare, the concerns of family love
for those of rough justice.

It is this valorization of virile, militaristic virtue and unsentimental
fairness that ultimately pushes the Israelites to repeat against their own
women a similar offense to the one that gave rise to the war in the first
place, and this offense constitutes the climax of the story's second movement. The avenging tribes successfully combat the Benjamites—so successfully, in fact, that "virtually the entire tribe of Benjamin, to the number of twenty-six thousand men, died by the sword of Israel, such that
only six hundred men, the last remnant of that unhappy tribe, escaped

the deadly blade..." (*Lévite* 1219). Once they survey the full extent of the damage they have done, the victorious armies suddenly realize that this tribal annihilation actually constitutes a form of *self*-destruction. The Benjamites, after all, are themselves Israelites: the Levite had originally sought shelter in their town because they were his "brothers," and now those that fought on his behalf are horrified at the fratricide they have committed. They resolve therefore to rebuild the community that they themselves tore asunder. Not surprisingly, the catalyst for this resolution is, once again, the spectacle of a mutilated body—this time the body politic itself: "But the victorious tribes, seeing the blood that they had spilled, felt the wound they had inflicted on themselves. The people came and, gathering together in the house of their strong God, erected an altar at which they mourned, they mourned their victory" (*Lévite* 1220). With the sight of blood, of a wound inflicted on their own tribal body, the Israelites are confronted with an image of castration, a mark of feminine vulnerability at the heart of their successful military campaign. As when the Israelites received the body parts of the Levite's dead lover, here too the lamentation of a feminine-coded wound actually proves to be *constitutive* of male-coded sociopolitical identity. It compels them to "gather... together in the house of their strong God," to unify under the heading of might and religious right. And so, repeating the dialectical pattern that made a man out of their Levite cousin, the Israelites decide to help repopulate the moribund Benjamite tribe by giving them their own unwed daughters. Everything happens as if the Israelites needed to expel this feminine element from their midst, in order to affirm their own wholeness and repair the wound that the civil war opened up in the body politic.

This second sacrifice of a female body assumes a slightly less gory cast, but it nevertheless serves as a clear pendant to the vignette of the Levite's dismembered mistress. As in the section devoted to the Levite, Rousseau structures this part of the story around a central couple, Axa and Elmacin, whose love has to be renounced for the greater good of the community (and who, as Thomas Kavanagh stresses, are inventions of Rousseau's, altogether absent from the biblical tale).[79] Axa's position is particularly difficult because she is not only one of the many young women slated to be handed over to the endangered Benjamite tribe but also the daughter of the city elder who devised this repopulation plan.

At first, Axa puts up some level of resistance to her father's proposal, so deeply does she love "the young Elmacin, to whom she had been promised" (*Lévite* 1222). Axa's tearful glances when she is presented to her new Benjamite master betray her reluctance, to the point where her father takes her aside and counsels her thus:

> "Axa," he said to her, "you know my heart; I love Elmacin, he would have been the consolation of my old age; but the salvation of your people and the honor of your father should be more important to you than he is. Do your duty, my girl, and save me from humiliation in my brothers' eyes, for I am the one who counseled everything that has been done." (*Lévite* 1223)

This paternal pep talk outlines the same opposition that surfaces throughout *The Social Contract,* between affairs of the heart on the one hand ("you know my heart; I love Elmacin") and those of the state ("your duty," "the salvation of your people") on the other. Public obligation is, moreover, in this case explicitly associated with a patriarchal and fraternal order (the old man refers both to a father's honor and to his brothers' judgments), while private emotion is implicitly associated with Axa's sentimental, womanly hesitation to do the right thing. In the name of the national salvation and filial duty, Axa's personal preferences must, in her father's solution, be sacrificed—just as the Levite suppressed his "love, pity, and regret" upon viewing his lover's corpse, and just as the exemplary citizen kills off his "passions" under the social pact.

Accordingly, the maiden responds with compliance to her father's words of wisdom:

> Axa lowers her head and sighs without responding, but when she finally lifts her eyes again, she meets those of her venerable father. His eyes said even more than his mouth: she takes his side. Her weak and trembling voice scarcely pronounces, in a weak and final adieu, the name of Elmacin, at whom she dares not look. Then, turning around immediately, half dead, she falls into the Benjamite's arms. (*Lévite* 1223)

The old man's gaze here plays a critical role similar to that of earlier specular tableaux: the mangled cadaver and the wounded body politic. Even more than his speech, it is the father's unmediated gaze that impels Axa to overcome her hesitation, operating on the sublime register of the transcendental discourse, whose efficacy Rousseau praises in other writings. Furthermore, when, prompted by this powerful nonlanguage,

Axa does abandon her sentimental weakness and turn herself over to the Benjamite, she herself is, in a sense, killed off. In Rousseau's exact words, she is "half dead": part of her, the part that values Elmacin more than the good of the state, has been put to death. With this part of her, excised, Axa becomes, like the Levite's unlucky lady, a sort of fragmented body: robbed of her own inclinations and exchanged between men for the sake of national security.

Predictably, this reprised display of a mutilated feminine corpse inspires the men of Israel to greater courage one last time. Elmacin, leading the charge, steps forth and announces that out of respect for Axa's courageous gesture, he will henceforth devote his life to serving God—again, the ultimate guarantor of the Israelites' patriarchal virtue. But more unexpected and fascinating than the young man's newfound civic devotion is the reaction of the other young women, Axa's companions in distress awaiting forced marriage to the Bejamites. When they see one of their own deliver herself, albeit in a dead faint, into the arms of an enemy soldier, the rest of the maidens are moved to imitate Axa's behavior. In so doing, they repeat the pattern of feminine self-sacrifice and political consolidation for the third time in the text: "Immediately, as if by a sudden inspiration, all the girls, carried away by Axa's example, imitate her sacrifice, and, renouncing their first loves, deliver themselves over to the Benjamites, who had been following them" (*Lévite* 1223). In this concluding episode, Axa's self-sacrifice is generalized, undertaken by all the Israelite women—also in an "immediate," quasi-sublime fashion. The critical component in this self-sacrifice is, as in Axa's case, the renunciation of their primordial attachments ("their first loves"), necessary once more to the unity of the state as a whole. In stifling their own sentiments in the interest of public harmony, these maidens become another, and the final, inspirational tableau for the Israelite tribes as a whole. Rousseau ends *Le Lévite d'Éphraïm* with these lines: "At this touching sight, a cry of joy bursts forth from the People: 'Virgins of Ephraim, through you, Benjamin will be reborn. Blessed be the God of our fathers. There is still virtue in Israel'" (*Lévite* 1223). The touching sight of the women's collective self-immolation assures the assembled tribesmen that all, at last, is right with the world. "The God of our fathers" receives heartfelt praise; the restoration of the patriarchal Israelite lineage is guaranteed; and virtue, that indispensable quality of socially motivated self-abnegation, carries the day. Affirmed by a single cry of disinterested, patriotic joy, uttered by the people as one, the Rousseauist republic of virtue is indeed reborn in *Le Lévite d'Éphraïm*, which thereby showcases, and genders, the terrible Terrorist aspects of *The Social Contract*.

CHAPTER TWO

The Terror That Speaks
The Unspeakable Politics of Robespierre and Saint-Just

> Let us always focus on *things,* without letting ourselves be seduced by *words.*
> —Maximilien Robespierre, "On the Freedom of the Press"

> So many traitors have already escaped from the Terror that speaks, who would not be able to escape from justice that takes crime into its own hands.
> —Louis-Antoine Saint-Just, "On Incarcerated Persons"

On March 31, 1794,[1] when Maximilien Robespierre sent his oldest friend and one-time political ally, Camille Desmoulins, to the guillotine as a counterrevolutionary suspect, he did so without explanation or comment. As Jules Michelet explains in his account of the incident: "A god who discusses things is lost."[2] This quotation suggests that for Robespierre, at the height of his powers in revolutionary France as the leader of the then near-omnipotent Montagnard party,[3] linguistic engagement was tantamount to vulnerability, weakness, a loss of control. In implying as much about the politician's silence, Michelet's observation speaks volumes about the precarious position of language under Robespierre's Reign of Terror. Given his staunch devotion to Rousseauist thought (rumor had it that he carried a dog-eared copy of *The Social Contract* everywhere he went), it comes as little surprise that he should have shared the philosopher's view of linguistic difference as inappropriate in a legislator and destabilizing in a polity.[4] Indeed, nicknamed the Incorruptible for his austere lifestyle and morals, Robespierre followed Rousseau in associating civic virtue with language of the purest, most universalizing nature. In the manifold speeches he made before the National Convention from 1792 to 1794, the Montagnard chieftain repeatedly articulated a poetics and politics of transparency, which he consistently prescribed to the fledgling republic and attempted to implement in his own discourse.[5] As this chapter should make apparent, the Incorruptible's aesthetic and political worldview construed silence to be the optimal, and perhaps even the sole, basis of radically inclusive public policy.

Robespierre was not the only Terrorist politician to bring such a markedly Rousseauist philosophical perspective to bear on the shape of the new French state. Louis-Antoine Saint-Just, Robespierre's right-hand man in the Montagnard party and one of its other most memorable spokesmen, also held up silence as an exemplary form of revolutionary expression. During the debate on the subject of Louis XVI's trial and execution, the event that perhaps more than any other paved the way for the Montagnard Terror, Saint-Just enjoined his fellow *conventionnels* to stop talking and start acting. "The truth," he intoned, "burns in silence in the hearts of men"[6]—the implication being that one moment of resolute speechlessness, accompanied by decisive action, would come far closer to expressing the truth of the Revolution than a thousand time-consuming, treacherous words ever could. Like Rousseau and Robespierre, Saint-Just attached supreme value to a discourse designed to overcome the hermeneutic and temporal slippages inherent in ordinary language. To kill Louis XVI (or indeed any alleged public enemy) without a word was for the Montagnards to attain a sublime discursive position worthy of Rousseau's quasi-divine legislator—whose two options, we recall, are "doing" and "keeping silent." Conversely, again: A god who discusses things is lost.

And yet, just as the *philosophe* held sublime discourse to be the flip side of totalizing expression, the masterminds of the Terror made claims for the complete discursive inclusiveness that coexisted alongside their valorized idea of wordless nonlanguage. In a March 1794 speech denouncing various "factions" working to undermine the nascent republic, Saint-Just opposes his interlocutors to this sinister group by declaring that "one can dare to say everything to *you,* you friends of liberty and enemies of tyranny."[7] The groups that Saint-Just accuses of anti-republican conspiracy can, he avows, be identified above all by their duplicitous, behind-the-scenes machinations, by their opaque dealings, artifice, and double-talk. By contrast, Saint-Just identifies the "friends of liberty"—the republican French—as those who engaged in a discourse of absolute totality, consistent with the notion of the general will that the revolutionary state supposedly reflected.[8] In theory, this new polity, officially known as "the republic one and indivisible," did not tolerate the divisive, the divided, or the partial. Like keeping silent, saying everything becomes a political imperative aimed, as in *The Social Contract,* at maintaining the unity of a society whose very existence is predicated on discursive sameness. "To say everything for the sake of the nation" (Soboul 166): Saint-Just announces this as his own most pressing political objective. "One must tell the truth in its entirety" (Soboul 122). Robespierre could not have agreed more: "When good citizens are not permitted to speak, then it is safe to say that the wicked are in power."[9]

Its totalizing promises notwithstanding, the sublimity of republican discourse invariably requires some fairly brutal discursive restraints at the margins, imposed upon those who do not qualify for inclusion in Robespierre's category of "good" citizenship. Considering a range of speeches by the Incorruptible and his chief henchman, this chapter identifies and investigates the limitations that inhere in the Terrorist leaders' attempts to transcend difference. It demonstrates how these men concerned themselves with eradicating elements and impulses very similar to those deemed inadmissible in Rousseau's political writing. Accordingly, the primary targets identified by Robespierre and Saint-Just, like those singled out by their esteemed Swiss forebear, made up: *(a)* the opaque, figural, and differential nature of language as such; *(b)* the obstacles that both time and words posed to the Montagnards' calls for immediate political action; *(c)* the presence of alternative voices or viewpoints, notably those held to betray "pathological" individuality; and *(d)* women's sexuality, conceptually equated with all other forms of difference. At the limit, the speeches and decrees through which Robespierre and Saint-Just constructed their Terror focus on purging society of all particularity—even though these texts repeatedly position themselves as disinterested, totalizing expressions of the common good.

As our examination of Rousseau has already revealed, however, the project of eliminating difference is not without considerable difficulties and contradictions, especially when it is undertaken in language. Indeed, despite the tremendous political power they enjoyed during the Terror, Robespierre and Saint-Just by no means escaped the problems proper to the linguistic medium that they necessarily, and prolifically, deployed.[10] Despite their attempts not just to preach but to practice sublime abstraction in speeches and published writings (they both favored a pseudoperformative style of oratory that Rousseau, not to mention Longinus, would have admired), these men displayed considerable self-awareness about the potential of language to undermine their homogenizing project. The difference between a word and its meaning, between the moment of a word's enunciation and the moment of its reception, between a subjectively perceived fiction and an objective fact, between a speaker's interpretation and that of his reader or listener, . . . the specter of this difference haunts the Montagnard politicians' every utterance, no matter how assiduously they strove to keep it at bay. Ultimately, Robespierre and Saint-Just resembled their revered *philosophe* not only in attempting to establish a nondiscursive discourse of political virtue but also in realizing and dramatizing the practical impossibilities of this project. In the final analysis, a thorough exploration of their semiotic struggles should enable us to determine, following Michelet, that even for the Terror's two most prominent figures, linguistic activity fatally undermined the pretensions of a regime alleged to reflect the will of all people. We might even go so far as to consider the possibility that Thermidor (July 1794), which brought the demise and death of both leaders, proceeded logically from their own destructive, untenable philosophy of language.[11]

The Beginning and the End: Rousseauism Redux

The silent inflexibility ascribed by Michelet to Robespierre was not always the latter man's trademark. To those who knew him before his meteoric rise to power—as a student at the prestigious Collège Louis-le-Grand in Paris, as a struggling provincial trial lawyer, and as a relatively unknown member of the first national legislature established after the Revolution—Robespierre could hardly have seemed a likely proponent of Terror. In 1788, he argued eloquently in the Arras courts against the arbitrary exercise of justice exemplified by the Old Regime's recourse to *lettres de cachet*,[12] conjuring up instead a vision of a justice system based on and sustained by equitable legal measures. Not only did he continue to promote this vision when he joined France's newly minted Constituent Assembly one year later; as a collaborator in the drafting of the nation's first Constitution, Robespierre was now advocating political reform at a much higher level and with much higher stakes. "Everything militates in favor of moderate laws," he announced to the Assembly in 1791, "everything conspires against cruel ones."[13] As an assemblyman, he continued his campaign against the injustice of the *lettres de cachet*[14]—but that was by no means the extent of his deep and exemplary liberalism. On questions of religious and racial equality (Should non-Catholics be allowed to hold government jobs? Should "men of color" enjoy the same civil rights as their white counterparts?), in debates over free expression and the freedom of the press, Robespierre's positions consistently surpassed those of his peers' in terms of inclusiveness and tolerance.[15] When in early 1792 his colleagues, as a means of nipping potential anti-republican sedition in the bud, called for the disarmament of all the nation's "suspect persons," he took a dissenting position, declaring that the government must by no means oppress or persecute its citizens.[16] But most progressive—and, in light of his subsequent activities, most surprising—of all was his demand for the eradication of capital punishment from the French penal code, made during his tenure in the Assembly. Inveighing against this "despotic" practice, Robespierre enjoined his colleagues thus: "Just listen to the voice of justice and of reason: it cries out to us that human judgment is never sure enough to justify the condemnation to death of one man by other men who are likewise subject to error" (Laponneraye I, 115). Despite these stirring words, Robespierre's fellow legislators outvoted him by a large majority, thereby laying the foundation for the execution-based platform that he himself would adopt less than two years later.

Striking not only for its glaring historical irony, the anti-death-penalty stance voiced by Robespierre in the early days of the French republic is noteworthy for the unmistakably Rousseauist terms in which it appears to be couched. Here as in Rousseau's work, rationality and equity are understood to be discursive phenomena; here as in the more self-conscious passages of *The Social Contract,* the acceptance of human fallibility is posited as a component of, rather than an obstacle to, true "justice." Robespierre's colleagues were in all likelihood primed to detect such overtones in their young comrade's oratory; he had after all made his intellectual allegiances crystal clear in the very first speech he delivered before the Assembly in 1789. The speech, aptly entitled an "Homage to the Shade of Jean-Jacques Rousseau," apostrophized the Swiss philosopher with unmitigated admiration: "Called to play a central role in the greatest events that have ever shaken [the foundations of] the world, . . . I have your example before my eyes. . . . I want to follow in your estimable footsteps, . . . lucky if, in the perilous path that an unheard-of revolution has just opened before us, I can remain faithful to the inspiration that I drew from your writings!" (Mazauric 81). Certainly Robespierre's fidelity to his intellectual idol comes across in the aspects we have already underlined in his declamation against the death penalty. Interestingly enough, however, this same speech also betrays one substantial difference between "early" Robespierre and Rousseau, who, as we saw in chapter 1, expresses unmitigated support for capital punishment. Whereas Rousseau postulates the "right to death" as a prerequisite of civil liberty, for his admirer from Arras it is the right to lead a human life of error and imperfection that seems, at the dawn of a new political era in France, to be a necessary feature of freedom.

This significant deviation from his master's thinking must not be read as a mere oversight on Robespierre's part. Rather, it demonstrates precisely the degree to which the budding politician is "faithful to the inspiration" of Rousseau's own self-contradictory statements about the role that contingent forgiveness and categorical severity have to play in government. What is more, it reveals that Robespierre was every bit as sensitive as his hero to language's capacity to lend itself to more than one side of an argument, to say more than one thing. The young assemblyman's allusion to "the voice of reason and of justice" resoundingly echoes *The Social Contract*. Yet in contrast to that text, where the discourse of reason and justice functions predominantly to silence or stem the proliferation of individual "pathologies," Robespierre invokes the very same discourse in order to advocate a more permissive attitude toward such idiosyncrasies.[17] Or in the language of structuralist linguistics: Robespierre attaches a Rousseauist signifier to a patently non-Rousseauist signified—just as, in *The Second Discourse*, the scared speaking subject attaches the term *giant* to a normal-sized man. The key point here is that linguistic malleability or subjective error makes substantial alterations even to a political program that seeks, like Rousseau's "right to death," to suppress all manner of disruptive heterogeneity. The paradox is that Robespierre soon found himself in the unpleasant position of sampling his own medicine. By the end of 1792, moved by a variety of factors to abandon the position of extreme tolerance that characterized his earlier political interventions, Robespierre exercised the right to change his mind and so to honor—following Rousseau's own apologia of human error—his own innate fallibility. His new stance, though, was one that categorically condemned above all the fallible, the flexible, and the different. His advocacy on behalf of "marginal" peoples (Protestants, Jews, African slaves) gave way to a zealous persecution of particularistic interest groups and "foreign bodies in the republic." His belief in unfettered journalistic expression transmuted into deep-seated anxiety about "conspiracies rooted in the freedom of the press" and utterances that could undermine his own unilateral political pronouncements.[18] And, most disappointing and dramatic of all, his privileging of forgiveness over the disenfranchisement and capital punishment of "suspect" persons reversed its terms, with deadly consequences for the new republic. With his stringently antidifferential politics made possible by an absolute shift in his own political agenda, Robespierre was perhaps both the best and the worst reader Rousseau ever had.

The Sublime Strikes Again: Lightning Rhetoric at the Trial of Louis XVI

Robespierre's transformation from a compassionate humanitarian to a pitiless enforcer of the general will emerged from a set of pressing circumstances that began to unfold in the summer of 1792. Prussia and Austria, both deeply threatened by the democratic turn that their neighboring country's politics had taken since 1789, went to war with France and began to win critical victories along its borders. On the domestic front, the famine that the Revolution had been expected to resolve continued to debilitate rural and urban populations alike; grain shortages, price-fixing scandals, and food riots were occurring with alarming regularity. Flouting the martial law that had been declared in Paris, formidable mobs of malcontents stormed the king's residence in the Tuileries on two separate occasions, once in June and once in August. After the second of these uprisings, in which the monarch failed to prevent his royal guard from firing on the crowd, Louis XVI and his family were thrown into prison while the people clamored for justice and the national legislators puzzled over the fate of a jailed monarchy. Finally, as summer turned to fall, evidence of the royal couple's secret, treasonous complicity with France's foreign enemies (relatives of the sovereigns

themselves) became more distressingly abundant by the day. The ramifications of these events for the authority of the Assembly, which had
declared a constitutional monarchy less than one year beforehand, were
fatal. Declaring the nation in danger and themselves incapable of con-
tending with its myriad problems, the Assembly decreed that a new legislative body should be convened to take on the mess. And although
this body, the National Convention, did indeed assemble in September,
it faced a powerful political threat from the Paris Commune, the local
governing body with extremist democratic leanings and a mandate to
advance the interests of the capital city's dangerously and volubly dissatisfied lower classes, the *sans-culottes*. Along with other left-leaning
members of the Convention, who coalesced into the party known as the
Montagne, Robespierre therefore faced considerable pressure to champion measures radical enough to appease the Commune and the urban
poor. When in the final months of 1792 the central question being de-
bated daily in the Convention was whether to place Louis XVI on trial
for crimes against the nation, the erstwhile bleeding-heart liberal was
compelled to abandon his characteristic empathy and equability for a
much more draconian stance. Fearing that reversion to a constitutional
monarchy, in the wake of the August 10 revolt, would constitute "a revolution without a revolution" (Mazauric 191), he found himself arguing
in favor of the deposed king's execution.[19]

Before going into the details of the trial, I would like to take a moment
to emphasize the homology between the radicality of Robespierre's
change of heart and the drastic nature of the change that the event of
the monarch's trial represented for the French people as a whole. Even
to propose the killing of the king—God's representative on earth and
the guarantor of all secular as well as religious authority—was to threaten
an entire nation with the sudden and violent stripping away of all their
most basic ideological reference points.[20] But by the fall of 1792, the
Montagnards had concluded that suddenness and violence were the
only viable means of solidifying the republic and securing universal suffrage. In the words of Saint-Just, the twenty-five-year-old legislative
novice whose chief political idol had long been Robespierre and who
pushed the older *conventionnel* himself into advocating regicide: "A revolution changes a people all at once" (Duval 492).[21] Making the same
point in a far more flowery fashion, Thomas Carlyle remarks as a preface to his account of the epic royal execution:

It is a change such as history must beg her readers to imagine, undescribed. An instantaneous change of the whole body politic, the soul politic being all changed; such a change as few bodies, politic or other, can experience in this world. Say, perhaps, such as poor Nymph-Semele's body did experience, when she would needs with woman's humor see her Olympian Jove as very Jove; and so stood poor nymph, this moment Semele, next moment not Semele, but flame and a statue of red-hot ashes! France has looked upon democracy; seen it face to face.[22]

In the historian's narrative of instantaneous political change as in the Montagnards' attempts to bring it about, the shadow of Rousseau looms unmistakably large. (Indeed, I should admit that if I am inclined to cite Romantic historians like Carlyle and Michelet from time to time in this chapter, this is because of the uncanny and enlightening mimetic relationship that exists between their rhetoric and that of their revolutionary subjects.)[23] *The Social Contract* narrates a "remarkable change"—occurring in a single "happy instant"—that marks the individual's passage from manhood to citizenship under the social pact (*Contract* 64). For Rousseau, Saint-Just, and Carlyle alike, radical social reform thus occurs all at once, without delay or temporal mediation: "face to face," the historian writes in a Pauline vein, further accentuating the unmediated nature of the transformation. The echoes of the Longinian and Kantian sublime that inflects Rousseau's articulation of an ideal polity reappear, thanks to an invocation of temporal transcendence, in the Montagnards' prescriptions for and the Scotsman's descriptions of the founding of a king-free state.

Shades of Rousseauist sublimity also inhere in Carlyle's insistence—taken up *ad absurdum* by Saint-Just and Robespierre—on the inherently painful nature of the social change in question. In good Longinian fashion, the historian describes a divine bolt of lightning (the sublime form assumed by Jove, the Law) striking "the whole body politic," figuratively identified with "poor Nymph-Semele's body," and destroying its existing attributes. Because this episode quite obviously involves no small degree of pain for its chief character, it recalls Rousseau's insight that man's transformation from savage to citizen is necessarily a painful process. More interesting still, Carlyle's image of a shattered woman recalls the slew of sacrificial female bodies in Rousseau's *Lévite*—emblems of the irreducible difference that no strong and unified polity should deign to tolerate. Like Rousseau's heartbroken heroine Axa, Carlyle casts his broken female protagonist here as a site of hopeless pathos ("*poor Nymph*")—and, correlatively, as the negative moment in a dialectical movement toward sublimation and political unity. A later portion of this chapter explores in more detail the ways in which Terrorist discourse feminizes the passions that it strives to suppress. For now, though, I shall merely acknowledge Carlyle's metaphor as a fruitful one, indicating as it does that the sublime, unmediated poetics of the Terror, like Rousseau's political discourse, calls for the destruction of certain specific elements even as it engenders a community based on other ones.

Let us return, though, to Louis XVI's trial, where it might be said that the seeds of political and discursive Terror first took root in the revolutionary polity. Schematically speaking, the terms and outcome of the debate about the future of the monarchy were dictated above all by the rivalry between the National Convention's two chief political parties, the Montagnards and the Girondins.[24] Whereas the former—with its affiliations to the principally leftist, *sans-culotte* Parisian population—were inclined to favor republican over royalist political solutions, the latter were by and large committed to the constitutional monarchy that had been declared in September 1791 and that seemed to appeal most to their constituents in the provinces. For the purposes of our analysis, the most significant result of this fundamental opposition was that it polarized deliberations about the king's future between emergency action demanded by the Montagnards and constitutional interpretation favored by the Girondins.[25] Evincing Rousseau's antithesis between the political leader who takes action in the practical sphere and the writer who "only" discusses issues of public policy, the clash between the two groups of *conventionnels* could be, and was, framed as a struggle between immediate, unmediated practice and textually mediated theory. Nowhere is this conception of the debate more starkly and effectively presented than in the speech Saint-Just delivered on November 13, 1792, which has earned deserved repute as "probably the most brilliant of all the speeches made at the king's trial."[26] In this urgent harangue, the young politician—like Rousseau, Carlyle, and the philosophers of the sublime—denigrated linguistic mediation and presented instantaneous violence as the necessary condition for the founding of a unified, morally sound community. "I have often noticed," he intoned, stepping to the Convention podium for the first time, that false precautionary measures [de fausses mesures de prudence], delays, reserve, were often in this case veritable acts of foolhardiness [de véritables imprudences]; and after the imprudent act that defers our moment for giving laws to the nation, the most deadly would be the one that would make us temporize with the king. Someday, perhaps, people will be surprised that in the eighteenth century, things were less advanced than they were in Caesar's day: then, the tyrant was sacrificed in the middle of the Senate, with no other formalities than twenty-three blows of a dagger, and with no other law than the liberty of Rome. (Soboul 62–63)

In the first part of this passage, Saint-Just decries the delaying tactics, procedural debates, and nitpicking negotiations to which the Girondins have resorted in their effort to spare the king. (Feeding the fires of this negative perception, the formidable Girondin supporter Madame Roland had addressed a letter to Robespierre some months before, begging him to comprehend that "time will make everything clear; its justice is slow but sure" [Michon 147].) In the new vocabulary forged by Saint-Just for the occasion, this party's failure to act, its "temporizing" precautions, justified as so many *mesures de prudence,* actually become—and I cite the French here for its neat parallelism—*de véritables imprudences.* Conversely, to take immediate and violent action against Louis is, according to Saint-Just, to engage in the highest form of prudence. Comparing the National Convention with the Roman Senate, he juxtaposes the Girondins' ineffectual "formalities" to the indisputably effective dagger blows that Julius Caesar, no more a tyrant than Louis, received in the name of freedom. In fact, Saint-Just holds up the abstract concept of liberty as greater than any other law. Whereas the law lends itself to interpretation, dispute, and delay, the concept of liberty calls simply for the speedy application of the blade. "A revolution like ours isn't a trial," he insists later, "but a lightning bolt that strikes the wicked."[27]

In his speeches on the subject of Louis's trial, Robespierre echoes the argument advanced so forcefully by his new colleague. As he declares in his first address on the subject: "This isn't a question of delivering a verdict for or against a man, but rather of protecting public safety and salvation [salut public]" (Mazauric 214). Like Saint-Just, he dismisses a traditional legal measure—"a verdict for or against"—as an irrelevant formality and presents its alternative—death to Louis—as a means of safeguarding and saving the republic. Similarly, in his second oration on Louis XVI's judgment, pronounced before the Convention on December 3, 1792, once more he represents public interest as a consideration that overrides and renders pointless any standard juridical proceedings. Asserting that "the people's freedom [demands Louis's] punishment," he continues: "People do not judge like courts of law; they do not issue verdicts, they throw lightning bolts; they do not condemn kings, they hurl them into nothingness; and this justice is every bit as good as the kind you find in courts" (Mazauric 216). In this as in Saint-Just's discourse, we find a clear opposition between two radically opposed ideas of justice. Denigrating the traditional legal procedures and verdicts proper to the courtroom, Robespierre maintains that republicanism can be upheld only by more drastic means—ones that, like lightning, their sublime metaphorical counterpart, have the virtue of overcoming the temporal hindrances decried by his fellow Montagnard. "I do not know how to debate something extensively when I am convinced that it is a scandal to deliberate" (Mazauric 217), Robespierre remarks later in the same speech, positing time-consuming deliberation as a politically and morally objectionable activity. What is more, the extreme measures designed to overcome such scandalous pursuits provide the additional benefit, likewise promoted by the logic and vocabulary of the sublime, of inflicting "punishment" on the people's enemies and "hurl[ing] them into nothingness." In theory, the reprehensible shilly-shallying of the Girondins and any other royalist or legalistic troublemakers is most effectively resolved by their unmitigated annihilation. To this end, Robespierre emphasizes that the Montagnards' sublime conception of justice should destroy not just Louis himself but also the very possibility of opposition from any quarter whatsoever. "Indeed," the Incorruptible asks of his audience, "what is the healthy tack to take for strengthening a nascent republic? It is to engrave deeply into [people's] hearts a disdain for royalty, and to strike dumb all the king's partisans" (Mazauric 214). In this case Robespierre yokes his idea of a language beyond representation, conveyed by the Rousseauist cliché of a principle that is engraved in people's hearts rather than "inscribed on marble or brass" (*Contract* 99), to a call for the destruction of political difference as well. Rather than engage in discussion or dialogue with those who would oppose Louis's death, one must strike them dumb, thereby eliminating their very ability to assert a point of view. To quote Saint-Just's infamous formula:

"What constitutes a republic is the utter destruction of everything that opposes it" (Soboul 136).

A similar injunction to paralyze any of the king's partisans appears earlier in the same speech by Robespierre, in a figure that rivals the lightning bolt for its sublime violence. Declaring that Louis's death is a necessary deterrent to other European monarchs, insofar as it will intimidate them into respecting the claims and demands of the newfound French state, the Montagnard exclaims with a menacing flourish: "What more surefire way to degrade [the other European monarchs] in the eyes of their people, and to strike them with fear, than the spectacle of their accomplice sacrificed to the betrayed liberty [of France]? This spectacle will be a Medusa's head for them" (Mazauric 212). The proposed political strategy again consists not in countering but rather in nullifying any possible argument in favor of Louis's life. In the name of "betrayed liberty," monarchist sympathizers must be struck dumb with fear, as if turned to stone by an unmediated—in Carlyle's term, "face to face"—encounter with Medusa. Robespierre's invocation of the notorious mythological Gorgon is not, however, noteworthy only for its overtones of the sublime. It is also provocative because it implies a parallel between Medusa and the monarch—a parallel that is later made explicit by a popular print issued to commemorate the king's beheading (Figure 1) but that serves a specific function within Robespierre's discursive universe. If, according to Freud, "the sight of the Medusa's head makes the spectator stiff with terror, turns him to stone,"[28] this is because such a spectacle (Robespierre's term, consistent with Freud's logic of spectatorship) suggests female genitalia, the absence of a penis, and therefore castration. In this context, to show Louis's fellow royals his severed head is to impress upon them the emasculated impotence of kingship as an institution.[29] Perhaps even more tellingly, Robespierre's attempt to cast the French monarch in the role of Medusa forges an implicit equation between monarchy and femininity, insofar as both of them stand for difference to which the republic cannot be reconciled. Although the Montagnards' relationship to gender is a disturbing and important one, before broaching that topic I want to pursue the question of what they construe to be Louis XVI's ontologically unassimilable alterity, feminine markings aside.

In an oration made during a debate about one of the many versions of the new republican Constitution, Saint-Just defends the document's

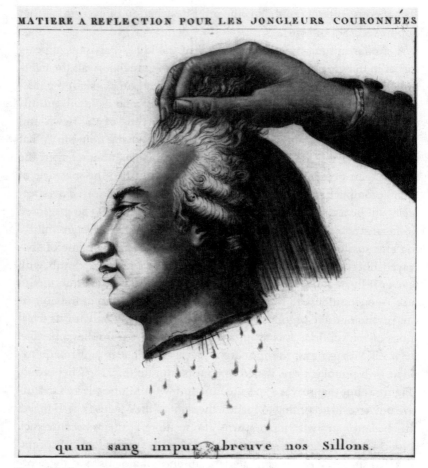

Figure 1. Villeneuve, *Matière à réflection pour les jongleurs couronnés* (Matter for the consideration of crowned jesters) (1793). Courtesy of the Bibliothèque nationale de France, Paris.

supposition of human universality by asking: "Do we not all have one and the same nature?" (Soboul 97). The syntax of this query, as well as the broader paean to universal suffrage that it is intended to conclude, quite obviously anticipates an affirmative response. The necessity of a positive reply becomes a problem, though, when we note that the very fact of posing a question rhetorically underscores a discrepancy between literal and figurative meaning—a discrepancy, as Rousseau's meditations on the origin of language suggest, that attests to the possibility of hermeneutic reversal and referential error. On the surface, Saint-Just's utterance is a question, ostensibly inviting an answer of any kind; but on a figurative or rhetorical level, it demands universal assent and so prevents the listener from taking its interrogative status literally.[30] Needless to say, the linguistic slipperiness manifested here could not be further from the crystal clarity and lightning immediacy of the Montagnards' own "revolutionary sublime," and their overarching mission is to eliminate such slipperiness wherever they find it. Nonetheless, at the moment of Louis Capet's trial, the loophole opened up by Saint-Just's own thinking permits him to turn the tables, just as Robespierre does on the issue of the death penalty, and to answer his own question in the negative. "To judge is to apply the law," he instructs the *conventionnels*. "A law is a relationship of justice: but what kind of relationship can there be between humans and kings? What does Louis have in common with the French people?" (Soboul 66). After a string of implacable definitions, Saint-Just concludes that kings and citizens, far from sharing some universal human nature, in fact have *nothing in common*. And according to his gnomic generalizations about law and judgment, justice can be meted out only to those who share in the common bond of the social contract. Two years later, when he and Robespierre are holding the reins of the French government and the Terror is in full swing, Saint-Just will articulate this same idea in a more concise and chilling fashion: "Between the people and its enemies, there remains nothing in common but the blade. Those who cannot be governed by justice must be governed by the blade" (Soboul 118). In short, just as Rousseau presents civil rights as the unique prerogative of the law-abiding citizen (and never of the outlaw), Saint-Just implies that republican justice applies solely to a group with which Louis, for one, can never have a "relationship." This group is moreover deeply homogeneous, and because the king is viewed as not having the "same nature" as the rest of the French, the usual rules do not apply to him. Instead, quite literally, the king is someone who can only "be governed by the blade." Saint-Just drives the point home by invoking the loaded, and dreaded, concept of foreignness: "Louis is a stranger among us" (Soboul 67). At a time when France was under siege by a host of foreign armies, the Montagnards held that no punishment could be severe enough for a disruptive stranger.[31]

Robespierre's orations during the king's trial develop the same irreducible opposition between Capet and the French people. Although the Incorruptible, like Saint-Just, insists elsewhere on the fundamental homogeneity of all human nature ("in every age, the human heart is at bottom the same" [Mazauric 319]), he too posits the king as the exception that proves this rule. Citing the "incommensurable distance between the mere memory of what [the king] was [ce qu'il fut] and the dignity of a citizen" (Mazauric 215), Robespierre concludes: "Louis was king [fut roi], and the republic is founded [est fondée]: the famous question that has been preoccupying you is decided by these words alone" (Mazauric 215). Here the unbridgeable ontological divide between the two entities is expressed in temporal terms. The erstwhile king belongs, in keeping with his backward-pointing moniker, squarely in the past: in the realm of memory, of completed action and essence ("ce qu'il fut"; "Louis fut roi"). The overtly literary nature of the *passé simple* only serves further to accentuate the noncoincidence of Louis's history with the present order of things. Indeed, when speaking of the latter, Robespierre uses the performative verb *est fondée*—a combination of durative present and colloquial *passé composé*, as opposed to the unidiomatic *passé simple*—to show that the new polity exists in an entirely different time frame from that of the former monarch. The republic's "founding," which constitutes its immediate past and its continuing present, requires the sovereign's expulsion to an era that exists prior to and outside republican reality. It is this belief, in fact, that gave rise during the revolutionary period to the creation of a new calendar, beginning with "Year I of Liberty" and patently effacing the thirteen centuries of monarchy that went before.[32]

Also of interest in Robespierre's attempt to establish the radical difference between Louis and the people is that he ascribes that difference to semantics and speech. "The famous question that has been preoccupying you is decided by *these words alone*": Robespierre designates his choice of words, "Louis *was* king, and the republic *is* founded," as the crux of the issue. He implies that once they recognize the appropriateness and significance of his loaded verb tenses, his fellow *conventionnels* will no longer need to debate the "famous question" of Louis's trial. They will know that the king is ancient history and has no place in the new republic. Robespierre then goes on to inform his colleagues that applying a vocabulary of desuetude to the monarch is not only fitting but also necessary, because "to say what displeases kings is to say what pleases peoples" (Mazauric 212). Once again, Robespierre places the king and the people in separate and mutually opposed discursive spheres.

The decisive differentiation between the powerful and the disempowered—a reversal of the long-standing relationship between kings and peoples—occurs at the level of language itself. In Jean-François Lyotard's parlance, Louis finds himself on the losing side of a differend: a situation in which a person "is deprived ... of the freedom to make his or her ideas or opinions public, or simply ... [finds his or her] testifying phrase ... deprived of authority."[33] At the limit, Lyotard postulates, such radical discursive disenfranchisement reduces the person who endures it to the status of a trapped or domesticated animal, whose utterances quite literally fail to register in the symbolic network of its human "masters."[34] Similarly, when Robespierre symbolically thrusts him outside the republic and its laws, the one-time king is stripped of all power to make his opposition heard in any meaningful way.[35] In this context it is by no means incidental that Louis's fall from grace coincided with a proliferation of popular images depicting him as an animal, and usually (because of his pudgy physique and penchant for rich foods) as a pig (Figures 2 and 3). Although all of these depictions attest to the king's profoundly compromised symbolic stature,[36] one of them represents Louis engaged with Robespierre himself in a communication breakdown that illustrates Lyotard's logic of the differend. This image, entitled *Leçon donnée par Ro*... (Lesson given by Robespierre), shows the monarch sitting down for a snack—he is in human form this time, but metonymically figured by the pig who stands next to him, also eating—while Robespierre utters some words into his ear through a long tube. Louis's body language betrays extreme resistance to his interlocutor's proposals, and the cartoon's subtitle, *C'est semer des perles devant les pourceaux* (It is like casting pearls before swine), indicates that the Incorruptible's instructive message is hopelessly wasted on its recipient. In this instance, the deposed king appears every bit as incapable of grasping the great Montagnard's meaning as the pig, who continues his chewing in placid ignorance of the interchange. This image thus graphically realizes Robespierre's own suggestion that Louis and the people (represented literally and figuratively by the *conventionnel* himself) occupy separate discursive arenas— and that the swinish, incomprehensible concerns of the former monarch merit no further attention.

Subjecting the monarch to such a differend—or "putting [him] to death through words," as Marc-Éli Blanchard aptly describes the situation[37]—is a vital maneuver on the part of the Robespierrists. After all, if

Figure 2. Anonymous, *Ah! Le maudit animal!* (Ah! The cursed animal!) (1791).
Courtesy of the Bibliothèque nationale de France, Paris.

Louis retains any authority whatsoever, then the very basis of the Montagnards' exclusionary republic disappears. In their view, the king has to be irreducibly different, and his power radically incommensurable with that of the republic, if the citizen is to exist at all. Jules Michelet negatively confirms this point when narrating Louis XVI's appearance before the Convention during his actual trial, at which the fallen monarch's unexpected *similarity* to the average Frenchman became disturbingly apparent to the assembled audience: "When the 'tyrant' was brought to the bar, and when people saw that *he was a man like any other*, a middle-class type, a family man, a simple fellow, a bit myopic, already pale-skinned from prison and smelling of death, everyone was troubled."[38] Michelet explicitly attributes the "trouble" experienced by those present at Louis's trial to the king's failure to live up to his radically different identity, constructed and promoted by Robespierre and Saint-Just, as a tyrant. (The Romantic historian was perhaps too delicate to mention the pig caricatures.) It is worth noting, moreover, that Louis's unsettling resemblance to "any other" human being derives, in Michelet's account, at least in part from his fatherly, patriarchal aspect and from his myopia. With both of these features, he seems a far cry from Robespierre's Medusa, whose deadly, irresistible gaze acts as a harbinger of castration

Figure 3. Anonymous, *Leçon donnée par Ro . . .* (Lesson given by Ro . . .) (1791).
Courtesy of the Bibliothèque nationale de France, Paris.

and antipatriarchal subversion. If, as Michelet's narrative suggests, the
defendant Louis XVI is in fact horrible to behold, it is not because of his
petrifying, feminine difference, but rather because of his disturbing resemblance to the men seeking his condemnation. Admittedly, the "smell
of death" that emanates from him attests to his symbolic status as a
dead man: when a person's very discourse is deemed invalid—as with
Lyotard's animal or Rousseau's outlaw—he is "between the two deaths,"
dead to the world of symbolic exchange despite his living body.[39] Such a
deathly taint, however, is downright uncanny when detected in a person
who appears to be "just like us," for it implies that anyone, not just an
overthrown king, could wind up in such an unspeakable position. Indeed, when the Reign of Terror commences and everyone becomes a
potential enemy of the state, the wretched Louis's former subjects will
learn this "lesson given by Robespierre" the hard way.

It is in light of the anxiety allegedly produced by the possibility that
Louis could actually be akin to his fellow Frenchmen that we can perhaps begin to comprehend the impetus behind the Montagnard ora-
tors' recourse to sublimely incendiary, anti-oppositional speech. While
the decimation of all dissent and the construal of the king as thoroughly
irreconcilable with the republican community may seem like rhetorical

overkill, Robespierre and Saint-Just view these means as unquestionably justified by the primacy of their ends. After all, what is at stake in their portrayal of Louis Capet is the vocabulary that upholds and validates revolutionary ideology. As the Incorruptible explains, alluding to the insurrection of August 10:

> Louis denounced the French people as "rebels"; to punish them, he called upon the weapons of his tyrannical cohorts; victory and the people decided that he alone was a rebel: Louis can therefore not be judged, he is already condemned, or the republic is not absolved. Any proposal to put Louis XVI on trial, in any manner whatsoever, . . . is a counterrevolutionary idea, because it places the Revolution itself on trial or in doubt [en litige]. (Mazauric 215)

One of the most striking features of this statement is its adroit reappropriation of Louis's own one-time condemnation of the revolutionary crowd as rebels. Whereas the king allowed his guards to fire on the supposedly insurgent masses outside his palace, in fact, "he alone was a rebel." In the antiroyalist lexicon of the Montagnards—which Robespierre here, in a characteristic rhetorical move, ascribes to "victory and the people"[40]—the monarch himself merits the punishment he had hoped to apply to his foes. Once his criminality has been established, "Louis can therefore not be judged"—the word *therefore* reveals the causal link between the king's newly declared position as an outlaw and his lack of actual, judicial rights under the ideal Robespierrist regime. By dint of his status as a rebel, "Louis is already condemned": with another *passé composé*, the Montagnard leader's speech performatively condemns the sovereign and strips him of the civil rights belonging to a law-abiding republican. If one ignores the king's a priori exclusion from the social pact, then the Revolution itself stands to lose its validity ("is not absolved," is placed on trial/put into doubt). Its claim to legitimacy is constituted by and based on the construction of Louis's claims, such as they may be, as illegitimate. It is in this context that Robespierre coins the term *counterrevolutionary*—one that will gain tremendous currency during the Terror itself—in reference, precisely, to anything that could call his master narrative of revolutionary authority into question. Like the denunciations that will feed the Terrorist killing machine in the aftermath of Louis's execution, the speech-act designating the ex-king as a traitor functions to banish him symbolically from the republican community. Thus marked, he loses his capacity to undermine the revolutionaries' authority.

Highlighting for his auditors this critical aspect of Louis's symbolic annihilation, the Incorruptible continues:

> Indeed, if Louis can still be the object of a trial, then he can be absolved; he can be innocent; what am I saying? He is presumed innocent until he is judged otherwise; but if Louis can be absolved, if Louis is presumed innocent, then what is to become of the Revolution? If Louis is innocent, all the defenders of liberty become liars, all rebels were really supporters of the truth and defenders of oppressed innocence, all the protests of foreign courts are simply legitimate objections to a dominant faction.... The people of Paris, all the patriots in the French empire are guilty: and that great trial pending in the tribunal of Nature, between virtue and crime, between liberty and tyranny, finally gets decided in favor of crime and tyranny. (Mazauric 215)

According to this formulation of the problem, with its litany of paradoxical predications, any trial of Louis would also involve a trial of revolutionary language and dogma. If, in other words, the thundering new rhetoric of the Revolution is designed to stamp out all opposition and to posit its tenets beyond question, this is because any such opposition could topple a whole system of doctrinaire definitions like a house of cards. As far as Robespierre is concerned, to permit interpretive dissent or dispute would be to risk destabilizing the rigid categorizations whereby "supporters of the truth" can never be confused with "rebels," "virtue" with "crime," "liberty" with "tyranny," and so forth. "Either this solemn declaration means what I just said it means," Robespierre had noted anxiously on the eve of Louis's trial, proclaiming his own unshakable patriotism but worrying about the lack of interpretive fixity inherent in his language, "or else it is nothing but a betrayal" (Bouloiseau 391). The very term *king*, he points out, is infinitely elastic: because it can refer not only to "a man who is honest, but weak and unenlightened" but also to "a corrupted pervert" and a whole host of additional personality types, "there is only the slightest difference between a king and a *king*" (Bouloiseau 410). The Montagnards' task in the trial, however, was to establish the king once and for all as a *king* in the worst sense(s) of the word: a friend to crime, tyranny, piggishness, and countless other, fundamentally synonymous evils. Saint-Just summarizes the issue nicely in his own discussion of the king's status as public enemy: "For the want of these distinctions, we have fallen into forms without principles" (Soboul 62).

Forms are problematic for Montagnard ideology insofar as they hinder the course of unmediated action and the emanation of transparent principles; highlighting this dilemma, Saint-Just announces to the other *conventionnels,* "Forms are hypocrisy; you will be judged according to your principles" (Soboul 67). In order to move beyond or outside the realm of formal malleability and obfuscation, and in order to attain the essence of principled republicanism, the properties of conventional language must be left behind. Saint-Just, for instance, feels that a tribunal is an inappropriate forum for the expression of that greatest of all abstract generalities, the general will, because he "cannot conceive of . . . how the general will could be cited before a tribunal" (Soboul 66). In proclaiming the inappropriateness of "citation" for the general will, Saint-Just designates the problem of iterability that also surfaces in *The Social Contract,* when Rousseau grapples with the tension between the legislator as a unique being who transcends time and space and the legislator as an exemplar (e.g., Peter the Great) whose actions are subject to imitation, repetition, and deformation. Like any possible objection to Louis's execution, these elements, intrinsic to language itself, constitute a significant threat to republican indivisibility. By their very nature, they allow for the proliferation of difference, which the Terrorist order cannot abide.

One partial solution to this problem consists in the Robespierrists' heaping generality upon generality in a massive system of tautological definitions that Albert Camus has characterized as a "cascade of peremptory affirmations, [an] axiomatic and sententious style" and that Marc-Éli Blanchard has termed a "language circle."[41] Both leaders, we have seen, devote a tremendous amount of energy and effort to establishing precise definitions for heavily loaded terms such as *innocent* and *rebel, liberty* and *tyranny,* and *virtue* and *crime.* The gnomic generalizations characteristic of both men's oratory—including Saint-Just's best known one-liner, "*One cannot reign innocently*" (Soboul 66; Saint-Just's emphasis)—reflect the same impulse to control and stabilize meaning. Of course, such an enterprise is fundamentally political in its intentions and its consequences, as Friedrich Nietzsche observes when pondering the phenomenon of predication: "The lordly right of bestowing names is such that one would almost be justified in seeing the origin of language itself as an expression of the rulers' power. 'This *is* that or that'; they seal off each thing and action with a sound and thereby take symbolic possession of it."[42] In the case of Louis XVI, however, the aggressive, predicative language of the Montagnards does not establish their complete "symbolic possession" and control of the king, nor does it cement republican homogeneity and transcendence of legal and linguistic forms. On the most elementary level, the speeches of Robespierre and Saint-Just refute the notion that Louis Capet, in his capacity as enemy-Medusa-tyrant, could be tried at all, and yet they make the bulk of their speeches in the context of a trial that does in fact take place. More generally speaking, they are constantly compelled to repeat principles and terms that, according to their own sublime political philosophy, could not and should not be repeated, discussed, or interpreted. That is why, over and above the suppression of royalist discourse, Robespierre and Saint-Just insist above all on unmediated action, beginning with the prompt execution of Louis XVI. This instance of supralinguistic violence—"force used . . . to make the people listen to reason" (Duval 978)— emerges as the Montagnards' supplementary mode of political containment.[43] And that mode, in the wake of the king's execution, achieves its ultimate expression in the violent Terrorist policies and practices of 1793–1794: policies that the Incorruptible presents to his countrymen as "one last effort [to liberate] the world from freedom's enemies" (Bouloiseau 98). It is therefore the Terror itself—a "Terror of pikes and bayonets,"[44] theoretically geared at overcoming language's differential pitfalls—that will now occupy our attention.

The Despotism of Liberty: Violence Terminable and Interminable

Although it constituted a clear victory for the Montagnards, the successful prosecution of Louis XVI, resulting in his execution on January 21, 1793, did not immediately ensure their dominance as an uncontested political power. The pressures that had weighed so heavily on the country as a whole—the chronic famine and poverty, the wars with foreign powers—had not been alleviated by the king's death. Not only did all these problems persist; they were compounded by the outbreak of ever more factions in French political affairs, factions that vociferously contested the Montagnards' Rousseauist vision of a "republic one and indivisible," which the ritual destruction of a sacrificial outlaw had been intended to cement. From the Hébertist extremists with ties to the urban poor, who felt that much more aristocratic blood must be shed before the state could be born anew, to disgruntled royalists and Catholics, mostly in the provinces, who were still eager to fight for God and monarch, substantial political threats besieged Robespierre and his colleagues from all sides. As a preemptive strike against these threats, on December 16, 1792, the Montagnards led the National Convention to pass a law calling for the execution of "whosoever should propose or attempt to violate the unity of the French republic, or to separate from it any of its integral parts for the purposes of uniting them to a foreign territory."[45] This decree generalized a crime that had heretofore been attributed to Louis XVI alone—the crime of betraying the will of the people and conspiring with foreign powers. The former monarch was, crucially, no longer held to be the only source of divisiveness within the polity. Even before sending him to the guillotine, the Montagnard party primed itself to eliminate anyone and everyone (the boundlessly inclusive "whosoever") who stood to disrupt the unity of the newfound state. As Saint-Just had already cautioned in his "Second Discourse Concerning the Judgment of Louis XVI," the threat of counterrevolution would not die with the monarch: "People will say that the Revolution is finished, that we have nothing left to fear from the tyrant, that the law punishes the usurper with death: but, Citizens, tyranny is a reed that bends in the wind and then stands up again. . . . The Revolution begins when the tyrant is finished" (Duval 398). With this figure of speech, an indirect allusion to La Fontaine's fable contrasting the fatal vulnerability of the oak to the scrappy flexibility of the reed,[46] Saint-Just suggests that regicide alone will not suffice. Striking at the roots of France's royal family tree,[47] he intimates, will not do away with all possible manifestations of antirepublican dissent. That enterprise, targeting the potentially widespread reed of civil disobedience as well as the solitary oak of the monarchy, will require countless additional executions. Like the Rousseauist ideal of a polity where the citizen has "[no]thing left to demand" (Contract 60), Saint-Just's vision of political stability is one in which there is "nothing left to fear," because the alleged tyrant—or rather, the less specific and more potentially widespread phenomenon of tyranny— has been definitively eradicated.

It is with this end in mind that the Montagnards legally institute a program of Terror—the systematic and literal suppression of anyone perceived to be capable of anticommunitarian subversion—in September 1793.[48] With the Terror, the violence already implicit in the sublime rhetoric of Louis's trial (and tauntingly demanded by the militant Hébertists on a regular basis) becomes an explicit and generalized part of the Montagnard political program.[49] In the oration "On the Principles of Political Morality That Should Guide the National Convention in the Interior Administration of the Republic," Robespierre explains the new initiative in these terms: "Tame the enemies of freedom through Terror, and you will be doing the right thing, as founders of the republic. The government of the Revolution is the despotism of liberty against tyranny. . . . Is lightning not made for striking down arrogant heads?" (Mazauric 301). As in Saint-Just's reference to La Fontaine's reed, Robespierre here broadens the target of his ire from a single tyrant, such as the king, to the abstract category of tyranny, whose multiplicative possibilities appear in the plural number of the "enemies of freedom." Accordingly, the lightning he once called upon to strike Louis out of existence is now enjoined to decimate a veritable population of counterrevolutionary agitators, figured by a host of "arrogant heads." In fact, the Incorruptible will later devise a more gruesome way of expressing this idea of multiple tyrannical heads, by referring to "the hydra of despotism"[50]—a figure that again evokes both the endless proliferation of enemy factions and the importance of making yet another effort to combat political dissent. In the case of the "arrogant heads," moreover, lightning is presented as a by-product or instrument of such an effort; it is placed in the service of Terror, a sustained, rational system of killings by which the alleged enemies of the republic are to be "tamed." On a semantic level, Robespierre's question works to enact a similar taming of potential enemies by structuring itself in such a way that no disagreement appears to be grammatically possible. The negative interrogation "Is lightning not made . . . ?" demands an affirmative answer; the logic of the sentence cannot incorporate or acknowledge any dissenting opinion. As we noted apropos of one of Saint-Just's rhetorical questions, the underlying danger of such a rhetorical move is that, when read thoughtfully, it calls attention to its own duplicity: the question is not really a question at all. Nevertheless, taken as an exercise in discursive brute force, the gesture retains some degree of efficacy insofar as the (non)question here contains an element of demagogical manipulation designed, as Hans Robert Jauss would say, "to steer [an] already inflamed crowd toward an unconditional 'Yes!'"[51] Against the backdrop of the increasingly active guillotine, Robespierre's rhetorical query about the fate of enemy noggins certainly did not invite rhetorical hairsplitting.

The shift in emphasis that this query betrays—a shift from a single adversary to a host of subversive (and unrecognizable) others—is significant, because it bespeaks the fear of plurality and pluralism that underpins the Terror as a whole.[52] Just before demanding that an unspecified number of counterrevolutionary heads be decimated (or, more precisely, removed), Robespierre defines Terror and republican virtue as two sides of the same strictly antidifferential coin:

> The resource of a popular government during a revolution is simultaneously virtue and Terror; virtue, without which Terror is disastrous; Terror, without which virtue is impotent. Terror is nothing other than prompt, severe, inflexible justice; it is therefore an emanation of virtue; it is less a particular principle than a consequence of the general principle of democracy applied to the most pressing needs of the state. (Mazauric 300)

Here again, Terror emerges as a literalization of the rhetorical values associated with the sublime. Prompt, it defies time and translates virtue's dictates into immediate action. Severe and inflexible, it makes no allowance for ontological or interpretive difference, for what Rousseau in his more permissive moments terms grace. "Crime is the child of error!" (Soboul 89), Saint-Just fulminates before the Convention, supporting with a pithy gnomic generalization Robespierre's call for unpolluted civic goodness. To err is human, and the concept of republican virtue, rendered potent by the praxis of Terror, has nothing human about it. In Robespierre's words, virtue consists in the repudiation of particularity ("particular principle[s]") and in the concomitant valorization of unified generality. "Simultaneously virtue and Terror": the two will forevermore be conjoined under the Robespierrist regime, and to both of them will be ascribed the temporal and ontological immediacy ("simultane[ity]") of the sublime Terrorist lightning bolt.

Every bit as destructive as a lightning bolt and just about as random, the Terror's most direct attack on the forces of heterodoxy takes the form of the Law of Suspects, passed on September 17, 1793. Pursuant to this law, individuals could not only be arrested and killed for proven counterrevolutionary activities; they could also be executed for *potentially* counterrevolutionary beliefs, for speech or behavior deemed insufficiently enthusiastic about the Terrorist republic. According to Robespierre: "It is necessary to hunt down without pity . . . not only nobles and rascals, but all dubious citizens, all schemers, all those people who have given proof of civic opposition [incivisme]" (Mazauric 232). Although no evidence was required to establish such proof, the Robespierrist injunction ruthlessly to "hunt down" suspects unleashed a flurry of denunciations in the polity.[53] Delivered in a political club or before the newly formed Revolutionary Tribunal, aspersions against a fellow citizen's character now carried the weight to put their target to death both performatively and literally. The result was a political climate steeped in fear and mutual suspicion, where even to challenge a convincing denunciation represented potential evidence of treason. "There exists nobody," explains the Incorruptible, "who can oppose these measures without declaring himself to be a bad citizen" (Mazauric 232). Like the Rousseauist outlaw and the late Louis XVI, the so-called bad citizen enjoys no civil rights: "The revolutionary government owes its full protection to good citizens; to enemies of the people, it owes only death" (Mazauric 288). Here again, the Manichaean nature of Robespierre's worldview is apparent: an individual is either good or bad, worthy of life or slated to death. "I know only two sides—good citizens and bad citizens" (Mazauric 338).

Political opposition or "bad citizenship," however, is in fact virtually impossible to define under the Montagnards' Terrorist regime. Maurice Blanchot, whose Hegelian reading of the Terror we examined in part in chapter 1, meditates in another essay on the Law of Suspects' philosophical underpinnings:

> Each time the universal is affirmed in its brutal abstract exigency, every particular will and every thought apart falls under suspicion. It is no longer enough to act well. Every individual carries within himself or herself a set of reflections and intentions, that is to say reticences, that commits each one to an oblique existence. . . . And through the part always held back that he figures forth, [the suspect] tends not only to interfere with the work of the State, but also to place it under accusation. From such a perspective each [person] governed is suspect; yet each suspect accuses the one who governs and prepares him to be at fault since he who governs must one day recognize that he does not represent the whole, but still a particular will that only usurps the appearance of the universal. Hence the everyday must be thought as the suspect (and the oblique) that always escapes the clear decision of the law, even when

the law seeks by way of suspicion to track down every indeterminate manner of being ... (The suspect: anyone and everyone ...).[54]

Before addressing the vitally important question of Robespierre's and Saint-Just's own imperfect attempts to "usurp the appearance of the universal," what I would like to emphasize is that the suspect can in effect be "anyone and everyone." The term's definition derives its radical open-endedness from the fact that no one at all can live up to or embody the "brutal exigency" of abstraction and universality that the Terror prescribes. This indeed is the overriding threat figured forth by the suspect: the demands of the common good notwithstanding, the suspect is an individual with a "particular will," a private life, a propensity toward what Blanchot elsewhere calls "intimacy."[55] More than simply a structural withholding from the public sphere, obliqueness and intimacy—like Rousseau's concept of forgiveness—imply an openness to or even an engagement with difference. And, as the Montagnards' speeches at the trial of Louis XVI worked to establish, to tolerate difference in any philosophical or interpretive sense is to call the entire legitimacy of the Revolution, as understood by the Robespierrist cadre, into question. "If Louis is innocent, then what is to become of the Revolution?" Thus, following Blanchot's analysis of the Law of Suspects, this question could be reformulated: If thought is oblique, private, and particular, then what is to become of thought under the Terror?

That is not to say that the Law of Suspects targets thought alone. Blanchot is right to identify thought, in good Hegelian fashion, as the form of self-expression that is most difficult to recuperate into a discourse of public activity. Nevertheless, the leaders of the Terror, like Rousseau before them, by no means neglect the specifically *linguistic* manifestations of individual psychology. The following citation from the text of the Law of Suspects makes this abundantly clear:

> Are *suspect*, and must be arrested as such: those who, in popular assemblies, interrupt the energy of the people with artificial discourses, turbulent shouts, whispers; those more prudent ones who talk mysteriously about the misfortunes of the republic; ... those who do not attend their section meetings, and who try to excuse their absence by saying that they do not know how to speak.[56]

This passage is fascinating in that it targets a virtually unlimited range of verbal expressions as counterrevolutionary utterances: from shouts to murmurs, from eloquent speeches to admissions of defeat in the face of the Terror's stringent linguistic rules. In short, the Law of Suspects explicitly defines its victims as people who fail to speak correctly—a category that appears to be infinitely elastic. The paradox here, of course, is that while the elasticity of the category is designed to guard against semiotic deviations, its very vagueness opens it up to a whole host of different interpretations. What is artificial, as opposed to natural, discourse? What is the difference between speaking patriotically, with legitimate concern, about "the misfortunes of the republic," and discussing this topic "mysteriously," in a manner that invites suspicion? What transcendental linguistic standard is there against which to judge each individual instance of speech? In light of these unanswerable questions, the Law of Suspects neatly illustrates the psychoanalytic precept according to which the repressed and the return of the repressed ultimately amount to the same thing.[57] Rather than eliminating linguistic heterodoxy and confusion, this text, at a formal level, performs and propagates it, thereby conforming to Saint-Just's great avowal of discursive and political slippage: "Nothing resembles virtue so much as a great crime." Once again, this is why the guillotine served such an important purpose in the new republic. Whoever controlled its operations had the power "to monopolize the terms of the [revolutionary] agenda" and so to identify with apparent certainty who was damned and who was saved; language itself, with its own inherently suspect potential, cannot and does not definitively enforce such categories. (Not so incidentally, it was at this very time that the Montagnard *conventionnel* Bertrand Barère, supporting the efforts of one Abbé Grégoire, decided to take his party's repressive new philosophy to heart. At his urging, the Convention sponsored a rigorous suppression of different languages, from foreign tongues to local dialects, within the republic—yet another expression of the revolutionary state's systematic repudiation of polyvalent expression.)[58]

Given, however, that their own Terror was still in large part "a Terror that speaks," the Montagnard leaders did not let language's aporetic qualities prevent them from trying desperately to establish a distinction between good (abstract) and bad (particularized) forms of verbal expression. "Citizens," Robespierre declares on May 7, 1794, "sometimes peoples, like individuals, have to collect themselves to listen, as it were, in the silence of the passions, to the voice of wisdom" (Mazauric 306). Just as Rousseau describes a discursive shift wherein "the voice of duty tak[es] the place of physical impulse" (*Contract* 64), this pairing of the silence of the passions and the voice of wisdom suggests the latter as a clear alternative to, and replacement for, the former. In the Terrorist schema, the generalized discourse of wisdom and reason must over-write the particularities and differences proper to the passions. In an-other speech, Robespierre admits that submitting one's passions to such constraints may be difficult, but encourages his audience: "Go ahead and cry, . . . but console yourselves if, silencing all vile passions, you want to ensure the well-being of your country and the world; console your-selves, if you want to bring back the exiled values of equality and jus-tice" (Mazauric 195). Opposing vile passions to a vision of public happi-ness, equality, and justice, with the passions belonging to individuals and their opposite to the nation and the entire world, Robespierre comes down squarely in favor of disinterested public virtue. As he states in yet another variation on this theme, stifling individual desires is necessary "so that all friends of the nation can make a show of support for the voice of reason and public interest" (Mazauric 298). Reason and the common good, held to be universal values, are alone thought to be ex-empt from the "vile" contaminations of personal difference.

Joining Robespierre in overriding concern for the individual as such, Saint-Just coins a memorable truism: "Justice is not clemency, it is sever-ity" (Soboul 139). This inflexible gnomic generalization is based first on a negative definition of justice and then on a contrived opposition be-tween the two abstract nouns, *clemency* and *severity,* with which it has been associated. In Saint-Just's eyes, any attempt to equate justice and mercy clearly betrays counterrevolutionary sentiment, for clemency al-lows, precisely, for the proliferation of "suspect" alternative feelings.[59] In fact this statement, proffered on February 26, 1794, as a justification for the countless imprisonments and executions prompted by the Law of Suspects, responded directly to a protest issued by Camille Desmoulins, which I treat at length in chapter 3, decrying the merciless persecution of victims under the Terror. Saint-Just continues his invective against Desmoulins's call for mercy—a position that, to Saint-Just, announces the journalist's adherence to a group of dissidents known as Indulgents, led by Robespierre's great rival Georges-Jacques Danton—by demand-ing that accused suspects and their sympathizers alike be silenced: "The pity that people display for crime is a glaring sign of betrayal, in a re-public that can only be based on inflexibility. I defy all of those who

speak in favor of the detained [suspects] to open themselves up to public accusation in a courtroom. Can the voice of criminals and corrupt,
tainted men really be taken into account in the judgment of their peers?"
(Soboul 139). Starting from the premise that the "republic...can only
be based on inflexibility," Saint-Just deduces the necessary exclusion and
elision of any alternative, more indulgent attitude toward the Terror's
suspects. These suspects, criminal by definition, are revealed by the
"glaring sign" of pathos to be antirepublican and therefore, like Louis
Capet, have no right to speak or be spoken for. It is moreover interesting that pity should be associated with the potentially traitorous order of
signs, of differential mediation—as against the inflexibility, the "prompt,
severe, inflexible justice" of the Terror. With this opposition in place,
Saint-Just echoes Rousseau's idea from *The Social Contract* of "voice[s]...
taken into account" in the ideal republic, and declares that any voice
sympathetic to the suspect cannot possibly be heeded in the determination of the criminal's fate. Again, the logic of the Terror demands the silence, the discursive annihilation, "of everything that opposes it" (Soboul
136), and that opposition is located in the irrecuperable sphere of pathos
and linguistic difference. "People," Saint-Just urges in another speech,
"listen neither to indulgent voices nor to irrational voices!" (Soboul 176).
An outgrowth of the Terror, rigid censorship becomes the rule of the
game: "It is difficult to establish a republic by other means than inflexible censorship" (Soboul 142).

In a report delivered before the Convention on February 5, 1794, Robespierre supports and reiterates his colleague's denunciation of Camille
Desmoulins's merciful political stance. Like Saint-Just, the Incorruptible forges a link between clemency and divisive passions, deploring
Desmoulins's attempt to "awaken in the [the people] all those passions
that could feed into [its] sinister schemes" (Mazauric 304). Also like
Saint-Just, Robespierre not only condemns the discourse of personal
sentiment but also demands that it be altogether overruled for the sake
of public harmony: "Let no particular and hidden interests encroach
upon the influence of the general will of the assembled people and the
indestructible power of reason" (Mazauric 305). In this injunction, the
usual opposition between particular interests and the general will is fortified by the qualification of the former as "hidden," opaque, and therefore resistant to the sublime, radically public transparency demanded
by the Terror. Because under the Law of Suspects that which is hidden

is condemnable and indeed condemned, the particularistic pathos of Desmoulins and of his all-too-indulgent comrades does not stand a chance. According to Robespierre, it must crumble before the indestructible power of the Terror, here aligned with the assembled people and reason. The image of the assembled people, borrowed from Rousseau's *First Discourse*,[60] obviously suggests communitarian togetherness: the generating and genitive root of the general will in this passage. And reason, which he frequently associates with a discourse of generality (as in his evocation of "the voice of reason and public interest" [Mazauric 298]), here remains exactly that: the "indestructible," transcendental opposite of differential feeling.

In evincing the manifold dangers of difference, Robespierre and Saint-Just sought not only to censor it but also to promulgate a countervailing discourse of utter generality. To this end, both men strove to position themselves and their pronouncements as abstract, disinterested, preoccupied solely with the common good. In the Incorruptible's case, his nickname alone bespoke his well-known will to overcome personal interests and sentiments, to use Saint-Just's phrase, "by reducing everything to the cold rule of justice" (Soboul 210). According to one of Robespierre's biographers, Camille Desmoulins sensed this trait in his old school friend as early as 1790, telling the man who would one day send him to his death: "You are faithful to your principles, however else it may be with your friends."[61] Similarly, Thomas Carlyle, a passionate soul with little patience for Robespierre's sanctimonious austerity, speaks of the man derisively as "a poor spasmodic incorruptible pedant, with a logic-formula instead of [a] heart."[62] Neither Carlyle nor Desmoulins, however, can be accused of putting words into Robespierre's mouth. Even during Louis XVI's trial, the Incorruptible insisted that he was acting out of purely disinterested motives when he advocated the monarch's death: "I have neither love nor hate for Louis, . . . but Louis must die, because the nation must live" (Mazauric 218–19). The first sentence establishes Robespierre's absolute exemption from the passions; the second, another of the many implacable gnomic generalizations we have come across in this body of texts, exemplifies the sort of heartless "logic-formula" ascribed by Carlyle to the Montagnard leader. The all-important republican motto, "The nation must live," stands, consistent with Desmoulins's characterization of Robespierre, in absolute opposition to personal sentiments such as love and hate.

Nonetheless, later in the same speech Robespierre appears to deviate from this principled rejection of feeling when, addressing his audience, he expresses sympathy for "the weakest ones among you," subject to "all the particular affections that can make you concerned about the fate of the accused." Describing how he personally handles difficult situations such as remaining inflexible in the face of human (albeit counterrevolutionary human) suffering, he remarks:

> Inexorable, when it is a matter of calculating, in an abstract manner, the degree of severity that the justice of laws must use against the enemies of humanity, I have felt republican virtue falter in my own heart. But, citizens, the ultimate proof of devotion that the representatives of the people owe to the nation, is to sacrifice these first movements of natural sensitivity to the safety and salvation [le salut] of a great people. Citizens, . . . clemency that negotiates with tyranny is barbaric. Citizens, it is to the supreme interest of public safety and salvation [le salut public] that I hereby call you back. (Mazauric 224)

At first seeming to undermine his nickname and his reputation, the Incorruptible begins this monologue with a confession that even he, despite his "inexorable" public record and his ability to calculate in an abstract manner what is good for the state, has experienced difficulty in maintaining rigid republican virtue. It is hard not to see in this startling allusion to his faltering heart the traces of the leader's self-proclaimed debt to Rousseau's *Social Contract,* in which the author's conflicted heart prevents him from passing definitively harsh judgment on those inclined to be soft on error. As we have already seen, however, by the final months of 1792, Robespierre sensed that the milk of human kindness had passed its expiration date. Parting ways, then, with the conflicted *philosophe*'s lessons in clemency, Robespierre recommends that his countrymen harden their hearts against tender mercies. Instead of calling for tolerance and pity, the Incorruptible commands his fellow delegates to "sacrifice these first movements of natural sensitivity to the safety and salvation of a great people." He even goes so far as to establish his implicit moral superiority to his colleagues by presenting himself as the individual best qualified to guide them on the path of civic-minded virtue. With the conclusion "I hereby call you back," Robespierre alone performatively rallies his addressees to the cause of public safety and salvation.

Once the Terror was fully underway, Robespierre took to punctuating virtually every speech with such avowals of his all-consuming commitment to the common good and refrained from making any further disclosures about the "particular affections" of his own heart. For example, insisting on the importance of distinguishing between "friends of liberty" and "criminals," he asks and then answers two questions designed to establish himself as the ultimate judge of such matters: "Who, then, will untangle these nuances? Who will draw the line of demarcation between these contrary excesses? The love of the nation and the truth will do it" (Mazauric 291). With their parallel interrogative pronoun *who*, these questions appear to anticipate that a human being will be named in reply. Strangely, however, Robespierre answers them with an abstract value: "the love of the nation and the truth." In this way, the orator is on one level semantically dramatizing the philosophical and political enterprise that he privileges in almost all of his texts—that of replacing individual sentiment with disinterested patriotism. But that is not all. Behind the pure, impersonal abstraction evoked here lurks the figure of Robespierre himself, who, as a matter of historical and contextual fact, was with Saint-Just the driving force behind the passage of the Law of Suspects. Despite the referential vagueness we have already discerned in this piece of legislation, its principal function was precisely to "draw the line of demarcation" between the guilty and the innocent, to weed out the good citizens from the bad. A contextually based interpretation would therefore see in Robespierre's statement an implicit equation between "the love of the nation and the truth" (the avowed source of the Law of Suspects) and himself (its actual origin). Like Rousseau's legislator, Robespierre would, according to this reading, be "working in secret" for the good of his people—a hidden figure like the Longinian sublime.

Robespierre's elliptical self-referentiality is, however, problematic, because it is indisputably a function of *interpretation*—of the very type of individual, particular (i.e., context-driven) hermeneutic activity that Terrorist discourse so zealously endeavors to eradicate. Insofar as Robespierre wants to be recognized as a paragon of forthrightness and patriotism, his listeners or readers must read in between the lines, instead of engaging in the discursive transparency that is his political and philosophical ideal. In the same way, they must suspend knowledge of his own rhetorical duplicity—manifested in yet another imperative question masquerading as a genuine query—and follow his oratory toward the conclusion that he forces upon his listeners. A similar set of problems resurfaces later in the same speech when Robespierre intimates only by way of considerable indirection that perhaps he alone can legitimately root out and repudiate the "excesses" of conspiracy and counterrevolution. First, he stresses that he has repeatedly distinguished himself by having the courage to tell the complete and patriotic truth ("to say everything") on the unpleasant subject of traitors and counterrevolutionaries. He then initiates yet another series of questions that begin with *who*—questions that defy the audience to see the unspecified referent of the interrogative pronoun as anything other than the consummate public servant: "Who defended the National Convention and risked his life in the process? Who has dedicated himself to its conservation, ... who has dedicated himself to its glory, ... when so many others maintained a criminal silence on the subject of their accomplices' crimes?" (Mazauric 334). Here again, an interpretive leap of faith, grounded in historical reference, is required if one is to place Robespierre in the textually unfilled position of national hero. Numerous *conventionnels* could perhaps be construed as dedicated to the conservation and glory of the republican legislative body, but only Robespierre—who had eluded an assassination attempt earlier that year—could readily be identified as someone who "risked his life" on behalf of the Convention. The more significant point, however, is that Robespierre's own text does not guard against alternative interpretations: it answers its own series of "who's" with a void, with nothing. Of course, this very answer could be taken as the ultimate reflection of Robespierre's radically self-annihilating stance, of his privileging of patriotic concerns over personal well-being. Nevertheless, this aporia makes Robespierre's speech *structurally* susceptible to other interpretations, invited literally—if only to be denied figuratively—by the interrogative form that it adopts. And these interpretations could run counter not only to his immediate political goals (nothing in this series of questions formally prevents one from answering with the name of one of the Incorruptible's Girondin, Hébertist, or Indulgent foes) but also to his generalized project of eliminating difference from political discourse. It was not, we shall soon see, much longer before the very polyvalent qualities of the language he was compelled to speak led Robespierre, along with Saint-Just, to conceive of silence as his only viable discursive strategy. At this stage, however, Robespierre held that silence could—following the Law of Suspects, which chastised those people who remained silent in their section meetings—be "criminal." Why? Because the silence is designated here, compared with Robespierre's own silent position as the subject of his own harangue, as the mask of crime, the very opposite of the republican transparency that the Incorruptible preached, even if he could not always practice it.

In fact, Robespierre changed his mind about the political applications and implications of silence in another, contemporaneous diatribe against his Girondin detractors. Faced with this party's accusation that he reverted to tyranny in governing the republic, the Incorruptible conjoined silence not with criminality but with its ostensible opposite: his own unimpeachable virtue. "What remains for me to say against these accusers?" he demands:

> Let us bury, if possible, these loathsome maneuvers in an eternal forgetfulness. Let us remove from the gaze of posterity these far from glorious days in our history, when the people's representatives, led astray by cowardly schemes, appeared to forget the great destiny to which they had been summoned. For myself, I will make no conclusion of a personal nature. I have renounced the easy advantage of responding to my adversaries' calumnies by even more redoubtable denunciations. I wanted to suppress [this] part of my justification. I renounce the just vengeance with which I would have had the right to pursue these slanderers; I ask for no other [vengeance] than the return of peace and the triumph of liberty. (Mazauric 197)

Robespierre here explicitly associates a program of silence and selective censorship with a conception of universal virtue and discursive totality to which he himself is the key. His opening line, "What remains for me to say," again recalls the position of the Rousseauist legislator, in that it locates the speaker beyond the ineffectual mediations of language. We recall that in the *philosophe*'s ideal republic, there is "[no]thing left to demand," just as in Saint-Just's, there is "nothing left to fear," because in both cases, lack and difference have been abolished. In this particular harangue, Robespierre presents himself as the inventor of a "sublime mission" geared toward overcoming the "senseless discourses" of the dissenting Girondins (Mazauric 196). This movement past language and toward supposed universal plenitude requires several critical erasures, all of which are paradoxically effected by first-person pronouns that include Robespierre and exclude his nemeses. First, there is the prohibition of factional discord, recommended by Robespierre when he urges the people to join him in erasing from historical record ("let us bury...

in an eternal forgetfulness"; "let us remove from the gaze of posterity") the Girondin efforts ("cowardly schemes") to challenge his power. In these statements, an all-powerful, unanimous "we," similar to Rousseau's "one" (more than to the *philosophe*'s highly personal "we"—always a community of readers), opposes and overrules the viewpoints of an inadmissible minority. Second, as Robespierre's repetition of first-person singular verbs makes clear, his concept of totalizing republican virtue involves the abolition and renunciation ("I have renounced.... I wanted to suppress....I renounce") of personal concern, however legitimate ("just") it may appear to be. In marked contrast to his scheming, self-serving enemies, the Incorruptible purports to be preoccupied only with his "great destiny" as a leader and with universal values such as "peace and the triumph of liberty." The contrast serves above all to secure the morally superior position that Robespierre is attempting to establish for himself, even though this position is explicitly a function of the speaker's subjective and partial linguistic activity.

Asserting that "one has to be [il faut être] a sublime man to consolidate one's nation" (Soboul 195), Saint-Just likewise seeks to cast himself in a transcendental light—and meets with similar difficulties when he attempts to achieve this in language. In this declaration, Saint-Just more or less succeeds in his effort at self-depersonalization, through his decision to put an impersonal command *(il faut)* in the position of the statement's subject. To bolster his self-presentation as a "sublime man," he skillfully and paradoxically elides his "I" altogether, hiding himself and denying his passions in the fashion of the radically disinterested Rousseauist legislator. The young Montagnard, whom one historian has described as "cold as marble and as inaccessible as stone to all the warm passions,"[63] resembles Robespierre in his efforts to cultivate a persona marked by radical, civilly obedient apathy. Also like his senior colleague, however, Saint-Just's pretensions to exclusively patriotic motivations and feelings do not always serve their original intentions. The following invective against foreign factions is a case in point: "So I come today, in the name of the Committee of Public Safety [salut public], to pay you the severe tribute of love of country; I come to denounce to the French people a perverse plot [un plan de perversité] designed to overturn the guarantee of the government, a conspiracy against the French people and against Paris" (Soboul 154). In this speech, Saint-Just emphasizes his heroic devotion to the republic with the dramatic repetition of what he alone has set out to do: "I come . . . to pay you the severe tribute of love of country; I come to denounce to the French people a perverse plot." In the first half of the statement, the speaker endows his "I" with noble sentiment of "love of country," a sentiment that he qualifies as "severe" just so that all his listeners understand there is nothing soft, subjective, or sentimental about it. This love, moreover, stands in direct contrast to the antirepublican "perversity" that Saint-Just attributes to his enemies, just as Robespierre had a few years earlier identified the possibility that a monarch might be a "corrupted pervert" (Bouloiseau 410). The explicitly sexual connotations of this term—and indeed their political associations with the notoriously debauched Old Regime—only serve to enhance the desexualized, disinterested, and purely patriotic nature of the love that Saint-Just arrogates to himself in this instance.[64] But unbeknownst, surely, to Saint-Just, the classic Lacanian definition of "perversion" is the condition of a subject who views himself not as the personal agent of his own desires but as the passive puppet of outside forces.[65] Saint-Just's positioning of his own "I" as speaking "in the name of the Committee of Public Safety" thus establishes him as something of a discursive pervert, even if his aim in this assertion is to strip his "I" of its pathological valence and affiliate it with a larger group. Even without this latter-day psychoanalytic perspective, however, Saint-Just's claim to speak "in the name of" the committee places his utterance under the sign of substitution and thus, as we saw in our analysis of the substitutive logic at work in Rousseau's text, of representation. As Saint-Just's much repeated "I" itself indicates, there *is* a difference—if only on the most basic grammatical plane—between the individual speaker and the broader political body he represents. His claim to speak in its place means the committee itself must be elsewhere, outside or beyond his necessarily subjective utterances. And this in turn means that Saint-Just's effort at a radical reconciliation of the personal and the political betrays its own goal.

This failure notwithstanding, Saint-Just sticks to his guns and persists in posturing as a sublime figure standing above the petty divisiveness and dangerous personal bias with which the Convention, and the entire French republic, is rife. "I belong to no faction; I will combat all of them" (Soboul 202), he informs his colleagues, declaring his enmity for all things divisive. If, later in the same speech, Saint-Just proclaims that he "cannot embrace evil" (Soboul 211), it is therefore understood that this virtuousness, like Robespierre's, derives from his alleged ability to overcome and stamp out political antagonism. Along these lines, he makes a grandiose promise for his future conduct on behalf of the nation: "I will say everything that [tout ce que] integrity advises for the good of the nation; I will picture to myself the image of an honest man, and of all the things that [tout ce que] virtue would demand of him at this moment; and everything that [tout ce qui] fails to resemble a pure love of the people will receive my hatred" (Soboul 211). In this case, Saint-Just insists that the only motives underlying his actions will be integrity and virtue, understood as "a pure love of the people." This purity, which alone characterizes the "honest man" in the republic, does not allow for any preoccupation other than "the good of the nation." The repetition of the correlative *tout ce que/qui*, with its obvious accent on totality, works further to underline the universalizing nature of Saint-Just's avowed commitment. Once again, the will to say everything is theoretically marked by, and marked for, pure patriotic devotion. Nonetheless, in proclaiming his hatred for "everything that fails to resemble" his own ostensible "pure love of the people," the orator reveals once more how explicitly intolerant the Terrorist notion of discursive inclusiveness really is. In Saint-Just's own words: "Liberty must conquer at any price" (Soboul 117).

The brutally exorbitant nature of this price becomes even more apparent when the young *conventionnel* maintains that his virtuous disinterest allows him not only to rise above but in fact mercilessly to sever the ordinary bonds of human intimacy. "A revolutionary man is inflexible," he generalizes, again dissimulating his own subject position behind an unspecified third-person pronoun, "he is the irreconcilable enemy of all indulgence" (Soboul 183). To prove that he himself possesses these qualities to a dazzling degree, he refutes the claim made by some of the Montagnards' detractors that partisanship and friendship have led him to side blindly with Robespierre in every debate. And so he takes up the first-person pronoun, in order to allege that he is not prone to such base, personal biases: "At least you must not believe that it could possibly have occurred to me to flatter a man. I am defending him because he struck me as irreproachable, and I would accuse him myself, if he were to become a criminal" (Soboul 205). In this instance, Saint-Just

emphasizes that his alliance with Robespierre is based solely on the latter's "irreproachable"—Incorruptible—nature and that his own political
sympathies are therefore entirely impersonal. To prove his point, Saint-
Just ventures to pledge that he would not hesitate to denounce his long-
standing partner and friend should the latter turn out to be a criminal.
By no means, then, would he engage in the sort of "criminal silence"—
the refusal to say everything about counterrevolutionary activity—
mentioned by Robespierre. For Saint-Just, the best political leader is
someone who not only says everything but who also manages, like
Rousseau's legislator, to separate himself from human pathos in the
process. To cast himself in this exemplary light, Saint-Just therefore consistently conjoins his "I" with declarations of his lack of personal sentiment. "I will say everything that I think of them, *without pity*" (Soboul
204; my emphasis), Saint-Just declares in reference to his existing foes,
threatening them with denunciation and death. "I know not how to express my thought halfway," he contends in another speech, "I am without indulgence for the enemies of my country, I know only justice"
(Soboul 135). Or again: "I speak to you with utter frankness of integrity,
determined to undertake everything, to say everything [tout dire] for
the safety of the nation" (Soboul 166). But as usual, the direct correlate
of such totalizing speech is the condemnation and elimination of alterity:
"I would accuse him myself, if he were to become a criminal." Friend
and friendship alike are to be cast aside if the general will demands it.

A similar link between Saint-Just's discourse of totality and his conception of virtue as the obliteration of pity also appears in his March
1794 tirade against foreign counterrevolutionaries:

> So I come today, in the name of the Committee of Public Safety, to pay
> you the severe tribute of love of country; I come to denounce to the
> French people . . . a conspiracy against the French people and against
> Paris. I come to tell you, in a completely blunt fashion [sans aucun
> ménagement], some bitter truths that until today have been veiled. The
> voice of a peasant from the Danube was not scorned in a corrupt senate:
> one can therefore dare to say everything to you, you friends of the
> people and enemies of tyranny. Where would we be, citizens, if it were
> truth that had to keep silent and hidden, and if it were vice that could
> attempt anything with impunity? . . . When a free government is estab-
> lished, . . . it must destroy everything that opposes public prosperity; it
> must courageously unveil all conspiracies. We have the courage to
> announce to you, and to the people, that it is time for everyone to return

to morality, and for aristocracy to return to the Terror; that it is time . . .
to plunge back into nothingness the enemies of the people who, by
flattering corrupt men's vices and passions, create factions, . . . rebuild
the throne, and serve the foreigner. (Soboul 154–55)

We have already examined the paradoxically metonymic relationship
that Saint-Just, in an effort to establish the absolute generality of his "I,"
draws between himself and the Committee of Public Safety. And we
have seen how he underscores his purportedly universal subject position when he ascribes to himself no sentiment other than the love of
country, a "tribute" motivated by severity instead of sentimentality. What
should now attract our notice is Saint-Just's claim that it is his pitiless
severity that allows him to adopt a vocabulary of absolute transparency
and utter plenitude: "I come to tell you, in a completely blunt fashion
[sans aucun ménagement], some bitter truths that until today have
been veiled." As at the trial of Louis XVI, where Saint-Just and Robespierre
lambaste the Girondins' delaying tactics and debates over constitutional
interpretation, the Montagnard approach to politics is presented as sublimely unmediated by formal manipulations (ménagements). To be sure,
the substitutive and subjective grammatical logic of this passage suggests otherwise, but Saint-Just does not seek to reconcile this with his
self-proclaimed discourse of radically transparent unveiling. Instead, he
constructs a privileged discursive position from which to expose "bitter
truths" that will make dead men of his opponents.

And so, like Robespierre's supposedly transparent language of virtue,
Saint-Just's notion of complete unveiling requires the suppression of
difference and enforces a strong bias against those "vices and passions"
that are held not to merit expression within the republic. Whence the
parallelism between Saint-Just's two prescriptions for a "free government"—"it must destroy everything that opposes public prosperity; it
must courageously unveil all conspiracies"—wherein the rhetoric of
revelation coexists with and accompanies that of partial concealment.
"It must destroy" stands as the precise correlate here to "it must unveil":
the two imperatives are inextricably linked in Saint-Just's political vision. As so often happens in Saint-Just's speeches, he then proceeds to
assign principal weight to the destructive side of his proposed project:
"We have the courage to announce . . . that it is time . . . to plunge back
into nothingness the enemies of the people. . . ." It is highly significant
here that when he advocates this Terrorist measure, Saint-Just's "I"

becomes a "we."[66] Impelled by a pure "love of country," his desire to crush all dissenters emerges as a communal project, belonging to "us" republicans without exception.

Illustrating both Montagnard leaders' tendency to construct themselves as purely impersonal mouthpieces of the general will (the historian Stanley Loomis references them collectively as "the self-appointed advocate[s] of humanity"),[67] the rhetorical transformation of Saint-Just's "I" into a pluralistic, unified "we" touches on the larger paradox of political representation during the Terror. In discussing the Rousseauist legislator, we have already become attuned to the problems inherent in the idea that a single individual at a specific moment in history can embody a truly general, transhistorical will. For the very role of the sublime lawgiver as a mediator between the general and the particular is a double-edged sword. On the one hand, his ability to transcend time and passion enables him to reconcile the differences among ordinary citizens in such a way that the common good can prevail. On the other hand, however, because he exists as a representative, or synecdochal extension, of the people, and because he stands in relation to them as an exemplar whose virtue is worthy of imitation, his position depends on precisely the mimetic and differential logic that he is supposed to overcome.

This contradictory logic not only surfaces in Robespierre's and Saint-Just's self-promotion as "sublime men" in the service of the general will; it also underpins their formulation of the *conventionnels*, and thus their own, function as "representatives" of the French people.[68] Attempting to justify his and his colleagues' status as delegates and spokespeople for their countrymen, Saint-Just tells his fellow legislators that "everything depends on our example and on the firmness of our measures" (Soboul 138) and that they must serve as "examples of rigidity" (Soboul 161) for the nation. Nevertheless, in the same speech, he refers to his enemies' supposed facility with fictions and dissimulations and concludes that "an imitative spirit is the mark of crime" (Soboul 159), thereby making problematic his own implicit suggestion that the elected representatives are models to be copied by their constituents. "One does not imitate virtue" (Soboul 161), he avers; in the same vein, he decries political representation in its specifically linguistic manifestations: "Liberty should not be in a book: it should be in the people" (Soboul 105). Because imitation and "that demon, writing" (Soboul 130), involve division and difference, representation is irreducibly at odds with the Terrorist understanding of virtue. It is, moreover, revealing that in his pronouncement about the impossibility of imitating virtue, Saint-Just resorts to the completely impersonal, undifferentiated pronoun *one*. With this shift, he calls attention to the fact that even the "we" he uses elsewhere to designate the *conventionnels* ("our example," "our measures"), as distinct from the people, implies a theoretically discomfiting separation of the two groups. Indeed, when he apostrophizes the Convention and the citizens together, it is to remind them that their fates are completely and utterly intertwined: "Your cause is inseparable" (Soboul 156).

Robespierre adopts the same problematic line of reasoning when he argues in favor of raising a new revolutionary army to stamp out the latest Girondin conspiracies (accordingly, the Girondins were executed en masse on October 31, 1793). Announcing that every citizen's duty is "to die for liberty," he continues: "I have taken a stand: let all citizens imitate me. May all of Paris take up arms, may the people keep watch, may the Convention declare that it is the people [se déclarer peuple]. . . . Patriotism and the people must dominate, and dominate everywhere!" (Mazauric 232–33). Although his closing exclamation asserts the incontestable, universal dominance of the people, Robespierre undermines this claim in both of the sentences that precede it. First, in defiance of Saint-Just's invective against "the imitative spirit," Robespierre connects the issue of political leadership to an inherently differential logic of imitation. He positions his "I," which stands both apart from and in the place of his fellow citizens, as the exemplar upon which they should pattern their common stance. In this way, he articulates and prescribes a mimetic relationship between himself and the people from whom his own position ought to emanate: the part and the whole do not perfectly coincide, but instead enter into an endless feedback loop of reflections, imitations, and refractions. Second, and similarly, in exhorting the Convention to "declare that it is the people," Robespierre evokes an underlying division between the people and the legislative body. Even if this gap can be bridged by the sublime semiotics of a performative utterance (as Robespierre here, with his reflexive and hortatory grammatical constructions, appears to assume), the need for such a declaration attests to an originary difference between the two spheres. Despite their universalizing pretensions, the Montagnards' concept of political representation inevitably bears the partial, divisive, and differential characteristics of its linguistic counterpart.

It is in this context that we should read Saint-Just's exasperated exclamation, quoted as an epigraph to and in the title of this chapter, about
the imperfections of "the Terror that speaks." Originally conceived as a
supralinguistic means of silencing the passions and expressing republican virtue, the Terror itself fell prey to the structurally suspect vicissitudes of language. "What language can I speak to you?" an exasperated
Saint-Just asks of his fellow representatives in July 1794, when he finds
himself hopelessly entangled in the differential discourse his political
platform had aimed to suppress. "And how can I make discernible the
evil that one word reveals, that one word corrects?" (Soboul 252). The
very fact that one word is capable of serving two opposing functions—
of revealing evil and correcting evil—means that language has the potential to spiral out of control, despite the best laid plans of the speaker
himself. As Michelet has already hinted, the architects of the Terror
were ultimately forced to conclude, a mere day after Saint-Just made
this speech, that there was indeed no "language to speak" consistent
with the radically antirepresentational tenets of their public policy. But
before this final defeat, they would turn one last time to Rousseauist
philosophy with a view to bolstering their flagging Terrorist tactics.[69] If
"a god who discusses things is lost," and if Robespierre and Saint-Just
were starting to realize that even they were not safe in speech, then perhaps their salvation, and that of the public, resided in the rehabilitation
of a sublime, unspeaking god. Saint-Just, peevishly lamenting the difficulties of conveying virtue in speech, accordingly invoked the need for
"virtue [to] show itself, a thunderbolt in its hand, to call vice to order"
(Soboul 209). While Saint-Just was to spend many of the last months of
his life on military missions throughout France,[70] calling vice to order
the old-fashioned way, Robespierre remained in Paris and concocted a
"Supreme Being" through which counterrevolutionary difference would,
ostensibly, likewise be defeated. It is this latter effort that we shall examine in the pages to follow.

"Fraternity or Death": Misogyny, the Supreme Being, and la Grande Terreur

Religion in revolutionary France has a complicated history all its own,
but for our purposes, the element to be stressed is the fact that, as the
Terror wore on, Robespierre became increasingly interested in a Supreme

Being as a political, moral, and philosophical tool and solution. First hatched in the final months of 1793, his Supreme Being was designed not only to fulfill the people's evident need for a religious governing principle but also to guarantee, in a way that language had not or could not, privileged Montagnard notions such as civic virtue and Terrorist justice. In terms of the former imperative—that of providing a deeply Catholic populace with a replacement for the God upon whom they had long depended and whose traditional earthly manifestation had disappeared with the last Louis—the first governmental attempt to address this issue on a grand scale was the Cult of Reason, upon which Robespierre's Supreme Being provided some important variations. These variations, in fact, have everything to do with the Montagnard leader's second objective for establishing a state religion (i.e., upholding the "truth" of antidifferential Robespierrist dogma). We cannot, however, appreciate the significance of the changes that the Supreme Being brought about without first briefly reviewing what preceded it—and specifically what failed—in the Cult of Reason.

Held on November 10, 1793, in Notre-Dame Cathedral in Paris and in other churches throughout the country, the Cult of Reason was a religious ceremony designed to celebrate a secular value straight out of the Revolution's intellectual arsenal. After a long, hard period of unprecedented sociopolitical turmoil, the majority of the *conventionnels,* following Rousseau and Voltaire, had conceded that some form of deity would assist both the people and the government. That is to say, it would help the populace in the usual business of confronting poverty and mortality, and their representatives in the necessary task of impelling the nation to civic virtue. Although Robespierre himself opposed the precise form that this version of secular religion was to take, he conceded the general need for faith, citing Voltaire's famous maxim, "If God did not exist, one would have to invent him" (Mazauric 285). Given the premium attached to rationalist thought by the *philosophes* and their republican disciples in the National Convention, it made sense to assign to "the Reason" the position that a Catholic God had occupied before the Revolution destroyed His earthly delegate. So it was with high hopes and great fanfare that the *conventionnels*—led by Robespierre's extremist nemeses, Jacques-René Hébert and Pierre-Gaspard Chaumette—voted on and organized a nationwide festival in honor of Reason.[71]

Reason "herself" was represented in each city by a suitably beautiful and virtuous *citoyenne* dressed in pseudo-Grecian allegorical garb, parading down the aisles of central places of worship and summoning onlookers to espouse a rational, public-minded morality.

At first blush, the worship of Reason might strike us as consistent with the philosophical principles of Robespierre and Saint-Just. The term *reason* certainly recurs in both men's speeches, where it almost always enjoys the status of an abstract, universal value worthy of and crucial to a disinterested people governed by a general will. It is, however, precisely on the issue of generality that the Cult of Reason deviates dramatically from the Robespierrist political ideal.[72] By *personifying* Reason, Hébert and Chaumette undermine the idea of a transcendental value that exists beyond individual persons. As one disgruntled festivalgoer, citizen Picard, writes in an editorial to the *Annales patriotiques et littéraires*, objecting to the worship of Reason's particular embodiments:

> Is not every man the temple of Reason? I feel strongly that one can consider Reason in an abstracting manner, outside of man [abstractif et hors l'homme]: and that is the only spirit in which it would be possible to gather for paying homage to Her. Let the people be told: "You should not come here looking for a statue of gold, silver, or marble erected to Reason, nor [should you come] to contemplate Her on a speaking canvas."[73]

The final lines of this passage recall the Mosaic interdiction against graven images, alluded to by Rousseau in *The Social Contract*. For Picard as for Rousseau, religious transcendence requires an overcoming of all things earthly, including and especially mediation and mimesis. Picard also espouses the idea that the point of transcending traditional representation is to attain a political condition that is properly "abstracting" and "outside of man." Under no circumstances can a specific person claim to represent the general will.

Especially if that person—as my deliberately feminine translation of the French pronouns attached to *la Raison* aims to indicate—happens to be a woman. Even worse, according to Picard, than the simple decision of a handful of individuals to portray Reason is the fact that these people are women. "It seems to me," he muses,

> that the philosophers' senses and imaginations are equally shocked by the idea of a *woman* representing *Reason,* and by the youthfulness of this woman. In women, this pure faculty [Reason] is identified, as it were,

with the *weakness,* the *prejudices,* the very *attractiveness* of this enchanting sex. In man, its empire [that of Reason] is exempt from all error: *force, energy,* and *severity* gather there instead. But, above all, Reason is *mature, serious, austere,* qualities that would hardly suit a young woman.[74]

Here again, Picard's vocabulary draws on that of the Terror. Force, severity, and austerity: these are the values, impersonal and implacable, that citizens ought to adopt and revere. Femininity, for Picard, is irreconcilable with such values. Referring to Reason's "exceptionally scandalous place in the French Revolution," Mona Ozouf wonders, after herself quoting Picard's letter: "Was it not, perhaps, in some obscure way, this triumph of the feminine that was found so shocking in the [Cult] of Reason?"[75]

Not only did this triumph of the feminine shock hard-line Terrorist sensibilities; it was also targeted by Robespierre's Festival of the Supreme Being, held on June 8, 1794, and obliterated from public memory.[76] Minutes from a meeting between Robespierre's Committee of Public Safety and the Committee of General Security, on May 29, 1794, catalog a general consensus that the Supreme Being should replace deities such as Reason, because "they [the Committees] regard the idea of three divinities (liberty, equality, fraternity) represented by three women as contrary [not only] to the principles that the French people has proclaimed through the organ of the Convention—[but also] to all notions of common sense."[77] This statement makes clear the degree to which the Supreme Being was designed to eliminate women from the central, figural position they had occupied in the Cult of Reason. Accordingly, Marie-Hélène Huet describes the Festival of the Supreme Being as a palimpsest, created for the express purpose of erasing the Cult of Reason and its scandalous display of sexual difference.[78] The aptness of this argument becomes evident when we examine the mechanics of Robespierre's Supreme Being and the celebration he more or less single-handedly organized to honor it. First off, evoking the spectacle of nothingness lauded by Rousseau in his *Lettre à d'Alembert,* Robespierre declines to give any visible or tangible form to his deity of choice.[79] Instead, the people are told to gather around a small artificial mountain, which, in the words of the festival's organizer, Jacques-Louis David, "becomes the altar of the Nation,"[80] to celebrate nothing but themselves, each other, "the republic one and indivisible."[81] Robespierre's Supreme Being itself surmounts the problem of divisibility, because it has no discernible form: it manifests itself simply in the flames of the torches that are set to effigies of counterrevolutionary forces such as "Atheism, upheld by Ambition, Egoism, [and] Discord."[82] Like the burning bush accompanying God's tautological announcement to Moses, "I AM THAT I AM," the Supreme Being conceived by Robespierre and staged by David shares the attributes of the sublime, for it self-destructs in its very self-manifestation. As the Incorruptible's loyal ally Claude Payan puts it, in a helpful formulation also cited by Huet: "When it comes to defining the Supreme Being, we shall have an idea of him that is so *sublime* that we shall not degrade him by giving him a face or a body similar to our own."[83] Just as Rousseau's legislator achieves superiority with respect to his fellow mortals by appearing to transcend the space and time of traditional representation, so does the Robespierrist deity seem to exist beyond the "degraded" realm of figurality.

It bears noting, moreover, that the sublime presentation of the Supreme Being rests on a denigration not only of figurality and of corporeality (in its self-consuming flames, it is a disembodied body) but of femininity as well. Anticipated by the opposition established in Rousseau's *Lévite* between virile, unmediated social bonding and the pathologically, divisively oriented female body, Payan's axiomatic statement about the Supreme Being displays an emphatic prejudice against "degrading" the divinity with a specifically feminine form. This notion is also implicit in Marie-Hélène Huet's reading of the Supreme Being as an antifeminine palimpsest. For Huet, the deliberate invisibility and intangibility of Robespierre's republican divinity derives largely from the psychoanalytic relationship, articulated by Jean-Joseph Goux, "*between the Judaic prohibition against image adoration and the incest taboo with the mother.*"[84] Goux's point is that Mosaic law, as conceptualized by Freud, involves an abandonment of the maternal, sensory realm for the repressive realm of the father's abstract legal codes: "By tearing oneself away from the seduction of the senses and elevating one's thoughts towards an unrepresentable god one turns away from the desire for the mother, ascends to the sublime father and respects the law."[85] Applying Goux's schema to the Cult of Reason, with its material portrayals of femininity, Huet observes: "The image and the maternal are inextricably linked. They were linked as well for the backers of the Cult of the Supreme Being, who sought, in their determination to create a 'sublime' religion, the double repudiation of idols and the feminine.... The Cult of Rea-

son had been too feminine; the Cult of the Supreme Being would be resolutely virile."[86]

Before turning to some examples of the Supreme Being's implicit
"virility," we would do well to consider Huet's analysis of the execrated
figure of Reason as a forbidden maternal body in light of Lynn Hunt's
superb study of Marie Antoinette as the quintessential "bad mother" in
the collective revolutionary psyche.[87] Denounced in widely disseminated
popular pamphlets as "the mother of all vices," Louis Capet's widow
was rumored to enjoy unspeakable sexual activities (including lesbian-
ism and incest with her own son, a charge that the revolutionaries
raised at her trial as one of numerous indications of her overall criminality).[88] According to Hunt and other historians, these exploits became
something of a national obsession during the revolutionary era, to the
point where female sexuality, aristocratic decadence, and antirepublican
politics became synonymous in the public imagination. We have already glimpsed this combined preoccupation in Robespierre's reference
to Louis XVI's head as a Medusa's head—a castrating, profoundly
threatening, and radically unassimilable female figure that, in the engraving from Villeneuve (Figure 1) has the added feature of displaying a
bloody (read: castrated) "hole" at the neck. In his analysis of this representation, Jacques André even sees menstrual imagery in the blood that
drips from the dead king's neck—referred to in the engraving's caption,
taken from the militant anthem "La Marseillaise," as "an impure blood
nourishing our fields"—and reads this fertilizing flow of blood as
strong evidence of the popular conflation of Louis with his notoriously
"impure" queen.[89]

Payan further exhibits this politically loaded distrust of femininity
when, not content simply to praise Robespierre's idea of a sublime,
formless deity, he execrates the *conventionnels* who dared to promote a
feminized version of reason:

> But what was this Reason to whom they were building temples? . . . This
> word, *reason*, assumed in their mouths all the meanings that could be
> useful to their interests. Sometimes it meant an insurrection against
> liberty; sometimes it was the wife of a conspirator carried triumphantly
> in the middle of the people; [sometimes] it was an actress who, the night
> before, had played the role of Venus or Juno. . . . Degraded goddesses
> were going to reign in France. The Convention identified these
> conspirators—they are no more.[90]

This passage reveals several interesting facets of Terrorist sexual politics. First, it suggests a direct connection between feminized figurality and a dangerous, differential hermeneutics. The allegorically costumed women, according to Payan, inspire an interpretation of the word *reason* that is both open-ended and particularistic, allowing for "all the meanings that could be useful to their interests." From the Terrorist perspective—which, as we have seen, demands fixed and stable meanings in the service of indivisible generality—nothing could be less acceptable. Robespierre admits as much when he denounces the Cult of Reason above all for the "open predication of atheism" (Mazauric 349) that it makes possible. The corollary that such dreaded interpretive *openness* assumes in the gendered sociopolitical sphere is, perhaps not surprisingly, the intimation that the female allegories of Reason are somewhat too open to both sexual and antirepublican "vice." Payan establishes the former by observing that the actresses dressed as Reason were also known to portray such promiscuous characters as Venus. (This was in fact the name of Paris's leading courtesan in the 1790s, though we might also be reminded of the actress-courtesan Nana's first appearance in Zola's novel by the same name.) That Robespierre himself was horrified by such a display of debauched female sexuality is advanced by Mona Ozouf, who quotes the Incorruptible as having been "shocked in his 'instinct of respectability'" by the goddess Reason."[91] But the virtue to which the feminine figures of Reason failed to demonstrate is political as well as sexual. For "the wife of a conspirator" to whom Payan alludes is, in at least one historical interpretation, none other than Madame Momoro, whose husband had broken definitively with Robespierre and aligned himself closely with the Incorruptible's militant Hébert, founder of the Cult of Reason. Momoro would later earn the Robespierrists' undying enmity by covering the carved tables of the Declaration of the Rights of Man with a black cloth to protest their leader's omnipotence in the Convention and the Committees.[92] As her husband's wife, marching in an Hébertist parade, Madame Momoro herself thus implicitly carries the taint of conspiracy. It matters little to Payan whether the degradation to which these female figures bear witness is sexual or political or both. The bottom line for him is that women are incapable of representing the public interest and dangerously liable to compromise it.

At least to a certain extent, this view can be construed as an outgrowth of the misogyny that existed on a broader scale during the Terror. Ever since July 1793, with Charlotte Corday's assassination of Marat, and October 1793, with Marie Antoinette's widely publicized trial and execution, women had become "an explicit object of hatred" in the new republic.[93] On November 3, an author named Olympe de Gouges was guillotined for papering the nation's capital with her profeminist, neo-royalist, anti-Robespierrist literature;[94] less than a week later, the influential Girondin patron Madame Roland met a similar fate. In a broader-based effort to quell feminine activism, which had been considerable in the earlier stages of the Revolution, on November 5 the *conventionnels* declared women's political associations and meetings illegal and forbade female attendance in men's clubs. Finally, in order to discourage unwholesome sex on the part of the female population, the Convention urged its special police force, the Committee of General Security, to crack down on prostitution. Its masculinist ideology bolstered by these directives, the Montagnard government took every opportunity to promote a constrictive kind of sexual politics, repeatedly emphasizing that French women's principal duty was to bear and raise republican children, preferably sons.

Robespierre himself entered directly into the fray about a month before his antifeminine festival. As a conclusion to his speech on republican political morality, delivered on May 7, 1794, he invoked Rousseau's "upright male eloquence" (Mazauric 321) as the guiding inspiration behind the Supreme Being. Having thus phallicized his greatest philosophical influence, Robespierre then proceeded to read aloud a list of landmark days in the history of the Revolution and the new republic (Mazauric 329). These dates, he declared, should be commemorated annually, "so that all friends of the nation might rally to the voice of reason and public interest" (Mazauric 298). From this list, he pointedly omitted one particular day that had been submitted to him by the Convention as worthy of inclusion, and that day was October 6, 1789, when the *sans-culottes* of Paris, led by women, marched on Versailles and demanded the king's return to the capital. In dropping this date from the official history of the Revolution, the Incorruptible was essentially discouraging any future mobilization on the part of the female population. Granted, Marie Antoinette, Charlotte Corday, Olympe de Gouges, and Madame Roland had all been executed by this time, but a raging horde of women threatened to be considerably less manageable. Having elsewhere railed against his enemies in explicitly feminine terms—presenting the Girondin concept of liberty as "a vile prostitute" (Mazauric 272), and the Hébertist and Indulgent notions of republicanism as a "Bacchante" and a "prostitute" (Mazauric 302), respectively—Robespierre did indeed conflate femininity and political dissidence and opposed both of them to his antidifferential conception of civic virtue. This is why his discourse of supposed republican generality, "the voice of reason and public interest," unabashedly silenced women's voices and the multiple forms of difference with which he associated them.

It is against this ideological backdrop that some additional features of the Festival of the Supreme Being assume their full significance. For example, the choreography for the event showcased many a mother "holding to her breast her son, who is her most beautiful adornment,"[95] and singing a song about how she was only as good as her husband's and sons' patriotic endeavors. For Robespierre's part, in his capacity as the president of the Convention and the star of the pageant, he capped off his participation by applying the purifying torch of the Supreme Being to the effigy of Atheism, associated by way of the Hébertists with a feminized conception of Reason. "Armed with the torch of Truth," the Incorruptible set fire to the figure, declaring: "It has returned into nothingness, that monster that the kings, in their genius, once vomited onto France."[96] In this case, the Incorruptible deploys the usual Terrorist vocabulary of annihilation against the feminine "monster" of the Hébertist celebration.[97] In alluding to this monster as a product of France's former kings, he also suggests a connection—one that we have already seen in the discourse of his colleague Payan and that Olympe de Gouges, with her royalist leanings, personified in a discomfiting way—between the monster of feminized Reason and the monstrous, Medusa-like, effeminate former monarchy. Once again, the Terror associates female sexuality with deviant, antirepublican politics and the incontestable truth (represented by Robespierre's tellingly phallic "torch of Truth") with their opposite. In an attempt to contrast his newly created divinity with the unacceptable, womanly one promoted by his opponents, Robespierre reminds his listeners of the new religion's purely republican underpinnings: "The idea of the Supreme Being is a continual call [rappel] to justice; it is therefore social and republican" (Mazauric 317). Given that Robespierre figures this call by setting fire to the monstrous statue of the former feminine cult, he recalls *(rappelle)* his fellow citizens to a type of justice according to which femininity joins other politically suspect categories in a pantheon slated for outright annihilation. Here as in Rousseau's *Lévite*, the republican instantiation of a supposedly universalizing, transparent community demands that sexual as well as ontological and political difference be suppressed.

In keeping with this exclusionary bias, the proceedings for the Festival of the Supreme Being as a whole required pronounced segregation of the sexes at the level of audience participation. David's script called for a strict separation of women from men as the crowd marched through Paris to the mountain at the Champ de la Réunion. Men and women, the former carrying guns and the latter flowers (as well as babies), were given separate verses to sing in a hymn composed for the occasion by Marie-Joseph Chénier. This poem, whose misogynist sexual politics are fascinating in their own right, merits an extensive analysis that I lack the time to give it in this chapter.[98] The chief point of interest here, though, is that the hymn highlighted the Supreme Being's ability to create and rule the universe without female assistance, thereby defeating the corrupt, aristocratic "bad mother" once and for all. And then, for the festival's grand finale:

> A formidable discharge of artillery inflames the courage of our republicans; it announces to them that the day of glory has arrived [le jour de gloire est arrivé];[99] a male, warlike song, the forerunner of victory, responds to the sound of the cannon. All the Frenchmen commingle their sentiments in a fraternal embrace; they no longer have any but one single voice, from which the general cry *Vive la République!* rises toward the Divinity.[100]

In David's script as in Rousseau's writings, the claim to absolute discursive unity ("they no longer have any but one single voice") and homogeneity ("the general cry") coexists in apparent harmony with the suppression of differential elements. Consistent with Robespierre's attack on the Hébertists' "degraded goddess," feminine difference is implicitly subsumed in, or erased by, male-gendered expressions of republican loyalty: the "male, warlike song" and the "fraternal embrace." Yet again, the voice of the people is represented as a masculine one.[101]

This passage from David's script also, if inadvertently, anticipates Sade's insistence on the homosexual subtext of republican fraternity. It would indeed be difficult to overlook the sexual connotations of the participants' prescribed "fraternal embrace," especially when it is considered in conjunction with the "formidable discharge" that serves as

the festival's climax. As Jacques André theorizes in his study of paint-
ings by David and speeches by Robespierre and Saint-Just: "The love of
brothers is the love of men; *revolutionary fraternity and misogyny are in-
dissociable complements.*"[102] From a psychoanalytic as well as a political
perspective, the idea of fraternity as the love of men is a highly suggestive one; accordingly, both André and Lynn Hunt have employed a neo-
Freudian methodology to demonstrate the homosexual underpinnings
and implications of republican brotherhood.[103] In this light, the psycho-
analyst Colette Soler, when speaking of the homosexual and gynopho-
bic aspects of Kantian philosophy, might just as well be referring to
Robespierrist republicanism when she writes: "By claiming to determine a will by excluding all motives and so-called pathological objects
of the senses, what the categorical imperative of the moral law and its
extremism ends up proscribing is, obviously, woman. In this option, we
can see, the subject 'removes itself from or fortifies itself against' Alterity in order to hole itself up in the refuge of the phallic One. It is a strategy
for the eradication of the Other."[104] Soler's analysis of Kantian morality
as a "bachelor's ethic" (the expression is originally Lacan's) unquestionably applies to the Incorruptible's cult of the Supreme Being, a religion
that vigorously forecloses not only femininity but also related "pathologies" such as figurality, the expression of female sexuality, and the articulation of anti-Montagnard political views. In response to this multifaceted, threatening alterity, Robespierre creates a supposedly transparent,
unified deity to preside over a homogeneous fraternity of citizens, which
corresponds to the "refuge of the phallic One" described by Soler. The
Supreme Being stands as the perfect manifestation of and mascot for
the "strategy for the eradication of the Other" upon which the Terror is
based.

With this perspective, we are in a position to understand the otherwise puzzling fact that on June 10, 1794, a mere two days after universal
fraternity was joyously proclaimed at the Festival of the Supreme Being,
Robespierre prevailed upon the *conventionnels* to pass the infamous
Law of Prairial. This decree's blanket suspension of defendants' rights
put the already stringent Law of Suspects to shame and initiated the
seven-week period of unprecedented bloodshed known as la Grande
Terreur. (To be precise: The fifteen hundred executions that occurred
during this period exceeded the total number of deaths remanded by
the Revolutionary Tribunal in all twelve months of 1793.)[105] Although

Robespierre was credited with the decree, it was perhaps Saint-Just who best described the philosophy underlying the Law of Prairial, when, returning to Paris after his lengthy absences overseeing republican troops in the provinces, he announced on behalf of the Committee of Public Safety: "Our goal is to create an order of things such that a universal inclination toward goodness be established; such that all factions suddenly find themselves flung upon the gallows; such that a male energy inclines the spirit of the nation to justice..." (Soboul 141–42). Significantly, Saint-Just positions the hallmark combination of Terrorist politics—the desire simultaneously to establish a universal "order of things" and to annihilate all dissident factions by means of the gallows—under the gendered rubric of "male energy." Confronted with this explicitly masculine proclamation of violent intolerance, we can now read the "male, warlike song" offered up to the Supreme Being as a precursor to the repressive measures of the Grande Terreur. Just as the Law of Suspects aimed to destroy anyone perceived to be suspect, the Law of Prairial, following so closely on the heels of the misogynistic Supreme Being, targeted anyone perceived to lack the "male" attribute of radical intolerance for difference.[106]

We recall, however, that the Law of Suspects construed its target category in such a way that every citizen ran the risk of falling into it, just by virtue of being an individual and a speaking being. In the same way, the paradox of the Law of Prairial is that it both sought to annihilate heterogeneity in all its forms and at the same time expanded the field of potential victims to a dizzyingly open-ended degree. Quite literally, François Furet points out, after Prairial, anyone could be accused of anything, and the "simple accusation" was enough to send a person to his or her death.[107] In a speech delivered one day before his overthrow, Robespierre acknowledged: "The penal code must necessarily have something vague about it, because, given that the current character of conspirators is dissimulation and hypocrisy, it is necessary that justice be able to seize them in all their forms" (Mazauric 360). The capacity of the Terror to root out *all forms* of potentially objectionable behavior left Robespierre himself vulnerable to its deadly workings. Indeed, as Michelet remarks with pithy insight about these final weeks of the Incorruptible's reign: "It seems that Robespierre, from one challenge to the next, would have ended by arresting and guillotining himself."[108] This is the thrust of one darkly funny political cartoon from the period, which shows the executioner who operates the guillotine, Sanson, using the machine against himself after all the nation's other inhabitants—from regular citizens to *conventionnels*—have submitted to its blade (Figure 4). The banner draped over this dramatic scene of self-destruction reads clearly "Gouvernement de Robespierre" (Robespierre's government). Accordingly, the logic of Prairial was geared to destroy anyone and everyone, including its creators, and to leave the law alone to uphold the abstract ideals of republican "energy."

In this context, it comes as little surprise that for the Robespierrists presiding over the Grande Terreur the discourse of energetic virility is often linked to the discourse of death. For Saint-Just, at the limit, death appears as the converse of legal rigor, its negative consequence: "Peace and abundance, public virtue, victory, everything resides in the vigor of the law; outside the law, everything is sterile and dead" (Soboul 95). Here the male-coded fertility and vigor of the Supreme Being, that harbinger of public virtue, are located exclusively in the law, with sterility and death looming large on the margins of this lofty realm. Elsewhere Saint-Just charges that counterrevolutionaries "have no energy" and bear "the mark of impotence" (Soboul 63), again equating the anti-republican and the unmanly, but when he ascribes this double quality to the law alone, he leaves very little hope for the mortals who have to follow it. To deviate in any way from Prairial's abstract imperative of absolute intolerance—in short, to demonstrate one's capacity for humanity—is to mark oneself for death, and so one is best advised to kill off one's human, differential impulses.[109] Herein lies the true meaning of the popular Terrorist slogan "Fraternity or death." The fraternity celebrated by the Festival of the Supreme Being and legalized by Prairial demands the destruction not only of feminine and political difference but of human difference broadly defined. Republican brotherhood, as Blanchot demonstrates in "Literature and the Right to Death," is just another way to die.[110]

Perhaps this is what Robespierre was driving at in the strange statement he made in the middle of his famous oration "On the Principles of Revolutionary Government": "A vigorous body, tormented by an overabundance of sap [sève], leaves more resources than a corpse" (Mazauric 290). The crucial qualifier here is *tormented*, evoking as it does the necessary mediation of pain in the development of a "vigorous" body politic. More interesting still is Robespierre's identification of an overabundance

Figure 4. *Gouvernement de Robespierre* (Government of Robespierre) (1794).
Copyright Snark/Art Resource, N.Y. Musée de la Ville de Paris, Musée Carnavalet,
Paris, France. Courtesy of Snark/Art Resource, N.Y.

of sap as the source of republican torment. His allusion to a pained body full of too much fluid has evident sexual overtones: the fraternal body, having been forbidden all contact with alterity, has no (heterosexual) outlet for its "seed." It is not sterile and impotent, as Saint-Just would have it, but its "resources" cannot be channeled into anything else, anything *other* than the tormented, literally self-destructive body politic. Most tragically of all, the only alternative that Robespierre could envision to this vicious circle of pain is death, "a corpse." No third way appeared to the Incorruptible; no possibility of difference offered itself as a way out of the fraternal bloodbath. "What do those people want who want neither virtue nor Terror?" (Duval 978) asked a puzzled Saint-Just when Camille Desmoulins tried to propose precisely such a nonbinary alternative.[111] This was a question to which the Montagnards—for whom truth, in Saint-Just's unforgettable phrase, was "like a light in a tomb" (Duval 401)—would never find an answer.

Post Scriptum on Thermidor: The Gods Are Mute

On July 27, 1794 (9 Thermidor Year II), a motley crew of anti-Robespierrist conspirators, fed up with the excessive bloodshed of Prairial and with the threats that hung over their own heads, overthrew the Incorruptible's government. They took over the floor of the National Convention and, in a maneuver that can be described only as poetic justice, prevented Robespierre and Saint-Just from uttering a word. The latter had devised a speech for the occasion, in which he dwelled presciently on the difficulties of speaking in the current political climate: "One no longer dares either to speak or to keep silent [ni parler ni se taire]" (Soboul 209), he had wanted to say. But when he was in fact forbidden to speak, Saint-Just "dared" to be silent: he stood speechless at the lectern until the mutinous *conventionnels* had him carted away to prison.[112] Robespierre dealt with his newfound disenfranchisement somewhat differently. He too maintained a steady silence in front of the Convention—and once in prison, he sustained a gunshot wound to the jaw, delivered either by his own hand or by a soldier sent by the deposed leader's enemies to do the job.[113] The following day, a nearly unconscious Robespierre, along with Saint-Just and a group of his other closest allies, was led to the guillotine and executed to vociferous public applause.

When considering the events of Thermidor, it is difficult not to conceive of them as the logical conclusion of the Robespierrist ideology of

Terror. In the most obvious sense, the Incorruptible and his followers died in accordance with the procedures that they themselves had sanctioned and perfected, from the Prairial-style lack of due process they received before their "judges" in the Convention, to the means of execution itself. "You will be judged," Saint-Just had prophetically informed his colleagues during the king's trial, "according to your principles . . ." (Soboul 67). In the context of this study, though, the event possesses an additional dimension of significance, which lies in the cluster of silencings and silences that marked the last day of their lives. When the rest of the *conventionnels* denied them the right to speak, Robespierre and Saint-Just experienced firsthand, and for the first time, the essentially censorious nature of the republican freedom to "say everything." From Louis's trial to the Law of Prairial, the duo had always conceived of totality as a deeply constrictive force, eradicating difference in the name of political expediency and artificial unity. On 9 Thermidor, their colleagues turned this policy against them. "I ask for the curtain at last to be torn away" (Soboul 202), shouted Thermidorian ringleader Jean Lambert Tallien when announcing the Robespierrists' overthrow to his colleagues. With this proclamation, Tallien made use of the same rhetoric with which Robespierre and Saint-Just had always silenced their opponents: counterrevolutionary opacity (the "curtain" of Robespierrist tyranny) must be eliminated in the name of republican transparency (the passage from obfuscation and particularism to a general will unencumbered by deceptive mediation). In a Terrorist system, the pretension to discursive totality always requires that at least one voice be suppressed. "Limitation," as Slavoj Žižek has remarked of the Kantian sublime, "precedes transcendence";[114] such that even when endeavoring to transcend the limits placed upon them by Robespierre's government, the victors of Thermidor revealed their collusion with the system they purported to despise.[115]

Perhaps more telling even than the Thermidorians' Terrorist strategies, however, is the fact that the Robespierrists' silence on the day of their demise was at least partly *self-imposed*. By standing in front of his colleagues and remaining visibly, defiantly speechless, Saint-Just appeared not simply to conform to his own party's censorious practices but to honor them. "What language can I speak to you?" he had asked in the statement he was not permitted to deliver on that day. "And how can I make apparent the evil that one word reveals, that one word corrects?"

(Soboul 252). Although I cited this question earlier, only now is it entirely apparent how Saint-Just and his incorruptible colleague decided to answer it. Once the Terrorist silencing tactics were directed at them, the only language that remained for these men to adopt was in fact silence. Because fraternity, with its imperative of absolute homogeneity, could by no means tolerate the deviations and differences made possible by language, the deposed leaders were left with death, which they themselves had deemed fraternity's sole alternative and which they themselves had meted out in the name of the republic. Robespierre's speechlessness before the Convention reportedly provoked the outraged cry: "Danton's blood is choking him!"[116] How chillingly appropriate, then, that the Incorruptible should go to the guillotine choking on his own blood from a wound that was intended, in the vein of the instantaneous destruction that was his trademark, as either a murder or a suicide. With this in mind, there remains little else for me to say on the subject, except perhaps to conclude with Carlyle's typically evocative account of the leader's gruesome silence:

> Robespierre lay in an anteroom of the Convention hall, while his prison escort was getting ready; the mangled jaw bound up rudely with bloody linen: a spectacle to men. Men bully him, insult him . . . he speaks no word. He had on the sky-blue coat he had got made for the feast of the Être Suprême; oh reader, can thy hard heart hold out against that? His trousers were nankeen; the stockings had fallen down over the ankles. He spake no more in this world.[117]

CHAPTER THREE

The Bridle and the Spur

Collusion and Contestation in Desmoulins's Vieux Cordelier

I am not Robespierre.

—Camille Desmoulins, *Le Vieux Cordelier*

I am not certain that only rhetoric is at stake.

—Jacques Derrida, "How to Avoid Speaking: Denials"

Shortly after her brother's death, Charlotte Robespierre discovered a stack of Maximilien's private papers, which included a note scribbled in the spring of 1794 in response to the publication of Camille Desmoulins's controversial journal, *Le Vieux Cordelier* (The Old Cordelier). Infuriated by his former best friend's traitorous reflections on the political value of compassion, the Montagnard leader had scrawled: "The people need to be enlightened, but what are the obstacles to their instruction? Those mercenary writers who lead [the people] astray through their daily, impudent impostures. What should we conclude from this? That writers must be eliminated as the nation's most dangerous enemies."[1] In this invective against men of letters, Robespierre reveals in no uncertain terms the antipathy to representation that is his hallmark. Authors' interventions in the public sphere can be viewed, the Incorruptible here opines, only as "obstacles," manifestations of difference that endanger the ostensible totality of the general will. At a time when the Montagnard government was struggling to rally the people around a homogeneously and unilaterally defined vision of the "republic one and indivisible," any challenge to this ideal could and had to be written off as divisive, self-interested, and erroneous. Thus, whether or not they accepted money for their efforts (Desmoulins himself made a great point of refusing the profits from *Le Vieux Cordelier*),[2] Robespierre felt that these men betrayed mercenary tendencies; and whether or not they were striking artificial poses, their writings warranted condemnation as "impudent impostures." Be it particularist, fictitious, or both, the work of the author—shades of Plato here—had no rightful place in the republic. With this unequivocal condemnation of authorial activity, the Montagnard leader provides us with a very precise idea of what Camille Desmoulins was up against in his dream of saving France from the Terror with "the boldness of my babbling pen, and its republican independence."[3] Desmoulins's attempt to realize this dream in *Le Vieux Cordelier* came to an abrupt end a few months before Thermidor, when Robespierre and Saint-Just had the author and his fellow Indulgents— including the group's most prominent figure and the Incorruptible's principal rival, Georges-Jacques Danton—sent to the guillotine as counterrevolutionaries. For those close to Robespierre, the decision to execute Desmoulins was particularly startling given that the journalist was Maximilien's oldest and dearest friend. Camille's inseparable companion during their school days at Louis-le-Grand and a witness at the journalist's wedding to Lucile Duplessis, Robespierre had recently even become godfather to the couple's infant son. Desmoulins returned these affectionate favors by praising the powerful Montagnard's virtue and vision to the skies in practically all of his journals (he founded several publications during his short life as an outlet for his "babbling pen"),[4] including the first few issues of *Le Vieux Cordelier*. What, then, could possibly have gone wrong? How and why did Camille wind up going so far afoul of his beloved Maximilien? For what reason did the politician see fit to condemn his old chum's journal as self-serving, untrue, and downright dangerous?

Although any study of *Le Vieux Cordelier*, concerned as it is with the day-to-day political events of the Terror, requires that serious attention be paid to historical data and detail, we will not find the answer to these questions in the official legal charge leveled against its creator at the time of his arrest. Penned by Saint-Just on the basis of a note from Robespierre, the indictment issued by the Committee of Public Safety on March 30, 1794, accused Desmoulins of being in league with conspirators seeking to restore monarchy to the throne. This, however, was little more than the habitual charge that the Montagnards trumped up in order to do away their enemies, whatever the political record of the accused. (On March 24, just six days before the journalist's arrest, all top members of the Hébertist faction had also been beheaded as monarchist agents; and their political platform, which held that the Robespierrists were not slaughtering *enough* suspects, could not have been more at odds with that of Danton's Indulgents.) Certainly the accusation—which shocked Desmoulins's contemporaries and which Alphonse de Lamartine later dubbed "the sacrilege of the Revolution"[5]—made no sense in the context of Desmoulins's own record as a revolutionary hero. He was legendary throughout France for having first sounded the insurgents' call to arms on July 12, 1789, donning the first cockade, and inciting the Parisian mob to storm the Bastille.[6] In the years that followed, Camille further enhanced his reputation as freedom fighter. He used his publications as bully pulpits for rabid Montagnard proselytizing, supported Robespierre's zealous persecution of counterrevolutionaries (beginning with Louis XVI) in the Convention, and even participated in the debilitating symbolic "pig-hunt" of the monarchy—depicted in Figures 2 and 3—by describing Louis XVI on more than one occasion as a swinish "animal-king."[7] When Danton became minister of justice, Camille served as one of his most trusted undersecretaries, juggling these responsibilities with a continued high profile in the political clubs and in print. By the time of the Terror, the only perceptible blight on Desmoulins's image was his association, through Danton, with an unscrupulous politico and playwright named Fabre d'Églantine, who in early 1794 was revealed to have accepted bribes and perpetrated fraud in the crooked liquidation of the Company of the Indies.[8] Undoubtedly, Fabre's shady dealings tainted the moral and political authority of the Indulgents as a group and gave Robespierre and Saint-Just, growing daily more uncomfortable with Danton's popularity and his cadre's anti-Terrorist views, a reason to retaliate against the faction as a whole. Nonetheless, if Desmoulins, who had had no direct involvement in the Company of the Indies debacle, suffered from the slightest hint of guilt by association, even this seemed insufficient to account for his sudden demise. Aware that neither royalism nor racketeering nor even a poor choice of bedfellows could legitimately be invoked to justify his fall from grace, the journalist proffered a much more convincing explanation on the day of his death. Addressing the mostly mute and somber crowds that gathered at the foot of the scaffold on April 5, 1794, Desmoulins cried out: "They are lying to you [on te trompe], people! They are sacrificing [on immole] those who most want to serve you! I am the one who first uttered the cry of liberty! My crime, my only crime, is to have spilled tears for the republic!"[9]

By juxtaposing the machinations of an abstract and repressive collective force, figured by the Rousseauist and Robespierrist pronoun *on*, with the tearful indignation of an individual "I," Desmoulins deftly touches on what can in fact be understood to be the real nature of his crime against the state. Spilling tears, after all, has something in common with the monarchist politics ascribed to Desmoulins in his official indictment and with the self-interested fictions attributed to him in Robespierre's private writings. Like monarchism, mercenary activity, and lying, the expression of soft or effeminate emotion could be taken as a betrayal of the disinterested and virile generality that the Montagnard leaders equated with civic virtue. Accordingly, I argue in this chapter that *Le Vieux Cordelier* represented a threat to the Montagnard state because it gave voice to the very forms of difference—political, ontological, and linguistic—that Robespierre and his acolytes strove to annihilate. In deep disagreement with the Robespierrists' Manichaean logic, whereby anyone not with the Terror was against it, Desmoulins attempted to formulate an answer to Saint-Just's own anguished question: "What do those people want who want neither virtue nor Terror?" (Duval 978). As a way out of this grisly deadlock, the journalist offered up the two-pronged, anti-Terrorist alternative of discursive freedom and play on the one hand and political tolerance and clemency on the other. Desmoulins's tears, spilled literally and figuratively in the pages of his last publication, expressed both passionate commitment to this program and, in the final months of his life, despair at the Robespierrists' failure to embrace it.

This is not, however, to say that *Le Vieux Cordelier* entirely avoids the Terrorist elements that it calls into question. As Ross Chambers has shown in another context, discourse designed to oppose authoritarian power structures tends to betray the very poetic and political biases it seeks to overcome.[10] So it often was with Desmoulins, who did, it must be noted, come up through the ranks of the Revolution by demanding that noblemen be hanged from lampposts, that suspects and spies be ferreted out of the republic, and that "schemers, climbers, aristocrats, and counterrevolutionaries of all stripes tremble" in the face of his journalistic revelations.[11] *Le Vieux Cordelier,* undertaken once Desmoulins and Danton's other Indulgents had begun to recoil from the Terror's excesses,[12] in many ways constitutes a dramatic shift away from this fanatical mindset. Nevertheless, certain parts of the journal betray an uneasy tension between the author's overarching commitment to the freedom of expression and his belief, conditioned by Montagnard ideology, that discursive and political repression are necessary conditions of liberty. Straddling the fine line between anti-Terrorist detraction and Terrorist collusion, Desmoulins's publication treads it with varying degrees of success. "When I come to visit the wounds of the state," he proclaims in December 1793, "I am not afraid that people will confuse my surgeon's scalpel with an assassin's stiletto" (*Vieux Cordelier* 41). For better or worse, though, the possibility for confusion inhabits his very medium; and in many instances Desmoulins pushes the obfuscating properties of language as far as they will go, cultivating ambiguity and reveling in the irony that he cannot prevent from undercutting his own self-proclaimed, salutary purpose. In the Incorruptible's words: "Either this solemn declaration means what I just said it means, or else it is nothing but a betrayal" (Bouloiseau 391). Paradoxically, in fact, because *Le Vieux Cordelier* combines party-line Robespierrist rhetoric with elements of subversive political critique, it was capable of striking both the Terror's partisans and its opponents as a betrayal.[13] As far as the Montagnards were concerned, the journalist undermined his promotion of an orthodox, appropriately restrictive understanding of "saying everything" by refusing to present it consistently and unequivocally as gospel. By contrast, for those troubled by the Terror's restrictions on free speech and freedom *tout court,* Desmoulins's efforts to explode the Robespierrist paradigm may have appeared insufficiently unorthodox, insofar as they retain notable traces of the repressive ideology that triggered them in the first place. This conundrum notwithstanding, it seems to me safe to make two overriding claims about *Le Vieux Cordelier,* claims that the rest of this chapter works to substantiate. The first is that at its best, its author uses a series of sophisticated textual maneuvers to deterritorialize, to borrow a term from Deleuze and Guattari, his opponents' theory and practice of discursive suppression, thereby transforming the Terrorist assassin's stiletto into a deft surgeon's scalpel.[14] The second is that even when the journal appears uncritically to propagate the biases of the Robespierrists—whether out of residual Montagnard commitment, ideological blindness, or a simple desire for political survival—it never "freezes" them into a dogmatic doctrine intended to oppress Desmoulins's fellow man. In this way, Desmoulins's journal differs significantly from the writings of his contemporary detractors and so stands to teach readers of any historical and critical stripe a great deal about the Terror and its discontents. Not only does *Le Vieux Cordelier* dramatize the uncomfortably symbiotic relationship between these two positions; it also designates the elusive possibilities of redemption that inhabit even the most restrictive of discursive systems.

Terrorist Challenges and Blessings in Disguise

Published on December 5, 1793, the first issue of *Le Vieux Cordelier* was openly devoted to the question of free expression, as the title itself likely suggested to anyone who got the reference.[15] The allusion was to one of Paris's two foremost revolutionary clubs, the Cordeliers Club (the other being the Jacobin Society), and the implication was that the club held value only in its "old" incarnation, before being taken over by the intolerant Hébertist thugs with whom it was now associated. Hébert and his followers had not always dominated the Cordeliers; in the early days of the Revolution, the society had been, at least in Desmoulins's view of things, a forum for healthy and earnest debate among thoughtful "true confessors of liberty" (*Vieux Cordelier* 37) like himself and Danton. A veritable "little Rome," as he had dubbed it in *Les Révolutions de France et de Brabant,* the place had metamorphosed under Hébert's stewardship into an outlet for narrow-minded, doctrinaire ranting, for the menacing mantra that Robespierre's Terror was not going far enough in rooting out the republic's bad seeds. For Desmoulins, on the contrary, the Terror was already going too far as it was, and the Hébertists' vitriol— regularly disseminated in a popular journal called *Le Père Duchesne* (Father Duchesne)—was only part of the problem. Another, bigger source of concern was that de facto freedom of the press had recently been suspended in France, and official censors had begun preventing the publication and dissemination of texts deemed "royalist" or "federalist."[16] Viewing this situation as a serious threat to the liberties he and his comrades had fought for in 1789, Desmoulins presented it to his readers as the chief reason behind his decision to take up journalism again after a few years of private study. "Ah, Pitt," he exclaims by way of an opening, apostrophizing the prime minister of England (currently at war with France) as the ostensible reason behind the disappointing turn republican politics has taken of late,

> I have trembled at your progress, and I have felt your strength even in our midst. I have seen, in the very cradle of liberty, Hercules on the verge of being strangled by your tricolor snakes. . . . So it is necessary that I write, that I relinquish the slow pencil of [my] history of the Revolution, which I was sketching by the fireside, in order to take up the rapid and breathless pen of the journalist, and, dropping the reins and the bridle, follow the revolutionary tide. (*Vieux Cordelier* 37–38)

This passage marks the beginning of a back-and-forth between Terrorist poetics and anti-Terrorist critique that runs throughout the first issue of *Le Vieux Cordelier*. Although the author explicitly intends his demand for a free press as a challenge to the policy currently in effect under the Montagnard regime, his statement to this end bears notable traces of Robespierrist textual strategy. Most obviously, Desmoulins betrays his militant conditioning by declaring English counterrevolutionaries to be the real force behind recent attempts to nip liberty in the bud, as if the Hébertists, the government censors, and the other opponents of free expression were acting solely at the behest of France's sworn enemy. This gesture directly inscribes his rhetoric in the vein of accusatory Montagnard militancy, for ever since the trial of Louis XVI, dismissing one's opponents as partisans of Britain and other foreign powers had functioned as an efficacious insult. (Saint-Just's damning formulation, "Louis is a stranger among us" [Soboul 67], is a case in point.) During the Terror, as the nation's massive war effort continued to drain its chronically dwindling resources, this practice had only intensified.[17] Foreigners "infiltrate our clubs, they sit in the very sanctuary of our national representation," Robespierre warned, "they lurk around us, they discover our secrets, they flatter our passions, they even try to alter our opinions . . ." (Mazauric 293). Desmoulins's vision of British secret agents "in our midst" conforms to this pattern of xenophobic denunciation and thus hardly seems a likely springboard for a simultaneous gibe at the Terror's own tyrannical aspects. But so it is; for though Hercules is, as has been demonstrated elsewhere,[18] a common figure for the French republic in revolutionary discourse, the snakes strangling the heroic polity are "tricolor." In ascribing to Pitt's alleged agents the signature colors of the new French flag, Desmoulins is effectively suggesting that the "foreign" agenda to undermine the Revolution has in fact taken a distinctly domestic shape. The stranglehold on freedom of expression in France is a function of Montagnard policy; in insinuating that such policy really operates in the service of Pitt, the journalist is chiasmically linking "good" (French, Robespierrist) republicanism with the "bad" machinations of England's insidious spies.

It is telling, perhaps, that this unheard-of gesture should be accompanied by a declaration of Desmoulins's desire to write, an activity which itself runs the risk—as the invocation of the tricolor snake performatively indicates—of destabilizing basic categories of "good" and "bad." At this point in his career, however, Desmoulins does not engage in a metadiscourse about the slipperiness of meaning. Rather, he reverts to a more properly Terrorist position by declaring that he is replacing the scholar's "slow pencil," wielded in private ("by the fireside"), with a purely public and unmediated form of discourse ("the rapid and breathless pen of the journalist"). Like Robespierre and Saint-Just, Desmoulins here adopts a rhetoric of pure public interest and immediate political engagement. The activities of the cozily homebound "I" cede in this formulation to the impersonal demands of the Revolution: "it is necessary that I write . . . and, dropping the reins and bridle, follow the revolutionary tide."

The other pronounced feature of Robespierrist poetics that informs the new journal's introductory passage resides in the figure of the reins and bridle that Desmoulins claims he must abandon in order to trace and denounce the progress of freedom's enemies. In a later and more overtly contentious issue of *Le Vieux Cordelier,* the bridle becomes an important metaphor for the type of strategic self-censorship that Desmoulins, through praeteritio and ellipsis, adopts as a way of both defying and evading his powerful Montagnard critics. In this first issue, however, the journalist purports to let go of the bridle altogether, and so, figuratively, to shake off all discursive constraints—to say everything, as his powerful peers are wont to proclaim. He develops this idea when explaining why his journal will be an important contribution to the current political scene:

> I was wrong to put down my periodical pen, and to give intrigue a
> chance to start falsifying public opinion and corrupting that immense
> sea with a wash of newspapers, as with so many rivers ceaselessly filling

it with poisoned waters. We no longer have a single journal that tells the truth, at least not the whole truth [dire toute la vérité]. I am reentering the arena with all the frankness and the courage for which I am known. (*Vieux Cordelier* 38–39)

The implicit claim here, of course, is that unlike other newspapers (notably the one most despised by Desmoulins, the Hébertists' rabble-rousing *Père Duchesne*), *Le Vieux Cordelier* will manage to "tell . . . the whole truth [dire toute la vérité]." Operating in the same rhetorical vein as Saint-Just, who promises to "say everything [tout dire] for the safety of the nation," Desmoulins invokes the well-being of the republic as his guiding principle and invokes his own unimpeachable patriotism as proof of his discourse's legitimacy. By stressing that he is "reentering the arena," he indirectly reminds his audience of his earlier exploits in the revolutionary sphere, exploits that have made his courage, commitment, and honesty a matter of public record. This record implicitly gives him the right to exclude other writers' ideas from his definition of the "whole truth," in contrast to journals like Hébert's, which have, he claims, functioned as so many "poisoned waters," corrupting the "immense sea" of public opinion. With this charge, Desmoulins also rejoins the Terrorist policy against free expression. While proclaiming his desire to "say everything," the journalist simultaneously emphasizes the relative illegitimacy or inadmissibility of positions with which he disagrees. Specifically, he dismisses the Hébertists, who have recently criticized both Danton and Robespierre in the clubs and the papers, averring that it is "impossible to raise your voice against [these men], without publicly declaring yourself to be in Pitt's pocket, as it were" (*Vieux Cordelier* 38). However wide the range of expressive freedom that Desmoulins stakes out for himself, it does not extend to the voices raised in opposition to his friends and political allies; in true Terrorist fashion, these opponents are disqualified as self-interested servants of the enemy.

This partisan posturing notwithstanding, it would be inaccurate to qualify Desmoulins's first issue as unequivocally Montagnard in its discursive and political dimensions. At the end of his first issue, he intimates that his idea of saying everything, while perhaps structurally similar to that of the Robespierrist government, may not actually involve what his more powerful political friends would like to hear. Slipping this suggestion into a seemingly banal paragraph on the intended publication schedule for future issues of *Le Vieux Cordelier*, Desmoulins writes: "This journal will appear two times every *décade* [the ten-day period that replaced the week on the new revolutionary calendar], and each issue will have more or fewer pages, depending on the abundance of new material and the indulgence of my masters in the Convention and at the Jacobins, for the boldness of my babbling pen, and its republican independence" (*Vieux Cordelier* 40). Like Robespierre and Saint-Just, Desmoulins displays a taste for abstract nouns, but the two key substantives he chooses in this statement, *indulgence* and *independence,* by no means form part of the accepted lexicon of Terrorist virtues. The former term, which Robespierre and Saint-Just will adopt a mere few weeks hence to disparage the relatively lenient politics of the Indulgent circle, already belies the fact that Desmoulins's idea of politically salutary speech, unlike that of the Montagnards, may require forgiveness. Reminiscent of Rousseau's call for grace in *The Social Contract,* the allusion to indulgence implies a potential for error—for deviation from Robespierre's "severe, inflexible" idea of republican justice—and for the forgiveness of error.[19] As Desmoulins will write in his third issue, by way of a preemptive apology for the extremely controversial political views it puts forth: "If, in a democracy, the people can be mistaken, at least it is virtue that they love" (*Vieux Cordelier* 49). The Laws of Suspects and Prairial, however, make no allowance for well-meaning infractions of the party line. By daring to hint at an alternative conception of civic goodness, Desmoulins is thus starting to make good on his pledge to act and write with intrepid frankness. His self-proclaimed personal "independence"—another word that is banned from the Terror's vocabulary of collective, anti-individualistic action—manifests itself in his willingness to proffer this bold proposition.

The journalist makes an even riskier statement at another point in the first issue, when, declaring his unequivocal commitment to a free press, he supports his argument by couching it in terms of a comparison with England, the country most hated and feared by the Robespierrist regime:

What man would, in good faith, dare to compare France to England nowadays, for relative freedom of the press? See how boldly the *Morning Chronicle* attacks Pitt and his military operations! What journalist in France would dare to talk about the gaffes and idiocies of our Committees, and our generals, and the Jacobins, and our ministers, . . . in the same way that the opposition catalogs those of the British minister? And

I, a Frenchman, I, Camille Desmoulins, should not have as much
freedom as an English journalist? This idea makes me absolutely
indignant. (*Vieux Cordelier* 39)

This praise for British liberty of expression, albeit delivered in a back-
handed manner, runs directly and flagrantly counter to French republican
orthodoxy. Although Desmoulins himself has very recently exploited
such jingoistic rhetoric (heavily loaded because of the war with England)
to discredit the likes of Hébert, he now nuances and even reserves his
terms. First, he draws an implicit parallel between himself and the free-
speaking English journalists by referring to their boldness, a quality that
he has already ascribed to his own pen. Going even further, he compares
a French public policy unfavorably to its British counterpart: "And I, a
Frenchman, . . . should not have as much freedom as an English journalist?" Even phrased hypothetically, the question is inconceivably daring. At a time when the workings of the government (the Committees,
the political clubs, the ministries) are forcibly held to be beyond re-
proach, and crucially so for the sake of the war effort, Desmoulins is suggesting that the republican powers that be are in error. Not only have
they made a mistake in limiting freedom of the press; they are capable
of any number of other "gaffes and idiocies" that could further weaken
their position vis-à-vis the English enemy. At the limit, this heretical
charge calls into question the viability and even the legitimacy of the
new regime; and if this is the case, then what, in Robespierre's words, "is
to become of the Revolution?" (Mazauric 215). For Desmoulins, however,
this is precisely the point: the Revolution ought to allow for a few human blunders, and the press ought to be able to discuss them freely
with a government open to all thoughtful perspectives.

Desmoulins then levels an even more unambiguous blow to Terrorist
dogma. Referring to the standard Montagnard argument that the suspension of certain civil liberties is perfectly justifiable when effected
"for the safety of the nation," he protests: "Do not tell me [qu'on ne me
dise pas] that we are in the middle of the Revolution, and that freedom
of the press must be suspended during the Revolution" (*Vieux Cordelier*
39). With this riposte to an anticipated objection, Camille contests the
Robespierrist notion, appropriately rendered by the impersonal pronoun *on*, that limitations on freedom constitute a sine qua non of republican unity. Like his Montagnard colleagues, he claims to believe in
and strive for a "republic one and indivisible" (*Vieux Cordelier* 37): this

phrase appears at the top of the cover page on every issue of *Le Vieux Cordelier*. Unlike Robespierre and Saint-Just, however, the journalist does not necessarily equate the difference of opinion with the outright dissolution of the state. Carefully conceding to his audience's anti-English sentiment, the journalist assures his fellow compatriots that, unlike their British counterparts, they have nothing to fear from a free press:

> Are the principles of freedom of the press less sacred in Paris than in London, where Pitt should be so very afraid of the light? I said it five years ago: only crooks are afraid of lampposts.... Is reason afraid to do battle with stupidity? I repeat, only counterrevolutionaries, only traitors, only Pitt can have any interest in preventing, in France, even the unlimited freedom of the press; freedom and the truth need never fear the penholder [écritoire] of servitude and mendacity. (*Vieux Cordelier* 39)

Here Desmoulins implicitly guarantees the political correctness of his call for freedom of expression in two ways. First, he once again reminds readers of his own revolutionary exploits. The term *lampposts* and the imagery of light that accompanies it are allusions to his "Discourse de la Lanterne," of 1789. Delivered by Desmoulins from atop a table in the Palais Royal, this rousing patriotic speech encouraged the Parisian crowd to rush off to the Bastille and start hanging aristocrats from lampposts—and its legendary status stayed with Desmoulins in the nickname it earned him: "the Lantern Advocate." Second, he charges that only a true enemy of the republic—as usual, Pitt—could favor the constrictions placed on journalists under the new order. Attributing the existing limitations on the French press to the British prime minister, he then throws in a few other groups of commonly deplored personae non gratae, "traitors" and "counterrevolutionaries," for good measure. With this last epithet in particular, Desmoulins uses the Terror's own language against it, striking preemptively at those who would accuse *him* of counterrevolutionary intent. At the end of his diatribe, Desmoulins adopts much the same strategy when he takes up the Terrorist rhetoric of gnomic generalizations and abstract nouns in order to protect his unorthodox position from Montagnard criticism. "Only crooks are afraid..."; "only counterrevolutionaries... can have any interest..."; "freedom and the truth need never fear...": all three of these pronouncements are couched in the language of eternal and immutable verity that we recognize from Robespierre and Saint-Just. The first two statements declare the outright invalidity of any objection to a free press—a gesture that recalls the Montagnards' devalorization of dissidents and their dismissal of their opponents' right to speak. In a related vein, the third statement calls upon the irreproachable values of liberty and truth. As Desmoulins knows full well, these are privileged revolutionary abstractions that, according to the Robespierrists' own rules of discursive combat, only a traitor or a counterrevolutionary could disregard. Whatever rantings might issue from such a person's "penholder" cannot possibly stand up to the mighty veracity of the Lantern Advocate.[20] In this instance, Desmoulins's rhetorical maneuverings work to annihilate his potential opponents just as surely as the Montagnards' language crushes theirs.

In the next paragraph, Desmoulins simultaneously assumes and subverts yet another keystone of Terrorist discourse. Although he has just asserted the importance of "even the unlimited freedom of the press," Desmoulins suddenly turns around and, seemingly contradicting himself, makes a concession to the Montagnard practice of keeping some things silent in the name of public security. "I realize," he acknowledges,

> that in the management of important affairs, it is permissible to deviate from the austere rules of morality; this is sad, but inevitable. The demands of the state and the perversity of the human heart render such conduct necessary, and have made this necessity into the first maxim of all politics. Should a man in a position of power decide to say everything he thinks, everything he knows, he would lay his country open to certain ruin. (*Vieux Cordelier* 39)

In this striking passage, Desmoulins appears to defer to the government's restrictions on free speech while actually highlighting the gap that separates the Terrorist theory of saying everything from the Terrorist practice of selective censorship. Even if the "man in a position of power" is *predisposed* to say everything, he is not *capable* of doing so: "Saying the truth in its entirety [la dire toute]," as Jacques Lacan has quipped, "is impossible, materially; words are lacking."[21] Never does such an admission cross the lips of a Saint-Just or a Robespierre; until Thermidor, when language fails them altogether, they strive to maintain the illusion that they are able, in the younger Montagnard's parlance, to "say everything for the sake of the nation." Desmoulins shatters this myth. Radically totalizing discourse may be the "austere rule" of Robespierrist morality, but it is also a rule from which, "sad[ly] but inevitabl[y]," the Terror's own creators cannot help but to deviate. Sometimes these deviations are political, occasioned by "the demands of the state"; sometimes they spring from the human condition itself, which Desmoulins curiously and cautiously describes as "the perversity of the human heart." Like Saint-Just, who speaks of counterrevolutionary activity as "perversity," the journalist sees the deviation from strict republican intentions as perverse; but like Rousseau, Desmoulins differs from the Montagnards in acknowledging the role that the human heart can play in matters of self-expression. Errors, interpretive differences, omissions of an inadvertent, deliberate, or structurally inevitable nature: for Desmoulins these are simply part of the human condition.[22] "Words are lacking," but they do not, as Robespierre and Saint-Just would have it, make every man or woman into a suspect.

This startling theoretical framework enables the author of *Le Vieux Cordelier* to advance a related hypothesis, equally unheard of in the context of the Terror. Despite its common currency as a Terrorist buzzword, "saying everything" may not actually be the best strategy for protecting the republic ("Should a man in a position of power decide to say everything," the journalist maintains, "he would lay his country open to certain ruin"). Instead of explaining what he means by this assertion, the journalist carries on as if it requires no further elaboration. Like his Terrorist counterparts, he refuses to encourage any real debate and simply assures his readers that he, arguably a "man in a position of power," will use his powers of persuasion responsibly: "Let good citizens not fear the deviations and indiscretions of my pen. My hand is full of truths and I will be careful not to open it entirely; but I will let out enough [truths] to save France and the republic, one and indivisible" (*Vieux Cordelier* 39). Although Desmoulins begins here by admitting that, like anyone else, he is prone to discursive "deviations and indiscretions," he immediately sets about seeking to remedy these potential flaws in his readers' eyes. To begin with, in addressing them as "good citizens," he is explicitly appealing to their goodness, just as he asks for his political leaders' indulgence in their reception of his journal. What is clever about this appeal is that it conveys an anti-Terrorist message by drawing on, rather than departing from, the commonly accepted vocabulary of the Terror. A starkly binary notion of goodness, after all, underpins the Montagnard notion of political virtue as formulated by Robespierre himself: "I know only two sides, good citizens and bad citizens" (Mazauric 338). But whereas the Incorruptible invariably invokes "good citizens" in order to level threats against their "bad" counterparts, Desmoulins

makes a rhetorical juxtaposition of quite a different kind. In his terminology, good citizens are those who tolerate journalistic deviations, not
those who decry or denounce them.

Nevertheless, these words attest to a two-sided paradox. On the one
hand, Desmoulins appears both to seek forgiveness for his potential discursive excesses and to define such forgiveness as the very nature of
civic goodness. On the other hand, he follows on the heels of these
statements with the claim that his journal is in fact based on rigorous
self-censorship and that it is through careful editing and incomplete
disclosure that he intends to "save the republic." "My hand is full of
truths and I will be careful not to open it entirely," he proclaims, "but I
will let out enough [truths] to save France." Like the Montagnards' self-
contradictory practice of "saying everything" by silencing certain parties,
Desmoulins's own proposal for "the unlimited freedom of the press" is
problematically paired with an admission that he himself will not reveal
all the "truths" at his disposal. But despite this surface resemblance to
conventional republican discourse, utterances released from his hand
(which, like his much-invoked pen, is an obvious metonym for his writerly
activity or position) in subsequent issues of *Le Vieux Cordelier* will
prove not to validate the Montagnards' intolerant suppressions but rather
to oppose them. The author intimates as much by requesting in advance the indulgence of his more powerful readers: he knows that eventually, he will need their forgiveness.

But at this point Desmoulins refrains from making any more particularly audacious remarks in his first issue, with the exception of a veiled
denigration of the ideal of unmediated linguistic engagement cherished
by Robespierre and his cronies. Whereas he opens his journal by forsaking "the slow pencil" of the historian in favor of the "the rapid and breathless pen of the journalist," he closes it with precisely the opposite claim.
Here, he presents the spatial, temporal, and psychological distance of
the historian as the optimal condition for understanding current events,
and he explains why he, as opposed to his more politically active comrades, is best suited to provide such understanding to the public:

> My colleagues have all been so busy with and carried away by the whirl-
> wind of current events—some of them in the Committees, others on
> governmental missions—that they have not had the time to read, I might
> almost say the time to think. I, who have been part of no mission and no
> Committee . . . ; who, in the midst of all this work my Montagnard

colleagues have been doing for the strengthening of the republic, have composed, almost entirely by myself alone [à moi seul] (if I may be forgiven that expression), a Committee of readers and thinkers, will I be permitted, at the end of a year, to present them [the Montagnards] with a report from my Committee, and so to offer them lessons from history, the only master—no matter what people may say—in the art of government, and to give them the advice that the greatest political philosophers of all time, Tacitus and Machiavelli, would have given them? (*Vieux Cordelier* 39–40)

While conceding that his busier Montagnard colleagues have been striving to strengthen the republic, Desmoulins suggests that the work they have done—Robespierre in the Committees, say, and Saint-Just on his military missions—does not alone suffice to further the goals of the Revolution. Consistent with the latter men's privileging of immediate action over the mediations of language and thought, the other revolutionaries have lacked the time, precisely, "to read, I might almost say... to think." For the first but not the last time in the history of *Le Vieux Cordelier*, the journalist therefore proposes an alternative committee— one whose sole purpose will consist of demonstrating the value of reading and contemplation. "To read—This practice—," Stéphane Mallarmé muses some hundred years later, in a similar injunction to his contemporaries about the importance of embracing, rather than glossing over, the deferrals and difficulties proper to textual interpretation.[23] These deferrals and difficulties, so thoroughly reviled by the Robespierrists, resurface under Desmoulins's pen as significant discursive desiderata. For example, he exponentially increases the temporal mediations of his own reading by proposing "lessons from history, the only master— no matter what people may say—in the art of government" as his primary subject matter. The phrase "no matter what people say" bespeaks the journalist's anticipation of potential objections from those who disapprove of "wasting one's time saying what ought to be done," as Rousseau puts it. However, even if he has to do it "myself alone"—an expression by which he mock-heroically implies a parallel between himself and, of all people, the author of *The Social Contract*[24]—Desmoulins will get the message across. He will broaden his distracted and recalcitrant colleagues' perspective by confronting them with the opacity of language and the lessons of history.

Despite this lofty and enthusiastic statement of purpose, however, the journalist does not manage to make good on it right away. A few days after the first *Vieux Cordelier* appeared on the newsstands, Robespierre, already sensing the journal's explosive potential, prevailed upon Desmoulins to let him have a hand in writing and editing the subsequent issue.[25] The journalist consented, and his publisher, Victor Desenne, released the next issue of *Le Vieux Cordelier* on December 10, 1793, bearing all the marks of direct Robespierrist involvement. Largely an extended attack on Hébert's Cult of Reason, which Robespierre was very much preoccupied with discrediting at the time, the issue praises the Incorruptible for having "lifted the veil" (*Vieux Cordelier* 43)—Terrorist transparency featuring heavily in this expression—and revealed the counterrevolutionary underpinnings of the Hébertists' festival. These anti-Robespierrist troublemakers, the journal alleges, "think they are furthering the cause of reason, when in fact they are furthering the cause of counterrevolution" (*Vieux Cordelier* 48), a claim that echoes Robespierre's parallel arguments in the Committees and the Convention. Desmoulins even offers up the same quote from Voltaire ("If God didn't exist, one would have to invent him" [*Vieux Cordelier* 44]) that Robespierre had used in a report before the Jacobin Society less than three weeks earlier to decry the atheistic nature of his rivals' secular religion.[26] Finally, as in the first issue, when he blamed France's lack of a free press on Pitt's machinations, Desmoulins resorts to the Montagnard rhetoric of conspiracy to condemn the Hébertists' Cult of Reason. This time, the king of Prussia, with whom France was also at war, emerges as the foreigner behind the insidious plot (*Vieux Cordelier* 47); the orthodox Robespierrist content (a condemnation of the Hébertists) assumes an equally unexceptional Terrorist form. By way of a justification for such overtly partisan remarks, which quite clearly undermine his own earlier pretensions to uncompromising honesty and scholarly truthfulness, the author announces: "For me to fall silent would be for me to desert [déserter]" (*Vieux Cordelier* 41). To have stated his position more precisely, Desmoulins ought to have used *desert* as a transitive verb and the Incorruptible or the Robespierrist cause as its object. The very fact, however, that Desmoulins elides Robespierre as a transitive reference is revealing, for it recalls the Terrorist leader's own self-presentation as a man who exists, like the Rousseauist legislator, beyond language.[27] In other words, Robespierre's textually designated invisibility in this issue, which he edited so heavily, paradoxically attests to his influence on its formulations.

Although the second issue thus seems to represent a move away from risky anti-Terrorist propositions and toward the imperatives of partisan friendship, shortly after its publication everything changed between Desmoulins and his closest friend. The era's denunciatory climate being what it was, the notoriety that the journal had begun to attract—its Incorruptible imprimatur notwithstanding—reminded the leaders of the Jacobin Society, the Cordeliers Club's equally influential counterpart, that it was time to investigate the purity of the journalist's principles. Having embraced Robespierre's "absolute mania for purification" since the passage of the Law of Suspects three months earlier,[28] the Jacobins were primarily interested in determining the nature of Desmoulins's attitude toward one Théobald Dillon, a general in the republican army who had been accused of treason by his own troops and murdered in the Vendée. Desmoulins had publicly defended Dillon at the time of his death, deploring the rude justice to which the general had been subjected, but to the Jacobins, closely aligned with Robespierre and Saint-Just in such matters, anyone who demonstrated leniency toward a counterrevolutionary was blatantly undermining the Revolution itself. Although Desmoulins convincingly reminded the society in his verbal testimony that he had spoken "neither good nor ill about Dillon" for several months,[29] its members pushed this extremely vocal member of their club to agree not to commit any more such grave errors of judgment. Provisionally quelling the Jacobins' doubts on his account, the journalist delivered an eloquent mea culpa that turned, characteristically, on the question of human fallibility, but he left the society in a fit of mortified pique. "I, Camille Desmoulins," asked to prove his fidelity to the republic and the Revolution? "I, Camille Desmoulins," called to the carpet for counterrevolutionary leanings? The third issue of *Le Vieux Cordelier,* published a matter of days after his trial at the Jacobins, carried the full weight of his indignation and hit its mark. For the inflammatory observations this publication made about the repressiveness of militant revolutionary politics, Robespierre would never be able to forgive him.

Transparent Obstacles: A Hazardous Political Parable

The controversial centerpiece of the third *Vieux Cordelier* springs from the objective announced by Desmoulins in the first issue, that of bolstering his current observations with the "lessons of history" and specifically of Tacitus. The third issue, he states in its opening lines, comprises a translation and exegesis of the Roman historian's reflections "on the reign of the Caesars and on the river of blood that flowed continually" (*Vieux Cordelier* 50) under that regime. Desmoulins further prefaces his Roman parable with the assertion that it will make contemporary readers grateful to be living in a republic rather than under a monarchy:

> In the fight to the death that the republic and the monarchy are waging in our midst, and given that one of the two will necessarily win a bloody victory over the other, who can lament the triumph of republicanism, after reading the description that history has given us of the triumph of monarchy; after casting a glance at the crude and schematic copy of Tacitus's descriptions, which I am going to present to the honorable circle of my subscribers? (*Vieux Cordelier* 50)

By the author's own account, lest there be any doubt about it, "the triumph of republicanism" remains his most cherished goal. If he includes in his retelling of Tacitus certain obvious, and critical, references to contemporary politics, these allusions must be taken not as antirepublican heresy but, on the contrary, as antiroyalist wisdom. His choice of scholarly reference matter—a favorite among French republicans for his outspoken disparagement of royal rule—seems only to cement these assertions of patriotism.[30]

Even the choice of a beloved classical author could not, however, guarantee that Desmoulins's musings on Tacitus would be taken as allegedly intended. This was a time when everyone was drawing on the rhetoric of ancient Rome—"alternately the Roman republic and the Roman empire," as Marx later sniffed[31]—to further his or her own political agenda. Remarking on this tendency during Louis XVI's trial, Desmoulins himself teasingly deflated the self-important *conventionnels* and goaded those arguing in a royalist direction with the remark: "All of us with different opinions, disputing among ourselves the right to the surname Brutus, here we are, seven hundred and forty Brutuses debating as to whether a tyrant is inviolable! The Brutus from Nancy, . . . the Brutus from Perpignan . . . ," and so on.[32] For Desmoulins, ever sensitive to the multiplicity of possible meanings associated with a single word, the point was that invoking Brutus was not necessarily tantamount to possessing his exemplary virtue. Likewise, when one year later Desmoulins starts talking about Tacitus, it is clear that the esteemed proper name does not necessarily correspond to an orthodox political objective. As both the substance and the language of Desmoulins's allusions to the historian indicate, they are motivated by an aversion not so much to monarchy—be it Roman or French, ancient or modern—as to the Terror itself.[33] The die is cast as soon as he relates the following "citation" from Tacitus: "*Once upon a time in Rome, there was a law that defined crimes against the state and crimes of 'lèse-majesté.'... Augustus was the first to apply this law, in which he included writings that he called counterrevolutionary*" (*Vieux Cordelier* 50–51; Desmoulins's emphasis). With the term *conterrevolutionary,* the author irrevocably tips his hand to his already suspicious Robespierrist readers; for this label clearly belongs to the Terror alone. Desmoulins implies as much in the footnote that he appends to this passage, in which he urges his readers not to "poison my sentences, by claiming that my translation of an author from fifteen hundred years ago is a counterrevolutionary crime" (*Vieux Cordelier* 51n). His own insistence that the entire passage from Tacitus "is, from beginning to end, simply a literal translation of the historian" (*Vieux Cordelier* 51n) does nothing to remove the stinging contemporary resonance from the loaded adjective in question.[34] His having already, and so recently, gone on record as an avid defender of a free press only further underscores the topical nature of Augustus's suppression of "writings called counterrevolutionary."

Desmoulins's remarks on this fragment from Tacitus encourage additional anti-Terrorist readings of his allegedly antiroyalist text. "Under his successors," he writes of Tacitus's Augustus, "the applications [of this law of *lèse-majesté*] no longer had any limits: as soon as speech and ideas became crimes against the state, with that as a starting point, one didn't have to go very far to condemn simple facial expressions—sadness, compassion, sighing, even silence itself—as crimes" (*Vieux Cordelier* 51). In informing his readers about the infinitely elastic definition of politically unacceptable expressions under Augustus, Desmoulins is alluding to nothing less than the Law of Suspects itself. The language of that decree, worth importing here from chapter 2, reads as follows:

> Are *suspect,* and must be arrested as such: those who, in popular assemblies, interrupt the energy of the people with artificial discourses, turbulent shouts, whispers; those more prudent ones who talk mysteriously about the misfortunes of the republic; ... those who do not attend their section meetings, and who try to excuse their absence by saying that they do not know how to speak.[35]

As we have already determined, the wording of this law makes it virtually impossible not to speak in a manner that could be construed as suspect—and Desmoulins's invocation of a whole range of potentially illegal statements and emotions under Augustus casts a glaring light on this parallel between Roman past and Parisian present. Furthermore, Desmoulins's allusion to "silence itself" as a potential crime recalls Robespierre's condemnation of his opponents' "criminal silence" in the Terror's widespread denunciation game. In the last issues of *Le Vieux Cordelier*, Desmoulins will fully exploit the possibilities of silence as a discourse of political opposition. For the time being, though, he contents himself simply to remark upon its construction as criminal under a regime that, while purporting to reward linguistic totality, places severe restrictions on a variety of "expressions," ranging from compassion—that "pathological" personal sentiment so regularly reviled by the Montagnards— to "even silence itself."

Desmoulins further highlights the contemporary resonances of the reign of the Caesars by continuing to couch his summaries of Tacitus in the vocabulary of the Terror. He does so by rehearsing a litany of "crime[s] of counterrevolution" committed under Augustus and his imperial successors, beginning as follows:

> Soon it was a crime of *lèse-majesté* or counterrevolution in the city of Nursia, to have erected a monument to its inhabitants who were killed in the siege of Modena, fighting under Augustus himself, because at the time Augustus was fighting with Brutus, and Nursia met with the same fate as Perusia [where . . . all the leading citizens had their throats slit, after which the rest of the inhabitants were slain by sword]. . . . Crime of counterrevolution by the journalist Cremutius Cordus, for calling Brutus and Cassius the last of the Romans. Crime of counterrevolution by one of Cassius's descendants, for having a portrait of his ancestor in his home. (*Vieux Cordelier* 51)

For Desmoulins, Tacitus proves a veritable font of anecdotes relevant to political life in contemporary France—where the "crime of counterrevolution" indeed plays the same role as the "crime of *lèse-majesté*" of yore. The mention of Augustus's brutal massacre of the people of Nursia, for instance, is a transparent reference to the republican army's obliteration of the population of Lyon (renamed Commune-Affranchie [Liberated-Commune] after its "recapture") following a royalist uprising there. On a more personal note, Desmoulins describes the plight of the "journalist" Cremutius Cordus in language that seems pointedly to refer to his own interrogation by the Jacobin Society on the subject of General Dillon. After Desmoulins managed to justify the error of his ways as far as the general was concerned, one of his antagonists reminded the society that the journalist had a history of being overly lenient toward numerous enemies of the republic, not just Dillon. More precisely, earlier in 1793, when the Montagnards expelled the Girondins from the National Convention and had them all guillotined, Desmoulins had decried this course of action as a travesty of revolutionary justice. He declared that the Girondins had died "like republicans, like Brutus,"[36] and the Jacobin Society subsequently used this remark against him, holding it up alongside the Dillon association as evidence of Desmoulins's "suspect" proclivities. In this light, by alluding to the unfairly persecuted writer who had dared to deem republican martyrs "Brutus and Cassius the last of the Romans," Desmoulins makes his point and gets his revenge. He then expresses sympathetic ire on behalf of the manifold victims of the Law of Suspects, who were indeed being carted before the Revolutionary Tribunal and off to the guillotine for such minor infractions as retaining mementos of their aristocratic relatives.

As damning as these few references are, Desmoulins has still not exhausted the vast array of Roman "crime[s] of counterrevolution" that beg comparison with contemporary infractions. He continues to list these crimes *ad absurdum*, each one a more ludicrous cause for punishment than the last, but most of them bearing an unmistakable resemblance to those that the Montagnards are so ruthlessly persecuting:

Crime of counterrevolution by Mamercus Scaurus, for writing a tragedy in which some verses could be interpreted as having a double meaning. Crime of counterrevolution by Torquatus Silanus, for spending his money. Crime of counterrevolution by Petreius, for having had a dream about Claudius. Crime of counterrevolution by Appius Silanus, because Claudius's wife had a dream about *him*. Crime of counterrevolution by Pomponius, because a friend of Sejan had gone seeking asylum in one of his country houses. Crime of counterrevolution to go about without having emptied one's pockets, and to have left in one's vest a coin with a royal face on it, showing a lack of respect for tyrants' sacred faces. Crime of counterrevolution to complain about the difficult times, because to do so was to challenge the government, to put the government on trial [faire le procès du gouvernement]. (*Vieux Cordelier* 51–52)

This passage bears a considerable amount of commentary, for it attacks the Terror on virtually all sides. In the last line, for instance, when Desmoulins speaks of the citizen accused of trying to "put the government on trial," it is hard not to read this phrase as an echo of Robespierre's noted demand that words such as *criminal* and *virtuous* be given one fixed interpretation, in theory and in practice, so as not to "place the Revolution itself on trial or in doubt [en litige]" (Mazauric 215). Furthermore, in the first of the offenses outlined here, Desmoulins pointedly alludes, as in the case of the persecuted journalist, to the limitations under which he himself is compelled to write. Recalling the footnote in which he urges people not to "poison his sentences" and assign a suspect intention to his words, the journalist anticipates that certain readers (notably the Committees' and the clubs' more rabid affiliates) will take exception to his "literal translation" of Tacitus. He knows that by using Roman history as an allegorical vehicle for anti-Terrorist polemics, he is laying himself open to the accusation of a crime of counterrevolution—especially given the Montagnards' oft-proclaimed belief in discursive transparency and their antipathy toward linguistic opacity and artifice. He attempts once again to use the age of Augustus both offensively and defensively, to point out the injustice of an era where a man could, as he himself soon would, be indicted for writing lines that "could be interpreted as having a double meaning."

Desmoulins then shifts the focus from his most cherished topic, the freedom of expression, to a more general range of problems occasioned by the Terror. Not only does current governmental policy prevent citizens from using words or phrases with more than one meaning; it also prohibits them from making the most personal decisions—about what they spend, with whom they fraternize, what they dream. This enumeration of basic privileges no longer deemed innocent anticipates Hegel's and Blanchot's critique of the Terror as a denial of individuality taken to ludicrous extremes. Moreover, at least one commentator sees in the reference to Torquatus Silanus, whose crime was spending his money, a reference to the smear campaign that the Montagnards were busy conducting against Danton, whose notorious financial (and sexual) profligacy did not sit at all well with the abstemious Incorruptible.[37] While this interpretation is certainly convincing, I believe we can also construe the mention of Torquatus Silanus as an allusion to the journalist's broader condemnation of a culture that privileges, in Robespierre's parlance, "a vigorous body, tormented by an overabundance of sap" (Mazauric 290). By recalling this sexually charged phraseology, Desmoulins confirms the view that the "virtue" of the Terror consists in the severe limitation not only of private sentiment (as expressed in friendship and dreams) but also of all forms of "natural" human release, including sexuality and economic exchange.[38] With their motto, "fraternity or death," the Montagnards did not allow for nearly such a wide range of options: all personal resources must be channeled into the sublimated and impersonal condition of patriotic brotherhood or the deathly cessation of all expenditure.[39] From the people hosted in citizens' houses to the people harbored in their dreams, no other relations are tolerated in the radically *public* space of the republic.

If basic human expression is ultimately a crime of counterrevolution, then the category of potential offenses is virtually infinite. "Everything," Desmoulins avers of Augustus's reign, "gave umbrage to the tyrant" (*Vieux Cordelier* 52); then, inserting the loaded word *suspect* into his text, he launches into a new catalog of actions construed as political affronts in imperial Rome:

> Were you rich; there was an imminent danger that the people could be corrupted by your generosity. *Auri vim atque opes Plauti principi infensas.* Suspect.
>
> Were you poor; what's this? Invincible emperor, this man needs to be watched closely. No one is as enterprising as a person who has nothing. *Syllam inopem, undè praecipuam audaciam.* Suspect....
>
> Finally, had one earned a good reputation during wartime; one was all the more dangerous for this talent.... The best thing to do was to get rid of him: at very least, milord, you cannot avoid dismissing him promptly from the army. *Multa militari famà metum fecerat.* Suspect.
> (*Vieux Cordelier* 52–53)

This litany of injustices, which I have abbreviated in the interest of space and time, simply represents a variation on the theme of ridiculously all-consuming "criminality" that Desmoulins stresses throughout the third issue. This particular passage, however, is also noteworthy for two other key reasons. First, the example of the fallen hero, the general who is perhaps unfairly condemned as a traitor, appears to allude to the disgraced hero Dillon.[40] In pairing a current event with a highly contemporary word, Desmoulins thus invites his readers yet again to confront the similarity between Augustan and Montagnard despotism; and above all he taunts his hard-line critics by indirectly rehabilitating the man with whom they forced him to disavow all ties. The second important aspect of this passage resides in the journalist's provision of the Latin text here, as in the footnote asserting that his is a "literal translation" of Tacitus, only to demonstrate its nonliteral nature. More precisely: Like the word *counterrevolutionary,* the word *suspect* is conspicuously absent from Tacitus's original, further betraying the pointed thrust of the commentary. In the Latin phrases cited by Desmoulins, the closest analogue to *suspect* is the term *infensas:* "dangerous" or "hostile." Even in this case, however, the political danger in question ("dangerous to the prince": *principi infensas)* is imputed to the citizen's wealth and influence *(auri vim atque opes Plauti)* alone.[41] By contrast, the French Terror always attributes the threatening or suspect quality to a person—witness Robespierre's aforementioned qualification of Desmoulins as a "dangerous writer." Under the Montagnards, it is the writer and not his writing, the rich man and not his riches, that is slated for destruction, although Robespierre, we shall soon see, makes a special exception to this rule for *Le Vieux Cordelier.*

In fact, despite his deep-seated frustration with the Jacobins and the Terror, Desmoulins still goes to some pains in the third issue to express his personal faith in the Incorruptible. Before concluding his list of those whose republican virtue was unfairly besmirched under Augustus, he includes a reference to Robespierre himself: "Should he be virtuous and austere in his morals; well then! He was a new Brutus, who was trying, by means of his pallor and his Jacobin wig, to criticize a happy and well-coiffed court. *Gliscere aemulos Brutorum vultús rigidi et tristis quo tibi lasciviam exprobrent.* Suspect" *(Vieux Cordelier* 52–53). With these lines, Desmoulins lashes out at the Hébertists, who had responded to Robespierre's recently expressed disapproval of their "debauched" Cult of Reason by disparaging his own ascetic morals as hypocritical and pompous airs. "Pallor" and "austerity" were widely recognized hallmarks of Robespierre's demeanor;[42] by substituting these qualities for the "rigid and sad" *(rigidi et tristis)* ones designated in the Latin text, Desmoulins draws an obvious parallel between Tacitus's maligned figure and his own ill-used friend. What is more, the journalist coifs the Roman historian's protagonist in a late-eighteenth-century "Jacobin wig" like the one unfailingly sported by Robespierre, a fashion statement that never ceased to annoy the militant Hébertists and their *sans-culotte* constituency, who had long since abandoned the fashions of the Old Regime.[43] Lest any doubt remain as to the identity of this "new Brutus," the journalist shows his hand altogether by lamenting the fact that for some corrupt politicians—Hébert's bullying crew—"the greatest crime [is] to be Incorruptible" (*Vieux Cordelier* 52). Whether Desmoulins's rush to defend Robespierre against the Hébertists is motivated by an instinct of political self-preservation or by some vestiges of friendship and good faith, it is hard to determine on the basis of the text. In either case, the favorable allusion to Robespierre does not, either in our current reading of *Le Vieux Cordelier* or in the reception with which it met in 1793, alter the fundamentally anti-Terrorist challenge that the journal delivers, in Carlyle's words, "prick[ing] into the Law of Suspects itself and making it odious!"[44]

Nevertheless, in the remainder of the third issue, Desmoulins resumes the strange balancing act between anti-Terrorist gadfly and Montagnard supporter that characterizes the first two issues of *Le Vieux Cordelier*. After his barely disguised attack on the Law of Suspects, Desmoulins returns to a more disingenuously capitulatory mode. To those, for example, who have discerned parallels between Tacitus's Rome and Desmoulins's Paris, the journalist offers the following words of pseudoconsolation: "Under the emperors, all those suspects did not simply get off, as they do in our day, with being sent to [prison at] the Madelonnettes, Irlandais, or Sainte-Pélagie. The prince sent them an order that they should call for their doctor or apothecary, and choose, within twenty-four hours, the type of death that suited them best" (*Vieux Cordelier* 53). With these lines, Desmoulins reverses the strategy he uses in the Tacitus passages, but obtains a similar, guardedly subversive result. In his litanies of "suspect" and "counterrevolutionary" characters from Roman history, he purports to provide a mere transcription of historical fact—a purely apolitical, or at least antiroyalist, enterprise—while nevertheless allowing the implicit parallels between Augustan past and Robespierrist present to surface in his text. Inversely, Desmoulins appears to make a direct, patriotic comparison between modern French "suspects" and their Roman counterparts ("all *those* suspects did not . . . , as . . . in our day . . ."), but the information he uses to support the relative good fortune of the French is, given the undeniable fact of the guillotine, patently false. "Camille well knows," writes biographer Jacques Janssens, "that in 1793,

suspects do not always 'get off simply' with a brief sojourn in the Madelonnettes, or some other prison, and this countertruth, coming from his
pen, is a disguised barb."[45] Thus, even when Desmoulins appears to
offer explicit praise of the current regime, his meaning cannot readily
be taken at face value. Here as in the rest of the third issue, he cloaks his
message in subtlety and sarcasm, equivocation and fiction.

Similar complexities underlie what seems to be the unequivocal ca-
pitulation to orthodox Montagnard conspiracy theory that Desmoulins
makes in the third issue's concluding pages. Echoing his own reasoning
from the first issue, his argument here is as follows: if "Terror, the sole
instrument of despots" (*Vieux Cordelier* 55) has been allowed to run
amok in France, "to make our liberty look like tyranny" (*Vieux Cordelier* 56), then it is not the French republicans but the English royalist
conspirators, sent and led by Pitt, who are to blame. The British prime
minister, whom Desmoulins piously deems a sworn and "clever enemy"
of French republican freedom, has "understood that the only way to
defame and destroy it [liberty in France] was to assume himself its costume and its language, . . . secretly instructing all his agents, all aristocrats, to don the red bonnet of liberty, to trade their narrow breeches
for trousers, and to make themselves into 'patriots'" (*Vieux Cordelier*
56). Thus attired, Pitt and his agents have managed to infiltrate the up-
per echelons of the French government and so to request, "in a certain
petition, *that nine hundred thousand heads be made to fall;* [and] in a
certain request, *that half of the French people be thrown into the Bastille,
as suspects*" (*Vieux Cordelier* 56; Desmoulins's emphasis). In this scenario, the journalist again posits the Terror's manifold horrors as origi-
nating in Pitt's plot to compromise and destroy revolutionary liberty.
That these acts of so-called justice are patently unjust, Desmoulins only
allows himself to declare once he has established that they were perpetrated by the royalist English, not the republican French. No sooner
does he risk calling Terror "the sole instrument of despots" than he takes
umbrage in a reference to Pitt, the Robespierrists' favorite scapegoat, as
the despot in question. Moreover, even beyond this qualified condemnation of Terror, Desmoulins manages to lace his pro-Montagnard rhetoric with subversive intent, for instance, in his explanation of how the
British minister actually managed to achieve his pernicious ends. When
the journalist asserts that Pitt aimed to bring down the republican
order by putting on "its costume and its language," on the one hand he

betrays typical Robespierrist anxiety about the fluidity of categories such as virtue and vice, patriotism and treason. On the other hand, Desmoulins avails himself of this very fluidity to realize the Terrrorists' own worst fears about poetic and political malleability; for in accusing Pitt of injustices perpetrated by the Convention, the Committees, and the Parisian clubs, he cloaks his critique of these institutions' intolerance in the language that they themselves habitually employ. We might say that in warning his readership against the British prime minister, "that clever enemy," Desmoulins is at the same time cautioning them against his own cleverness as well, particularly in the realm of seditious doublespeak.

Needless to say, this approach represents a flagrant departure from the discursive transparency favored by Robespierre and Saint-Just. Given this discrepancy, the riskiness of the issue's political propositions was immediately obvious to the Parisian public—such that, according to historian Louis Blanc, the publication of the third issue on December 15, 1793, "triggered an immense scandal" in the nation's capital.[46] Robespierre himself, in no way placated by the studied allusions to his own irreproachable virtue, was deeply troubled by his friend's rhetorical sleights of hand and sly anti-Terrorist observations. He joined Desmoulins's Jacobin detractors in the conclusion that the journalist had to be censured once again and more severely than in the Dillon affair. Robespierre was temporarily distracted from this issue, however, by the arrival of a group of women—wives and mothers of imprisoned suspects—on the floor of the National Convention, seeking clemency for their loved ones and demanding an audience with the Incorruptible himself.[47] He dealt severely with these women, offering them nothing more than a new "Committee of Justice" that would examine the suspects' cases and provide evidence in support of their detention. This decision, handed down on December 20, so troubled Desmoulins that he delayed the publication of his fourth issue by one day in order to comment on it exclusively. This issue decried in harsh and relatively unequivocal terms Robespierre's latest display of republican "justice"—and sealed Desmoulins's fate as a man marked for death.

"Let Me Speak": Clemency and Its Consequences

From the very first lines of *Le Vieux Cordelier*'s fourth issue, published on December 21, 1793, Desmoulins makes it clear that he intends to pull no more punches on the subject of the Terror. Abandoning the relatively cagey tone that marked his introduction of veiled anti-Montagnard comments in the first three issues, he admits right away that his journal has caused no small amount of displeasure in some quarters. "Certain people," he writes,

> have expressed disapproval of my issue #3, in which, they say, it pleased me to establish comparisons that tend to show the Revolution and all patriots in a bad light: they should have said the *excesses* of the Revolution and all *professional* patriots. They think that my issue can be refuted, and everyone else justified, by these words alone: *We know perfectly well that our present state is not one of liberty, but patience, you will be free someday.* (*Vieux Cordelier* 61; Desmoulins's emphasis)

Gone from this opening is Desmoulins's tendency to sugarcoat his impolitic assertions and protect himself against charges of counterrevolutionary intention. Adopting the Robespierrists' own practice of forceful predication, he dogmatically replaces the privileged abstractions marshaled against him by his critics, "the Revolution" and "all patriots," with emphatic substantives that can only discredit them: "the *excesses* of the Revolution" and "*professional* patriots." Here for the first time, Desmoulins explicitly ascribes the uncontrolled violence of Tacitus's Rome to the political situation in modern-day France. Having thus abandoned the pretense of alluding to anyone but his own contemporaries, the journalist continues his direct attack by putting words in the mouths of the powers that be—words that effectively acknowledge the lack of freedom that characterizes the republic. "*We know perfectly well that our present state is not one of liberty, but patience, you will be free someday*": Desmoulins has already, in his first issue, alluded to logic of this variety, when seeming to endorse the Montagnards' belief that certain liberties, such as those of expression and the press, can justifiably be suspended during tumultuous times. In this case, however, the author is willing to brook no such argument. Instead of condoning postponement as a necessary revolutionary measure, he lashes out at those who have stood by and allowed true freedom to be compromised in the here-and-now:

> These people apparently think that liberty, like childhood, needs to go through stages of screaming and crying before it can reach maturity; on the contrary, it is in the nature of liberty that in order to enjoy it, a person has only to desire it. A nation is free from the moment it wants to be free (we recall this saying of Lafayette's); ... otherwise, those who get

themselves killed for the sake of the republic would be as stupid as those fanatics in the Vendée who get themselves killed for the delights of a paradise which they will never enjoy. (*Vieux Cordelier* 61)

This passage challenges Terrorist orthodoxy on several fronts. First, it flies in the face of the republic's current position with respect to Lafayette—like Dillon, a one-time revolutionary hero now reviled as an enemy of the state—by locating its definition of liberty in the sayings of the discredited general himself.[48] In more far-reaching terms, the passage also exposes the mystification that underlies the idea of liberty as a dream necessarily deferred. To suffer now in the belief that one will be rewarded hereafter, according to Desmoulins, is to be just as superstitious and self-deluded as "those fanatics in the Vendée who get themselves killed for the delights of a paradise which they will never enjoy." The Vendéens, still loyal to counterrevolutionary notions of God and king, had been engaged in bitter civil war with the republican army since March 1793, and Montagnard policy makers justified the merciless extermination of these men by classing them as ignorant and dangerous fanatics.[49] In this context, Desmoulins's suggestion of an underlying philosophical similarity between true revolutionary believers and anti-republican religious insurgents could hardly have failed to offend those in the former camp. In the logic of the journalist's analogy, the Vendéen rebels did not have a monopoly on fanaticism or stupidity: these qualities existed in spades among those who supported the Terror and its tyrannical suspension of civil liberties in the republic.[50]

The accusation of fanaticism is not, however, the only criticism that Desmoulins levels against the Montagnards in this contentious passage. Just as significantly, he challenges the notion—one that we have encountered in Rousseau, Saint-Just, and Robespierre—that the mediation of pain, attending the suppression of personal inclinations, is fundamental to the experience of liberty and the establishment of the general will. In direct contrast, Desmoulins disputes the notion that "liberty, like childhood, needs to go through stages of screaming and crying before it can reach maturity" and avers instead that freedom is not a function of pain but of desire: "a person has only to desire it." Although desire is in fact implicit in the Terrorist buzzword *will* (the French words *volonté* and *vouloir* deriving from the same root), the generality that is invariably imputed to that term works, in the Robespierrists' schema, to stamp out the traces of individuality that might otherwise disrupt public consensus. Desmoulins, on the contrary, presents desire as a constitutive feature of freedom and proposes it as a salutary alternative to the Montagnard ideology of painful sublimation.

It is in fact precisely as an antidote to the destructive, repressive policies of the current government that Desmoulins develops the idea that constitutes the crux of his fourth issue. As mentioned earlier, the impetus behind this particular issue was Robespierre's refusal to pardon and release the imprisoned suspects whose wives and mothers came to the National Convention seeking clemency. In keeping with Saint-Just's dictum—"justice is not clemency, it is severity" (Soboul 139)—the new Committee of Justice that the Incorruptible offered to create as a means of appeasing these women had as its mandate the review of the suspects' cases and the confirmation of their guilt. Thus, while treated with appropriate severity, the prisoners would at least be guaranteed this basic level of justice: such was the cold comfort extended by Robespierre to the suspects' loved ones. To this harsh, unfeeling proposal Desmoulins offers a truly singular alternative: a "*Committee of Clemency* . . . the establishment [of which] I hold to be a great idea, one worthy of the French people" (*Vieux Cordelier* 66; Desmoulins's emphasis). To introduce this committee, the journalist boldly avows, in direct opposition to Terrorist dogma, that "clemency, used wisely, is the most revolutionary and the most effective strategy there is, whereas the Terror is nothing but the *Mentor of one day*, as Cicero so aptly says: *Timor non diuturnus magister officii*" (*Vieux Cordelier* 65; Desmoulins's emphasis). Clemency is a viable and desirable political strategy, because, unlike Terror, it is not predicated on fear *(timor)*. According to Desmoulins's Cicero, the bloody rhetoric and realities of the Law of Suspects cannot be sustained; the systematic intimidation of the populace is no replacement for an abiding *(diuturnus)* sense of justice and duty *(officii)*. Clemency, by contrast, is "revolutionary and effective" precisely because it is livable and sustainable: "love is stronger and more lasting than hatred" (*Vieux Cordelier* 67). In addition to their promotion of the political stability and durability so often invoked by Rousseau and the Robespierrists, notions of love and mercy have, in Desmoulins's view, the supreme virtue of being humane and of being human. True freedom, he concludes, "cannot exist when there is neither humanity nor philanthropy; [all that can exist under such circumstances is] an arid and desiccated heart. Oh, my dear Robespierre! It is to you that I am addressing these words..." (*Vieux Cordelier* 66).

In his capacity as the nation's chief Terrorist, however, the Incorruptible prided himself on his "arid and desiccated heart," as well as on an approach to justice that accommodated "neither humanity nor philanthropy." Given that Desmoulins was intimately acquainted with this fact,[51] his attempt to "address" Robespierre might thus be said to manifest itself less in this undisguised call for clemency, which was bound to displease the Montagnard leader, than in the underhanded intimations that follow in its wake. Whether to trick Robespierre into sharing his point of view or to protect himself from the political repercussions should that all-powerful reader fail to be converted to the ethos of clemency, Desmoulins promptly abandons the note of combative frankness on which the fourth issue ends, and returns to his earlier strategy of roundabout reasoning and cunning quasi assertion. Right after remarking on the efficacy of mercy, for instance, he reminds his readers that ancient Greece was saved by recourse to clemency and that ancient Rome fell by refusing such an alternative. "Nevertheless," he continues, "I am refraining from proposing such a measure to you. Down with the proposed amnesty! A blind and generalized policy of forgiveness would be counterrevolutionary indeed..." (*Vieux Cordelier* 66). Signaling an apparent change of heart with the conjunctive adverb *nevertheless,* the journalist mitigates the radical impact of his call for institutional clemency by resorting to praeteritio. "I am refraining from proposing such a measure," he writes, having already brought up just such a measure with his Committee of Clemency. In this way, even as he appears to concede to Terrorist politics, he violates the cardinal rule of Robespierrist poetics, linguistic transparency, by obscuring and undermining something that he had appeared to assert without equivocation—"proffering the word, only to plunge it back into its emptiness," as Mallarmé would say.[52] Desmoulins extends the pattern of praeteritio to his next sentence, a vigorous denunciation of amnesty that seems to represent a further concession to the Terrorist party line. For with the exclamation "Down with the proposed amnesty!" the journalist again purports to negate the very stance—clemency and forgiveness—that he has just suggested. In subsequent issues of *Le Vieux Cordelier,* Desmoulins will hone this tactic of simultaneous concealment and revelation to perfection. Here already, it plays a powerful role in his attack on Robespierre's regime: opaque insult added to anti-Terrorist injury.

The duplicitous and subversive force of this passage derives not only from its recourse to praeteritio, but also from Desmoulins's tongue-in-cheek appropriation of the term *counterrevolutionary*. As in his loose translation of Tacitus, where his use of the word *suspect* establishes damning parallels between the imperial Caesars and the Montagnards, Desmoulins draws here on mainstream Terrorist vocabulary in order to maintain the semblance of political propriety while delivering a message that is none too politically correct.[53] If we look closely at his condemnation of "a blind and generalized policy of forgiveness," for instance, we see that Desmoulins is decrying not clemency per se, but rather the practice of sweeping, general, and all-inclusive accusations upon which the Law of Suspects itself is based. In this context, even Desmoulins's apparent dismissal of "blind and generalized . . . forgiveness" as counterrevolutionary becomes a critical remark directed not so much at his own Committee of Clemency as at Robespierre's Committee of Justice. Needless to say, the corollary to this proposition is that some other type of clemency, one abandoning depersonalized abstractions to concern itself with the specifics of individual cases, would not run counter to the Revolution at all. At least, it would not run counter to Desmoulins's ideal of revolutionary justice.

After these artful maneuvers, the journalist adopts a different, if similarly indirect, strategy for making Robespierre understand his point of view. "Oh, my old school chum," he apostrophizes, "remember those philosophy and history lessons" (*Vieux Cordelier* 67). True to his promise in the first *Vieux Cordelier* to provide busy politicians with the insights of history, Desmoulins corroborates his own arguments, in this case aimed directly at Robespierre, with the assertions of canonical historical thinkers. Beginning with another classical author who enjoyed great popularity in contemporary republican circles,[54] Desmoulins writes that although "acts of clemency are the ladder of dishonesty, as Tertullian tells us, by which the members of the Committee of Public Safety have climbed to lofty heights, people never really get there except by means of a bloody staircase. . . . Rather, it is a *Committee of Justice* that has been proposed" (*Vieux Cordelier* 67; Desmoulins's emphasis). In this statement, Desmoulins establishes an opposition between clemency and justice and privileges the former as Tertullian's recommended antidote to bloody excesses. It is impossible, according to the historian, to ascend to the summit of political power "by means of a bloody staircase"; for this reason, Desmoulins infers, the violent "justice" promoted by Robespierrist institutions is bound to fail. The applicability of past to present is, in fact, made explicit in this case: as in his commentary on Tacitus, Desmoulins couches the "lessons" of Tertullian in thoroughly modern vocabulary, addressing the Roman's admonition against unforgiving politics to the unmistakably present-day Committee of Public Safety. The implication, of course, is that the existing committee cannot maintain its formidable position through force alone. If Tertullian and "the lessons of history" are to be believed, the bloody ascendancy of Robespierre's omnipotent government agency must yield to the path of forgiveness.

Not content to base the legitimacy of his Committee of Clemency solely on one classical authority, Desmoulins immediately turns to another to lend additional support to his case. After noting that Robespierre's proposal of a Committee of Justice bears little resemblance to the more merciful measures prescribed by Tertullian, he continues: "But why would clemency have become a crime in the republic? Are we claiming to be more free than the Athenians, the most democratic people who ever lived, and who erected an *altar to mercy*, before which the philosopher Demonax, over a thousand years later, still required tyrants to prostrate themselves?" (*Vieux Cordelier* 67; Desmoulins's emphasis). Marshaling "the Athenians, the most democratic people who ever lived" to his side as he proclaims the importance of clemency, the author presents the Greeks' "altar of mercy" as a validating antecedent, and analogue, to his own proposed forum for institutionalized mercy. Moreover, he challenges anyone to find fault with the means by which that legendarily democratic people succeeded in keeping tyranny at bay. "Are we claiming to be more free than the Athenians . . . ?" With this rhetorical question, the author deploys the familiar Montagnard strategy of corralling his readers into providing the answer he wishes to hear. He adopts this Terrorist form, however, to get across a thoroughly anti-Terrorist message, one that Desmoulins conveys by extending his plea directed to Robespierre alone ("oh, my old school chum, remember") to an abstract group of citizens identified by the first-person plural. With this shift in address, he indicates that the stakes of clemency are too high to concern Robespierre alone. Desmoulins wants all of his readers to join the Incorruptible and himself in seriously pondering the questions of freedom, democracy, and mercy, to which the Athenians attached such importance. While he knows that his compatriots cannot honestly profess to be "more free" than the citizens of classical Athens, he invites them to consider and aspire toward a more appealing conception of liberty.

As fruitful a springboard as it again proves for Desmoulins, ancient history is not, however, the only source where he locates evidence of clemency as a paramount political value. To conclude his meditations on the subject, he turns his attention to more recent authorities. Claiming, in reference to his Committee of Clemency, that he has "done a good job in demonstrating that healthy politics require such an institution" (*Vieux Cordelier* 67), he completes the demonstration with a reference to Machiavelli:

> And our great teacher, Machiavelli, looks upon this establishment [the Committee of Clemency] as the most important and of the utmost necessity for any government, since the sovereign should sooner abandon its obligations as a Committee of General Security than its obligations as a Rescue Committee. *It is to this body alone,* he counsels, *that the depository of national sovereignty should assign the distribution of pardons, and everything of that order.* (*Vieux Cordelier* 67; Desmoulins's emphasis)

With these words Desmoulins offers up a boldly distorted interpretation of Machiavellian political philosophy. As anyone familiar with *The Prince* knows full well, the Italian thinker views clemency as little more than a *pis-aller,* a last resort to fall back on when a leader is not controlling his people sufficiently through fear: "Every prince . . . ought to be both feared and loved, but as it is difficult for the two to go together, it is much safer to be feared than loved."[55] Far from postulating the dangers of excessive cruelty, Machiavelli furthermore warns against the "misuse [of] mercifulness" and an "excess of tenderness."[56] Nonetheless, Desmoulins uses this philosopher's evocation of institutionalized mercy to bolster his own belief that grace—a reprise of Rousseau—is the supreme political virtue and that the hypothetical Committee of Clemency is "the most important" of all governmental bodies. In addition, the superlative status he assigns to his own proposed committee stands as a direct challenge to Robespierre's competing Committee of Justice—and, more audaciously still, to the two committees that already do govern all of France. One of those, to which Desmoulins alluded earlier, is of course the Committee of Public Safety: the small executive branch of the government, composed of *conventionnels,* through which

the Robespierrists, in a sublime blurring of legislative and executive powers, turned their policies into fact. The other, the Committee of General
Security, served as the police force behind the Terror; its charge was to
carry out promptly the Committee of Public Safety's ineluctable decrees. Here, Desmoulins dares once again to call this frightening contemporary institution by its name, openly questioning its primacy and
subordinating it (in supposedly Machiavellian terms) to a "Rescue Committee" like the one he himself has devised. Clemency alone, he concludes with another daring superlative, constitutes "the best way of revolutionizing" (*Vieux Cordelier* 67).

Having, with this explicit depreciation of Montagnard politics, gone
well beyond the bounds of acceptable Terrorist expression, Desmoulins
brings his fourth issue rapidly to a close. He maintains the pose of an
objective historian and impartial scholar, thanking his readers for having afforded him "the honor of attending my lessons" and reminding
them that he has based his insights on "examples from history and from
authorities like [Tertullian] and Machiavelli" (*Vieux Cordelier* 67). These
remarks—like the claim that the second issue's translation of Tacitus is
merely literal—are quite obviously intended to deflect some of his
readers' anticipated outrage from his own subversive political program.
Desmoulins realizes, however, that he cannot entirely hide behind the
received wisdom of history and that no examples and authorities are
going to make his assertions palatable to the revolutionary hard line. He
therefore moves from this defensive posture back to the offensive one
with which he opened the fourth issue. In the closing paragraph, he
imagines and repudiates the disparagement with which his ideas on
forgiveness are likely to be met—and compares himself to a great revolutionary martyr in the bargain:

> If, I say, my Committee of Clemency strikes some of my colleagues as
> inappropriate and smacking of moderantism, to those who will reproach
> me for being "moderate" in my fourth issue, I can only respond, as time
> goes by, like Marat did in a very different day, when we were reproaching
> *him* for being too extreme in his newspaper: *You don't understand a thing
> I'm saying here, eh? My God! Let me speak: people will only be too ready to
> cut me off.* (*Vieux Cordelier* 67–68; Desmoulins's emphasis)

At this particular moment, *moderantism* was arguably the dirtiest word
in the republican political arena. In the speech he delivered on December 25, "On the Principles of Revolutionary Government," Robespierre

declared that the republic "must navigate a course between two rocky reefs, weakness and temerity, moderantism and excess" (Mazauric 289),[57] referring to Danton's and Desmoulins's Indulgents on the one hand and to the Hébertists on the other. Anticipating this criticism by four days, the author of *Le Vieux Cordelier* defuses its explosive potential by comparing it to its opposite, the adjective *extreme,* which the late militant revolutionary Jean-Paul Marat's detractors leveled against him "in a very different day." Desmoulins's point in comparing his alleged "moderantism" to Marat's "extremism" is that such labels, however different the political context in which they are used, invariably serve the same function, which is to devalue and demean the opinions of the persons to whom they are applied. Marat's response to this strategy, which Desmoulins now emulates in turn, was first to declare that in misconstruing his message, his readers showed no real comprehension of it ("*you don't understand a thing I'm saying here*"). Second, when faced with his readers' bad faith, Marat was simply to keep writing anyway. "Let me speak": as Desmoulins has emphasized from his first issue, devoted to the question of a free press, his main concern is that liberty of expression be restored to the republic. Even an insult like "moderantism" cannot detract him from that supreme purpose, even though he realizes, prophetically enough, that "people will be only too ready to cut [him] off." More pointedly still, the comparison between himself and Marat lends the author of *Le Vieux Cordelier* an unmistakably heroic aura. Although the late politician's inflammatory pronouncements had met with frequent censure while he was alive, his murder by Charlotte Corday had turned him into one of the republic's most beloved martyrs, eulogized in a vast, government-sponsored and David-orchestrated public funeral on July 16, 1793, as well as in subsequent festivals around Paris.[58] The invocation of Marat's example thus not only attests to the protean nature of political opinion (a hero one day becomes a suspect the next, and vice versa); it also invites Desmoulins's readers to see proof of his own revolutionary authority in the very opposition his journal is generating. The implication is that even if he is sorely misunderstood during his own lifetime, his countrymen will someday come to recognize the underlying value of his writings.

Despite this savvy bit of self-promotion on Desmoulins's part, the freedom to make his viewpoint known was in fact precisely what the author's influential foes were determined to deny him. Even more than its predecessor, his fourth issue caused an absolute sensation in Paris and immediately became the topic of fierce discussion and debate in the clubs, the Committees, and the Convention. Matters came to a head on January 7, 1794, when the Jacobin Society met to discuss the provocations of *Le Vieux Cordelier,* and Robespierre promptly took the floor. Addressing some members' demands that the author be jailed and executed for having dared to question their stringent conception of justice, the Incorruptible made a rare exception in favor of his friend, but one that would deal a tremendous blow to Desmoulins's campaign for a free press. "Camille's writings are condemnable, without a doubt," Robespierre began. "But we should be careful to distinguish the person from his works. . . . We must crack down on his journal, . . . and retain Desmoulins in our midst. I request that, as an example to the public, Desmoulins' issues be burned [here] in the Society."[59] The logic of the Terror, we will recall, tended to equate people's thoughts, words, and actions with their "person": any attribute or act was sufficient to reveal the individual's "suspect" essence. But in the case of his old school companion, Robespierre urged his fellow Jacobins to separate, for a change, the writings from the man and to preserve the latter while destroying the former. Despite this gesture of friendship, however, the call to burn the collected issues of his *Vieux Cordelier* struck Desmoulins with all the force of a personal affront. Present at the meeting where Robespierre made this recommendation, Desmoulins jumped out of his seat and replied in a rage: "That's very well said, Robespierre, but I will answer you like Rousseau: *Burning is not the same thing as responding* [Brûler n'est pas répondre]!"[60] To which a stunned Robespierre replied, angrily dismissing Desmoulins as a journalist only a nobleman could love: "The flattery of aristocrats prevents you from abandoning the path that error has laid out for you."[61]

This exchange brought about the definitive rupture between the two long-time friends. Robespierre, already irked by the fourth issue's critique of his Committee of Justice, was livid at Desmoulins for challenging his authority so heedlessly in front of the assembled Jacobins and for doing so in the name of his own hero, Rousseau, to boot. "Brûler n'est pas répondre" had after all been the Swiss philosopher's enraged response when censors banded together to burn the *Émile;*[62] so by quoting this exclamation against Robespierre, Desmoulins effectively classed the Montagnard leader as an antagonist of Rousseauist freedom itself. It did not help matters when the Incorruptible's charismatic Indulgent nemesis, Danton, rushed to the journalist's defense and castigated Robespierre: "Let us tremble to deliver [such] a blow to the freedom of the press!"[63] For his part, Desmoulins was incensed that his dearest friend and comrade-in-revolutionary-arms had refused to engage with him on the pressing topics of clemency and liberty, particularly given that he had addressed the fourth issue directly to Robespierre himself. When the Terrorist master sought to suppress the arguments of *Le Vieux Cordelier* instead of addressing them in earnest, the journalist had to abandon the idea that Robespierre would ever embrace or even consider his alternative proposals.

Ironically, Desmoulins had tried to recast his unorthodox arguments in more conventional Montagnard terms in the fifth issue of *Le Vieux Cordelier*, which he composed a few days before this meeting at the Jacobin Society and which he had unsuccessfully attempted to read aloud while there. Entitled "Camille Desmoulins' Great Justificative Discourse to the Jacobins" (*Vieux Cordelier* 69), this issue is clearly an effort at self-defense, written by the author's own admission "to defend myself" (*Vieux Cordelier* 70) against the accusations of counterrevolution that his Committee of Clemency had inspired from the outset. In the spirit of this enterprise, the fifth issue is characterized mainly by the sort of capitulatory Terrorist rhetoric that marked some of the journal's earlier issues. For instance, adopting the hackneyed discourse of paranoid incrimination, Desmoulins blames the Robespierrists' usual scapegoats, Hébert and Pitt, for all of the problems currently afflicting the polity inside and out. Judiciously avoiding any criticism of the Incorruptible and company, he instead issues a warning statement about "moderantism" and "extremism" that not only takes credit for Robespierre's recent pronouncement about navigating a "course between two rocky reefs" (Mazauric 289) but also espouses the leader's relatively uncompromising notion of republicanism: "The vessel of the republic is drifting, as I have said, between two rocky reefs, moderantism and extremism. I began my Journal with a profession of political faith that should have disarmed my slanderers: I said . . . that in the route the vessel was taking, it was still better to move closer to the reef of extremism than to the sand bar of moderantism" (*Vieux Cordelier* 69). This claim about his earlier expressions of support for extremism is a foolhardy one, because such expressions do not in fact appear in the earlier issues of *Le Vieux Cordelier*. Nonetheless, should any "slanderers" question his political credibility, Desmoulins plays the trump card of his privileged friendship with the ultimate arbiter of republican virtue: "Robespierre... has followed me practically since childhood, and... made this testimony about me which I oppose to all slander: *that he did not know a better republican than I ... and that it was impossible for me to be anything else.*" To continue this forceful assertion of his patriotic credentials, Desmoulins then describes himself as "incorruptible" (*Vieux Cordelier* 82) and, in a phrase worthy of the man who bears that nickname, identifies as his sole antagonists "the enemies of liberty, for I cannot have any others" (*Vieux Cordelier* 73). He insists that the public good alone has guided all his actions and that his critics have been wrong to read his Committee of Clemency as an outgrowth of unpatriotic sympathy for counterrevolutionary friends (viz., Dillon). "I have been more faithful to the nation than to friendship," he protests, "and my love for the republic has triumphed over my personal affections" (*Vieux Cordelier* 74). With statements like these, Desmoulins sounds more like a Robespierrist suspect-monger than a spokesman for anti-Terrorist mercy. Only one line retains a trace of his erstwhile philosophy of tolerance: "Since when is man infallible and exempt from error?" (*Vieux Cordelier* 75), although even in this case, he is not so much stressing the ethical importance of forgiveness as he is demonstrating that he has returned to, or indeed never strayed from, the Montagnard fold.

Despite this cultivation of unimpeachable republicanism, Desmoulins was prevented from reading his "Justificative Discourse" at the Jacobin Society; and after his break with Robespierre, he made no further effort to reenter the leader's or the Jacobins' good graces. The falling out seems to have filled him with a renewed sense of vigor and purpose, as Michelet observes in high-flown but fitting terms: "Camille felt himself coming back to life. After he, like Samson, had trembled, suffered, and languished, he felt that his hair was starting to grow back. Not content to have crushed the Philistines, I mean to say the Hébertists, under his heel, he was, driven by an unknown force, going to shake the columns of Robespierre's temple and reputation."[64] Desmoulins's fire gained additional fuel on January 12, when Robespierre had his fellow Indulgent Fabre d'Églantine arrested in the middle of the night for his collusion in the Company of the Indies fraud.[65] Although Fabre's hands were hardly clean in the affair, Desmoulins took issue with the Robespierrists' treat-

ment of his colleague as a common criminal and with the lack of gratitude that they showed for Fabre's history of substantial contributions to
the revolutionary project. Among other tasks, Fabre had participated on
the Convention's subcommittee for the creation of a new "republican era"
calendar, an enterprise geared at cementing the nation's radical break
with her royalist past. The sometime poet and playwright had created
the new month names that were now in effect throughout France, functioning as regular reminders to citizens that the days of France's imperial and monarchical history (figured in months named after Roman
deities) were long gone.[66] It is in foregrounding this lynchpin of revolutionary ideology and custom that Desmoulins indignantly breaks the
news of Fabre's arrest on January 15, at the start of his sixth issue:

> Considering that Fabre d'Églantine, who invented the new calendar, has
> just been imprisoned in the Luxembourg, before getting to see the
> fourth month of his revolutionary calendar; considering the instability
> of [political] opinion, and wanting to profit from the fact that I am still
> in possession of ink, pens, and paper, and both feet still on the
> floorboards, to set my reputation straight and to stop the lying of all my
> slanderers past, present, and future, I am going to publish my *profession
> of political faith,* and the articles of the religion by which I have lived and
> will die, be it from a bullet or a stiletto, be it in my sleep or from the
> *philosophers' death.* . . . (*Vieux Cordelier* 95; Desmoulins's emphasis)

In this opening, Desmoulins's anti-Terrorist stance is apparent in the
very fact that he broaches the subject of Fabre's demise. Despite his un-
savory exploits in the Company of the Indies, Fabre's arrest sent waves
of fear through the Parisian political community. With his record of
service to the Montagnards and his close affiliation with the indomitable
Danton, he had appeared untouchable even at a time when the Terror's
infinitely expanding net of suspicion promised to spare no one.[67] This is
precisely the grim suggestion that Desmoulins is aiming at when he invokes Fabre's history of public utility: the Revolution has reached a
point where even its most faithful servants may suddenly be destroyed
as traitors. Accordingly, the journalist presents Fabre's detainment as a
function of fickle political tides. As in his comparison in the fourth
issue—between the accusation of "moderantism," used to discredit his
writings, and the epithet "extreme," which had dogged Marat "in a very
different day"—the implication here is that the Terrorists will attack
anyone for any reason. Patriotic commitment itself is no safeguard

against such "instability." By emphasizing this quality of the Montagnards' persecutions, Desmoulins undermines the aura of immutable truthfulness in which they envelop their dicta. At the same time, he flouts their oft-expressed wish for a nonexistent fixity of meaning, for a language through which the Revolution as they conceive it could never be alternately construed or radically called into question (*mis en litige*). In emphasizing the vulnerability to interpretive shifts that is every current citizen's lot, however, Desmoulins is not simply taunting his and Fabre's enemies or raising consciousness among his other readers. In terms that hit much closer to home, he recognizes that even the possession of writing materials—"ink, pens, and paper"—cannot be taken for granted under such political conditions. The twin specter of censorship and the guillotine casts long shadows on this issue, and Desmoulins does not deceive his readers or himself about the immediacy of such threats.

While there was still time, then (and Desmoulins's days were indeed numbered at this point), the journalist launched into his political credo. In many ways, this statement reiterates themes and ideas that Desmoulins has explored in earlier issues of the journal: notably the irreproachability of his own republican record, his tolerance for error, and his belief in a free press. Initially, Desmoulins addresses the first of these topics. Referring sarcastically to Robespierre's comment about the aristocratic sympathies of *Le Vieux Cordelier,* he writes:

> It has been claimed that my favorite activity was to charm aristocrats by the fireside, during long winter evenings, and . . . that Pitt is the one who paid for me to start this journal in the first place. The best response that I can make is to publish the political credo of *Le Vieux Cordelier,* and I call upon every honest reader to judge whether Mr. Pitt and the aristocrats can accommodate my credo, and if I am one of them. I *still believe* today, just as I believed in July 1789, when I dared to publish in my *La France libre,* page 57: "that popular government and democracy are the only constitution suitable for France and for all those who are not unworthy to be called men." (*Vieux Cordelier* 95–96; Desmoulins's emphasis)

In this paragraph, Desmoulins makes powerful use of his own earlier writings. The expression of unequivocal support for popular and democratic government that he uttered in 1789 leaves little room for doubt about his soundly republican leanings. In so doing, he points up the hollowness of the denunciations linking him to Pitt, as well as the obvious and dangerous "instability of public opinion" that he has already established apropos of Fabre. Taking the high road away from character assassination, Desmoulins explicitly presents his credo as a *response* to Robespierre's and the other Jacobins' slurs against his virtue. Whereas the Incorruptible saw fit to burn *Le Vieux Cordelier* instead of replying to its contents, the author attempts to engage with his adversary in a battle of opinions. Unlike Robespierre, he thereby acknowledges and expresses some degree of tolerance for his interlocutor's point of view— despite its radical difference from his own. That is not to say that Desmoulins makes the least bit of pretense about agreeing with the Robespierrists' perception of him: his snide remark about charming the exiled aristocrats "by the fireside, during long winter evenings" makes clear his departure from the Jacobins' collective opinion. Crucially, though, Desmoulins *allows* such disagreement into his text. The meaning of *credo*, after all, is "I believe," as the journalist's use of that very verbal construction makes clear. By highlighting the "I" in this manner, he suggests that every individual has a right to his or her own beliefs—a notion that is starkly at odds with the anti-individualistic philosophy of the Terror. With his belief in mutual recognition and the right to self-expression, Camille's republican value system is now revealed to be worlds apart from Maximilien's.

This is the precise point that Desmoulins stresses when, instead of resting on his revolutionary laurels, he changes the subject to the need for broad-based tolerance in a republic. Ever the self-styled historian, he couches his lesson in terms of Roman history, but this time he makes no effort to disguise the parallel between contemporary France and ancient Rome: "It is possible to be in disagreement, as were Cicero and Brutus, about the best revolutionary measures and the most effective means of saving the republic, without Cicero concluding from this mere difference of opinions that Brutus was being paid off by Photinus, Ptolemy's prime minister" (*Vieux Cordelier* 96). In this scenario, Desmoulins quite obviously identifies with Brutus, that exemplary republican to whom he once compared not only the mass-executed Girondin deputies—but also, we recall from his angry riposte to the Hébertists' criticisms of his friend, Robespierre (*Vieux Cordelier* 52). Here, however, Desmoulins claims Brutus's unimpeachable virtue for himself and compares Robespierre unfavorably to Brutus's respectful opponent, Cicero. Where the Roman orator accepted the validity of Brutus's "difference of opinion," the Montagnard leader seeks to discredit his adversary's utterances by deeming them part of an aristocratic, anti-republican plot (with Photinus being an obvious stand-in for Prime Minister Pitt). The real Cicero, according to Desmoulins, allowed for genuine debate to occur on important political subjects, such as "the best revolutionary measures" and "the most effective means of saving the republic." Both of these expressions are in fact quotations from earlier issues of *Le Vieux Cordelier:* the former recalls Desmoulins's self-proclaimed desire, expressed in the fourth issue, to determine "the best way of revolutionizing" (*Vieux Cordelier* 67), and the latter echoes the promise he makes in the first issue, not to "say everything," but to "let out enough [truths] to save France and the republic, one and indivisible" (*Vieux Cordelier* 39). By indirectly quoting his own past political pronouncements in this discussion of Brutus, Desmoulins reinforces the parallels between himself and the exemplary citizen and calls into question the republican viability of Robespierre's dogmatic narrowness, incapable as it is of tolerating a "mere difference of opinions."

These implicit quotations from previous issues of *Le Vieux Cordelier* also serve another purpose—one with even more profound implications for Desmoulins's political credo. The journalist's veiled evocation of his earlier challenge to the Terrorist rhetoric of "saying everything" lays the groundwork for the complex pattern of self-censorship that occurs in the remainder of the sixth issue and that he will amplify in novel ways in his seventh and final issue. In order to understand this dynamic, we must first reexamine the full version of the quotation from the first issue that resurfaces in part in the sixth: "My hand is full of truths and I will be careful not to open it entirely; but I will let out enough [truths] to save France and the republic, one and indivisible." This passage, as we have already seen, constitutes a notable anti-Terrorist admission on Desmoulins's part; for it implies that the so-called discursive totality championed by the Montagnards is not necessarily the best way to "save France and the republic." In large part, of course, this observation is true because of the censorious mechanisms that the Terror has, contradicting its own pretensions to "saying everything," put in place. It is to this unacknowledged feature of Terrorist politics that Desmoulins draws attention in his sixth issue when he comments about selective disclosure shortly after alluding to his earlier comment on the subject. Having affirmed as a part of his credo that he "persists in believing that our liberty is the inviolability of the principles in the Declaration of the Rights of Man" (*Vieux Cordelier* 99), he adds:

> At the same time, I believe... that in a time of Revolution, sound politics required the Committee of Public Safety to cast a veil on the statue of liberty, in order to prevent us from spilling all at once the entire horn of plenty that the goddess holds in her hand, but rather to suspend the emission of some of her benefits, so that we will later be assured the enjoyment of all of them. (*Vieux Cordelier* 99–100)

This passage is one of the most politically risky and rhetorically audacious in the entire *Vieux Cordelier*. Desmoulins's principal challenge to the Montagnards assumes the form of a figure of speech: a veiled statue of liberty.[68] Reminiscent of a fragmentary essay written by Rousseau, which depicts a nightmarish dystopia whose subjects are all forced to prostrate themselves before a blindfolded, cruel, and bloodthirsty idol, this image represents the very opposite of the virtuous transparency promoted by the Robespierrists.[69] What the figure of the veil suggests is obviously that Terrorist "liberty" is not complete and unmediated, whatever the Jacobins and the Montagnards may say. The veiled statue therefore not only invites comparisons between Rousseau's imaginary Terrorist state; it also implies that the concealment of certain truths is fundamental to the disclosures permitted and practiced by the Committee of Public Safety. In Desmoulins's hands, the orthodox republican conception of freedom becomes a goddess selectively doling out information—and deferring a complete revelation of all political "benefits" ("the enjoyment of all of them") indefinitely into the future. It is this statement, which describes truth as a process of filtering and deferral, that recalls Desmoulins's promise to let his valuable insights "escape" a few at a time. Even more strikingly, it points up the common ground between the rhetoric of the Terror and Desmoulins's own journalistic modus operandi. If, in short, Robespierre's utterances are as mediated, differential, and incomplete as those of the widely execrated, much-censured, and censored Desmoulins, then we might ask, punning on Robespierre's famous question from the king's trial, "What is to become of the Terror?"

In this context, when the journalist deems the veiling of the statue of liberty the upshot of "sound politics," he can be taken to be not so much complimenting the Committee of Public Safety as designating the deep-seated hypocrisy of its methods and mind-set.[70] Two, furthermore, can play at this deceptive game, as Desmoulins proves when he makes an abrupt about-face on the now-infamous topic of clemency. Informing his readers that he has come under considerable fire from the government for proposing a Committee of Clemency, he goes through the motions of retracting all his scandalous ideas:

> In my fourth issue, even though the footnote and the open parenthesis show right away that it is a *Committee of Justice* that I meant, when I said a *Committee of Clemency,* since this new expression struck patriotic types as scandalous, since Jacobins, Cordeliers, and the whole Montagne have censured/censored it [l'ont censuré], . . . I would become guilty if I didn't hasten to suppress my Committee myself, and to say *mea culpa,* which I am doing here with perfect contrition. . . . (*Vieux Cordelier* 97; Desmoulins's emphasis)

Given the patent flimsiness of his supposed mea culpa, we might wonder how "perfect" Desmoulins's contrition really is here. His ex post facto "suppression" of the Committee of Clemency, for instance, was bound to strike his critics as too little, too late—and as somewhat beside the point, since the proposal had already been quite definitively shot down in the actual Committees and clubs. Perhaps more provocatively still, Desmoulins ventures to declare that a handful of metatextual and diacritical markings ("the footnote and the open parenthesis"), properly understood, should suffice to transform his anti-Terrorist Committee of Clemency into a Committee of Justice à la Robespierre. With this proposition, he essentially denies ever having favored clemency at all and pretends instead to see no difference between his own notion of justice and that of the Montagnard leader. In keeping with this message, what Desmoulins is doing here is of course blatantly emulating "Jacobins, Cordeliers, and the whole Montagne."[71] He demonstrates that he has chosen to exercise not a right to say everything but a right *not* to say everything, a right to suppress the facts where he sees fit. For all intents and purposes, Desmoulins has in this sense followed the lead of the Committee of Public Safety and thrown a veil on his Committee of Clemency. Sound politics indeed.

To provide one more dramatic instance of such self-suppressing discourse, Desmoulins again resorts to metaphorical language—itself a bald-faced application of the opacity and polyvalence that the Terror's chieftains tried to avoid. First Desmoulins half jokes that he must repudiate his Committee of Clemency, if only because "clemency would be out of season in the port of the Montagne." This line refers simultaneously to the political party led by Robespierre and to the port city of Toulon, which the republican army had, at the time Desmoulins drafted the sixth issue, just taken back from counterrevolutionary insurgents in one of the bloodiest civil clashes of the Terror (a clash, in fact, second only in brutality to the one that occurred in Lyon, deplored in the third issue of *Le Vieux Cordelier*). Continuing in this metaphorical vein, he apostrophizes Fréron, the general who led the "bloody repression against the rebels of Toulon,"[72] to point out the vast discrepancy between the call to mercy issued in his journal and the treatment of the rebels in the besieged port city: "Beware, Fréron, that I did not write my fourth issue in Toulon, but here, where I assure you that everyone is on board, and that there is a need not so much for the *Père Duchesne*'s spur, as for *Le Vieux Cordelier*'s bridle . . ." (*Vieux Cordelier* 97). Like so many statements in the sixth issue, this proclamation can be read in two ways. On the one hand, it suggests that if Desmoulins's fourth issue had been composed in Toulon, then Fréron's republican army would not have gotten away with the merciless atrocities they perpetrated there. On the other hand, the journalist appeases the general—and the committee members who dispatched him to the seaside—by insisting that he, Desmoulins, is not about to spur on the Parisian public to any kind of dissident uprising. Unlike the *Père Duchesne*, the incendiary Hébertist journal that the Robespierrist government also attempted to censor, *Le Vieux Cordelier* is, according to its author, a model of discursive restraint. Desmoulins's choice of equipment is the bridle, not the spur: he professes to abide by an ethos of controlled self-censorship rather than outright provocation.[73] Taking advantage of the enmity between Robespierre's faction and the one surrounding the publisher of the *Père Duchesne*, Desmoulins asserts his own republican virtue in the Manichaean method so dear to the Robespierrists: by identifying an opponent's lack of virtue.

Nonetheless, this opposition between bridle and spur can be read as much more than a self-promoting attestation of constrained speech or a politically astute dig at the Hébertists. In many ways, the equestrian conceit as a whole—the bridle in conjunction with the spur—describes beautifully the dialectic that underpins and structures *Le Vieux Cordelier* in its entirety. Desmoulins alternates deftly and sometimes dizzyingly between explicit anti-Terrorist diatribes (uttered after the proverbial "reins and bridle" have been dropped [*Vieux Cordelier* 38]) and superficially "bridled" pro-Robespierrist concessions. The sixth issue follows this pattern to the hilt. Beginning with an openly irate reference to the Fabre affair, it closes with an apparent repudiation of the Committee of Clemency and contains lots of double-edged rhetoric—partly provocative, partly conciliatory—in between. The effect of this back-and-forth was radical enough that Desmoulins's publisher, Desenne, hesitated to print the sixth issue when he first received it on January 15 and waited almost a month to release it. This issue was in fact the last to appear during the author's lifetime: its provocations, however veiled and restrained, provided the final impetus for Robespierre and Saint-Just to arrest Desmoulins at the end of March. At that time, however, the journalist was already hard at work on the seventh and final issue of *Le Vieux Cordelier,* drafted as a "continuation of my political credo" (*Vieux Cordelier* 105) and where the dialectic of the bridle and the spur can truly be said to reach its apogee.

Desmoulins's Dialogic Imagination

The history of *Le Vieux Cordelier*'s seventh issue has long been cloaked in mystery and surrounded by conjecture. Historians have ascertained that Desmoulins was working on it at the time of his arrest on March 30, 1794, and that he continued to expand upon it from his prison cell in the Palais du Luxembourg. One point on which scholars have failed to achieve certainty is the possibility that someone from Robespierre's camp managed to steal a few incriminating pages of the issue from Desmoulins's home before his arrest and that these pages, ranting mostly against the Committee of General Security and even more outrageous than the already shocking material of the sixth issue, served as the final nail in Desmoulins's coffin. Be that as it may, it is certainly true that in terms of both political and rhetorical audacity, the author of *Le Vieux Cordelier* outdoes even himself in his final issue. After Desmoulins was executed on April 5, Desenne faithfully attempted to cobble together a handful of drafts he had rescued from the journalist's quarters but, before he could publish them, was executed as a counterrevolutionary for his involvement with *Le Vieux Cordelier.* So fear-inspiring was the mythology that developed around the seventh issue that even after Robespierre and his allies fell in July 1794, it took forty years before anyone dared to make it public. To reiterate and refine the question with which we began this chapter: What made the seventh issue in particular so threatening to its author, its potential publishers, and, according to Robespierre, the Terrorist republic as a whole?

To confront this question is necessarily to consider at greater length the tension, evoked by Desmoulins, between the bridle and the spur as both figures relate to discursive expression. Entitled "Freedom of the Press: Pros and Cons," the seventh issue is of interest less for its restatement of the problem of free speech in itself than for its stylistic sophistication and subterfuge and, above all, for its remarkable dialogic form. Written as a debate between two revolutionary thinkers, the text represents an interplay of extreme positions on either end of the free-speech issue. While a debater named "Desmoulins" argues for political and linguistic prudence (the bridle), his interlocutor, labeled simply "the Old Cordelier," waxes eloquent about the vital importance of a free press (the spur). This model is suggestive for two important reasons. First, it again demonstrates an ethos of balanced and mutually respectful interchange that the Robespierrist camp, with its systematic denial of alterity, clearly cannot abide. Second, because the author never intervenes to privilege any one position, potential censors are prevented from ascertaining that politically offensive doxa have been asserted one way or another. The "real" Desmoulins thus manages to put forth even the riskiest notions by allowing his sparring alter egos to undermine them before they can solidify into definitive statements worthy of Robespierrist censure.[74] The two interlocutors in Desmoulins's seventh issue may represent the full range of revolutionary beliefs, but never do they—or does their author—claim to outline a unitary, unified set of republican "truths." The latter approach, of course, is the Terrorist claim to "say everything." As we shall see, the power of Desmoulins's warring narrative voices derives much more from speaking in part than from purporting to speak fully.

A prime example of the author's efficacious dialogism and understatement surfaces in the series of radical rhetorical questions with which the fictitious Old Cordelier attacks his pro-Terror opponent, Desmoulins. To the latter's claim that there are certain things "that are more useful to the nation when they are kept silent than when they are said" (*Vieux Cordelier* 114), the former responds with about six pages of incendiary invective against Robespierre and all those who would hypocritically seek to compromise republican liberties. The following is an abbreviated version of the diatribe:

It's Robespierre who is forgetting . . . that liberty . . . does not need to hide behind battlements to conquer cities; but rather, that as soon as one sees [liberty], one is taken by and runs ahead with her. But would you dare to make similar comparisons and, through these contradictions, throw back on Robespierre the ridicule that he has been pouring on you with open hands for some time now? . . . Would you dare to express yourself with the same frankness about the Committee of General Security? Would you dare to say that this very Committee that . . . has imprisoned thousands upon thousands of citizens as suspects, for not loving the republic enough, has Vadier for its president, . . . that same Vadier who, on July 16, [1791,] announced on the floor of the National Assembly: *I adore the monarchy and I hold republican government in utter contempt?* Would you dare to say that Vouland, the secretary of the Committee of General Security, was also a royalist . . . ? Would you dare to say that . . . Monsieur Héron, a former aristocrat, went into the prisons soliciting false testimonies and trying to buy witnesses, to help him send an excellent, white-haired patriot to the Revolutionary Tribunal? Would you dare to say . . . that this same Héron . . . has in his house a stack of blank arrest warrants and *lettres de cachet,* in which he has only to fill in the names, . . . today, when laws and democracy supposedly reign supreme? (*Vieux Cordelier* 120–21; Desmoulins's emphasis)

This passage deftly and simultaneously conceals and reveals its political incorrectness, not only by dint of its dialogic form, but also by its recourse to praeteritio—the device of which Desmoulins made limited use in his fourth issue, when he disingenuously professed that he "refrain[ed] from proposing" clemency as a political strategy. A similar dynamic of simultaneous concealing and revealing is at work here. Even as the journalist purports to downplay or censor certain scandalous opinions, his insistent refrain of "would you dare to say?" in fact introduces the very things that the interlocutor of the Old Cordelier could not, under pain of death, openly venture to assert.

This passage is also noteworthy for an image reminiscent of the veiled statue described in the sixth issue, where Desmoulins graphically depicted his own partly self-censoring discourse and at the same time called attention to one of the Terror's more censorious tactics. The image that performs this same function here is, of course, the "blank arrest warrants and *lettres de cachet,* in which [one] has only to fill in the names." On one level, the blank letter aptly figures the poetics of understatement and indirection that prevails in this passage, where the author's wily use of praeteritio basically allows the reader to "fill in the blanks" that have been ostensibly, and ostentatiously, left in the text.[75] On another level, the allusion to such a letter represents a none-too-sly gibe at the Terror's unselfconscious appropriation of one of the Old Regime's most reprehensible practices. The implication here is that the *lettre de cachet*, a document through which an individual's family could guarantee his or her imprisonment without involving any other legal proceedings, still played a role in French political life, even though the Revolution was fought to eliminate injustices of this very kind. In fact, despite its royalist associations, the *lettre de cachet* can be read as a metaphor for the collapse of public and private spheres effected by the Terror itself.[76] For, in harking back to a time when people's families could ship them off to prison for infractions not necessarily suitable for trial in public courts (an ill-advised liaison or comment), Desmoulins's attack on Héron emphasizes that even "today, when laws and democracy supposedly reign supreme," the government not only permits but rewards invasion into its citizens' personal lives. From Rousseau's proposed dissolution of the "I" into the collective sphere to the Law of Suspects's injunctions about incorrect public and private speaking habits to the related mania for denouncing one's fellows, Terrorist philosophy and praxis in this way mimic the corrupt legal machinery of the monarchy.

Characteristically, however, the journalist's evocation of the *lettre de cachet* does not serve solely as an unambiguous indictment of his enemies' actions. Taken as a figure for his own discursive strategies, the image of the unmarked letters harbored by Héron prefigures as well a tactic that Desmoulins employs later in the issue to condemn his detractors while appearing to refrain from doing so. More specifically, he achieves this end by using only the initials of his foes in his personalized attacks on their politics. The first of Desmoulins's nemeses to bear the brunt of this device is Bertrand Barère, a militant Jacobin and vindictive member of the Committee of Public Safety who had literally been engaged of purging linguistic difference from the French republic and whose Terrorist mentality the Old Cordelier disparages as follows:[77]

Yes, I would rather see people denouncing one another up and down, I almost said calumnying each other, even like the *Père Duchesne* does, but with the kind of energy that characterizes strong, republican souls, than to see, as we do today, all this bourgeois politeness, all these timid monarchical manipulations, all this circumspection, all these chameleons and cloak-and-dagger faces, in a word, all this B...ism[...]. Better the

language of democracy, with its indiscretions, than the cold poison
of fear, which paralyzes thought in the bottom of people's souls, and
prevents it from pouring forth at the tribunal, or in writing! (*Vieux
Cordelier* 112–13)

The outspoken Old Cordelier prefaces his invectives against Barère with
more praeteritio, using the statement "I almost said" to qualify his reference to certain extremists' daily denunciations of potential counterrevolutionaries as calumnies. But these outbursts, which Desmoulins
criticized in the sixth issue when he denigrated the "spur" of the *Père
Duchesne,* are the least of his concerns at the moment. Far worse, the
Old Cordelier observes, is the "cold poison of fear" with which the Committees of Public Safety and General Security have infected French society and which prevents people from saying, writing, or even thinking
anything that this powerful political body could deem offensive. The
Old Cordelier goes on to baptize this oppressive "B...ism," allowing
the infamous, household name of "Barère" to shine through even in the
ellipsis that follows his first initial. As if to remove any doubt as to this
individual's identity, the Old Cordelier concludes his long "would you
dare to say?" harangue with an explicit inscription of Barère's name—
but in the same sentence, he suppresses all but the initials of two other
Robespierrists whose role in the Terror he decries. Addressing "Desmoulins," he asks:

> But would you dare to say these truths to Barère? Would you dare to say
> that that H..., for example, that M..., (that A..., B..., C..., D...,
> E..., F..., G..., H...)
> ....
> ....
> .... (*Vieux Cordelier* 122)

Although the multiple lines of ellipses that follow the alphabetical series
destroy any possibility of conclusively determining a context, it seems
likely, on the basis of the rest of the seventh issue, that "H" and "M"
refer to Héron and Momoro, two bitter foes of Desmoulins's on precisely the subject of the freedom of the press. Héron, we remember, is
identified by name shortly prior to this harangue as the loathsome man
who keeps blank *lettres de cachet* at the ready. Momoro is mentioned by
name elsewhere in the seventh issue, receiving the journalist's ire for
working to get him expelled from the Cordeliers Club and for posturing
as "the Premiere Publisher of Freedom" but refusing to publish certain

unnamed revolutionary works (most likely Desmoulins's own).[78] Even without this referential specificity, however, the initials function to underscore the radically oppositional poetics that the seventh issue puts into play. In putting the names of "that H..." and "that M..." under erasure, Desmoulins designates the simultaneous presence and absence, in his text, of the men he is attempting to lambast. The initials serve as a titillating trace of a meaning that, thanks to the writer's ellipses, can never be definitively established. He radicalizes the gesture still further by following this allusion to two apparently specific enemies with a parenthetical listing of the first eight letters of the alphabet—the last one in the series, "H...," rejoining the initial with which he began his mini-tirade. In this way, Desmoulins explicitly reduces the target of his political diatribe—whose specificity is suggested by the demonstrative, "*that* H..."—to nothing more than an empty, arbitrary signifier, a purely neutral term in a grammatically determined series. Coming as it does at the end of the six-page denunciation by the Old Cordelier of virtually all the Terror's kingpins, this play on the arbitrariness of the sign, this sudden breakdown of political decipherability, is itself a profoundly political act. It constitutes yet another effort on the part of the beleaguered journalist to get a message across about the near impossibility of unfettered speech in a society where only certain utterances are permitted to "pour forth at the tribunal, and in writing." It comes as little surprise at this point that "Desmoulins," the more politically astute interlocutor of the Old Cordelier, should reply to this outburst with a self-protective praeteritio of his own: "Permit me to throw into the fire, without pity, these six long and caustic pages" (*Vieux Cordelier* 122). An obvious allusion to Robespierre's recommendation that all extant copies of *Le Vieux Cordelier* be burned, this response calls attention to the fundamentally destructive imperative of Terrorist discourse: destroy that to which one cannot respond. Or, as Robespierre and Saint-Just were soon to decide in the case of the maverick journalist, guillotine the person to whom one cannot respond. "A god who discusses things," Michelet says in reference to this very episode, "is lost." And so Desmoulins perished in order that the Robespierrists' highly constrictive discourse of unity and totality might live, at least for a few more months. As the journalist himself had written in the last line of the seventh issue, later adopted by François Mauriac in a play by the same name: "The gods are thirsty!" (*Vieux Cordelier* 134).

While obviously a regrettable betrayal of "genuine" liberty, equality, fraternity (whatever those might look like), Desmoulins's obliteration at the hands of the Robespierrists is also perfectly illustrative of the phenomenon that we have traced throughout this work. The totalizing discourse of Terrorist communities invariably has its limits, and Desmoulins paid with his life the price that irreducible individuality, pity, and linguistic play all pay, rhetorically and philosophically, in the writings of the Robespierrists and, albeit in a qualified manner, of Rousseau as well. Toward the end of the seventh issue, the circumspect speaker named Desmoulins advances a sad and disturbing theory: "I do not know whether human nature is capable of the perfection that the unlimited freedom of speech and of writing would presuppose. I suspect that in no country—republic or monarchy—have those who govern been able to endure such unlimited freedom" (*Vieux Cordelier* 129). In this cogent formulation, Desmoulins postulates that the problem of political correctness—speech that limits people's liberties in the name of freedom itself—is fundamentally a problem of power. Having lived under both a monarchy and a republic, he aptly observes that neither regime tends to be particularly receptive to an "unlimited freedom" poised to undermine its authority. After all, his own journalistic enterprise has given him ample opportunity to observe how Robespierre and Saint-Just, like their monarchist predecessors and their Hébertist nemeses, use restrictions on language to translate their ideological vision into reality. In his quest, however, for "neither virtue nor Terror," Desmoulins uncovers a phenomenon that is related to but infinitely more unsettling than the issue of how governments handle discursive potentiality. In the above-cited passage, he wonders not only if kings and republican leaders have the capacity to tolerate truly free, unfettered speech but also if human nature itself "is capable of that perfection that the unlimited freedom of speech and of writing would presuppose." Like his unexplained mention of the "perversity of the human heart" in the first issue, Desmoulins seems here to be designating something endemic to human communication, or to the psyche itself, that prevents a full engagement with diversity and alterity. The problem may be fundamentally structural, as in Jacques Lacan's assertion, cited earlier, about the impossibility of saying everything—"saying the truth in its entirety is impossible, materially: words are lacking"[79]—but it has profound ontological ramifications as well. In the broadest philosophical sense, Desmoulins's vocabulary of perversion (to draw on the same psychoanalytic terminology we applied to Saint-Just) might be taken to suggest that we are all "perverts," that is, all instruments of an intrisically limited and limiting discursive framework over which we have little control.[80] When Rousseau, a man not unknown for his own arguably perverted penchants, calls for radical empathy in the realms of both human interaction and textual interpretation, he, like Desmoulins in this passage, does not really seem to think it possible, and most likely for the same reasons. For if we are all ensnared in a symbolic system that purports to be all-inclusive when in fact it is predicated on division and difference, then we can only oscillate uncomfortably between the dream of totality and the experience of lack. If our fundamental condition as speaking and social beings is, as *The Social Contract* asserts, "alienation," then the advent of some genuinely "unlimited freedom of speech and of writing"—some real transcendence of existing discursive conditions—would dissolve human nature as we know it. Under these circumstances everyone would become a Rousseauist legislator, "a special and superior function which has nothing to do with the human condition" (*Contract* 85). At that point our very connection to and need for a human polity would, pace Marx, wither away.

In the final analysis, Desmoulins himself is just perverse enough to shy away from such a drastic scenario. Despite his sophisticated understanding of language as a fragmentary and differential medium, he does not abandon the dream of a human community where "love, more lasting than hatred" (*Vieux Cordelier* 67), would bridge, if not close, the ontological, linguistic, and political gaps among its members. "I had dreamed of a republic," he writes to his father from the confines of the Luxembourg prison, "that everyone could have adored."[81] Because joined to others by love, Desmoulins's idealized "everyone"—unlike the purportedly totalizing communities envisioned by his detractors—does not, in *Le Vieux Cordelier*, appear to exist at the expense of someone or something else. As we noted earlier, the journalist does not assign discursive privilege or truth-value to either of the two interlocutors in the seventh issue. Here as in the rest of the journal, the bridle and the spur coexist in undeniable if unsettling harmony. Terrorist and anti-Terrorist, Montagnard and suspect, all varieties of political antagonism and philosophical discourse make themselves heard in *Le Vieux Cordelier*. That is one reason Desmoulins's journal, while obviously not overcoming the inherent imperfections and structural limitations of all language, begs at least to be remembered as a text that, in truth, everyone might adore.

CHAPTER FOUR

The Second Time as Farce

Sade Says It All, Ironically

> Ah, Enlightenment, Enlightenment, were you nothing more than a
> preparation for Darkness? Rousseau, you eternal fucker, has your
> reign finally come? . . . Aren't we simply trading one tyrant for
> another, worse one?
> > —D.-A.-F. de Sade, *Sade contre l'Être suprême*

> Ironically, the Terror always claims to combat its double. It thus gives
> way to an infinite series of reversals. Who is speaking? A hangman
> and a victim . . . the one and the other at the same time.
> > —Laurent Jenny, *La Terreur et les signes*

In *A Place of Greater Safety*, a novelized account of political life during
the Terror, Hilary Mantel imagines a brief but suggestive encounter between two republican writers. One of them, Camille Desmoulins, sits in
his home one afternoon in late November 1793, poring over Tacitus and
muttering to himself about the parallels between modern Paris and ancient Rome. The other, one former Marquis de Sade, appears uninvited
on Desmoulins's doorstep, introduces himself, and requests an audience.
Both men have already achieved some degree of notoriety in their respective fields—political journalism and libertine fiction—but on the
surface they could not be more different from one another. Desmoulins
is young and fervently devoted to the Revolution. As yet, he is also devoted to his friend Robespierre, despite their increasingly divergent ideas
on how the state should be governed. Sade, by contrast, is middle-aged
and jaded; his involvement in republican politics strikes his friends and

family as opportunistic at best, and, predictably in light of his quasi-pornographic opus and lifestyle, he is no fan of the man known as the Incorruptible.[1] These differences notwithstanding, in Mantel's fantasy scenario the two unlikely bedfellows find common ground in their deep-seated aversion to the Terror and in their anxiety about what it means for the future of civil liberty in France. The libertine author has come to Desmoulins, he explains, "to air [his] views" about the repressive political climate of the day, because he has detected similar frustration in some of the journalist's recent writings.[2] Despite his initial reluctance to discuss current events with a stranger (and an erstwhile nobleman at that), Desmoulins eventually comes around to confessing his distaste for the atmosphere of intolerance engendered by the Law of Suspects. Not only, the younger man complains, are "people . . . being killed who need not be," but also—and almost worse—"we dare not speak freely to our best friends, or trust our wives or parents or children."[3] The older gentleman concurs, adding that what appalls him the most "is not the deaths, [but] the judgments, the judgments in the courtroom."[4] With these words, Sade turns tail and goes off, consistent with his prediction, to face arrest for having expressed similar ideas in public.[5] Galvanized by this interchange, Desmoulins pens the controversial third issue of *Le Vieux Cordelier* and, like Sade, is soon jailed for his trouble.

Although Mantel's focus in this improbable tête-à-tête is on how it impacts Desmoulins's journalistic endeavors, in my view what is most interesting is the specific objection to the Terror that she ascribes to Sade. Her ex-marquis deplores the revolutionary government not because of its cruelties per se but because of the justifications given for these activities and the stringent attitude that underpins them. The problem for the Sade of *A Place of Greater Safety* lies in the Montagnards' rationalized "judgments": the methodical intolerance behind the bloodshed. "You see," he admits earlier in the conversation with Desmoulins, "I approve of the duel, the vendetta, the crime of passion. But this machinery of the Terror operates with no passion at all."[6] To repress the passions as the Robespierrists so vehemently do is for Mantel's Sade to undermine the promise of liberty for which the Revolution itself was fought. In fact, this fictitious portrayal offers an interesting potential explanation for the "real" Sade's otherwise puzzling complaint, conveyed in a letter to his lawyer, Gaspard Gaufridy, in 1795, about his imprisonment under the Montagnard regime. (Scheduled to die on July 27, 1794, or 9 Thermidor Year II, he lived to tell about his experiences thanks only to the Robespierrists' fortuitously timed overthrow.)[7] Unfavorably comparing the short sentence he served during the Terror to the decade he spent, courtesy of a *lettre de cachet,* in the Bastille under the Old Regime, he wrote: "My *national* detention, which placed the guillotine under my eyes, did me a hundred times more harm than all the imaginable Bastilles ever did."[8] How to make sense of this enigmatic statement? Having a window that overlooked the daily operations of the guillotine, as Sade did in his confinement at Picpus,[9] could hardly have appealed to the ordinary citizen, but was it not bound to gratify a man who spent most of his time narrating elaborate scenes of torture and carnage? In light of Sade's notorious literary output (not to mention his personal experience with poison, whippings, and prostitutes),[10] how could having "the guillotine under [his] eyes" possibly have displeased him? A potential answer to these questions resides, I think, in the Picpus veteran's sarcastic emphasis on the term *national.* As in *A Place of Greater Safety,* he does not object to imprisonment itself—his prompt dismissal of "all the imaginable Bastilles" indicates as much—but rather to the rationale attached to it by the Terrorist regime. Whereas the monarchy at least made no bones about its arbitrary judicial practices[11]—shamelessly reveling, as the Montagnards themselves argued at Louis's trial, in despotism and bloodlust—the revolutionaries justified their killings in the abstract, joyless language of public interest.[12] To witness countless scenes of death and suffering: not a problem. But to watch these slayings carried out, in Mantel's phrase, "with no passion at all" and in the name of a polity that construed passion itself as a threat to liberty: this, perhaps, was to Sade the Terror's ultimate outrage. Having expected the Revolution to consecrate "the right to say everything,"[13] as he wrote in a mock republican political treatise from the era, he instead found that the Robespierrists' rhetoric of universal liberty in fact imposed severe restrictions on this right. Especially when "saying everything" meant speaking honestly and exhaustively about one's desire.

Speak about desire, though, Sade irrepressibly did—before, during, and after his run-in with the Montagnards. What concerns me in this chapter is how he evinced the events of the revolutionary period when speaking about it, how he ironically appropriated and inverted key components of republican *liberté* for a project of *libertinage.* To take just one example, a death by guillotine merrily depicted in his massive novel *Juliette,* written in the years immediately following his release from Picpus:

In this scene, the novel's eponymous heroine is visiting Rome and staying at the house of one Cardinal de Bernis—a man who, historically speaking, was Louis XVI's ambassador to the Vatican, a legendary profligate, and a personal friend of the author himself. After participating in a round of orgies organized by her host, Juliette decides that to complete her pleasurable sojourn, she will rob Bernis of all his treasure and concoct a scenario to make the cardinal's virtuous niece appear guilty of the crime. All goes according to plan—since the niece angered her uncle by refusing his sexual advances, even he is not predisposed to intervene on her behalf—and Juliette stays in Rome just long enough to gloat at the girl's beheading:

> The trial ends on the seventh day with the poor creature's sentence to death. She was decapitated on San Angelo Square, and I had the pleasure of watching her execution, seated beside Sbrigani who maintained three active fingers in my cunt during all those grisly and arousing proceedings. "O Supreme Being!" I cried inwardly once the blade stood in the block and the severed head lay in the basket, "thus is innocence avenged by thee. . . . I rob the Cardinal, that niece of his he lusts after flees him to prevent a grave sin from being committed: my crime is spasms of joy, she perishes on the scaffold. Holy and Sublime being! Such are thy ways, such the fates whereunto thy loving hand guideth us mortals—aye, 'tis fitting, is it not, that we adore thee!" (*Juliette* 695)

In this extravagant vignette, the dispassionate activity of the Terrorist guillotine metamorphoses into a pretext for erotic pleasure. Juliette revels in her scapegoat's demise, thanks not only to the "three active fingers" with which her lover stimulates her during the execution, but also to the knowledge that, instead of meting out justice, the executioner's blade carries out a profound injustice—prompted by her own false denunciation. Gone is the Terror's unwavering faith in what Robespierre had called "justice prompt, severe, inexorable, and thus an emanation of virtue"; in this case, the inexorable decapitation springs directly from Juliette's private vice, her capricious wish to denounce another for no reason. Gone, too, is the self-abnegating logic of the Montagnard polity, which demands that I destroy myself—my predilections, my difference—for the sake of my fellow citizens. Instead of suppressing her inclinations, Juliette actively and gleefully brings about another human being's demise, her "spasms of joy" being more than sufficient justification for the innocent niece's suffering. Conversely, Juliette also transgresses the

Robespierrist embargo on pathos when, albeit ironically, she qualifies her victim as a "poor creature." The point is that whether it triggers her arousal or her false pity, the beheading unleashes the libertine heroine's affect: she is free to feel whatever she pleases, and thanks none other than the "sublime" Supreme Being for her good fortune.

In light of Robespierre's religious program, this allusion to the Supreme Being is a loaded one to say the least. Coupled with the representation of the guillotine—one of only two, to my knowledge, in Sade's entire oeuvre[14]—it emphasizes the topical nature of the scene. In its most heavy-handed capacity, because the passage establishes a direct link between the beheading and the heroine's outpouring of gratitude to the deity ("'O Supreme Being!' I cried inwardly once . . . the severed head lay in the basket"), it clearly evokes the temporal contiguity of Robespierre's festival and the bloody Law of Prairial that directly succeeded it. Sade's reversal of the chronology, whereby the bloodshed precedes and prompts the religious fervor instead of the other way around, of course highlights the more substantive ironic reversal that is at work in the pairing. After all, the brutal crackdown of Prairial appeared to attest to the Robespierrists' inability to cement their "despotism of liberty" through spiritual propaganda alone, to their dependence on violence as a supplement to ideology. By contrast, Juliette's apostrophe credits the Supreme Being with establishing the ascendancy of her own desires over her fellows' basic well-being. Sade thus adds blasphemous insult to anti-Terrorist injury: not only does private inclination triumph over the public good, but the Being that failed to usher in the latter is presented as the catalyst and guarantor of the former. Leveling one final blow at his former republican persecutors, the author adopts one of their own most cherished textual strategies, the rhetorical question, to complete the picture: "'Tis fitting, is it not, that we adore thee?" Syntactically speaking, only an affirmative answer will do, but no orthodox Terrorist worth his salt could proffer such a reply in any but the most begrudging manner. A "holy and sublime being" that furthers the destructive self-interests of the wicked could only, for a Robespierrist, represent a travesty of the divinity conceived to inspire the citizenry to virtue. From such a perspective, to worship such a being is unthinkable; to be railroaded into doing so by Sade's rhetorical maneuvering is downright unforgivable.

Before engaging in further expositions of Sade's discursive slyness, however, I should comment briefly on the principal pitfall that attends what Ross Chambers has termed "reading (the) oppositional (in) narrative."[15] As I mentioned in chapter 3, Chambers stresses that the decision to interpret a given utterance as "ironic" and "oppositional" (or, for that matter, as "earnest" and "collusive") is precisely a *decision,* made by the reader and determined by his or her desire.[16] I raise this point again here because Sade's texts, perhaps even more than Desmoulins's, are terribly slippery, frequently self-contradictory, and invariably too complex to reduce to doctrinaire formulations of any single problem. It would take tremendous bad faith—or in Chambers's more generous parlance, tremendous desire—to flatten Sadean discourse into strict dogma, even though the author's own texts, which favor pedantic asides such as "only an idiot would dare dispute this eternal truth," frequently invite such a reading. Informed as it is by the political and ideological pressures of the 1790s, my own reading tends to take Sade's outrageous musings as critical responses to this historical context, and thus may appear at the limit to construe them as patently politicized antidogma. Sadistic joy in an innocent woman's beheading becomes an "oppositional" commentary on the Montagnard refusal of *jouissance;* a jubilant prayer to the Supreme Being constitutes an "ironic" rewriting of Robespierrist religious propaganda; and so forth. I wish to clarify at the outset, then, that this approach cannot help but gratify my own desire, which has been shaped negatively by immersion in two distinct strains of Sadean scholarship. The first is exemplified by critics who tend unproblematically to equate Sade's pronouncements with those of the Montagnards;[17] and the second, by readers who overlook the revolutionary context altogether, positing the Sadean catchphrase "say everything" as a largely apolitical proclamation of boundless libertine discursivity.[18] My approach differs from these by insisting on the places in Sade's writings—those composed during the Reign of Terror and in its aftermath—where Terrorist discourse returns to the reader in inverted, anti-Terrorist form. If, as Angela Carter has noted, Sade appears to be "still in complicity with the authority which he hates,"[19] this is because his complicity is, in its relation to Robespierrist discourse, largely ironic; following Lucienne Frappier-Mazur, I read his pseudorepublican pronouncements as "parodic utterances ... both magisterial and divided."[20] Along the same lines, paraphrasing the motto of one character in *La Nouvelle Justine* (1797), the "prequel" to *Juliette,* Pierre Saint-Amand has aptly remarked that Sade's entire "doctrine could be summed up in a [single] phrase ...: *imitate, but while hating; copy, but while cursing.*"[21] In the following pages, without for my part proclaiming a definitive Sadean doctrine, I present this statement as an illuminating lens through which to comprehend the almost constant vacillation between Terrorist collusion and anti-Terrorist critique that marks his postrevolutionary output. The lens is on some level a product of my interpretive desire, to be sure, but I attempt as much as possible to anchor its potential implications strongly in the language of Sade himself.[22]

Anchored it is, as well, in Hilary Mantel's imaginary meeting between the authors of *Juliette* and *Le Vieux Cordelier,* which seems to me a most appropriate starting point for an analysis of this kind. If Sade is suitable company for Desmoulins, it is because, like the dissident journalist, he can be understood effectively to deterritorialize the discourse of the Terror, revealing its hateful nature even as he imitates it and pointing up the exclusions that underpin the Rousseauist/Robespierrist pledge to "say everything."[23] To illuminate this aspect of the libertine writer's work, I focus in this chapter on three of his most revealing texts from the mid- to late 1790s: *(a)* a private letter written to the aforementioned Cardinal de Bernis in 1793, in which Sade explicitly denounces the Montagnards' ideological mystifications; *(b)* the *Philosophy in the Boudoir* (1795), in which he parodically theorizes an ideal republic and demonstrates its limitations as a practical reality; and *(c)* the aforementioned *Juliette* (1797), whose shamelessly self-interested, sexually avaricious protagonist surfaces as the Terror's disavowed evil twin. Read alongside one another, these writings can be construed as damning criticisms and ironic subversions, by turns explicit and implicit, of Terrorist poetics and politics. Like Desmoulins's *Vieux Cordelier,* Sade's texts evince the false totality and repressive tactics that underpin Robespierre's polity. Along philosophical, political, and sexual lines, the repressed elements constitutive of republican virtue return in the libertine's work under the guise of glorified egoism and hypocritical intolerance. As he writes in *La Nouvelle Justine* (1797): "Remember to tear through all veils [and] to depict everything without artifice; cast a veil over virtue, if you like, but let crime always walk about uncovered."[24] In adhering to this ironic precept, Sade presents a face of the Montagnard regime that its own creators endeavored not to recognize.[25] Because the first and perhaps most direct gesture of anti-Terrorist unmasking occurs in Sade's overtly political letter to Bernis, recently published by Philippe Sollers under the fitting title

Sade contre l'Être suprême (Sade against the Supreme Being), it is with that document that our inquiry begins.[26]

Nastiness, Negativity, and the Marionette's New Clothes

Drafted on the evening of December 7, 1793, just hours before Sade was arrested as an enemy of the republic, his letter to Cardinal de Bernis may very well be his only surviving Terror-time missive in which the fear of interception does not compel him to mince his words. "I am sending you this letter by secure means," he informs the cardinal. "So whatever you may learn about me later, rest assured that this letter expresses my real beliefs. I have had to mask myself a lot in recent times" (*Contre* 90). Indeed, aware of the precariousness of his liberty under an antiaristocratic government, the one-time marquis had been careful to conduct himself as an exemplary citizen in both public and private. "Citizen Louis Sade," as he called himself during this period, had not stopped at renouncing his title and dropping his *particule*. He had also distanced himself from his children when they emigrated to escape potential persecution, accepted a series of posts in the government of his Parisian neighborhood, the Section des Piques, and regularly peppered his correspondence as well as his official speeches with assertions of his "patriotic principles."[27] Convenient and even convincing proof of the latter lay in his somewhat extraordinary behavior during his final days in the Bastille. On July 2, 1789, having shoved a pipe through the stones of his cell wall to make himself heard in the surrounding neighborhood, he shouted into it that the guards were slaughtering his fellow inmates and that the good people of Paris ought to storm the place to save them. Although Sade was transferred to another facility the day after this subversive stunt, he later—when freed in 1790 by the new legislature's repeal of the *lettre de cachet*—took every occasion to remind his compatriots that he had inspired the Revolution's finest hour. His persecution under the monarchy itself became a feature of his patriotic pedigree: "Sade moaned in the dreadful dungeons of the Bastille, how could he not cherish the reign of liberty?"[28] Above all, however, it was his abiding hatred of religion, already apparent in much of his prerevolutionary literature,[29] that lent Citizen Louis's republican pronouncements an unmistakable air of sincerity. When in the fall of 1793 the nation seemed to be well on the way to unilateral de-Christianization, he decided to declare his own atheistic leanings in a public eulogy to Marat and in a speech delivered before the Convention. Unlike the exaggerated pastiches of fervid revolutionary discourse that he often produced during this time[30]—flagrant examples of the "self-masking" to which he confesses in the letter to Bernis—both of these antireligious texts are generally held in Sade scholarship to "express sincere convictions."[31] Unfortunately for their author, however, he chose the wrong time to make such a proud show of atheism. As we saw in chapter 2, the Cult of Reason, celebrated by the Hébertists in November, provoked their rivals' horror and led Robespierre to proclaim atheism "aristocratic" and his own newly minted Supreme Being the sole valid guarantor of republican morality.[32] As a result, Sade's hopes for survival underwent a dramatic change for the worse. "A great misfortune threatens us, my dear Cardinal," his letter of December 7 begins, "and I still can't get over it. The tyrant and his men are preparing to reestablish the deific chimera" (*Contre* 61). Although Sade penned these words several hours in advance of his arrest, they reflect his awareness that his hard-won liberty was already at the mercy of a tyrant.

Nevertheless, afforded some relative degree of freedom by the secure means he had found to correspond with Bernis, the old aristocrat devotes several dozen pages to sounding off on the travesty that is the Incorruptible's "deific chimera." Living in self-imposed exile in Rome because of the Terror's unkind policy toward church officials and former servants of the throne, Bernis was bound to receive these rantings with sympathy, and not just because of his presumed Catholic biases. Despite his lofty position as a Vatican insider, Bernis was known less for his faith than for his savvy political abilities and prodigious romantic exploits. Adviser to kings, friend to king's mistresses, consummate ladies' man, and highly cultured "Cardinal of Pleasures": this was the reputation of Sade's chosen confidant. Accordingly, the author seems to assume in his letter that Bernis shares his disdain not only for the new state religion of France but for the one that it replaces as well. The difference being, Sade notes with disgust, that in its attacks on the Church, the Revolution had promised to do away with belief systems designed to undercut men's autonomy, and therefore that the republicans ought to have held themselves to a higher standard. "Were the altars of superstition and fanaticism destroyed," he demands of his correspondent, "only so that the same crude dogma could be reconstructed in an inverted form? Just when we thought hypocrisy had been rooted out, well, all they're really doing is preparing another spectacle for us. After the rivers of blood, what next? I'll tell you...the *Supreme Being!* Don't laugh, that's the Chimera's lofty new name; they have merely changed the marionette's clothes" (*Contre* 61). The grounds for Sade's annoyance with the reinstatement of divinity are simultaneously clear and complex. On the most obvious level, he decries the revival of dogma and superstition—lynchpins of the monarchy—in a postmonarchical age. Like Rousseau and Robespierre, Sade is fully aware of religion's utility as a tool for popular manipulation, but unlike these men, he despises it for this very reason. Just because the republican conception of God has been assigned a "lofty new name" and tricked out in a different guise, it does not mean this deity has ceased to be a mechanism for social control. Such a being's "chains," Sade writes later, "are [no less] useful to the preservation of order" (*Juliette* 321), masquerade though "He" may as a disinterested spiritual principle. Under Sade's critical eye, the cultivated sublimity that the Robespierrists ascribe to their religious construct loses its supposed transparency and becomes artifice heaped upon artifice: deceptive clothing on a demagogue's marionette. The latter term in particular inverts the Montagnards' religious and representational ideal, given that a few months hence, they would represent their Supreme Being as a purifying flame doing battle with physical effigies of antirepublican vice. Since the author himself had been burned in effigy under the Old Regime (for an unfortunate incident at a brothel in Marseilles), the parallel between prerevolutionary and republican political rituals was unlikely to have been lost on him.[33] Accordingly, what he points out by means of the marionette metaphor is that far from eschewing the opaque logic of idolatry and mediation, the Terror's new cult actively embraces it, all the while hypocritically ascribing these qualities to their enemies (from Catholics to Girondins, and from Hébertists to Indulgents) alone.

Sade's next critique of the Supreme Being likewise calls the cardinal's attention to the "hypocrisy" of the new belief system, this time by noting that its sacred rituals call for "rivers of blood" to flow throughout the polity.[34] He notes, for instance, that the executioner's practice of "showing...heads to the public"—exemplified in the popular print of Louis's disembodied head (Figure 1)—"strangely resembles the [Church] ritual of the monstrance" (*Contre* 88). What such grisly ritual implies, according to Sade, is an ethos of hatefulness. "Will you believe me if I tell you that the new religion's secret gospel...can be summarized as follows: 'Hate thy neighbor as thyself'?" (*Contre* 61). While hardly inclined to

condemn hatred or killing on their own terms, Sade deplores the institutionalized sacralization of these forces, which simply inverts Christian
teaching ("Love thy neighbor as thyself") and as such remains quite
close to the Catholic orthodoxy that Robespierre and his acolytes claim
to have left behind. Worse still, this inversion of charitable humanitarian-
ism—of hatred toward all and love toward none—represents an egre-
gious travesty of revolutionary precepts. "Liberty? People have never
been less free; they're like a crowd of sleepwalkers. Equality? The only
equality is among guillotined heads. Fraternity? Informing [on one's
neighbors] has never been more active. Everyone wants everyone else's
death..." (*Contre* 70). Through the Terror's culture of beheadings, denunciations, and widespread fear, the ideals of 1789 have, Sade emphasizes, been corrupted through and through. "Of the program 'liberty or
death,' we have nothing left but death" (*Contre* 90); "And common graves
for everyone, equality and fraternity [indeed]!" (*Contre* 79). During his
brief tenure as president of the Section des Piques in the summer of
1793, Sade himself had become all too familiar with the death-based aspects of republican ideology, signing a decree that the motto "Fraternity
or death" be painted on the façade of all buildings in the neighborhood.[35]
And although he had resigned from this post shortly thereafter (after
refusing, not incidentally, to carry out some of the section's more san-
guinary mandates),[36] his "*national* detention" would soon bring him into
close contact with the carnage once again. Even before his stay at Picpus,
though, the violence of so-called republican virtue was readily apparent
to Sade. "Beware of your brother," he sarcastically cautions the cardinal,
"the walls are full of fraternal ears that are prepared to send you straight
to hell" (*Contre* 90); furthermore, he scoffs, such back-stabbing "fraternal" ways are protected and encouraged by the "Being-Supreme-in-
Nastiness" (*Contre* 66). With this last designation, Sade calls the cardinal's
attention to the deeply unpleasant "inverted form" in which the once-
banished Catholic God *and* the once-promised liberties of the Revolution had returned to haunt the blood-soaked nation.[37] As aficionados of
Lacanian psychoanalysis may have noticed, Sade's allusion to the discursive inversions performed by the propaganda of the Terror anticipates
quite clearly Lacan's famed statement about the message of the unconscious returning to the subject in its inverted form.[38] The libertine
author's related observation is that the "truth" of revolutionary ideology—
liberty, fraternity, equality—reveals itself precisely in the executions, the

denunciations, the widespread paranoia, fear, and readiness to destroy one's neighbor that poison all social relations under the Terror. Saint-Just, we may recall, put it thus: "Terror is a double-edged sword, used by some to serve the people, and by others to serve tyranny"; or, in a Sadean variation on this theme: "Nothing resembles virtue like a great crime." This is the very logic of inversion that Sade identifies here and that, as we shall see below, informs his own literary transmutations of republican virtue into libertine vice.

In his letter to Bernis, however, he proposes that a fundamental distinction be made between the Montagnards' "virtuous" deployment of violent means and his own "vicious" ideas about death and destruction. This distinction manifests itself along the lines of passion and pleasure. While these are things for which Robespierre and his colleagues have manifestly no tolerance, Sade sees them as the very raison d'être of any homicide:

> Everyone wants everyone else's death. But let them at least use a little inventiveness, a little spice, an infinite variety of forms, and not the mechanical, terrible coldness of the Revolutionary Tribunal. The *death penalty* repels me; death should always be linked to pleasure. So it's forbidden to make fun of death? Let's just see about that! Death is serious? Industrial? Morose? Technical? . . . Are you laughing? Are you screaming with laughter? (*Contre* 70–71; Sade's emphasis)

Here again the author deplores the Terrorists' ritualized bloodshed for its inherent lack of passion; he complains of the death penalty's "coldness," its refusal to allow enjoyment to enter into the experience of killing. That is not, he stresses, to say that murder cannot be delightful if gone about differently: if conceived in an inventive, imaginative fashion, then the act of taking another person's life can quite easily be "linked to pleasure." After all, the ability to envision "an infinite variety of forms" of murder and the willingness to revel in such creativity exemplify the intellectual eroticism (*jouissance de tête*) with which Sade's libertinage is often associated.[39] Under these circumstances, death itself, like the libertine's victim, becomes subject to the intellectual mastery of the person who carries it out; the libertine cheats or defies nature by taking charge of its operations and revels in his or her own superiority.[40] The Montagnards' "industrial" deployment of the guillotine, however, presents none of these possibilities: under their stewardship, everyone must submit to the same predictable and homogeneous fate, every bit as uniform and joyless as the general will itself. This, according to Sade, is one of the Terror's foremost failings; it has taken all the "spice" out of death, and has even gone so far as to forbid people from taking pleasure in it (à la Juliette). Murder should moreover be enjoyable not only to those who perform it, he argues, but also to those who witness it: people should be allowed to laugh at death. In its solemn proclamation of the soul's immortality, however, the Supreme Being forbids even this darkly pleasurable outlet. On the contrary: The government's campaign against discursive difference prohibits citizens from responding to its pronouncements with the sort of ironic distance that humor demands.[41] Obviously, the humorousness of death is itself a debatable proposition, but in a way that is precisely the point of Sade's grievance. Whereas the "serious," "morose" Terror does not tolerate any deviation whatsoever, the writer's lustful, laughing approach to mortality exemplifies just such a stance.

The libertine's next and related grounds for complaint against Montagnard orthodoxy are that it militates against other deviant passions that he adores, namely, those involving sex—or "*those* things," as he writes mock-euphemistically at numerous points in his letter (*Contre* 93, 95, 97). "We might ask if the intention behind this whole patriotic slaughterhouse is not to put to death the pleasures of an entire century" (*Contre* 77), he wonders, neatly juxtaposing the life-affirming qualities of the Old Regime with the morbid practices of its replacement. Accordingly, despite his long-standing hatred of Christianity, Sade suddenly waxes nostalgic about the occasional bursts of "lubricity" proper to the Catholicism of the fallen monarchy as against the puritanical cheerlessness of the Robespierrist cadre:

> You know that I am a lot of things, but certainly not a cold-blooded creature. But now we have upon us the age of abstract, rigidified, and frigid blood. The Christian fable may have been absurd, but at least it occasionally permitted some voluptuous flights of fancy. What do we see happening now? Pinched, disaffected, disinfected, hygienic bodies, regularly chopped in two without the least sign of lubricity. (*Contre* 62)

Once again Sade reiterates his staunch opposition to the Terror's cold and apathetic abstractions, which suppress any movement toward "voluptuous flights of fancy." No doubt to the great satisfaction of the lascivious Cardinal of Pleasures, he maintains that the Christian body is voluptuous, or, in Marcel Hénaff's term, "lyric." From the passion of Christ to Saint

Anthony's temptations to Teresa of Avila's *jouissance*, for example, the Catholic narrative is replete with delectable scenes of torture, fantasy, and ecstasy, of the body in all its painful and pleasurable glory. As such, it gives rise to voluptuous flights of lyrical fancy—to deeply personal sensations not susceptible to recuperation by a dry universal principle like "fraternity" or "patriotism." For this very reason, and in stark contrast to the Christian body, the Terrorist body is "disaffected, disinfected, hygienic," because radically purged of all affect; and Sade, for all the press he tends to get in today's critical circles as a champion of apathy, explicitly rejects this corporeal model here.[42] He rejects it because, at the limit, such physical purging culminates in an all too cheerless cult of self-abnegation, in a somber "right to death" that leaves little room for the sentient, sensuous individual. The author observes as much when he resumes his lament for old-time religion: "The old God demanded procreation and sacrifices. The new one has decided to abolish sex and to replace it with an incessant *decreation [sic]*. This one is truly a God of the dead; at least the old one pretended to be a God of the living" (*Contre* 90; Sade's emphasis). Most striking in this passage is Sade's decision to connect the Terror's morbid practices to a program of "decreation," his neologism for a moratorium on sexual reproduction. It must be admitted that this charge sounds a bit dubious, given that Robespierre and Saint-Just actively promoted, at least in theory, the repopulation of France by fecund mother-citizens, enjoined to bear as many sons as possible for the greater glory of the republic.[43] This fact notwithstanding, Sade construes the Montagnards' morbid policies as geared against procreation—a misperception that will inform the exaggerated antimaternal sentiments that his libertine protagonists express in the *Philosophy in the Boudoir*. I will pursue this line of inquiry in my reading of that novel, below; for now, it suffices to observe that Sade again takes exception to the Terror on the basis of its eradication of sexual pleasure and its promotion of death as a coldly calculated affair.

As Sade understands it, the underlying problem with this privileging of death and abstraction over life and passion is that it places the individual at odds with himself. The Terror's combined adoption of the guillotine and the Supreme Being results in the literal and figurative splitting of the subject—unacceptable to a man who, as Marcel Hénaff has argued, consistently rejects the very idea of an internally divided subjectivity.[44] "Isn't it funny, my dear friend, to see the absurd dogma of the soul's immortality being reasserted through increasing demonstrations of the body's mortality? ... The Eternal One carried by corpses to the basket beneath the guillotine, bodies on one side, and heads on the other! Yes, yes: the man on one side, and on the other the citizen!" (*Contre* 78–79). Sade's language here noticeably echoes that of *The Social Contract*, when Rousseau declares the mutual incompatibility of man and citizen, of individual feelings and collective duty. The fact that the machine with which Rousseau's revolutionary admirers enforce this separation literally leaves "bodies on one side, and heads on the other" is for Sade a coincidence too fortuitous, too laughable to be passed over in silence. But the guillotine in fact becomes downright absurd when, he points out, one realizes that it operates in conjunction with "the Eternal One," an allegedly universal principle that actually imposes stringent limits on citizens' bodies and minds. "In sum, the Supreme Being wants to *select its bodies* and turn them into its foundation, as it were. It's a selection process. Perhaps the day will come when it will be able to string them [citizens' bodies] together from different pieces and, annihilating their memory, their past, their beliefs, make them immediately obey its voice of iron" (*Contre* 80; Sade's emphasis). Traces of Rousseau once more surface in Sade's political commentary, although this time it is not so much *The Social Contract* as *Le Lévite d'Éphraïm* that comes immediately to mind. In this passage as in Rousseau's prose piece, the "foundation, as it were," of society is composed of literally and metaphorically dismembered bodies: some guillotined, some simply dispossessed of their beliefs, and all sacrificed to the unity and obedience of the populace. (Sade's *Philosophy in the Boudoir* will take this destructive fundamentalism to violent new heights, with a female body, *Lévite*-style, at the community's sacrificial center.) The people's allegiance to the republic's guiding principle is moreover "immediate," unmediated both by temporal delay and by independent remembrance of things past. The Supreme Being participates in a sublime aesthetics that is, as Jean Starobinski would say of Rousseau, more transparency than obstruction—all differential obstacles having been "selected" out of the body politic like so many undesirable genes.

That these obstacles and the selection process that roots them out are discursive as well as physical phenomena is implicit in Sade's own metaphor of the "voice of iron," a guillotine-oriented play on the clichéd Terrorist "voice of duty." Turning his attention to the problem of voices

and of self-expression under the Supreme Being, the author charges
that this dastardly deity restricts not only people's sexual identity but
their self-expressive potential more broadly defined. Republican virtue,
as we have noted throughout this study and as Sade reminds Bernis, entails that everything *not* be said, and the so-called passions are not even
the sole object of censorship. Representation itself has come under fire
in the new polity: "They are assassinating not only bodies, but also language, music, painting, architecture, theater. . . . The vandalism has become generalized, and illiteracy will certainly result from this regression. . . . Every person who knows how to read well has become a suspect;
having a book of Latin or Greek on your person can . . . cost you your
life" (*Contre* 71). On one level, these grumblings target the "new" revolutionary artistic style, best exemplified in Sade's view by the severe neo-
classicism of Jacques-Louis David, whom he despised.[45] They also refer
to the vandalism—the literal decimation of the Old Regime's images
and monuments—that the Montagnard leaders ordered to be carried
out as one physical manifestation of their destructive rhetoric. More
perceptively still, Sade insists here that the Terror is hindering the *language* of the French people, that it is performatively whittling away at
the population's very literacy. Insofar as "every person who knows how
to read well has become a suspect," and reading the classics is a criminal
offense, any serious engagement with language has become all but impossible. In this sense, Sade echoes the slightly less pessimistic assertion
made by Desmoulins in the first issue of *Le Vieux Cordelier:* that his
contemporaries "have all been so busy with and carried away by the
whirlwind of current events . . . that they have not had the time to read,
I might almost say the time to think" (39). Desmoulins himself, as we
already know, soon paid the price for his independent thinking and especially for his subversive mastery of Latin texts. (Similarly, one apocryphal story about Sade's run-in with the republican authorities holds
that he was arrested for owning an extensive library of classical tomes.)
Autonomous intellectual engagement—the opportunity "to read, I might
almost say to think"—has been stamped out in the "regression" over
which the Supreme Being presides.

The link between the freedom to read and the freedom to think, and
the dangers to which both are subjected under the Terror, becomes even
clearer in Sade's letter when he presents a snippet of Voltairean black
humor as an apt description of Montagnard France:

No doubt you remember that text that Voltaire wrote under the pseudo-nym of Joussouf-Chéribi—the one that we laughed over together a long time ago. It was about the dangers of reading. I copied some sentences from it awhile ago; they are only too true today: "For the edification of the faithful and for the good of their souls, we forbid them ever to read any book, on pain of eternal damnation. And . . . to prevent anyone from contravening our ordinance, we expressly forbid them from thinking, or they face the same consequences; we enjoin all believers to denounce through official channels anyone who pronounces four sentences linked together from which a clear meaning can be inferred. We command that, in all conversations, only terms that mean nothing be used. . . . (Decreed in our Palace of Stupidity on the 7th of the Muharem Moon . . .)"[46] (*Contre* 63–64)

Undoubtedly, the restrictive policies that emanate from Voltaire's Palace of Stupidity partake in the Terrorist regime's hostility toward uncensored linguistic activity, be it reading, thinking, or interpretation (the process by which "meaning can be inferred"). In the "official channels" through which denunciations of free-thinking citizens are to take place in the great satirist's dystopia, it is easy to discern the Revolutionary Tribunal and Committees charged with enforcing the Law of Suspects. And the latter itself, if we remember the vague and essentially meaning-less language in which its definition of the suspect was couched, might be said to exemplify the "terms that mean nothing" prescribed by the *philosophe*'s imaginary government. Furthermore, these restrictive measures are passed off as destined "for the edification of the faithful and for the good of their souls"—in short, for the same religious and moral reasons with which Robespierre justifies the republic's need for a Supreme Being. The bottom line, in Voltaire's story and the Incorruptible's government alike, is that "all conversations" are subject to censorship. "Philosophy itself," the ultimate exercise in reading, thought, and interpretation, "has become suspect" (*Contre* 83).[47] In light of the famous battle cry with which he concludes *Juliette*, "philosophy must say everything [doit tout dire]" (*Juliette* 1193), Sade thus sees the discursive totality promised by the Montagnards as a "term that mean[s] nothing": every bit as empty as the infinitely elastic, and destructive, term *suspect*. Given this severe limitation on the freedom of expression, the French republic cannot, in Sade's eyes as in Desmoulins's, be said to have come a particularly long way. Returning to his beloved, forbidden books of Greek and Latin, the old libertine again demonstrates his political kinship with Desmoulins by making a comment that directly anticipates the journalist's pointed "translation" of Tacitus in the third issue of *Le Vieux Cordelier* (which appeared only two weeks after Sade sent this letter to the Vatican). "You would think we were living under Tacitus rather than at the end of the eighteenth century" (*Contre* 77), Sade groans. In the realm of thought as in the realm of sexuality, the Revolution has violated its own ostensible commitment to freedom and turned into its opposite: a dead ringer for imperial Rome.

For documented evidence of the republic's now-violated intentions, Sade directs the cardinal's attention to the article of the Declaration of the Rights of Man that guarantees extensive liberty of expression to all French citizens:[48]

> The *Rights of Man*—decreed, you will recall, "in the presence and under the auspices of the Supreme Being"—will doubtless prove a poor defense against the rising tide [of the Terror]. It nevertheless amuses me to remind you of Article 11: "The free communication of thoughts and opinions is one of man's most precious rights; every citizen may there-fore speak, write, and publish freely...." I shall stop quoting here, for afterward the limit of the law comes back: "in the presence," "under the auspices"; reference is even made to the "gaze of the immortal legislator." It makes me shudder with disgust. (*Contre* 94–95; Sade's emphasis)

When Sade cites this passage, the discrepancy between Terrorist prac-tice (de facto censorship under the Law of Suspects) and revolutionary preaching (freedom of speech) becomes glaringly obvious. When he complains, however, that this contradiction is sustained by "the limit of the law" and stabilized by the Supreme Being, he puts his finger on an even larger problem, which is the transcendental status that the Terror grants to its logic of limitation. Sade's repetition of the expressions "in the presence" and "under the auspices," originally used in conjunction with the Robespierrist deity, emphasizes this figure's position as a guar-antor of meaning, however self-undermining. Under the auspices of the Supreme Being, the expansive letter of the law devolves into its own self-restricting spirit. Like the "immortal legislator" of *The Social Con-tract,* the Supreme Being exists above and beyond a realm of universal human freedom of which it secretly determines the limits. If this phe-nomenon elicits a "shudder [of] disgust" from Citizen Louis, this is due to its simultaneously dishonest and alienating nature: dishonest because republican law promises the opposite of what it actually delivers, and alienating because in order for this bait-and-switch to occur smoothly, citizens have to look outside themselves to a transcendental principle little different from a Catholic God or a French king. More precisely, the difference between the Terrorists' transcendental logic and the logic adopted by the Old Regime lies in the former's hypocrisy, its refusal to acknowledge that the liberty it offers to its people is a farce and a lie.[49] This is the meaning of the first epigraph to this chapter, in which Sade apostrophizes Rousseau and expresses serious concern that the *philosophe*'s Montagnard admirers are "simply trading one tyrant for another, worse one." Not only has the contingent nature of so-called immortal authority failed to disappear with the last of the Bourbons (the Supreme Being is no less an artificial master-signifier than its royalist precedents);[50] the new authority dares to pass its tyrannical agenda off as an affirmation of universal freedom.

Even on an aesthetic level, Sade notes, the new regime and the old one differ substantially only in the level of hypocrisy that attends their respective mystifications. Whereas the revolutionaries had distinguished themselves from the monarchy by decrying its opaque and artificial ruling techniques (numerous ministers and advisers as mouthpieces of the sovereign's will; obscure legal language; elaborate protocols dictating access to the seat of power), they are by no means above oppressive obfuscations of their own. Although the Robespierrists' poetics of sublime transparency offers the promise of universal inclusiveness, Sade holds that these leaders use ineffability itself as a means of fleecing the French people. "They will say, for example: the essence of the Supreme Being is closed off to us by an obscure cloud," he remarks derisively. "Without a doubt! And for a good reason! [Et pour cause!]" (*Contre* 89). Once again, the libertine writer's words foreshadow those of Jacques Lacan—this time on the falsity of any pretension to discursive totality: "One would not know how to say everything, and for a good reason [et pour cause]."[51] In his version of this utterance, Sade is suggesting that the very positioning of the Supreme Being beyond the realm of conventional representation, in the "obscure cloud" of sublime (non)language, serves the cause of universal freedom only insofar as it stamps out all particularity and difference. The radical insubstantiality of the Supreme Being—memorably deprecated by Hegel as the "vacuous . . . exhalation of a stale gas"[52]—can reflect each citizen's interests only by negating them all: "The condemned prisoners cry out: Long live the king! Or even: Long live the republic! In either case the crowd replies: Long live the nation! And the blade of the guillotine punctuates these cries with: Long live the Supreme Being!" (*Contre* 89). Whether the Terror's victims are sent to the guillotine for their royalist leanings (e.g., the Girondins) or their unwelcome variations on republicanism (e.g., the Hébertists and the Indulgents), they are dissolved into the three-pronged nothingness of abstract nationhood, death by beheading, and the Supreme Being. The Robespierrists' nihilistic public policy enshrouds the diversity of human expression in a cloud that is not only obscure but deadly; for "here," Sade laments to Bernis, "it must be said that the spectacle is mortal" (*Contre* 77).

The disgruntled Citizen Louis is not, however, willing to succumb to such machinations without a fight. For his part, he assures his correspondent: "I have no intention of applauding such a spectacle!" (*Contre* 89). In contrast to the Terrorists' pretensions to universal justice, propped up by a supposedly transparent deity, Sade offers up a highly particularized discursive and political ideal: "I want nothing to do with a king or a republic; I do not want a nation, nor do I want a Supreme Being! . . . Nor do I want a fatherland! Literature doesn't have one, and I have nothing to lose but my chains" (*Contre* 89). Repudiating the whole range of abstract principles through which Robespierre and his acolytes attempt to control human behavior, Sade puts forth "literature" as a countervailing discursive space in which these principles lose their efficacy.[53] Literature is after all a space that welcomes those who, as Desmoulins would say, take the time to read and to think; as such, it invites the free and inventive proliferation of opinion released from tyrannical master-signifiers like *nation* and *Supreme Being*. Thus performatively liberated in the space of his own text, Sade goes on to affiliate this utopian literary realm with his favorite particularist discourse of all, the passions:[54]

> Stories, variations, experiments in *those things*, that is what we need. That is my Torah, my Gospel, my Koran, my *Declaration of the Rights of Man*, or more modestly, if you prefer, my sextant, my compass. . . . I must now finish, my dear Cardinal, my messenger is knocking on the door in the code that he and I have established. Do not forget me in your prayers, and especially in your remembrance of *those things*, . . . and believe me ever to be your nonhumble, nonobedient servant, that is to say your friend. (*Contre* 95, 97; Sade's emphasis)

Forsaking fatherland and morality for "stories" and sexuality, the "nonobedient" Sade sees in *those things* the only sound alternative to Robespierre's restrictive categorical imperatives. (Even his inversion of the traditional French epistolary closing, "your humble and obedient servant," betrays this will to insubordination.) He recognizes that his passionate particularity will meet with little approval in a nation that has elected unilaterally to "hate thy neighbor as thyself." Nevertheless, true to his anti-universalist credo, the so-called common good of his compatriots is hardly Sade's concern. "If the French themselves have decided to start hating each other,...well, poor Frenchmen! Go ahead and annihilate yourselves! Yet another effort! Go ahead and embrace Mosaic theories and [extremist] babble!" (*Contre* 96). For now, then, the author seems ready to abandon his fellow citizens to the logic of generalized self-annihilation propagated by the Montagnards and personified by the Supreme Being. Nonetheless, in his next work on the Terror, the *Philosophy in the Boudoir*, he himself will make "yet another effort" to debunk the "Mosaic theories and [extremist] babble"—the bogus sublimity and vehement intolerance—by means of which his homeland is so methodically self-destructing.

"This Is Not Made for You," or Terror in the Boudoir

Sade was carted off to prison by the revolutionary police the day after writing this letter to Cardinal de Bernis. Consistent, however, with his optimistic closing comments about the subversive powers of literature, he appears to have spent much of his subsequent incarceration working on a novel, the *Philosophy in the Boudoir*, first published anonymously in 1795. At the level of rhetorical experimentation, the novel exploits the author's earlier apologia of linguistic freedom by subverting the Robespierrist government's discourse and dogmas. The text's principal means to this end, which confirms Georg Lukács's famed maxim about irony being the mode proper to "a world abandoned by God," resides in black humor and irony.[55] As the profoundly irreverent author of *Yet Another Effort, Frenchmen, If You Would Be Republicans*—the tract inserted into the middle of the novel—asserts: "Julian's sarcasm wrought greater damage to Christianity than all Nero's tortures" (*Philosophy* 306). Indeed, Sade's sarcastic formulations in the republican treatise and the novel that frames it take as their primary target the policies, religious and otherwise, of "the infamous Robespierre" (*Philosophy* 301). The Supreme Being and the sublime aesthetic from which it springs; the ideals of fraternity, equality, and liberty; the concept of republican nationhood; the sexual double standard—all these Terrorist hallmarks meet with blistering ridicule under Sade's pen. In addition to debunking these ideological lynchpins one by one, however, the *Philosophy in the Boudoir*'s primary objective and impact, we might say, is above all its revelation of their collective, untenable contradictions. When transposed into a boudoir full of ruthless and imaginative libertines, the Robespierrists' very idea of a "despotism of liberty" becomes grimly absurd; the self-styled despots of libertinage wrangle with neo-Rousseauist political discourse only to demonstrate that not "all voices [should] be counted" in the elaboration of communitarian freedom. More than in *Yet Another Effort* or the novel's dialogues taken independently of one another, the tension between the libertine characters' enlightened theories and their despotic practices plays itself out in the ways in which they respond to, interpret, and frame their pseudorepublican reading. For this reason, my analysis of the *Philosophy in the Boudoir* proceeds with an examination of how the Terror is systematically spoofed within *Yet Another Effort* itself and with an investigation of how this document's internal contradictions become manifest in its reception by the readers inside Saint-Ange's lair.

Yet Another Effort makes its dramatic entrance in the middle of the novel's "Fifth Dialogue." As this section heading—along with the book's subtitle, *The Immoral Instructors*—indicates, the *Philosophy in the Boudoir* as a whole has pronounced pedantic aims. Modeled less on *Le Vieux Cordelier* than on the Socratic dialogues of Plato, it is a send-up of a philosophical tutorial, and its premise is the initiation of a young girl named Eugénie into the erotic, social, and moral codes of libertinage. The project is undertaken by a pair of voluptuaries, Madame de Mistival and her brother's blackguard friend Dolmancé, and the tone they take in their immoral instructions, interspersed as these are with explicit sexual "demonstrations," is decidedly didactic. For this reason, the sudden eruption of a lengthy philosophical treatise into the group discussion appears to proceed relatively organically from the foregoing action; it is even directly prompted when Eugénie, fresh from an orgy, inquires about the role that morality should play in government. In response, Dolmancé informs her that he just happens, "while at the Palais de l'Égalité, [to have] bought a brochure that . . . will necessarily answer [her] question" (*Philosophy* 295) and that the text should be read aloud for Eugénie's benefit. (On the basis of what Dolmancé describes with humorous double-entendre as his "beautiful organ," Saint-Ange's brother, the chevalier de Mirvel, is asked to do the honors.) Although on a diegetic level this reply justifies the pamphlet's inclusion in the novel, it also designates the political and ontological commingling of what previously appeared to be two distinct discursive spheres. For whereas the libertines' dialogic interchanges occur in the seemingly timeless, thoroughly isolated zone of Saint-Ange's private boudoir, the republican tract hails from an "outside world" of specific historical significance: the Palais de l'Égalité. Formerly known as the Palais Royal and renamed as part of the Terrorist government's campaign to erase all vestiges of the monarchy from the national consciousness, this venue was from the Revolution's very beginnings the central public site of inflammatory debate and pamphleteering in Paris. It was here that Camille Desmoulins enjoined the populace to storm the Bastille; and it was here that heated discussion sometimes escalated into violence, as when a group of zealous Jacobins grabbed a noblewoman and spanked her for her presumed monarchist leanings (Figure 5). Dolmancé, we shall soon see, is a great believer in spankings and in even harsher punishments for women whose convictions controvert his own. But at this point it simply bears noting that in tracing the pamphlet to the Palais de l'Égalité, he links it to revolutionary political ferment, and at the same time, because the source's name is a palimpsest disguising its royal past, he implicitly reveals the document's discursively heterodox origins. When it appears in the "Fifth Dialogue," *Yet Another Effort* thus manifests not only a rapprochement between the democratically minded rabble of the Palais de l'Égalité and the decadent elite of Saint-Ange's boudoir, but also a confusion in the political origins and alliances of "republican" doctrine itself. If the French must make yet another effort to become republicans, it is because tyranny still inhabits their ideological touchstones, just as surely as the word *Royal* still lurks behind the term *Égalité* and just as surely as the language of the Terror informs that of Sade's ironic subversions.

By commencing with a discussion of revolutionary religion, the unnamed author of *Yet Another Effort*—who, significantly, Dolmancé hints might actually be himself[56]—straightaway indicates that the specter of tyranny still hovers over the French state. While he initially asserts that "we must have a creed, a creed befitting the republican character" (*Philosophy* 296), he quickly reaches the conclusion that no conventional cult, be it that of Catholicism or "pure theism" (*Philosophy* 299), fits

Figure 5. Anonymous, *Femme battue pour avoir craché sur le portrait de Necker* (Woman spanked for spitting on Necker's portrait) (1789). Courtesy of the Bibliothèque nationale de France, Paris.

this description. First he deprecates Christianity as a mere tool of an abusive monarchy and clergy and warns that its "platitudes of dogma and mystery... would, by blunting the fine edge of the republican spirit, rapidly put about the Frenchman's neck the yoke which his vitality but yesterday shattered" (*Philosophy* 296). Next, and more pointedly, he raises the possibility of a theistic deity reminiscent of the Supreme Being, only to discredit it at length:

> Will the acceptance of a chimera infuse into men's minds the high degree of energy essential to republican virtues, and move men to cherish and practice them? Let us imagine nothing of the kind; we have bidden farewell to that phantom and, at the present time, atheism is the one doctrine of all those prone to reason.... We have sensed that this chimerical divinity, prudently invented by the earliest legislators, was, in their hands, simply one more means to enthrall us, and that, reserving unto themselves the right to make the phantom speak they knew very well how to get him to say nothing but what would shore up the preposterous laws whereby they declared they served us... [while] serving their own interests.... Let the total extermination of cults and denominations therefore enter into [our] principles.... Let us not be content with breaking scepters; we will pulverize the idols forever: there is never more than a single step from superstition to royalism. (*Philosophy* 299–300)

The genius of this passage consists in its savvy adoption of standard Robespierrist rhetoric to undercut the regime's own moral tenets. Without explicitly naming this deity just yet, the author undermines the very idea of an invented God by marshaling buzzwords such as *energy, virtue,* and *reason* against it. (*Energy* is a favorite in this tract: "If he grows soft, if his energy slackens in him, the republican will be subjugated in a trice" [*Philosophy* 333], the pamphleteer cautions elsewhere, bringing an irreverent levity to the pronouncement with silly sexual innuendo.) He contrasts transcendental republican principles, which in theory have no need of fictitious, mediating structures, with "preposterous laws" reminiscent of the legalistic forms decried by the Montagnards in their showdown with the Girondins. The effect of this juxtaposition, however, is of course to prove that even allegedly formless religious principles work to shore up such forms—and thus operate in the service of self-interest, particularism, and domination. Like the architects of the Terror, and in language that bears all the marks of their categorical intolerance ("total extermination," "pulverize forever"), the pamphlet's author proposes that these elements be addressed through violence. He moreover suggests that anyone who opposes such measures is surely a royalist collaborator, thereby echoing the Committee of Public Safety's most common charge against counterrevolutionaries while also, as in Sade's letter to Bernis, highlighting the fundamental structural complicity between "*scepter* and *censer*" (*Philosophy* 298; Sade's emphasis). "Yes, citizens," he concludes in the axiomatic tone of a Robespierre or a Saint-Just, "religion is incompatible with the system of liberty" (*Philosophy* 301). The logical consequence of this truism is that "atheism is the one doctrine" capable of sustaining civil freedom . . . the Incorruptible's unequivocal denigration of atheism notwithstanding.

Sade's pamphleteer defies Robespierrist doctrine even more overtly in the following paragraph, when he declares on behalf of the French people:

We have no use for a dimensionless god who nevertheless fills everything with his immensity, an omnipotent god who never achieves what he wills, a supremely good Being who creates malcontents only . . . [and] who moves man at the moment man abandons himself to horrors; such a god makes us quiver with indignation, and we consign him forever to the oblivion whence the infamous Robespierre wished to call him forth. (*Philosophy* 301)

While the undisguised references to the Supreme Being's creator and its "dimensionless" nature make the political intent of this diatribe apparent enough, a slightly subtler critique of Robespierre's new religion also surfaces here. The author remarks that despite the Montagnard leader's exuberant claims about the Supreme Being's ability to dissolve all discord, the deity could not be further from achieving what he or his creator purports to offer the people. Instead of establishing universal happiness and well-being, the divinity "creates malcontents only"; the republican virtue that it ("he") prescribes to the citizenry is in fact (witness the guillotine's unrelenting industry) an excruciatingly painful brand of medicine. That the "horrors" of fratricidal bloodshed are carried out *for the sake of* this stringent morality is the cause of the pamphleteer's avowed indignation, just as it is of Sade's in his letter to Bernis. In *Yet Another Effort*, the proposed solution is again violent and again couched in unmistakably Terrorist terms: "we consign him forever to oblivion." Using this close variation on one of Robespierre's signature formulas ("hurl [the king] into nothingness") to condemn his pet political creation, the pamphleteer attacks the Incorruptible with his own weapons. The performative effect of this gesture is to reveal that absolutely no aspect of Montagnard dogma is sacred.

To underscore this point, the author of *Yet Another Effort* goes on to recommend as an antidote to the government's strict morality a force bound to prevent it from being taken seriously: humor. Already mentioned by Sade when ticking off to Bernis the Terrorist regime's many deficiencies, laughter is presented here as the most effective blow that true republicans can deal to religious propaganda:

> Yes, let us destroy for all time any notion of a god . . . [and] let them
> speak to us no more of their chimerical Being nor of His nonsense-filled
> religion, the single object of our scorn. Let us condemn the first of
> those . . . charlatans who comes to us to say a few more words either of
> God or of religion, let us condemn him to be jeered at, ridiculed, covered
> with filth in all the public squares and marketplaces in France's largest
> cities: imprisonment for life will be the reward of whosoever falls a
> second time into the same error. (*Philosophy* 306)

Interestingly, whereas in Sade's discussion of death's titillating aspects laughter is associated with enjoyment, here it emerges as a force for unmitigated (symbolic) destruction. The intermingling of pleasure and violence is of course not unusual in Sade's work—it even informs his remarks to Bernis about death's humorous aspects—but in this case, the violent reorientation of a pleasurable activity derives from a markedly Terrorist conception of discursive freedom. Insofar as they are to be deployed against anyone "who comes to us to say a few more words either of God or of religion," jeering and ridicule function in *Yet Another Effort* categorically to stifle certain types of expression. The fact that the pamphleteer deems such forbidden utterances erroneous further reveals his debt to the intolerant rhetoric of the regime he loathes. As we have seen, the leaders of the Montagne consistently dismiss political and philosophical difference as corrupt falsehood; once more, the treatise's author appropriates their discursive strategy in order to undercut the very system that strategy is intended to support. In the process, he again performatively establishes the instability of the principles in which his foes doggedly attempt to locate transcendental truth. If the Supreme Being itself is an error, then what is to become of the republic of virtue?

To add insult to injury, the author of *Yet Another Effort* continues his denigration of the Robespierrists' creed with another maneuver from their repertoire: the transparently fallacious pledge of discursive freedom and totality. Recommending that the government directly support expressions of ridicule, he writes:

> Let the most insulting blasphemy, the most atheistic works be fully and openly authorized, in order to complete the extirpation from the human heart the memory of those appalling pastimes of our childhood; let there be put into circulation the writings most capable of finally illuminating the Europeans upon a matter so important, and let a considerable prize, to be bestowed by the Nation, be awarded to him whom, having said and demonstrated everything [ayant tout dit, tout démontré] upon this score, will leave to his countrymen no more than a scythe to mow the land clean of all those phantoms, and a steady heart to hate them. In six months, ... God will be as naught, and all that without [your] ceasing to ... fear the blade of the law [le glaive des lois] or to be honest men. (*Philosophy* 306)

Yet again, the Terrorists' tactics are readily discernible behind those put forth as alternative republican practices. The writer provides a sweeping, if negative vision of religious tolerance—even "the most insulting blasphemy, the most atheistic works [are to] be fully and openly authorized"—only to laud its capacity to root out countervailing currents of thought. Like the propagandist program by which French place names were changed (e.g., the Palais Royal to the Palais de l'Égalité; the Place Vendôme to the Place des Piques) to erase all traces of the nation's monarchical heritage,[57] the unfettered proliferation of (anti)religious opinion serves to extirpate memories inimical to atheist conviction. Not only does the state reward such "extirpation"; it also hails the most effective extirpator's discursive negations as totalizing truth. As usual, the flip side of such totality is intolerance (it endows the citizens with "steady heart[s] to hate") and radical negation ("God will be as naught"). The by now familiar paradox is that these destructive impulses are held to serve "the blade of the law," a figure that reprises the Terrorists' hackneyed metaphor for justice,[58] and therefore to make honest men of those who display them. In the same sanctimonious vein, the author concludes his musings on religion by avowing that the true republican's "only guide is virtue and [his] one restraint is conscience" (*Philosophy* 307)—and thus, in a flagrant reversal of Robespierrist belief—that the true republican has no patience for the Supreme Being.

Although already apparent in these rhetorical appropriations and inversions, the tract's praise of ridicule really shifts from theory to practice when its author proceeds to elaborate on just what freedoms France's "honest men" ought to enjoy. Enjoy is the operative word: *Yet Another Effort* now becomes a treatise on mores (those interpersonal societal dealings that Rousseau charged the legislator with manipulating "in secret") and articulates these as a cluster of libertine activities that virtually any conventional legislation would deem unspeakable. Murder, prostitution, incest, rape, sodomy, and so on—these heretofore proscribed aspects of human comportment are included in the "freedom of action" that the pamphleteer posits as a necessary corollary to republican "freedom of conscience and of the press" (*Philosophy* 307). Having already conceived of freedom of conscience as the freedom to annihilate religious dissenters, the author now defines the individual's "proprietary right of enjoyment" (*Philosophy* 320) as a right to ignore the well-being of his or her fellows and so to suppress any considerations alien to his or her own pleasure. As Pierre Klossowski has argued in compelling detail, such a conceptualization of the individual's rights "den[ies] the reality of the neighbor, to empty the notion of the neighbor of its content."[59] In the context of the Terror's systematic disavowal of political, discursive, and sexual alterity, the kind of denial recommended here becomes another pointed commingling of Robespierrist jingoism and radical dissent. "The issue of [the other's] well-being," the pamphleteer states flatly, "is irrelevant" (*Philosophy* 320); as a result, the Montagnard ideology of the general good and of fraternal communitarianism appears to go out the window. At the same time, the author's dismissal of standard republican dogma invites the reader's laughter, because it patently exploits the Revolution's own foremost philosophical tenets. Counterintuitively enough, the "right" to kill, rape, sodomize, or rob the other in order to gratify one's own pleasure is presented as an outgrowth of a strong social pact. It is possible as long as everyone simply "yields a little of his freedom and of his wealth in order to assure and sustain the preservation of each" (*Philosophy* 313). Are such minor sacrifices not, the author asks innocently, the very "elements of the social contract?" (*Philosophy* 313).

According to the treatise's reconceptualization of the general good, this right to pursue one's personal pleasure in fact permits "equality, that foremost law" (*Philosophy* 309), to prevail in the republic. With a few important exceptions, of which more later, everyone is empowered to exercise his or her desires on everyone else. And although the pamphleteer couches this universal empowerment in the language of fraternity—"loving others as brothers" (*Philosophy* 309) paradoxically means accepting the mutual disregard in which citizens all hold each other's self-interest—he further subverts the Terrorists' fraternal ideal by promoting the inclusion of women. Borrowing from Rousseau's *Social Contract* (with its famous first line "man is born free") and the Declaration of the Rights of Man (which omitted women from its definition of citizens), the author writes against the grain of the conventional patriarchal notion of women as their fathers' or husbands' property:

> Never may an act of possession be exercised upon a free being; the exclusive possession of a woman is no less unjust than the possession of slaves; all men are born free, all have equal rights: never should we lose sight of these principles, according to which never may there be granted to one sex the legitimate right to lay monopolizing hands on the other.... The act of possession can only be exercised upon a chattel or an animal, never upon an individual who resembles us, and all the ties which can bind a woman to a man are quite as unjust as illusory. (*Philosophy* 318–19)

Now this correction to the Revolution's fundamentally masculinist *liberté* and *égalité* appears bold enough in an era when women's potential for political involvement was the target of severe government crack-

downs. But the pamphleteer has an even more subversive proposition
up his sleeve, as his repudiation of "the *exclusive* possession of a woman"
stealthily indicates. If women should be freed from paternal or marital
domination, it is not, according to the author, so that they might vote,
gather in clubs, or organize political demonstrations. Rather, it is so
they might engage in an activity that Robespierre and his comrades
found even more threatening to republican virtue: prostitution. "If we
wish to preserve the government we have adopted, I am going to try to
convince you that the prostitution of women who bear the name of
honest is no[t] dangerous" (*Philosophy* 318), the pamphleteer suggests,
going on to assert that the state will flourish only if *(a)* all women are
free to "give themselves to as many men as they see fit" (*Philosophy* 321)
and *(b)* "all men have an equal right of enjoyment of all women" (*Philosophy* 319). In stark and mocking contrast to the puritanical, dispassionate conception of liberty and equality put forth by the Incorruptible
and company, the true republican polity is here presented as a hotbed
of rampant lust and indiscriminate couplings. Perhaps most insultingly
of all, though, to the memory of Robespierre's misogynist cadre, the
key to this political consolidation lies in the unleashing of feminine sexuality: "O charming sex, you will be free.... For a bridle have nothing
but your inclinations, for laws only your desires ... like us, you are free"
(*Philosophy* 323). In Hegelian terms, the freely self-prostituting woman
with no constraints on her sexuality represents a "negation of a negation":
she is the inverted image of the straight-laced Robespierrist *citoyenne*
and the self-effacing Rousseauist heroine, figures who themselves in-
vert the "normal" human freedom to indulge one's sexual impulses.[60]
The same logic dictates the metamorphosis of the "bridle"—a paradigmatic figure, as Desmoulins demonstrates, for Terrorist discursive constraint—into a principle of unfettered feminine desire. Where freedom
and equality under Robespierre require women to stifle their sexual and
political inclinations, Sade's version of these values negates or overturns
them to bring to light what they suppressed in the first place.

This topsy-turvy schema includes a new take on fraternity as well; for
since women now entertain countless sexual partners and their offspring's
paternity can no longer be assured, children become, "as they must be,
purely *les enfants de la patrie*" (*Philosophy* 322). Wickedly citing the anthem "La Marseillaise" to summarize his proposal, the author suggests
that children are better off not having their "thoughts particularized" by

"only one family" (*Philosophy* 322) and that they should instead be raised in public institutions, thus directing all their loyalties toward the country as a whole. Moreover, he asserts, the blurring of biological origins will invariably lead to incest, which further "loosens family ties so that the citizen has that much more love to lavish on his country" (*Philosophy* 324). The impersonal love of country thus again becomes the unexpected ideological justification for overt depravity: "I would venture, in a word, that incest ought to be every government's law—every government whose basis is fraternity" (*Philosophy* 324). These "fraternal" bonds also stand to receive a boost from the practice of sodomy, which *Yet Another Effort* prescribes to both men and women but which it presents as especially suited to men. Citing a host of examples from around the globe—subverting the Terrorist discourse of abstract homogeneity and xenophobia with a litany of references to foreign peoples partial to the "vice"—the author concludes that sodomy is "useful . . . in a republic" (*Philosophy* 327) insofar as it brings its practitioners (literally) closer together. Such "attachments steady the republic" and encourage "patriots [to] sacrifice everything to the state's prosperity" (*Philosophy* 328), even if it means, as the pamphleteer quotes Plutarch as saying, "women must in no way figure in men's love" (*Philosophy* 327). In addition to pointing up the homosexual implications of male-gendered republicanism, these comments, as Lynn Hunt has ably demonstrated, seem flagrantly inconsistent with the text's earlier proclamation of female suffrage.[61] It is possible, however, to understand this very inconsistency as a parody of Robespierrist argumentation, which likewise does not hesitate to declare universal freedom and specific "unfree" exceptions (the people vs. Louis, the good citizen vs. the bad citizen) in the same breath. The case of the good citizen and the bad citizen is particularly illuminating here because it shows that beings from the same ontological category—be it "citizen" or "woman"—can fall on both sides of the Terror's Manichaean binary. In the mock-republican pamphlet, then, the "good" woman is the one who prostitutes herself to every man, while the "bad" woman is the one who protests when a couple of manly patriots want to have their fun without her. In the Robespierrist republic as in its parodic reincarnation, the value judgment is by no means consistent or transcendental. It is determined, rather, by the contingent agenda (or again, à la Chambers, the interpretive desire) of the person with the power to enforce it as law, who in both cases is expressly identified as male. (The pamphleteer takes pains to note that, women's new free-doms notwithstanding, the republican military still belongs to the men-folk.) Illuminating in this regard is Robespierre's recipe for distinguish-ing "friends of liberty" from "criminals": "Who, then, will untangle these nuances? Who will draw the line of demarcation between these contrary excesses? The love of the nation and the truth will do it" (Mazauric 291). Since "love of the nation" is not in and of itself an im-mutable principle—its subversive alignment with sodomy and incest in *Yet Another Effort* makes this clear enough—the real "line of demarca-tion" can thus be traced to political power and brute strength.[62]

As cynical as this insight may be, it in fact underlies Saint-Ange's and Dolmancé's own teachings, which resemble those of the pamphlet not only in their promises (e.g., unlimited liberty for men and women, the "right to say everything") but also in their contradictions (e.g., restric-tive sexual politics, instances of censorship). The latter become most ap-parent when we examine closely the reception with which *Yet Another Effort* meets among the assembled libertines, for the reading of the pam-phlet is framed by a series of gestures that would otherwise seem in-compatible with its overall message of (ostensible) all-inclusiveness. The first of these gestures immediately precedes the chevalier's recitation and occurs when Saint-Ange banishes her illiterate gardener, Augustin—whose enormous "member" has earned him temporary inclusion in the group's frolics—from the boudoir. "Out with you, Augustin," she com-mands as her brother prepares to read *Yet Another Effort* aloud, "this is not for you; but don't go too far; we'll ring you when we want you back" (*Philosophy* 295). This cursory and unexplained expulsion has puzzled many a reader; as Claude Lefort asks:

> Why . . . shouldn't Augustin listen? To put it another way, what is Sade trying to tell us, the readers, with this stroke? What complicity is he seeking to establish with us, such that he feels no need to justify the exclusion of the man of the people—an exclusion that occurs, moreover, at the very moment when the philosophy of the boudoir opens onto the philosophy of the city? . . . At this point, theory diverges from practice.[63]

While concurring with Lefort's point about Augustin's representative status among his aristocratic employer's friends as a "man of the people," I do not share his conviction that this episode represents a discrepancy between republican theory and libertine practice. On the contrary: Saint-Ange's arbitrary suspension of a person's right to say (or rather to hear) everything establishes a level of complicity not so much with "us readers" as with the Montagnard regime itself, by dramatizing the very theoretical inconsistencies that structure both *Yet Another Effort* and its real-life inspiration.[64] More specifically, Augustin's banishment anticipates the slight but significant exception that the tract posits to its definition of universal freedom. "Never may an act of possession be exercised upon a free being.... The act of possession can only be exercised upon a chattel or an animal, never upon an individual who resembles us." As I have shown elsewhere, the proliferation of animal metaphors in the *Philosophy in the Boudoir* functions principally to establish a discursive and ontological divide between libertine masters and their luckless victims.[65] Augustin, whom Saint-Ange first introduces to her comrades as a "great pig... [un]fit for civilized society" (*Philosophy* 266), merits unequal treatment before the libertines' law because he is not "an individual who resembles us." In linguistic terms, the difference between Augustin and the rest of the crew is pronounced indeed; composed entirely of short grunts and inarticulate argot, his speech bears no resemblance to that of his loquacious and eloquent "betters." A differend—as Lyotard understands the term—thus arises between the two sides, as in Louis XVI's trial, when the Montagnards deemed royalist discourse invalid in the eyes of the people. But as Lyotard stresses, and as the Montagnards' recourse to the guillotine made abundantly clear, a discursive differend is always an indication and an outgrowth of a pronounced power differential between two parties.[66] Ultimately, Saint-Ange (whose double-barreled, virtuous-sounding name clearly recalls that of Saint-Just)[67] bars Augustin from the boudoir *because she can*— because he does not resemble the aristocratic "us," whose far superior financial and sociopolitical means enable them to treat him as chattel.[68] This gesture thus becomes the negative mirror image of the "pig-hunt" that the popular press declared on Louis XVI in his disgrace, repeatedly depicting him in porcine form and in one instance showing a representative of the people chasing the "cursed animal" away (Figure 2). In Sade's novel, the pig's class affiliations are reversed, but the exclusionary logic to which he is subjected is identical—and the connection between Saint-Ange's boudoir and the Palais de l'Égalité, the birthplace of antiroyalist publications, becomes more apparent than ever.

Although Augustin is the only lower-class participant in the orgy, he is by no means the only person to meet with rigorous censure for violating

204 The Second Time as Farce

the libertines' superficially permissive, fundamentally restrictive norms governing speech and action.[69] Eugénie herself receives a notable slap on the wrist for unwittingly transgressing one unexpected libertine rule. Although she readily accepts every truism her masters dispense (e.g., the superiority of anal to vaginal sex, the delights of promiscuity and atheism, the invalidity of family ties), the girl is stunned when, immediately after the reading of *Yet Another Effort*, Dolmancé refuses to include her in one of his debaucheries. For the purposes of this particular affair, which Dolmancé, cagily forfeiting his "right to say everything," says is too disgusting to name, Augustin is summoned back into the boudoir only to leave again in the gentleman's company. "One must," Dolmancé declares ominously, "be alone and in the deepest shadow in order to give oneself over to such turpitudes" (*Philosophy* 348). Ignoring this warning, Eugénie volunteers to accompany the two men, only to be reprimanded by Dolmancé: "No, no, this is an *affaire d'honneur* and should take place between men only; a woman would only disturb us" (*Philosophy* 348). Quite clearly this dismissal recalls the pamphlet's assertion that "women must in no way figure in men's love." In this way, it reveals that women's liberty—which Saint-Ange and Dolmancé have already, anticipating the treatise's proclamation of feminine suffrage, decreed her birthright—is just as unstable in the libertine minisociety as it is in the pamphleteer's republic and in the treatise's Robespierrist counterpart. Up until her importunate request to join in Dolmancé and Augustin's private encounter, Eugénie has been the model initiate; her teachers have marveled at her unhesitating assimilation of all their principles and her aptitude in carrying out their orders. "Libertinage," she fervently declares, "is now my sole God, the unique rule of my conduct, the single basis of all my actions" (*Philosophy* 263). In a split second, though, her status in the boudoir changes from that of "good" citizen, as it were, to that of "bad" citizen—and the change is ratified by the very unitary principle ("libertinage") on which her behavior has without exception been based. With this sudden and arbitrary shift, Sade seems to me to be underscoring the contradictory, unreliable nature of the master-signifier around which sociopolitical and religious ideology is structured. Whether this signifier is designed to uphold libertine or Montagnard orthodoxy, whether it is a "God" of libertinage or of republican virtue, it can always be turned against its subjects, according to the whim of the person who has the power to pose as its spokesman. In Saint-Ange's love nest, Dolmancé and his hostess share that incontestable authority; the young girl, whose debauched father has sent her there to be "educated" by his friends, is indisputably in their hands. Well aware of her subordinate place in this sphere—"you will never have a more submissive scholar [than myself]," she assures Dolmancé (*Philosophy* 222)—Eugénie defers to her mentor's command, even though it contradicts both his own earlier instruction and that of the treatise.

In the next dialogue, Eugénie is encouraged to obey yet another male libertine, whose dictates likewise contradict the message of gender equality promulgated in *Yet Another Effort*, and not just in regard to the eager young pupil. This authority figure is the girl's father, Monsieur de Mistival, who sends a letter to the boudoir warning that his prudish wife is on her way to Saint-Ange's house to "rescue" Eugénie from the libertines' clutches. Although Mistival's foremost aim in the letter is to enjoin the group to punish his wife for meddling, he also consolidates their control over his daughter by urging them to corrupt Eugénie and by declaring that in so doing, "you will have labored in some sort on my behalf" (*Philosophy* 350). In this regard, the girl's father, whom Saint-Ange describes to her friends as a bona fide kindred spirit in libertinage, blatantly contradicts the dialogues' and the pamphlet's foregoing attacks on parental authority as an obstacle to both unrestricted pleasure (Dolmancé and Saint-Ange) and disinterested "republicanism" (*Yet Another Effort*). The letter also violates the treatise's clause that repudiates a husband's right to "monopolize" his wife's body, for it functions as a kind of *lettre de cachet* that assumes the right to dispose of Madame de Mistival as he and his surrogates see fit:

> I request you to punish her impertinence with exceeding rigor; yesterday, I chastised her for something similar: the lesson was not sufficient. Therefore, mystify her well, I beseech you . . . , and believe that, no matter what lengths you carry things to, no complaint [plainte] will be heard from me. . . . 'Tis a very long time this whore's been oppressing me . . . indeed. . . . Do you follow me? (*Philosophy* 350)

This elliptical missive recalls not only Dolmancé's parallel reluctance to "say everything" on the subject of his tryst with Augustin but also the blank *lettres de cachet* referenced in the last issue of *Le Vieux Cordelier*. The significance of the *lettre de cachet* in that text, as in this one, lies in the fact that the free-floating injustice of the Old Regime—the recourse to a private letter instead of to public legal channels—also informs Terrorist "justice." With its deconstruction of the private/public distinction and its readiness to condemn citizens for political or personal dealings, the Robespierrist regime's open-ended definition of the suspect makes everyone a potential target. In the same manner, Mistival's letter exploits the fundamental instability that inhabits the libertine system's concept of female freedom. Because Madame de Mistival wishes to interfere with the debauchery of the boudoir, her husband denounces her as a whore. The effect of this term is not simply to show how a conventionally "good" value (protecting a daughter's virtue) can be construed as "bad" in a different (libertine) context. More profoundly, it reveals the underlying malleability of the same term within a single framework and the utter contingency of how its valence is determined. Madame de Mistival is to be brutally punished as a whore, whereas other identically designated women are praised extensively in *Yet Another Effort* and the dialogues. The reason for this discrepancy lies entirely in the devout spouse's refusal to accept her husband's licentious principles as her own. Like Augustin, she is not, in the language of the republican text, "an individual who resembles us"; and like Augustin, she lacks the power to assert her alterity as valid.

That the relative strength of the libertines above all consists in brute force becomes evident as soon as Madame de Mistival bursts into Saint-Ange's inner sanctum. Aimed at coaxing Eugénie from this visibly dissolute venue, her expressions of religious piety and maternal concern meet with outright violence. The assembled crew holds her down and strips off her clothes, only to discover that Monsieur de Mistival's "lesson" of the day before has left her very badly injured. "I don't believe I've ever seen a body more mistreated than this!" Dolmancé cries joyfully (*Philosophy* 357). Inspired by their fellow libertine's example, the veterans of the boudoir begin fondling, prodding, and slapping their new prey and trump her protests with promises of more brutality:

MADAME DE MISTIVAL, *to Madame de Saint-Ange:* My God, where am I? Are you aware, Madame, of what you are allowing to be done to me in your house? Do you suppose I shall file no complaint?

MADAME DE SAINT-ANGE: It is by no means certain you will be able to.

MADAME DE MISTIVAL: Great God! Then I am to be killed here?

DOLMANCÉ: Why not?

MADAME DE SAINT-ANGE: ... Listen to me, you whore! You are a victim
   sent us by your own husband: you have got to submit to your fate; ...
   you are going to suffer. ... As for your cries, I warn you they will be to
   no purpose: one could slaughter a steer in this chamber without any
   risk of his bellowings being overheard. Your horses, your servants
   have already left; once again, my lovely, your husband authorizes what
   we are doing. ...

MADAME DE MISTIVAL: Merciful heavens! What an outrage!
   (*Philosophy* 356–57)

This exchange is highly suggestive for its juxtaposition of warring master-
signifiers. Against Madame de Mistival's invocations of secular and above
all divine justice—she addresses a god "merciful" enough to heed her
complaints—the libertines found the legitimacy of their actions in the
will of her "own husband." However, because the authority of the husband in general has been so extensively denigrated in their recent republican reading, the group's reliance on this as the basis for their actions
rings hollow indeed. The overt hypocrisy with which they rehabilitate a
man's authority over his wife is also the hypocrisy of the Robespierrists
rehabilitating a Supreme Being for the purposes of sociopolitical control.
Sade's diagnosis holds true in the one case as in the other: "the same
crude dogma [is] reconstructed in an inverted form." The disenfranchised husband of *Yet Another Effort* becomes an omnipotent guarantor
of libertine conduct, and the liberated "whore" of the treatise becomes a
desubjectivized victim with no means of making herself heard (an endangered "steer" corresponding to the reviled "great pig"). Across the
board, the ideological inversion is bolstered not by transcendental truth
but by sheer might.

   It nonetheless bears noting that Madame de Mistival's sufferings have
a clear linguistic basis, for her discursive touchstones are the very ones
that her captors are least inclined to tolerate. In this respect, Saint-Ange
and company are utterly faithful to the virulent atheism of *Yet Another
Effort*, which demands that "God ... be as naught" and which they reprise
in their harsh denigration of Madame de Mistival's beliefs. ("Implore
Him not, my dove," Dolmancé teases her while whipping her behind,
"He will remain deaf to your voice ... never has this powerful figure
bothered to entangle himself in an affair concerning merely an ass" [*Philosophy* 358].) They are faithful too—selectively so—to the tract's repudiation of the idea that parents should exert any influence on their children's

behavior. From the libertines' perspective, one of Madame de Mistival's greatest strategic errors consists in mentioning filial obligation and maternal concern as valid grounds for attempting to wrest Eugénie from their company. Dolmancé ripostes with disdain:

> And what, if you please, are these rights, Madame? Do you flatter yourself they are legitimate? . . . How can you expect [Eugénie] to be beholden to you today for your having discharged when years ago someone fucked your nasty cunt? Take notice, Madame: there is nothing more illusory than fathers' and mothers' sentiments for their children, and children's for the authors of their days. . . . Filial piety is a true chimera. . . . Pity, gratitude, love—not one of these sentiments is [your] due. (*Philosophy* 353–54)

Madame de Mistival is slow, however, to grasp her captors' utter disregard for the precepts that guide her conduct and her speech. As the tortures to which she is subjected become more excruciating, she persists in begging for special treatment from Eugénie: "Oh merciful heavens! . . . Eugénie, my beloved Eugénie, for the last time heed the supplications of her who gave you life!" (*Philosophy* 355); "Have pity upon me, I beg of you. . . . I . . . I am not well . . ." (*Philosophy* 359). The common denominator in these pleas, which Dolmancé also indirectly associates with the "chimera" of familial obligation, is pity. "In this world there is nothing dangerous," he cautions Eugénie right after the republican excursus, "except for pity. Let a keen observer calculate all of pity's dangers, and let him compare them with those of a staunch, resolute severity, and he will see [that] the former are greater" (*Philosophy* 340). In the logic of the libertines' minirepublic as in that of the Robespierrist state, severity must override pathos, because the latter engenders partiality in an arena where everyone should be equal, either to pursue one's self-interest like a Sadean libertine or to suppress one's self-interest like a Montagnard patriot. Pity can thus be understood as the affective equivalent of a filial or parental bond; as such, it threatens to introduce difference into a sphere that in theory requires absolute parity and sameness. These latter qualities are of course blatantly undermined by the libertine posse's very positioning of Madame de Mistival as someone whose perspective has no meaning, not to mention of Monsieur de Mistival as a Supreme Being who creates meaning for them. Nevertheless, the voiceless outlaw and the allegedly transcendental exemplar are two common, even constitutive, elements of Rousseauist and Robespierrist ideology. In its radical curtailment, the luckless mother's "right to say everything" corresponds directly to that of the social pact's outcasts and enemies.

Like Robespierre and his henchmen, the immoral instructors ultimately, as threatened all along, employ severe nonlinguistic measures to eradicate the language of difference definitively from their midst. And although flogging is certainly part of their repertoire—a recapitulation of the noblewoman's spanking by Jacobins in the Palais de l'Égalité (Figure 5)—they have far nastier humiliations in store for their victim. The libertines enumerate these measures in a mirthfully ironic improvisation of a trial, at which Dolmancé presides and which he opens by informing the defendant: "Must you not hear your sentence pronounced? Must it not be executed? Come, let's gather round our victim; let her kneel in the center of the circle and, trembling, hear what will be announced to her" (*Philosophy* 362). In a classic Terrorist conflation of speech and action, a stage direction in the dialogue announces that the libertines' various gory suggestions "*are pronounced while the characters are in full action*" (*Philosophy* 362; Sade's emphasis), culminating in Dolmancé's proposed grand finale:

> I have, waiting outside, a valet, and he is furnished with what is perhaps one of the loveliest members to be found in all of Nature; however, it distills disease, for 'tis eaten by one of the most impressive cases of syphilis I have yet anywhere encountered; I'll have my man come in: we'll have a coupling: he'll inject his poison into each of the two natural conduits that ornament this dear and amiable lady, with this consequence: that so long as this cruel disease's impressions shall last, the whore will remember not to trouble her daughter when Eugénie has herself fucked. (*Philosophy* 362)

Dolmancé's commands, like those of a Rousseauist legislator, are immediately realized: the syphilitic servant appears on the scene, he rapes Madame de Mistival vaginally and anally, and the rest of the company celebrates with some quick orgiastic couplings of their own. Madame de Mistival's message of mercy and piety, a poisonous element in the merciless and impious boudoir, is thus returned to her in the concretized, deadly form of the servant's disease. With this gesture, Sade's text performs another "negation of a negation": it shows how the republican antipathy to "corruption" itself takes the form of corrupt behavior. This black parody of revolutionary justice vividly realizes Saint-Just's dictum, "Nothing resembles virtue like a great crime." In this case, the "virtue" that is being upheld—Eugénie's sovereign right to "[have] herself fucked"—is quite obviously an inversion of the virtuous republican's "right" to sacrifice all personal desires to the general will. But the method by which the ironized right and its Terrorist model are sustained is structurally identical, with the sole difference that the members of the libertine tribunal, unlike those of the Revolutionary Tribunal, take the proceedings as a pretext for sexual gratification of their own.

Even with this punishment, however, Madame de Mistival's ordeal is not over; for her tormentors also resemble the Robespierrists in their conflation of undesirable discursive difference with sexual alterity. Whereas Madame de Saint-Ange has from the text's opening lines refused to be identified as a woman—"I am an amphibious creature, . . . I should like to combine every gender [tous les genres]" (*Philosophy* 187)— and Eugénie has followed suit by declaring her aversion to vaginal sex and her fondness for sporting a strap-on dildo,[70] the girl's mother is identified entirely, in the libertines' eyes, with her devalorized sexual organs. In yet another of the text's proto-Lacanian moments, Dolmancé presents the phallus as the ultimate guarantor of discursivity when he describes the penis to his pupil as "this member of which we shall be obliged to speak incessantly" (*Philosophy* 200).[71] "In [Sade's] schema," writes Angela Carter, "[the] vagina might be regarded . . . as a speaking mouth, but never one that issues the voice of reason."[72] Indeed, in contrast to Dolmancé's endlessly discourse-compelling penis—"the penis sublime," as another libertine puts it (*Juliette* 493)—the vagina emerges as the ultimate "unmentionable." Through her tireless mentions of maternal duty and affection, Madame de Mistival unfortunately encourages this association of female genitalia and unspeakable alterity,[73] which the libertines emphasize once and for all when they decide to sew her labia shut. This is the group's final exploit before the novel ends, and because Eugénie carries it out, it represents the completion of her libertine training, her internalization of mock-republican ideology. Lacan himself has interpreted this gruesome episode as a confirmation of Sade's own conformity to the Law—the law of castration, of the repression of maternal sexual difference necessary to the functioning of the symbolic order, and so forth.[74] In light of the novel's extensive allusions to the republican political context, however, the literal and figurative sealing of a dissident's lips can be understood not so much as an affirmation of (Robespierrist) symbolic law as a pointedly subversive parody of it. The reference becomes clearer still when Dolmancé notes with satisfaction as Eugénie puts the finishing touches on her embroidery: "Now everything has been said [tout est dit]" (*Philosophy* 366). Agonizing "between the two deaths," her vaginal lips bound together with thick red thread, the libertines' graphically silenced victim figures forth the flagrant limitations on free speech that sustain the Terror's promise of discursive totality. "Liberty? Never have people been less free. . . ."

Juliette's Story: One More Time, With(out) Feeling

In the libertine republic of late Sadean fiction, Justine and Juliette are "bad" and "good" citizens writ large. Fairy-tale sisters, one blond and one brunette, they are separated in their early adolescence when their father exposes the family to financial ruin, and both parents (so the girls are told) die of grief. They are dealt exactly the same lot—cast out into an unfeeling world without money or connections—but face their destiny in entirely different ways. Fair Justine is a stickler for virtue: her virginity, her Christian faith, and her immortal soul are her most valuable possessions. Even when she unwillingly loses the first of the three, she holds onto the other two in the face of endless tortures, betrayals, and humiliations, all meted out by people from whom she seeks love, protection, pity. A saint in mind if not in body, she remains a dogged martyr to probity right up to the day of her death, when the good Lord strikes her dead with lightning for no apparent reason. Raven-haired Juliette, by contrast, eagerly embarks upon a life of extravagant vice and licentiousness, turning society's moral bankruptcy to her advantage and loving every minute of it. She has no interest in God, charity, or chastity and in fact never finds greater delight than when she succeeds in trampling on these ludicrous "chimeras." Justine's tale is subtitled *The Misfortunes of Virtue;* Juliette's, *The Prosperities of Vice:* "They mutually reflect and supplement one another, like a pair of mirrors."[75] If Justine, who is perennially silenced by her tormentors and whose protests mean nothing to them,[76] is a younger and even more abject version of Madame de Mistival, then Juliette is Eugénie all grown up. Under the sway of no authorities and always prepared to cast off even her most useful accomplices, the wicked sister becomes the "good" citizen of Sade's topsy-turvy world by rejecting the general good, desecrating morality and religion, making false denunciations and carrying out unjust killings, and generally gratifying her desires at every turn. To revert one last time to

Hegelese: she is the negation of the negation that the prudish and devout Justine perpetrates against nature, sexuality, and cold, hard reason.[77] But she also, springing full-formed from Sade's quill less than three years after his "*national* detention," represents the Terror's own satanic double, a condemnatory reworking of the suppressions performed by the state in the name of communitarian virtue. Whereas Justine's plight had preoccupied Sade since his latter days in the Bastille and his first days of republican freedom,[78] Juliette is truly a child of her time—the Corruptible par excellence. Her great crimes *are* her great virtues, and she's not afraid to "say everything" as long as it means making a mockery of the tenets that the Robespierrists, and not just her sister, hold dear. At the same time, her ruthlessness also partakes of and casts in an ugly light the Terror's own foremost verity: that its totalizing pretensions in fact mask an all-consuming will to destruction. By parts collusion and critique, the doings of Sade's infamous heroine reflect and supplement those of the Terror itself.

As Annie Le Brun observes, *Juliette* is not only a fairy tale in which, "for the first time, a little girl comes into the world purely for her own pleasure"; it also may well be "the first fairy-tale narrated by the fairy herself."[79] Indeed, in formal terms *Juliette* differs from the other texts considered in this study in its deployment of a sustained first-person narrative voice. A writing "I" may occasionally intrude into *The Social Contract* or make itself heard in *Le Vieux Cordelier,* but in neither case does a specific, subjectively articulated perspective serve as the entire work's unifying thread. In *Juliette,* by contrast, a loose picaresque plot structure becomes the pretext for a detailed exposition of one woman's opinions and proclivities. Sade devotes over a thousand pages to cataloging his heroine's every dissolute urge, philosophical conviction, and sexual adventure. This libertine trinity—debauched desire, belief, and action—constitutes Juliette as above all a whirlwind of personal passion, a roving lone wolf with an insatiable appetite for adventure. Admittedly, her wanderings bring her into contact with many fellow "friends of crime" (also the name of a secret society for which she is recruited), each of whom relates his or her own debauched experiences and opinions to Juliette in elaborate detail. But because the penchants (e.g., vampirism, coprophagy) and rationalized biases (atheism, incest) put forth in these first-person monologues are always highly particularized, their cumulative effect is a dizzying *mise-en-abîme,* an infinite multiplication of the heroine's own multifaceted lusts. It should, moreover, not be missed that Juliette's first-person narrative encompasses these other singular viewpoints; in recounting them verbatim to her diegetic crew of listeners (of whom more in a moment), she regularly interrupts the stream of her "own" story and the continuity of her "own" narrative voice. The fact, however, is that at the level of both *récit* and *histoire*,[80] she folds all these other people's penchants into her own vast repertoire of vice. From Saint-Fond she learns to enjoy eating excrement, from Durand to appreciate the finer points of poison, from Minski to indulge in cannibalism, from Noirceuil to stimulate herself by placing birdseed on her genitals and allowing chickens to feed therefrom . . . and so on, ad infinitum. Directly reversing the movement of the Rousseauist/Robespierrist social contract, which absorbs the individual into the collective will, Juliette incorporates all these disparate and subjectivized voices into her own, becoming unto herself a discourse of virtually inexhaustible multiplicity. It is thus not without reason that of all the characters in his voluminous body of work, Sade reserves the epithet *unique* for Juliette alone.[81] The word connotes both radical singularity and absolute oneness; accordingly, our heroine stands as a single embodiment of endless variety. Even the deeply misogynistic libertine Belmor expresses admiration for our heroine's "lasciviousness, diversity, and energy" (*Juliette* 521).

Nonetheless, like the Terrorist totality whose structure she inverts, Juliette's expansiveness has its limits, and these are first and foremost designated in her narrative by the shadowy presence of the virtuous Justine. Significantly, the libertine sister's decision to tell her life's story is prompted by a chance encounter with the sister from whom she had separated after the parents' death and who at the end of *La Nouvelle Justine* crosses paths with Juliette on a remote country road near the latter's chateau. The perennially persecuted Justine has just escaped from prison, where she awaited capital punishment for a crime she did not commit, and is now staggering through the countryside in rags, tearfully wondering why her "fervid [prayers to] the Supreme Being" (*Justine* 401) have always gone unanswered. Juliette, meanwhile, is strolling in the same area with a group of men who are visiting her chateau for a pleasure party; she recognizes Justine as her sister and invites her back to the castle so that the girl might entertain them all with her wretched life's story. Ever dutiful, Justine relates the nonstop mortifications that have beset her since their parents' death, while Juliette and her houseguests listen with titillated interest. But although Justine—like Juliette after her—spins a first-person narrative brimming with sex and death, her "I" differs from her sister's in being a locus not of subjective preference but of alienated erasure. Instead of acknowledging its own desires, the ego of her *récit* and *histoire* presents itself as the mere instrument of other people's selfish caprice and/or of Providence's inscrutable will. In this respect, Justine fits the psychoanalytic profile of the pervert referenced in connection with Saint-Just's self-abnegating subject position. Like the young Montagnard and his mentor, Sade's virtuous maiden would recoil at the label, given her assiduous denial that personal inclination has ever played any role in her conduct. This denial, however, is the essence of perversion: like the self-sacrificing republican statesman or citizen, the pervert always claims to serve only the other. In keeping with this stance, Justine's very autobiographical narrative emanates not from a wish to open her heart but from the eager prompting of Juliette and her entourage. In contrast to her sister, Justine is a woman without qualities; her virtuous self-effacement causes her to blend with or bend to the will of those around her, thereby realizing the Terrorist subjective ideal just as surely as Juliette subverts it.

To a woman who lives to assert passionate selfishness, infinite heterogeneity, and active control over her own destiny, Justine's abject discourse represents a sorry excuse for existence. Her initial response to the younger woman's story is to proclaim axiomatically, "Heaven protects and rewards vice, while saddening virtue and laying it low" (*Justine* 405). Then, in order to illustrate this precept (itself a mocking inversion of Juliette's idea of heaven), she launches into her own autobiography. An immoral instruction manual unto itself, her narrative abounds in many more such truisms from which a less resolutely puritanical auditor than Justine might learn a great deal. (This would appear to be the hope of *Juliette*'s extradiegetic commentator/editor, who appends many a footnote to the heroine's monologues, encouraging women in particular to look to them for inspiration.)[82] Whatever her sister's own opinion in the matter, though, Juliette indicates from the outset that her libertinage "is not made for" Justine any more than the pseudorepublicanism of Saint-Ange's boudoir applies to Augustin and Madame de Mistival. Before beginning her narration, Juliette informs her audience that what she tells them will above all "persuade them that it is not without justification that Chabert and Noirceuil [two of the houseguests, who figure prominently in Juliette's tale] have often said that there are in the whole world few women as singular as I" (*Justine* 405–6). Her proclamation of feminine uniqueness implies an irreducible distinction between Juliette and her sister, who is the only other woman in the room and whose foregoing life's story—full of stereotypical feminine protestations against enjoying sex[83]—definitely confirms the divide. This divide is translated straightaway into markedly unequal seating arrangements, which Juliette orchestrates, in *La Nouvelle Justine*'s final lines, in preparation for her story. Sprawling out sultana-style on a loveseat, Juliette bids her male listeners recline on sofas, while the humble "Justine takes only a chair" (*Justine* 406). Emphasizing from the outset Justine's second-class citizenship *chez* Juliette, this interlude does not spoof a specific Terrorist practice so much as the elaborate, undemocratic seating rituals (reflective of significant power differentials) in the court of Versailles. Nevertheless, it foregrounds a certain degree of hypocritical reliance on old-school tyranny—Juliette peppers her yarn with feverish antimonarchical tirades—that sustains the libertine hostess's self-proclaimed singularity. Just as the Montagnards appropriate the Old Regime's "deific chimera" to further their despotism of liberty, so does Juliette institute inequality in her discursive domain as a prefatory illustration of her own despotic principles.

Her lowly seat, however, is the least of the virtuous maiden's concerns once the story gets underway. Although, not insignificantly, Justine receives almost no mention in the whole of *Juliette*, when Sade does describe her reactions to Juliette's tale, they reveal her utter shock and misery. Unlike Augustin, excluded from the boudoir and thus from the reading of Dolmancé's treatise, Justine is retained in her sister's "delicious salon" (*Justine* 405) and compelled to listen to her sister's depraved discourse. What the gardener's banishment and the prude's inclusion have in common, though, is the utter disregard for each person's wishes that the libertines' treatment of them reflects. Justine, for instance, has already told Juliette and her friends how painful the loss of their parents was, and still is, to her. Therefore, when her sister brightly reveals that their father had not died when they thought he had, but that he later tracked Juliette down and begged her for money, only to have his request refused, Justine is aghast:

"Great heaven!" cried the unhappy Justine. "My father lived and I knew him not? Dear God, had Thou but brought us together I would have been a comfort to him and soothed him in his distress, I would have shared with him the little I had and my sympathy might have compensated for the unkindness which, sister, he probably had to endure at your hands."

"My child," declared the marquis, all out of patience with Justine after the night he had spent with her, "if you are allowed the honor of being present at this gathering, it is not to afflict us by your jeremiads. Pray continue, Madame." (*Juliette* 466)

With protestations of this kind, which foreground religious belief, filial piety, and pathos, Justine reproduces Madame de Mistival's useless re-monstrances—and meets with the same kind of censure that the older woman endured in the boudoir. Juliette's friend the marquis wastes no time in silencing her and reminding her of her relative powerlessness in the libertines' midst. Additionally, this passage indicates rather omi-nously that Justine has had to do more than just listen to the discourse of dissolution; the remark that she has spent the night with the marquis suggests that she has also been forced to experience it in the real. Per-haps in punishment for a less than enthusiastic performance (it is rare that Juliette and her ilk are "all out of patience" after sex), Juliette com-pounds her sister's distress by announcing that she not only refused their father's request for charity but killed him, precisely because "pathos abounded in the wretch's [petition]" (*Juliette* 467). Before that, Juliette even seduced him—she laughingly tells of her "straying hands wander-ing up to the paternal legs to unbutton the paternal pantaloons and to fondle . . . the half-stiffened instrument that brought me into this world" (*Juliette* 471)—and got pregnant with his child, whom she carelessly aborted. "The scion of his excellency my esteemed father once dropped in the latrines, I came forth trimmer about the waist than ever before" (*Juliette* 523). Having already been chastened for speaking out, Justine is not shown to react to these additional horrendous reports: Sade's elision of her from the text parallels the censorship to which Juliette's friends subject the outsider's speech.[84] (In fact, Juliette's initial decision to aban-don her sister is provoked, at the beginning of *La Nouvelle Justine*, by the latter girl's unwillingness to "stifle [her] perfidious sentimentality" [34]; it is because Justine refuses to be silent on this score that Juliette leaves her to her own devices.) At the end of *Juliette*, the libertines will preside over Justine's physical death just as merrily as their counterparts in the *Philosophy in the Boudoir* orchestrate Madame de Mistival's downfall. But until then, Justine exists like the despised mother "between the two deaths," annihilated on a discursive level while awaiting her inevitable last agonies. In Rousseauist and Montagnard terms, she is *hors la loi*, cast outside the symbolic law that binds the rest of the community together. Justine's eventual murder will confirm this parallel by realizing quite literally some of the Terrorists' most memorable recommendations for the handling of outlaws. For the bulk of Juliette's narrative, however, her mute presence attests more subtly to the suppression of notions (pity, God, filial feeling) incompatible with the salon's predominant dogmas.

As in the *Philosophy in the Boudoir*, this uneven exercise of censorship appears to coexist unproblematically alongside the libertine characters' proclamations of complete sexual and discursive freedom: "philosophy must say everything [tout dire]" (*Juliette* 1193). For Juliette, such pronouncements surface more often than not in discussions of a political nature, and she demonstrates her immunity to the gender biases of Robespierrist dogma by spreading the gospel of republicanism to a number of extremely powerful men. Not content, like the victims of the Terror's misogyny, to bow out of political discussion and tend the hearth, our heroine travels far and wide, addressing everyone from Archduke Leopold (Marie Antoinette's brother and France's enemy during the Revolution) to Pope Braschi (burned in effigy by the Montagnards), on the subject of drastic societal reform. For her as for the author of *Yet Another Effort*, the end goal is a radically libertarian polity in which some citizens are nevertheless more equal than others.[85] In a nod, for example, to Desmoulins's qualification of Louis XVI as an "animal-king," Juliette informs Leopold that regicide is a valid measure, since a king is no different from a monkey (*Juliette* 617). The obvious effect of this statement is to downgrade Leopold's ontological status by drawing on the same terminology with which the Montagnards disenfranchised his brother-in-law. Echoing *Yet Another Effort*'s attack on both prerevolutionary and Robespierrist faith, Juliette commiserates with Belmor, the president of the Sodality of the Friends of Crime, about the problem of religious belief in France and concurs with his assessment that all nonatheists must die. To quote the exact recommendation, with its appropriation of a favorite Terrorist metaphor: "You don't confine yourself to severing one of the hydra's heads, it's the entire monster you must exterminate" (*Juliette* 500). The paradox of this particular metaphor is that when deployed by the likes of Robespierre, it emphasizes the explicit hatred of plurality behind his public policy. By contrast, the sodality to which Belmor and Juliette belong mirrors the latter's own much touted diversity of interests; its very first by-law "approves and legitimates everything [tout], and considers as [the Sodality's] most zealous and most estimable members those who, unhesitatingly and unrepentantly, acquit themselves of the greatest number of those vigorous actions fools in their weakness call crimes" (*Juliette* 418). Even this statute, however, draws on the logic of the Terror and so provides a loophole by which Juliette's or the Sodality's hydralike heterodoxy holds more validity than, say, the diversity of religious thought. In the language of the Sodality's by-laws, an individual's actions enjoy unrestricted freedom as long as they are unhesitating, unrepentant, and vigorous—"prompt, severe, and inflexible," to quote Robespierre's recipe for revolutionary morality. Like republican virtue, libertine crime is a totalizing principle—it "approves and legitimates everything"—as long as it remains based in unmediated action and in the pitiless extermination of its would-be detractors.

The dilemma that such a system poses to Juliette, despite her zealous preaching and practice of unfettered criminality, is that women themselves are invariably considered obstacles to its realization, even when they are not pious and virginal like Justine. The Sodality of the Friends of Crime, Juliette learns upon joining it, has very different rules for its male and female partners in debauchery, with the women explicitly ranked below men in terms of prestige and power. (Most notably, and humorously, only the men who attain leadership roles in the sodality enjoy the privilege of literally having their asses kissed by the female members: the women always remain on the subservient side of this relationship.) The sodality's president declares "the inferiority of females to males [to be] established and patent" (*Juliette* 506) and traces this shortcoming to women's intrinsic predisposition to—what else?—sentimentality and mercy. In an effort to help would-be libertine women overcome this essential flaw, the statutes intended for the sodality's female membership address the problem head on:

> Let a very hardened heart be her protection against an emotional sensi-
> tivity/sentimentality [sensibilité] which is certain to be her undoing; a
> woman susceptible of sympathies must expect nothing but the worst,
> for [being] weaker, more delicate, thinner-skinned than men, she will be
> rent much more cruelly by all that assails this sensibility; whereupon she
> may bid all pleasure farewell. (*Juliette* 435)

This passage's essentializing presuppositions notwithstanding, it at least
holds out the possibility that a woman could cultivate "a very hardened
heart": a guarantor and a badge of the apathetic stance required by the
Sodality. But not all Juliette's interlocutors, or even all her fellow Friends
of Crime, share this hope; President Belmor himself sees the libertine
woman as a contradiction in terms and admiringly draws the Sodality
members' attention to societies where men exercise "the right to life
and death" (*Juliette* 508) over women. (It is most likely not by sheer
happenstance that one of the peoples to whom he attributes this sexist
variation on Rousseau's great theme is the "people of Rome"—also the
preferred exemplum of Montagnards like Saint-Just.) Even Juliette's closest friend, Clairwil, and her first libertine mentor, Noirceuil, admonish
her more than once for her own proclivity to engage in her transgres-
sive activities "enthusiastically" instead of "calmly, deliberately, lucidly"
(*Juliette* 475), "in cold blood" (*Juliette* 450). They caution that her impassioned approach to crime—the very sort of approach that Sade proposes in his letter to Bernis—could at the limit degenerate into irrational-
ity or even "the virtuous impulse" (*Juliette* 450), when what libertinage
requires is on the contrary "a very chilly heart" (*Juliette* 475). Juliette
herself takes offense at these caveats, reminding her friends of her track
record of ruthless behavior and assuring them accordingly: "Had you
somewhat more carefully observed my comportment . . . of late, you
would not, I am sure, have formulated these criticisms" (*Juliette* 476).
The gauntlet, however, has been thrown down. In all her subsequent
shenanigans, especially those in which Clairwil or Noirceuil play a part,
she ostentatiously refrains from "relent[ing] in [their] presence" (*Juliette* 449). The tension between Juliette's wish to be recognized as a hard-
hearted evil-doer and the world's propensity to perceive women quite
otherwise will persist for the remainder of her crime-ridden bildungsroman and will in fact lead Juliette paradoxically to emulate her sister,
Justine, in adopting other people's desires as the basis for her conduct.

In light of this tension, Sade's decision to recount his catalog of criminal activities from Juliette's point of view does more than just challenge the Terrorist premise that women are too emotional to be capable of rigorous virtue (the libertine counterpart being, again, unremitting vice). The first-person female narration provides an additional, ironic dimension to this critique by dramatizing the discrepancies between how Juliette sees herself (i.e., a libertine and a criminal as "good" as any other) and how she *sees others seeing her*. The latter occurrence is a quintessential instance of ideological "quilting" *(captionnage),* the moment when the subject realizes the exact contours of the place that she is assigned to occupy in a given symbolic network—a place determined not by the subject herself but by the system that preexists and encompasses her.[86] Precisely because Juliette does not, at least for the first part of her *récit* and *histoire,* accede to the truth value of the misogynist ideology with which she is constantly coming into contact, her references to her colleagues' displays of sexism take on a subtly laconic edge. For example, when she interrupts her storytelling to show her audience an old copy of the aforementioned *Instructions to Women Admitted into the Sodality of the Friends of Crime,* she remarks dryly: "I have kept the paper, for it is interesting. Listen to its contents" (*Juliette* 431). With this understated introduction, Juliette invites her listeners to remark upon the discrepancy between what the *Instructions* say about her and what she has already said about herself (the blithe seduction and murder of her father being just one of the incidents that precede her induction into the Sodality). The discrepancy, of course, makes Juliette's sexist naysayers look ridiculous, as they do in another "interesting" incident she describes. Arriving at a wild orgy in a monastery, Juliette and her female companion attempt, knowing the sodomite predilections of the priests, to "make their asses available to all comers" (*Juliette* 494), only to meet with "cold glances" and the following rebuff:

> "You've nothing to offer us that would recompense infidelity on our part," they told us: "even were you to avail us of the shrine wherein we perform our customary sacrifices, there would yet be that other altar whose mere presence nearby is sufficient to defeat any attempt at homage. *Contrive what she will, however she turn, / A woman can be naught but a woman.*—Martial." From others we had a friendlier greeting, but to what trouble we had to go merely to stiffen their antique instruments! What ministrations, what lewd attentions! (*Juliette* 494)

Initially, Juliette retains her tone of neutrality, quoting the insulting epigram from Martial (another Roman authority) without commenting on it. She exacts her revenge, though, by indicating that the priests who disdained her charms were barely even capable of maintaining stiffened instruments. We detect here, between the lines, the same sort of indignation that Desmoulins expresses when sketching for his readers a shocking comparison between himself—his freedom of speech restricted by the government—and his British counterparts. "And I, a Frenchman, I, Camille Desmoulins, should not have as much freedom as an English journalist?" For the lusty Juliette, capable of having sex with dozens of people at once for days on end, all the while engaging in vigorous beatings, slayings, and other tortures, the quasi-impotent priests' denigration of her sexual pedigree is downright ludicrous. In a wider sense, Juliette's irony can be understood to critique any ideology of freedom, be it libertine or Terrorist, that founds itself on a theory of sexual inequality.

One of the problems with ideology, however, is its tendency to become a self-fulfilling prophecy, to absorb those individuals who are most critical of its dictates.[87] Such is the case for Juliette herself, perhaps not coincidentally, shortly after these illuminating brushes with sexual discrimination. Juliette has been living with a prominent minister in the French government, the evocatively named Saint-Fond,[88] who harbors a scheme to destroy the bulk of the country's population through war and famine, sacrificing them to his "Being-Supreme-in-Nastiness" (*Juliette* 399). In keeping with his own and his deity's Montagnard nomenclature, he echoes the party's anti-individualistic rhetoric to justify his intentions: "I have for a long time had the profound conviction that individuals can be of no account to the politician. . . . All the power resides in the sovereign" (*Juliette* 479). In the true interest of the general will, he argues, the weak and the stupid (who by his reckoning constitute at least two-thirds of all Frenchmen) must not be spared; the "right to death" must be exercised to spare the body politic any sap on its energy. (Like his namesake Saint-Just, Juliette's lover is preoccupied with an anthropomorphized nation's manly vigor.) When first apprised of her lover's scheme—an extreme version of the Terrorist "*decreation*" about which Sade complained to Bernis—Juliette responds: "Believe me, Saint-Fond, to all the principles you have just settled I adhere most cordially" (*Juliette* 481), and they drop the subject for the time being. But not long after the priests' dismissal of her on the grounds of gender and Belmor's lengthy speech to the sodality about how "the human female is no more than an animal" (*Juliette* 513), Juliette suddenly has a change of heart. In fact, the change follows on the heels of an actual prophecy that she receives from a sorceress—"*When vice doth cease, woe betide*" (*Juliette* 531)—and occurs when Saint-Fond, again raising the topic of the genocide, informs her that she will be charged with carrying it out: "I—yes, I confess it: corrupt to the core though I was, the idea made me shudder; O thou, the fatal start I gave, what wert thou not to cost me! Little impulse, why could I not have suppressed thee? Saint-Fond caught it . . . and went away without a word" (*Juliette* 549). The cruel minister's response to this hesitation is, again pace Robespierre, prompt, severe, and inflexible to say the least. Within a matter of hours, Juliette receives a note from a mutual friend of hers and Saint-Fond's, warning her that because her shudder betrayed an inherently weak and merciful nature, she must flee the country to escape the man's wrath. Furthermore, Saint-Fond will see to it that all her ill-gotten riches are confiscated, and none of her friends will speak to her anymore; from the point of view of the libertine community, she is—again to use the Rousseauist expression—*hors la loi*. "A bolt of lightning," she informs her listeners as she recalls these grim tidings, "would have smitten me less cruelly" (*Juliette* 550). Confronted with her lover's virulent repudiation of sentiment and error, Juliette now finds herself cast in the role of the pathos-bearing feminine victim evoked by Carlyle in his account of Louis's trial: "Poor Nymph-Semele, . . . [the] next moment not Semele, but flame and a statue of red-hot ashes! France has looked upon democracy. . . ." In the blink of an eye, Juliette has gone from an invincible virago to a defeated, disenfranchised woman on the receiving end of sublime Terrorist ire. Saint-Just's "lightning bolt that strikes the wicked" becomes a lightning bolt with which his namesake annihilates the virtuous.

An abrupt departure from everything she has ever believed in, Juliette's unwitting conversion to victimized virtuousness is all the more striking in that she conceives of it quite explicitly as a return of the repressed. Specifically, the repressed material that has returned to her psyche after years of conscious banishment is none other than the value system and person of her long-lost sister, Justine. While cowering in bed and contemplating the error of her ways, she narrates:

> I [fell asleep and] had a troubling dream: in it I saw a fearful figure
> putting a torch to my belongings, . . . to everything I owned: all was afire

and in the midst of it a young creature stretched out her arms to me, sought desperately to save me, and in the attempt perished herself in the flames. I awoke all asweat, and [recalled] the sorceress' prediction: *when vice doth cease, woe shall betide*. O Heaven, I cried in my heart, I stopped at being vicious for a fleeting instant, I shuddered at a proposed horror; misfortune is about to engulf me, it is sure. The woman I saw in my dream, she is the sister, the unregenerate and sad Justine with whom I fell out because she was bent on taking the virtuous way; she appeals to me, and in my heart vice falters. Fatal prognostic! (*Juliette* 549)

We might begin to parse this dense incident by noting that the very fact of dreaming attests to the dramatic change that Juliette has undergone. Sadean libertines, as I mentioned earlier following Marcel Hénaff, are by no means known for their psychological depth: their "individuality," such as it is, shines forth in their pet perversions and uncommon appetites, not in their refined self-reflectivity or complicated emotions. A dream, however, attests to at least some degree of psychic complexity— to a capacity for reserved or ambivalent thought, which is precisely what Saint-Fond cannot forgive in his mistress. (In a Freudian paradigm, her involuntary shudder is just as expressive as those other classic mines of psychic insight, the dream and the parataxis; it represents precisely the kind of unconscious error against which the Montagnards, in their attempt to cleanse the citizenry of all personal associations and reserves, militate so vigorously.)[89] If we recall, moreover, Desmoulins's politically loaded mention of the reverie deemed "suspect" under Augustus, the parallel between Juliette and a Terrorist suspect—a parallel already highlighted by the accumulation of Montagnard rhetoric and dogma in Saint-Fond's fateful scheme—becomes clear indeed. Above all, though, it is the content of Juliette's dream and her response to it that solicit our attention. The flames that consume Juliette's possessions and ultimately destroy Justine recall the metaphorical lightning bolt of Saint-Fond's/ Saint-Just's merciless violence, not to mention the torch brandished by Robespierre at the Festival of the Supreme Being. Because both Juliette and Justine fall victim to this force, they are for the moment aligned together on the powerless side of a differend enforced by those who, as Juliette's own interpretation of the dream suggests, have no tolerance for "the virtuous way." The similarity between the two sisters even manifests itself in Juliette's unprecedented invocation of the heavens, a gesture that confirms her as a partner in Justine's discursive disenfranchisement.

Nevertheless, it is the latter girl alone who perishes in the fires of un-remitting reprisal, a fact that is perhaps not lost on Justine as she listens to the dream narrative, forbidden though she may be from expressing her thoughts on the matter.

This fact is also not lost on Juliette, for whom the vision of Justine's death by fire functions as a deterrent to any further lapses into human-itarianism and a stern reminder not to infuse libertine ideology with her own impassioned deviations. Just as the Montagnards hoped that the fearsome spectacle of Louis Capet's severed head would prevent his potential allies from acting against the republic, so does our heroine's dream prompt her to steel her heart forevermore against the suspect temptations of clemency and feeling. Having narrowly escaped her own death—Noirceuil's letter enables her to emigrate from France before Saint-Fond can mete out her punishment—she intends to take no more chances:

> Come now, take hold of yourself, . . . I said to myself; I have learned from my youthful errors. O fatal virtue! Thou tricked me once; never fear, I'll never again come under thine execrable sway. Only one fault have I committed, only once have I slipped, and it was an infernal impulse to probity that tripped me. Let's now snuff it out forever within us, virtue is man's mortal enemy, capable of procuring him nothing but his doom; and the greatest mistake which can be made in a completely corrupted world is to want to put up a lonely fight against the general contagion. And, great God, how often have I told this to myself! (*Juliette* 550)

With this monologue, which the closing line suggests has been her mantra from the time of her nightmare up till the present day, Juliette declares her fidelity to those ruthless principles preached even and especially by her misogynistic detractors. Speaking in the Terrorist language of Saint-Fond, she performatively "snuffs out" human kindness in herself by de-claring it null and void. Furthermore, she describes a significant turning point in the motives behind her libertinage. In the early part of her ca-reer, Juliette had indulged her criminal appetites as an unabashed ex-pression of individuality: she rejoiced, for instance, in her parents' death because it freed her to do as she wished. But now she conceives of her viciousness as a necessary concession to what we might call a general-will-in-nastiness: individual feelings, even those she has previously chan-neled into feats of extreme corruption, have no place in the "general contagion" of dispassionate malevolence. Acting in accordance with this epiphany, Juliette proceeds consciously and systematically to sever any bond of sentiment that could, in that paradoxical libertine/Terrorist way, compromise a worldview based on apathetic abstraction. She marries a man, Monsieur de Lorsange, so that she can murder him; she wins people's confidence in order to enhance the betrayal when she kills them; she even conspires with her friend Clairwil to push their beloved accomplice Olympe (perhaps a stand-in for Robespierre's sworn feminist enemy, Olympe de Gouges?) into a volcanic crater, only to poison Clairwil soon afterward. Apart from Lorsange, in fact, almost all the people Juliette murders after her formative nightmare are women; the preponderance of female victims in the second half of her narrative attests quite graphically to the masculinist underpinnings of her newfound apathy. In this very vein, in one of the last episodes she describes to her listeners, Juliette sends for the daughter she bore by Monsieur de Lorsange and joins her old chum Noirceuil, himself an unabashed "hater of cunts," in roasting the girl alive. That the young girl just happens to be named Marianne (the allegory of the French nation first devised by the *conventionnels* in September 1792)[90] once again lends a more directly political resonance to Juliette's cruelties. Like the exponentially increasing violence of the Terror, which led in fact to the Robespierrists' own demise and in popular satire to the execution of the executioner himself (Figure 4), Juliette's trajectory toward perfect insensibility culminates in the extermination of her own flesh and blood. In the case of both the Montagnards' fratricide and Juliette's infanticide, the underlying principle is the same: self-destruction on an epic scale, and self-destruction that equates the dangers of pity with those of femininity.

When Juliette's story comes to a close, there nevertheless remains one feminine suspect whose presence betrays a chink in the protagonist's armor, who embodies the persistence of family ties in particular and of goodness and light in general. That unlucky suspect is, no surprise here, the hapless and long-suffering Justine. Because Juliette has finished speaking, it is now a third-person narrator who lays the groundwork for the unlucky sister's demise, finally describing the girl's reaction to the atrocities she has been forced to hear: "The tears which had just wet our unhappy Justine's cheeks . . . her sorrowing mien, the afflictions it told of; her native timidity, that touching virtuousness shadowed in all her features, everything about her incensed [the company], who must absolutely submit this luckless creature to their filthy and ferocious caprices" (*Juliette*

1189). Although the new narrator's tone evinces sympathy for the wholesome Justine and disgust with her wicked companions, the juxtaposition between the two moral codes in fact accentuates yet again the unchallenged dominance of vice over virtue: the former's will to subjugate the latter is described as inexorable, absolute. As in the *Philosophy in the Boudoir,* the libertines' relative power in a material sense (Justine is essentially a prisoner in Juliette's chateau, and like Madame de Mistival has no means of escape) enables them quite easily to "submit this luckless creature to their... ferocious caprices." They justify their destructive scheme in terms of Justine's discursive and ontological incompatibility with their group—"Madame de Lorsange refuse[s] to keep such a prude under her roof" (*Juliette* 1189)—but they also conclude that mere symbolic exclusion will not sufficiently punish their foe. Like the initiates of Saint-Ange's boudoir and the Robespierrist government, they resort to extralinguistic means to purge their community of unassimilable difference. Observing that a terrible storm is brewing outside, they decide to place Justine at the mercy of the elements; so they strip her of her clothes and possessions and unceremoniously turn her out of the castle, "bewildered [and] humiliated by so many abominations, ... but murmuring thanks to God" (*Juliette* 1190) for having spared her a still harsher fate. Notwithstanding this devout thanksgiving, as soon as Justine reaches the edge of the estate, "she is struck down, smitten by a lightning bolt that pierces her through" (*Juliette* 1190). Lightning, the recurring Terrorist figure for justice, here extinguishes the voice of piety and pity once and for all. What is more, as if deliberately targeting the two sites on Justine's body most closely associated with her alterity, the blast from above "enter[ed] by way of the mouth [and] had burst out through the vagina" (*Juliette* 1190). Justine's symbolic death, effected inside the chateau by the silence imposed on her protests, now achieves its physical manifestation in an appropriately brutal manner. In accordance with the dream that prompted Juliette to "snuff [virtue] out forever" within her own heart, Justine herself is snuffed out for having refused to stifle such leanings. Thus, paraphrasing Robespierre, we might say that libertines "do not issue verdicts, they throw lightning bolts ... they hurl their enemies into nothingness."

Needless to say, Juliette and her friends are ecstatic at this turn of events and make vicious fun of the prayer that preceded Justine's death. With shouts of laughter they encourage one another to "contemplate heaven's handiwork" and "praise . . . God" (*Juliette* 1190), thereby retroactively negating Justine's moral code and emphasizing instead that God is less a font of love and mercy than a Being-Supreme-in-Nastiness. As one last mocking affront to their victim and her belief system, they join together in violating her corpse, subjecting it to an uproarious orgy before abandoning it in a ditch. For Juliette, this episode represents definitive proof of her libertinage—"oh, these late events are most welcome, they consecrate my happiness and perfect my tranquillity" (*Juliette* 1191)—and enables her to rest secure in the knowledge that true freedom resides in cold-bloodedness alone. The political resonances of this lesson become clear enough when, immediately following the gang rape of Justine's dead body, Juliette's lover Noirceuil receives a letter from Paris informing him that he is "to assume the reins of the government" (*Juliette* 1193). He offers everyone present high-ranking posts in his new regime, reserving for Juliette the special but structurally subordinate position of unofficial adviser in all affairs. "From this," Noirceuil announces amid general rejoicing, "I foresee nothing but happiness accruing to all—save only virtue" (*Juliette* 1193); and this is the happy ending with which Sade concludes his parodic fairy tale. The distinctly serious point of all this, however, is that like the Terrorists' republic of virtue, the libertines' new republic of vice is to be based on one constitutive exclusion, which its leaders will stop at nothing to preserve. Although their reign, marked from its inception by gleeful necrophilia, is not likely to share the sanctimonious and humorless qualities that Sade deplores in Robespierre, France's fictitious new heads of state will remain true to the Incorruptible's fundamental principle of restrictive totality. Happiness will indeed accrue to all—save only those who, in their effeminate dissent, call forth the lightning bolt of doctrinaire apathy. *Justine est morte, vive Juliette. . . .*

EPILOGUE

The Revolution Eats Its Children

> "You charlatan," Juliette said to him with feigned naïveté, "you speak out against the drugs that you yourself are distributing."
> —D.-A.-F. de Sade, *Juliette, or the Prosperities of Vice*

> Do we have to look that far for examples?
> —Camille Desmoulins, *Le Vieux Cordelier*

On March 16, 1793, aghast at the increasing violence of his Montagnard rivals' policy recommendations, the Girondin politician Pierre Vergniaud sounded a note of alarm on the Convention floor: "Citizens, we now have cause to fear that the Revolution, like Saturn successively devouring his children, has finally given way to despotism and all the calamities that despotism implies."[1] Like the contemporary image of the Terror's executioner guillotining himself (Figure 4), this memorable figure of speech emphasizes the self-destructive turn taken by revolutionary politics under Robespierre's rule. In addition to highlighting the internecine nature of the purges, Vergniaud's image aptly evokes a violent absorption of plurality into unitary control, of the different into the same.[2] As I have tried to demonstrate in the foregoing chapters, such an absorptive maneuver characterizes precisely the Terror's approach to both politics and language. "To say everything for the safety of the nation": Saint-Just's lofty pledge in fact contains, Saturn-like, the seeds of its own undoing. Why? Because the promise of discursive totality is constitutively undermined by the definition the Montagnards, following Rousseau, attached to national interest. To preserve the general will as abstract emptiness, the self-proclaimed despots of liberty, in keeping with their own paradoxical moniker, had to subject all particular content to the very "calamities that despotism implie[d]." Whether this particularity manifested itself politically, discursively, or even sexually—and these three possibilities are, of course, by no means mutually exclusive—it found itself condemned to the garbage heap of alleged counterrevolution. But as Saturn and the Robespierrists alike learned the hard way, a single, totalizing principle can never definitively curtail the proliferation of difference, because the former and the latter are indissolubly conjoined.[3] At the level of language, Terrorist sublimity invariably, and in spite of itself, assumes the form of a "Terror that speaks": language does not lose its linguistic properties simply by declaring a hearty aversion to them. Perhaps it was due at least in part to the Montagnards' disavowal of this basic insight that their revolution ended by devolving, in Marx's famous diagnosis, into tragedy.[4] Or again, as Vergniaud suggested: The Revolution turned into tragedy because it devoured its children, literally and figuratively speaking.

This travesty of free expression has important implications well beyond the historical milieu in which it came to pass. However distant or inconceivable that period's militant politics and overactive guillotine may seem to us today, the fact is that twenty-first-century America has a bit more in common with late eighteenth-century France than any of us might like to admit. On the broadest societal level, the increasingly normalized rules of "politically correct" speech, though commendably designed to establish a more inclusive and less prejudicial discursive environment for all, impose restrictive parameters on permissible discussion and debate.[5] In the world of literary academe, the explosion of interpretive possibilities brought about by the post-structuralist revolution of a few decades ago has given way to a distinct *renfermement* in the range of approaches available to the contemporary scholar. Literary-critical discourse now largely stigmatizes ciphers like "de Man" and "deconstruction," to give two notable examples, and the ostensibly apolitical or politically suspect notion of the signifier's 'free play' has largely been replaced by an at times essentializing promotion of historical referentiality as the gateway to right-minded cultural analysis.[6] To get at the "truth" of a particular author, movement, or trend (this argument runs), it is far better to focus on "material conditions," far more helpful to consider "historical actuality" than the rhetorical or figural mechanisms of the text as such. "Nobody 'does' literature anymore," an old professor of mine from Harvard recently disclosed to me with a sigh, taking stock in a paradigm shift that has rendered her old-school semiotic orientation all but obsolete. Indeed, in today's intellectual climate "doing literature" often brands the doer as an academic suspect insofar as it seems to constitute a denial of history or an evasion of politics—and thus an affront to liberal thought itself.[7]

In response to any perceived incompatibility between literary and historical analysis, the goal of this book has thus been to lay bare the problems that underpin this opposition by emphasizing the political consequences that a deep-seated ambivalence toward textual and intellectual difference is capable of engendering. The unorthodox linguistic and philosophical positions adopted by Desmoulins and Sade, for instance, demand our attention because they posed such rigorous challenges to the dominant discourse, which, while promising to "say everything," in fact promoted a reductively homogenizing approach to self-expression. From a historical perspective, the most significant achievement of these two authors can be held to reside in their courageous affirmation of personal, political, and rhetorical difference as vital components of what the journalist called "a republic that *everyone* could adore." Conversely, their Terrorist opponents' most glaring philosophical shortcoming might be understood to consist in their refusal to think figuratively, to appreciate the expansiveness that figural or differential language could have brought to a discursive space that otherwise failed truly to reflect all its constituents' voices. It should by no means be overlooked, moreover, that Robespierre's enemy Vergniaud diagnosed the Montagnard fury for destruction with a metaphor. From Louis XVI's trial onward, did the Girondins not incite their rivals' hatred by countering the Montagnard demand for sublime immediacy with a labor of reading and interpretation? Was the putting into discourse of difference not the greatest perceived threat to the "republic one and indivisible"? Along these lines: I recently joined a walking tour of Paris led by a guide who, coming upon one stately *hôtel particulier,* explained that in the late eighteenth century it was inhabited by an elderly noblewoman no longer able to see or hear. Under the Law of Prairial, this woman was hauled before the Revolutionary Tribunal and sentenced to death for being *blind and deaf to the demands of republican justice.* This anecdote represents the Terror's literalism at its worst. The word and the thing, the rhetorical figure and the referential "truth" collapse into one another, and all tolerance for human difference disappears. In this respect Citizen Louis Sade was right: another effort still had to be made, in the mid-1790s, if his countrymen wished to establish once and for all the radical political and discursive liberties that the Revolution originally promised to everyone. "However much nature may shudder," concluded his Terrorist antiheroine Juliette, "philosophy must say everything." Similarly, another effort remains to be made today if literary criticism is to constitute itself as a field that—however much its irreducibly diverse specialists may shudder—actually says everything.

By the same token, the alternative toward which I am gesturing here should not be understood as a naïvely utopian response to the naïve Terrorist utopia, echoed today by a certain strain of Habermasian critic, that promises unproblematically transparent, "unbroken" communication for all. My allusion to academics' methodological infighting is in this regard intended as a negation of a negation: the presentation not just of a problem (i.e., the devalorization of particular scholarly voices) but also of an admittedly imperfect solution, a potential remedy located at the very root of the ailment. One of the Terror's crucial lessons is that universal agreement—a discourse of totality—is structurally impossible and that any attempt to enforce such an ideal represents at best an illusion and at worst a brutal violation of every subject's unassimilable alterity. Without even invoking Levinas's ethics or Lacanian psychoanalysis, both of which can be taken as extended meditations on the fundamental impossibility of closing the gap between self and other (Levinas) or within the symbolic order itself (Lacan), the case can easily be made that disagreement and mutual misunderstanding are necessary by-products of unrestricted intersubjective exchange. Transposed into the sphere of literary and/or cultural studies, a model of this kind might be as salutary as it is commonsensical, with the old cliché about "agreeing to disagree" becoming an ethical principle borne of structural as well as practical necessity. If we academics find ourselves respectfully divided by our "antagonisms," in the apt terminology of Ernesto Laclau and Chantal Mouffe,[8] we are in fact practicing freedom of expression at the highest level and in the greatest good faith. Rather than seek to impose a template of unilateral validity ("everyone's 'doing' cultural studies these days"; or "it's high time we returned to a formalist appreciation of the text 'in itself'"), we might, learning from the Montagnards' mistakes,

resist the temptation to organize our interactions around a single valorized principle.[9] Precisely because moral and political categories are as
malleable as the words that constitute them, today's "good" citizen may
very well be tomorrow's bad apple, and vice versa. Like Rousseau, I am of
course neither a prince nor a legislator and thus am in no way qualified
to advocate the antagonistic model as a feasible strategy for sweeping
sociopolitical change.[10] However, in the relatively controlled environment of the academy, it seems to me that an enhanced awareness of the
conflicts necessarily produced by our principal medium and object of
study—language—might at least engender tolerance where consensus
is lacking. An embattled department, conference panel, or editorial
meeting may never become a discursive space that everyone can adore.
Surely, though, to remain mindful of our colleagues' and our own limitations as speaking subjects, we might make yet another effort—and try
a little tenderness.

Notes

Prologue: The Revolution Is Frozen

1. Camille Desmoulins, *Le Vieux Cordelier,* ed. Pierre Pachet (Paris: Belin, 1987), 113.

2. Maximilien Robespierre, "Sur les principes de morale politique . . . ," in Claude Mazauric, ed., *Écrits* (Paris: Messidor/Éditions sociales, 1989), 301.

3. As Hegel comments in the *Phenomenology of Spirit,* trans. A. V. Miller (Oxford: Oxford University Press, 1977), under the Terrorist general will, "all that remains of the [citizen] . . . is solely [an] *abstract* existence" (360; Hegel's emphasis); this principle effects the erasure of all "inwardness of intention" (360) proper to the individual as such.

4. Kantian morality and sublimity, both characterized as categorical, noncontingent phenomena, are discussed further in chapter 1.

5. Maximilien Robespierre, "Sur les principes du gouvernement révolutionnaire," in Mazauric, ed., *Écrits,* 304.

6. These just are a few of the post-structuralist truisms to which I alluded above. I discuss these aspects of language—as understood not just by twentieth- and twenty-first-century literary critics but by the Terrorists themselves—at greater length throughout this study. As a basic introduction to these concepts, however, I refer the uninitiated reader to Jacques Derrida's notion of "differance," a view of language as necessarily unstable and constantly in flux. In very simple terms, Derrida's insight is that language always "differs" from itself in both space and time. On the spatial level, there are, for instance, physical differences between a word and the thing it designates as well as ontological "spaces" between different interpreters and interpretations of the same text. On the temporal level, even when I say something "directly" to you, there opens up a temporal gap between my utterance of a word and your aural perception of it; and still greater temporal divisions separate, say, the eighteenth-century author of a text from its twentieth-century reader. See Jacques Derrida, "Differance," in *Margins of Philosophy,* trans. Alan Bass (Chicago: University

of Chicago Press, 1982). In this crucial respect, my approach contests that of Alexis de Tocqueville, who in *The Old Regime and the French Revolution*, trans. Stuart Gilbert (Garden City: Doubleday, 1955), describes the revolutionaries' intellectual and ideological orientation—derived from *philosophes* such as Rousseau—as "abstract, literary politics" (138). Whereas this qualification implies an equivalence between abstraction and literary language, my reading of "literary" or figural language (which, following not only Derrida but also Rousseau himself, I equate with language in general) emphasizes its differential, particularizing nature, its capacity to disrupt the *soi disant* stable and unitary categories of "abstraction." For Rousseau's maxim, expressed in the *Essay on the Origin of Languages*, that "the first language was figural," see chapter 1.

7. Marc-Éli Blanchard, "The French Revolution: Political Line or Language Circle," in Jacques Ehrmann, ed., *Yale French Studies* 39: *Literature and Revolution* (1967), 68; translation modified.

8. Laurent Jenny, *La Terreur et les signes: Poétiques de rupture* (Paris: Gallimard, 1982), 16.

9. For an analysis of the Terror as "a concept of power that consciously makes use of fear" and violence as tools for political domination, see Bronislaw Baczko, "The Terror before the Terror?" in Keith M. Baker, ed., *The French Revolution and the Creation of Modern Political Culture*, vol. 4: *The Terror* (Oxford: Pergamon Press, 1994), 19–38.

10. See Jean Paulhan, *Les Fleurs de Tarbes ou la Terreur dans les lettres* (1941; Paris: Gallimard, 1990).

11. Paulhan, *Les Fleurs de Tarbes*, 46.

12. See Keith Michael Baker, "Introduction," in Baker, François Furet, and Colin Lucas, eds., *The French Revolution and the Creation of Modern Political Culture*, vol. 1: *The Political Culture of the Old Regime* (London: Pergamon Press, 1987), xii; as well as his "On the Problem of the Ideological Origins of the French Revolution," in Dominick LaCapra and Steven L. Kaplan, eds., *Modern European Intellectual History* (Ithaca: Cornell University Press, 1982), 198–99.

13. See Christie McDonald, "Words of Change," in Sandy Petrey, ed., *The French Revolution 1789–1989: Two Hundred Years of Rethinking* (Lubbock: Texas Tech University, 1989), 33–46.

14. Paulhan, *Les Fleures de Tarbes*, 30–31.

15. Longinus's and Kant's conceptions of the sublime are elaborated at length in chapter 1, below.

16. See Marie-Hélène Huet, *Mourning Glory: The Will of the French Revolution* (Philadelphia: University of Pennsylvania Press, 1997), chapters 2 and 3, "The End of Representation" and "The Revolutionary Sublime," 32–78.

17. Louis-Antoine Saint-Just, "Second discours sur le jugement de Louis XVI," in Michèle Duval, ed., *Oeuvres complètes* (Paris: Gérard Lebovici, 1984), 401.

18. This is also the principal thesis of Albert Camus's discussion of Rousseauist and Montagnard rhetoric in *The Rebel: An Essay on Man in Revolt*, trans. Anthony Bower (New York: Random House/Vintage Books, 1956), 105–32.

19. In addition to Huet, *Mourning Glory*, 69–71, see Jean Starobinski, *Transparency and Obstruction*, trans. Arthur Goldhammer (Chicago: University of Chicago Press, 1988), as well as Christie McDonald, *The Dialogue of Writing: Essays in Eighteenth-*

Century French Literature (Waterloo, Ontario: Wilfrid Laurier University Press, 1984), chapter 4, "The Model of Reading: *Les Dialogues, Rousseau Juge de Jean-Jacques*," 34–46.

20. On the lability of "truth" and "lie" and on their implication in a system of sociopolitically motivated "linguistic legislation," see Friedrich Nietzsche, "On Truth and Lie in an Extra-Moral Sense," in Walter Kaufmann, ed. and trans., *The Portable Nietzsche* (1954; London: Penguin, 1976), 42–47. Nietzsche's fundamental inquiry in this essay—"Do the designations and the things coincide? Is language the adequate expression of all realities?" (45)—points the way toward the post-structuralist findings referenced above and, like Derrida's article "Differance," presents a helpful introduction to the subject of linguistic instability.

21. Camille Desmoulins, *La Tribune des patriotes* (Paris: Société littéraire typographique, n.d.), 4.

22. For a provocative discussion of catachresis as a significant political as well as rhetorical structure, see Ernesto Laclau, "The Politics of Rhetoric," in Tom Cohen, Barbara Cohen, J. Hillis Miller, and Andrzej Warminski, eds., *Material Events: Paul de Man and the Afterlife of Theory* (Minneapolis: University of Minnesota Press, 2001), 229–53. The helpful example by means of which Laclau explains catachresis is the "wings of an airplane": "The expression," he comments, "was metaphoric at the beginning, but... there is no proper designation of the referent. I am not free to call the 'wing' in any other way.... The... defining feature of a catachresis is its being based in a figural name that has no counterpart in a proper one" (238).

23. Robespierre, "Sur les principes du gouvernement révolutionnaire," 288.

24. Saint-Just cited by Camus, *The Rebel*, 130. Unfortunately, Camus does not provide a source for this quotation, and I have been unable to locate it in Saint-Just's voluminous collected writings.

25. Jean-Jacques Rousseau, *The Social Contract*, trans. Maurice Cranston (London: Penguin, 1968), 70n.

26. See Maurice Blanchot, "Everyday Speech" and "Literature and the Right to Death," in (respectively): *The Infinite Conversation*, trans. Susan Hanson (Minneapolis: University of Minnesota Press, 1993), and *The Work of Fire*, trans. Charlotte Mandel (Stanford: Stanford University Press, 1995).

27. Interestingly enough, although Rousseau consistently devalorized "effeminate" emotional attachments in his political works, his novel *Julie, or the New Heloise*, widely popular among contemporary women for its supposed sentimentality, was one of the prime catalysts of the social and artistic trend of feminine *sensibilité* in the eighteenth century.

28. Slavoj Žižek, *Enjoy Your Symptom!* (New York: Routledge, 1992), 14. See also Sigmund Freud, "Dream and Delusion in Jensen's *Gradiva*," in *Standard Edition*, vol. 9: "It is precisely what was chosen as the instrument of repression... that becomes the vehicle for the return: in and behind the repressing force, what is repressed proves itself victor in the end" (35); as well as Jacques Lacan, *Le Séminaire III: Les Psychoses*, ed. Jacques-Alain Miller (Paris: Seuil, 1981), 21, 94.

29. Roland Barthes, "Literature and Signification: Answers to a Questionnaire in *Tel Quel*," in *Critical Essays*, trans. Richard Howard (Evanston: Northwestern University Press, 1972), 261–79.

30. See Jürgen Habermas, *Communication and the Evolution of Society*, trans. Thomas McCarthy (Boston: Beacon Press, 1979).

31. Louis-Antoine Saint-Just, "Sur les personnes incarcérées," in Albert Soboul, ed., *Discours et rapports* (Paris: Messidor/Éditions sociales, 1988), 147.

1. Rousseau's "Contradiction of Words"

1. Jean-Jacques Rousseau, *Sur l'économie politique*, in *Oeuvres complètes*, ed. Bernard Gagnebin and Marcel Raymond, tome 3 (Paris: Gallimard/Bibliothèque de la Pléiade, 1964), 252. Unless references to English editions are provided, all translations of French texts are my own, in this chapter and throughout the book.

2. Jean-Jacques Rousseau, *The Social Contract*, trans. Maurice Cranston (London: Penguin Books, 1968), 60. All subsequent references to this volume are designated *Contract* and appear in parentheses in the body of the text. Where necessary, I modify Cranston's translation and include the corresponding terms or phrases from the French original: *Du Contrat social* in *Oeuvres complètes*, tome 3, 349–472. Page numbers refer to the English edition.

3. It is worth noting—and by no means coincidental—that several of the most influential "post-structuralist" discussions of lack, instability, and difference as necessary components of linguistic expression surface in analyses of Rousseau's work. See, for example, Jacques Derrida, *Of Grammatology*, trans. Gayatri Spivak (Baltimore: Johns Hopkins University Press, 1974); Paul de Man, *Allegories of Reading: Figural Language in Rousseau, Nietzsche, Rilke, and Proust* (New Haven: Yale University Press, 1979); and Paul de Man, *Blindness and Insight* (Minneapolis: University of Minnesota Press, 1983).

4. The "Clarens section" of Rousseau's *Julie, or the New Heloise* could also be included as a work illustrative of this dynamic, insofar as it depicts the founding and functioning of a society of virtuous *belles âmes*, where transparent language (silence) predominates in what is nevertheless a highly mediated, artfully controlled environment. Because these aspects of *Julie* have already received considerable attention from Jean Starobinski and Paul de Man, I have chosen not to include the novel in my discussion of communitarian virtue in Rousseau. See Jean Starobinski, *Transparency and Obstruction*, trans. Arthur Goldhammer (Chicago: University of Chicago Press, 1988); and Paul de Man, "The Rhetoric of Temporality," in *Blindness and Insight*, 187–228. I do, however, briefly allude to *Julie* and to de Man's reading of it in note 15, below.

5. I have opted to exclude "practical" texts such as Rousseau's proposals for governmental reform in Corsica and Poland because of the considerable—and, within the framework of this French-oriented study, irrelevant—information about historical context that lengthy allusions to them would require. The interested reader, however, may wish to consult *Projet de Constitution pour la Corse* and *Considérations sur le gouvernement de Pologne*, in *Oeuvres complètes*, tome 3, 901–52 and 953–1044, respectively.

6. See Jean-Jacques Rousseau, *Discourse on the Sciences and the Arts*, in Donald A. Cress, ed. and trans., *The Basic Political Writings* (Indianapolis: Hackett Publishing, 1987). This text is renowned most of all for its prosopopoeia of the Roman general Fabricius, in which Rousseau narrates hypothetically the great man's horror at the sight of eighteenth-century society's corrupt and artificial trappings. Condemning the "vain pomp, . . . studied elegance, . . . [and] frivolous eloquence" of contemporary Europe, Rousseau's Fabricius proclaims his preference for a "sight

which neither your riches nor all your arts could ever display; the assembly of two hundred virtuous men, worthy of commanding in Rome and of governing the earth" (10). This, along with the transparent spectacle imagined by Rousseau in his *Lettre à d'Alembert* (see below), is the precise model that Robespierre has in mind when he organizes the Festival of the Supreme Being in 1794, discussed in chapter 2.

7. Jean-Jacques Rousseau, *A Discourse on Inequality*, trans. Maurice Cranston (London: Penguin Books, 1984), 171. All subsequent references to this volume are designated *Second* and appear in parentheses in the body of the text.

8. The two "passions" that Rousseau associates with man's praiseworthy, un-corrupted nature are self-love, understood as an instinct of survival, devoid of vanity (*Émile ou de l'éducation*, in *Oeuvres complètes*, tome 4, 491–93), and pity, "a feeling that puts us in the place of the sufferer" (*Second* 100). The latter feeling in particular serves in the *philosophe*'s worldview as a "salutary curb" on man's potential for egotism (*Second* 102); as such, it should not in theory register among the passions that, in promoting or manifesting interpersonal differences, he condemns to exclusion from his ideal polity. Rousseau's conception of love, Derrida notes in *Of Grammatology*, "is the perversion of natural pity. Unlike the latter, it limits our attachment to a single person. As always in Rousseau, evil here has the form of . . . comparison and of preference. That is to say of difference" (175). I, however, maintain that even pity is construed as a pathology when it inspires amorous softness of heart in opposition to the unsentimental and abstract commitment to public duty required by Terrorist communities. See my discussion of *Le Lévite d'Éphraïm*, below, and of the Montagnard government in chapter 2.

9. Although his account of life in despotic society recalls the bleak political visions of Hobbes, Rousseau is insistent about the deep philosophical differences between his own philosophy and that of his predecessor. One of his major points of departure from the English philosopher resides in his view of mankind as innately good, whereas Hobbes believes that man is naturally wicked (*Second* 98–99). There is also Rousseau's not-so-veiled reference to Hobbes at the beginning of that discourse, where he lambastes unnamed philosophers who "speak of savage man [but] depict civilized man" (78). See also his mention of Hobbes's "dangerous reveries" in the *Discourse on the Sciences and the Arts* (19).

10. "The savage man breathes only peace and freedom; he desires only to live and stay idle, and even the *ataraxa* of the Stoic does not approach his profound indifference toward every other object. Civil man, on the contrary, being always active, sweating and restless, torments himself endlessly in search of ever more laborious occupations. . . . He pays court to great men he loathes and to rich men he despises; he spares nothing to secure the honor of serving them; he boasts vaingloriously of his own baseness and of their patronage, and being proud of his slavery he speaks with disdain of those who have not the honor of sharing it. . . . In order for [the savage] to understand the motives of anyone assuming so many cares, it would be necessary for the words 'power' and 'reputation' to have meaning for his mind; he would have to know that there is a group of men who attach importance to the gaze of the rest of the world, and who know how to be happy and satisfied with themselves on the testimony of others rather than on their own" (*Second* 136).

11. See Jean Starobinski, *Le Remède dans le mal* (Paris: Gallimard, 1989). In his reading of Plato's "Pharmakon," Jacques Derrida likewise analyzes the linguistic and ontological commingling of disease and cure; see *Dissemination*, trans. Barbara

Johnson (Chicago: University of Chicago Press, 1981), 95–116. As Derrida himself points out in a footnote to this essay, the ambiguity of linguistic mediation in Plato—the power of his *pharmakon* both to improve and to worsen a situation—is analogous to the double-edged nature of language in Rousseau (96n).

12. Readers of Immanuel Kant—to whom I refer in this chapter's opening paragraph and who figures more prominently below—will recognize in this notion a crude precursor to the categorical imperative. In contemporary philosophy, the more pragmatic strain of this line of inquiry receives provocative treatment in Ronald Dworkin, *Sovereign Virtue: The Theory and Practice of Equality* (Cambridge, Mass.: Harvard University Press, 2000).

13. In positing discursive self-expression as a gesture that confers positive existence on the speaking subject, I am perhaps obviously distancing myself from the literary critical model, initiated by Hegel and reaching its apogee in Mallarmé, whereby the articulation of a sign (including "I") destroys or negates the referent. At bottom, the reason for my position is historically and ethically determined: the chapters that follow this one treat a historical period in which the right to speak was not, in spite of the Revolution's initial promise, a foregone conclusion—quite the contrary. Under these circumstances, what Hélène Cixous would call "coming to language" is, as for the women in Cixous's model, a profoundly political act. The daring and difficulty that attended, under the Montagnard Terror, the articulation of an explicitly personal speaking position should not be drained of their ethical import by being reduced to stock-in-trade examples of the truism that "the letter kills." For a thorough overview and, in the end, a thoughtful critique of the latter approach, see Jonathan Strauss, *Subjects of Terror: Hegel, Nerval, and the Modern Self* (Stanford: Stanford University Press, 1998).

14. Paul Hoffmann, *Théories et modèles de la liberté au XVIIIe siècle* (Paris: Presses Universitaires de France, 1996), 363. Similarly, Starobinski says of Rouseeau: "The equivocal is intolerable to him" (*Transparency and Obstruction,* 57).

15. The Elysium, the garden that Julie cultivates at Clarens once she has renounced her illicit love for Saint-Preux and married the reasonable, socially acceptable man selected by her father, in many ways resembles the social contract theorized by Rousseau in his political treatise. For the garden is an artificial construct designed to overwrite the passions that could tear its mistress's new, postadulterous household asunder. It functions quite literally as a palimpsest, erasing the traces of a little grove where Julie and Saint-Preux once shared their first kiss; in the language of the social contract, it imposes silence on the voice of the passions. At the same time, the garden is designed to look completely natural, as though no human artifice or mediation has gone into its creation—just as the social contract, as I will show in detail below, is supposed to transcend the mediating structures of conventional representation. The paradox of the Elysium's artificial naturalness, discussed in numerous studies of *Julie or the New Heloise,* receives arguably its most illuminating analysis in de Man, "The Rhetoric of Temporality," in *Blindness and Insight,* 187–228.

16. Rousseau, *Émile ou de l'éducation,* in *Oeuvres complètes,* tome 4, 248. All subsequent references to this volume are designated *Émile* and appear in parentheses in the body of the text.

17. In *Of Grammatology,* Derrida remarks that "the metaphor of the voice always indicates in Rousseau a law" (173).

18. In the *Émile*, contrarily, Rousseau does imbue desire with a voice when he speaks of the "murmur of nascent passions" (490)—but these are to be understood as the natural, unperverted (because unmodified by civilization), and salutary sentiments ascribed to "savages" in *The Second Discourse*. See note 8, above.

19. Rousseau, *Fragments politiques*, in *Oeuvres complètes*, tome 3, 510. This text was drafted in response to a questionnaire Rousseau had received from the Economic Society of Bern, inquiring as to the best "methods for removing a people from a state of corruption and ... the most perfect plan that a legislator can adopt to effect such a change" (1526).

20. On the role of mimesis, identification, and violence in the political thought of the *philosophes*, see Pierre Saint-Amand, *The Laws of Hostility: Politics, Violence, and the Enlightenment*, trans. Jennifer Curtiss Gage (Minneapolis: University of Minnesota Press, 1996). Although Saint-Amand provides a fine commentary on Rousseau's *Second Discourse*, among other texts, it is above all his brilliant examination of Montesquieu's *Lettres persanes* that helped to clarify my thinking on the (Girardian) relationship between imitation and jealousy in a despotic regime.

21. Personal desire and egocentrism always feature extremely prominently in Rousseau's writing. See, for example, his *Rousseau juge de Jean-Jacques*, in *Oeuvres complètes*, tome 1, 664, where Rousseau reflects on his oeuvre as a product of him having been "forced to speak ceaselessly of myself."

22. Martin Heidegger, *Being and Time: A Translation of "Sein und Zeit,"* trans. Joan Stambaugh (Albany: State University of New York Press, 1996), 119; Heidegger's emphasis.

23. Similarly, in his text on proposed governmental reforms in Poland, Rousseau describes individuals who resist the imperative of civic virtue as "slaves of the passions that must be stifled." See *Considérations sur le gouvernement de Pologne*, 974.

24. See Immanuel Kant, *Grounding for the Metaphysics of Morals*, trans. James W. Ellington (1928; Indianapolis: Hackett, 1991), 16–17, 22–25, 38–41, and, most succinctly, 49: "A free will and a will subject to moral laws are one and the same." See also Kant, *The Critique of Judgment*, trans. James Creed Meredith (Oxford: Clarendon Press, 1991), 124n: "Passions belong to the faculty of desire, and are inclinations that hinder or render impossible all determinability of the elective will by principles. ... In passion, ... freedom of the mind is ... abrogated." All subsequent references to this volume are designated *Judgment* and appear in parentheses in the body of the text. On the centrality of Rousseau's philosophy to Kant's conception of freedom as "rational self-legislation rather than sentiment," see Richard L. Velkley, *Freedom and the End of Reason: On the Moral Foundation of Kant's Critical Philosophy* (Chicago: University of Chicago Press, 1989), 12–88.

25. See Émile Benveniste, *Problems in General Linguistics*, trans. Mary Meek (Coral Gables: University of Miami Press, 1971): "'Ego' is he who *says* 'ego,' ... a reality of discourse" (224).

26. In *Transparency and Obstruction*, Starobinski sums up Rousseau's notoriously misanthropic stance in this axiom: "The proposition: society runs contrary to nature, has as its immediate consequence: *I* oppose myself to society" (53; Starobinski's emphasis). Examples of Rousseau's antisocial egoism are manifold in his own writings. See, for example, his *Confessions* (77), as well as the *Lettre à d'Alembert*, in which he identifies with the protagonist of Molière's *Misanthrope*.

27. The question of self-interest as a structurally nongeneralizable force surfaces throughout Rousseau's oeuvre, not just in his properly political writings. See, for example, the preface to his play *Narcisse*, in *Oeuvres complètes*, tome 2, 968: "For every two men whose interests are in agreement, there are perhaps one hundred thousand [men or interests] that are opposed to them."

28. Maurice Blanchot, "Literature and the Right to Death," in *The Work of Fire*, trans. Charlotte Mandell (Stanford: Stanford University Press, 1995), 319; translation slightly modified for the sake of grammatical correctness.

29. In *Subjects of Terror*, when discussing Blanchot's and Alexandre Kojève's readings of Hegel's "Absolute Freedom and Terror," Jonathan Strauss asserts that the former's interpretation is the more accurate of the two, in that Kojève "misread[s] ... the Terror as a positivity" (62). But insofar as Blanchot himself presents the "right to death" (even with irony) as a positive outgrowth of the Terrorist absorption of the individual subject into the general will, his reading of this phenomenon does bear a trace of the dialectical positivity that Hegel himself resists. It is indeed for this reason that I refer to Blanchot and not to Hegel at this point in my reading—precisely because Rousseau too dialectically recuperates as a "right to life and death" the private citizen's dissolution in absolute liberty.

30. Georg W. F. Hegel, "Absolute Freedom and Terror," in *Phenomenology of Spirit*, trans. A. V. Miller (Oxford: Oxford University Press, 1977), 359.

31. This exchange, it should be noted, receives a remarkably similar articulation in Freud's famous phrase: "wo *es* war, soll *Ich* werden," wherein the law-abiding, self-censoring, rational ego assumes the place of the passionate, unruly, antisocial id. See Sigmund Freud, *New Introductory Lectures on Psychoanalysis*, ed. and trans. James L. Strachey (London: Norton, 1933), 80.

32. Rousseau avows that all his thoughts on the social pact "are reducible to a single one, namely, the total alienation by each associate of himself and all his rights to the whole community. Thus, in the first place, as every individual gives himself absolutely, the conditions are the same for all, and precisely because they are the same for all, it is in no one's interest to make the conditions onerous for others" (*Contract* 60). More succinctly, placing individual interest on the side of bias and the general will on the side of fair impartiality, he states: "Private will inclines by its very nature towards partiality, and the general will towards equality" (*Contract* 69).

33. Jean-Jacques Rousseau, *Essay on the Origin of Languages*, trans. John H. Moran (Chicago: University of Chicago Press, 1966), 13; translation modified. All subsequent references to this volume are designated *Essay* and appear in parentheses in the body of the text.

34. Paul de Man, "Metaphor (Second Discourse)," in *Allegories of Reading*, 151. In the same passage, de Man continues: "The empirical situation, which is open and hypothetical, is given a consistency that can only exist in a text. This is done by means of a metaphor (calling the other man a giant), a substitutive figure of speech ('he is a giant' substituting for 'I am afraid') that changes a referential situation suspended between fiction and fact (the hypothesis of fear) into a literal fact. Paradoxically, the figure literalizes its referent and deprives it of its para-figural status. The figure dis-figures, that is, it makes fear, itself a para-figural fiction, into a reality. . . ."

35. Or as de Man puts it in "Metaphor (Second Discourse)": "Language is not conceived as a transcendental principle but as the possibility of contingent error" (156).

36. Jean-Jacques Rousseau, *Lettre à d'Alembert* (Paris: Garnier-Flammarion, 1967), 233.

37. For more detail on Rousseau's rejection of "deputies or representatives," see *The Social Contract,* 140–43. Predictably, Rousseau questions the value of such intermediaries insofar as they, like the mediations of language, stand to deform or extrude through a subjective lens the general will that they supposedly exist to protect. "The moment a people adopts representatives it is no longer free; it no longer exists" (*Contract* 143). Or, less harshly: "If the general will is to be clearly expressed, it is imperative that there should be no sectional associations in the state, and that every citizen should make up his own mind for himself" (*Contract* 73). This stance will have significant, complicating consequences for the leaders of the French Revolution and the Terror, as Keith M. Baker shows in his superb essay, "Representation," in Baker, François Furet, and Colin Lucas, eds., *The French Revolution and the Creation of Modern Political Culture,* vol. 1 (London: Pergamon Press, 1987), 469–92.

38. Rousseau also, it should be mentioned, presents Moses as an exemplary legislator in *Considérations sur le gouvernement de Pologne,* 956. Although her focus is not on the Mosaic sublime, Carol Blum remarks upon Rousseau's interest the Jewish people, led by Moses, as a model of political virtue; see her *Rousseau and the Republic of Virtue: The Language of Politics in the French Revolution* (Ithaca: Cornell University Press, 1986), 114–15.

39. Deuteronomy 5:8. Rousseau expresses his own religious bias against graven images in his *Confessions,* where he says of one curate: "But although M. de Pontverre was a good man, he was assuredly not a virtuous man, on the contrary, he was a zealot who knew no other virtue than the worship of graven images" (85). Tellingly, Rousseau posits virtue and the worship of graven images as mutually exclusive terms.

40. Exodus 3:14. See also Deuteronomy 5:6 and Numbers 15:41.

41. In analyzing the primal "cry" of affect (hunger or fear) that for Rousseau, as for his important predecessor Condillac, represents language in its nascent stages, Michel Foucault insists implicitly and explicitly on the temporal dimension that the cry assumes as it "becomes" a type of linguistic utterance: "It becomes language, but only at the end of definite and complex operations: the notation of an analogy of relations (the other's cry is to what he is experiencing—that which is unknown—what my cry is to my appetite or my fear); inversion of time and voluntary use of the sign before the representation it designates (before experiencing a sensation of hunger strong enough to make me cry out, I emit the cry that is associated with it); lastly, the purpose of arousing in the other the representation corresponding to the cry or gesture (but with this particularity, that, by emitting a cry, I do not arouse, and do not intend to arouse, the sensation of hunger, but the representation of the relation between this sign and my own desire to eat). Language is possible only upon the basis of this entanglement." See Michel Foucault, *The Order of Things: An Archaeology of the Human Sciences; a Translation of "Les Mots et les choses"* (New York: Random House/Vintage Books, 1973), 105.

42. In this way, the legislator further resembles the god of the Judeo-Christian tradition, of "the Law of the Hebrews," insofar as God is held to lie outside or beyond earthly time. This is the viewpoint expressed by one of Rousseau's favorite authors, Saint Augustine, who apostrophizes God in the following terms: "You are at once before all past time and after all future time. . . . Your years are completely present to you all at once, because they are at a permanent standstill. They do not

move on, forced to give way before the advance of others, because they never pass at all. . . . Your years are one day, yet your day does not come daily but is always today, because your today does not give place to any tomorrow nor does it take the place of any yesterday. Your today is eternity." See Augustine, *The Confessions*, book 11 (New York: Penguin, 1961), 263.

43. Rousseau, "[Fragment sur la puissance infinie de Dieu]," in *Oeuvres complètes*, tome 4, 1055.

44. Éliane Escoubas makes a similar observation about the "suspension of time" (60) inherent in the "simplicity" of the Kantian sublime. See Éliane Escoubas, "Kant or the Simplicity of the Sublime," in Jeffrey S. Librett, ed. and trans., *Of the Sublime: Presence in Question* (Albany: State University of New York Press, 1993), 55–70.

45. See Marie-Hélène Huet, *Mourning Glory: The Will of the French Revolution* (Philadelphia: University of Pennsylvania Press, 1997), 59–78. Huet is not, however, alone in identifying a strong commonality between the discourses of the sublime and of the French Revolution. Jean Starobinski makes an off-the-cuff remark about the parallels between Kant's conception of the sublime and the French Revolution's call for the "annihilation of our existence as feeling creatures" for the sake of political unity. But unlike Huet, Starobinski does not develop this idea; nor does he apply it to Rousseau—upon whose association of society with an "annihilation" of man's natural instincts I have already commented. See Jean Starobinski, *1789: Les Emblèmes de la raison* (Paris: Flammarion, 1973), 157.

46. That Longinus is—and, for at least the past three centuries, has been—considered the starting point of all serious European thought on the sublime hardly requires a footnote. Boileau's French translation of this work brought the sublime to the forefront of late seventeenth-century aesthetic debate, as did Dryden's contemporaneous criticism invoking Longinus as one of the "authors to whom I owe my lights" (John Dryden, *Essays*, ed. W. P. Ker [Oxford, 1900], vol. 1, 186). Addison, Akinside, and Burke soon followed suit in England, while Kant himself drew on Longinus in *The Critique of Judgment*. On the importance of the sublime in seventeenth- and eighteenth-century French aesthetic discourse in particular, see Louis Marin, "On the Sublime, Infinity, *Je ne sais quoi*," in Denis Hollier, ed., *A New History of French Literature* (Cambridge, Mass.: Harvard University Press, 1989), 340–45. I should add that despite many of the interesting parallels between Burke's ideas on sublimity and those advanced by the authors under investigation here, not to mention his critical analyses of the French Revolution, I have chosen not to include the British author in this study. Above all, this is because Burke, unlike Kant and Longinus, does not posit divine performativity and representational transparency as features of the sublime.

47. See Longinus, *Of the Sublime*, in *Classical Literary Criticism* (London: Penguin, 1965): "The effect of sublime language is, not to persuade the hearers, but to entrance them; and at all times, and in every way, what transports us with wonder is more telling than what merely persuades or gratifies us" (74). All subsequent references to this volume are designated *Hypsous* and appear in parentheses in the body of the text. As Kant will do some fifteen centuries later, Longinus here contrasts the sublime to notions of the beautiful (which "merely . . . gratifies") and of the rhetorically effective (which strives to "persuade")—as defined, for instance, by Aristotle, respectively, in *The Poetics*, trans. James Hutton (New York: W. W. Norton, 1982),

and *The "Art" of Rhetoric,* trans. John Henry Freese (Cambridge, Mass.: Harvard University Press, Loeb Classical Library, 1926).

48. *Hypsous,* the term that Longinus uses to describe his key concept, specifically means "an elevation of the spirit or the soul." Its Latinate translation, "sublime," does not adequately capture the connotations of moral superiority and literal transcendence or elevation implicit in the Greek term. It does, however, resonate nicely with the Freudian concept of sublimation, which is so clearly at work in the vexed "passage from the state of nature to the civil state" that Rousseau describes in *The Social Contract.*

49. Philippe Lacoue-Labarthe, "Sublime Truth," in Librett, ed. and trans., *Of the Sublime,* 104. I have taken the liberty of transliterating here the Greek characters used by Lacoue-Labarthe in his reading of the Greek text.

50. In fact, had Kant cited the interdiction's corollary commandment, "Thou shalt have no other gods before me," the similarity to Rousseau in particular would have been even more pronounced, insofar as the adverb *before* is evocative of both temporal and ontological privilege and recalls Rousseau's gesture of placing the voice of duty *before* the passions. The parallel with Longinus, moreover, would have been more apparent had Kant gone on to quote the allusion to thunder and lightning that follows Moses' receiving of the Ten Commandments, namely: "And all the people saw the thunderings, and the lightnings, and the noise of the trumpet, and the mountain [Mount Sinai] smoking . . ." (Exodus 20:18). Thus Longinus's favorite metaphor for sublime language, the bolt of lightning, also surfaces in the text invoked by Kant to demonstrate the capacity of the sublime to destroy traditional representation.

51. For Rousseau, too, morality is above all a comparative phenomenon—a point that surfaces repeatedly in his numerous autobiographical self-justifications. See, for instance, his *Confessions:* "Eternal being, gather around me the innumerable crowd of my fellows; let them listen to my confessions . . . and then let one single man among them say to you, if he dares: *I was better than that man*" (43); and: "People have imputed to me a desire to be original and to act differently from other men. In truth, I [only] wanted to do what was right" (93). *The Second Discourse'*s postulations about morality also betray this comparative bias, in that Rousseau ascribes natural man's ignorance of good and evil to his absolute isolation in the wild. Only when he starts living with other men and comparing himself with them does a sense of morality (as well as personal property, desire, jealousy, etc.) come into being.

52. Even Longinus's choice of a biblical citation—one that he posited, we will recall, as a testimony to "the power of the Divine Being"—suggests that the sublime, for him, has religious or moral undertones.

53. See Roman Jakobson, *Fundamentals of Language* (Paris: Mouton, 1971), 90.

54. Paul de Man, "Review of Harold Bloom's *Anxiety of Influence,*" in *Blindness and Insight,* 274.

55. Foucault speaks of "discourse understood as a *sequence* of verbal signs," in *The Order of Things,* 83; my emphasis. Derrida conceives of writing as "a detour, a delay, a relay, a reserve, a temporal and temporizing mediation, . . . *differance,*" in "Differance," 123. And de Man announces the "unveiling of an authentically temporal destiny" occasioned by any and every linguistic "play of substitutions." See "The Rhetoric of Temporality," in *Blindness and Insight,* 206. In the same essay, de Man's

concept of allegory takes up Jakobson's idea of (metonymic) language as repetition and substitution: "This relationship between signs necessarily contains a constitutive temporal element; it remains necessary, if there is to be allegory, that the allegorical sign refer to another sign that precedes it. The meaning constituted by the allegorical sign can then consist only in the *repetition* . . . of a previous sign with which it can never coincide, since it is of the essence of this previous sign to be pure anteriority" (207; de Man's emphasis). It is no accident that these reflections surface in de Man's (aforementioned) study of the republic of virtue established at Clarens— and allegorized in the Elysium—in *Julie*.

56. Locke discusses the "appeal to High Heaven" in his *Second Treatise of Government*, ed. Thomas P. Peardon (1952; New York: Macmillan, 1987), paragraph 168. For a superb, broad-ranging analysis of the "recourse to God" in European political philosophy from Machiavelli to the Terror, see Hannah Arendt, *On Revolution* (1963; London: Penguin, 1990), 39.

57. It is this normative, prescriptive aspect of Rousseau's thought that Christopher Kelly neglects to account for in his recent article, "Taking Readers as They Are: Rousseau's Turn from Discourses to Novels," in *Eighteenth Century Studies* 33, no. 1 (1999): 85–102. Interestingly enough, however, Kelly suggests that Rousseau's willingness to "take readers as they are" has something to do with his increased sensitivity, as he moved away from theoretical to novelistic writing, "to the subtle ways in which the effects of literature escape the intentions of the author" (93). This sensitivity, we shall see toward the end of this chapter, does manifest itself on occasion in Rousseau's *Social Contract*—which after all opens with a vow to "take men as they are"—in his vexed calls for the reader's mercy. Tolerance, however, is not the predominant philosophical or semiotic value promulgated in his political philosophy, focused as it is on the establishment of (often stringently) universal principles.

58. Rousseau, *Du Contrat social*, first, unfinished version (known as the Geneva manuscript), in *Oeuvres complètes*, tome 3, 288.

59. In *Sur l'économie politique*, Rousseau sidesteps this problem somewhat by displacing the possibility of art in the service of politics into a distant past: "If it is good to know what to do with men as they are, it is better still to make them into what one needs them to be. . . . You must train men if you wish to command them: therein lay the great art of ancient governments, in those distant times when philosophers gave laws to peoples . . ." (251–52).

60. Rousseau's assertion that genius, unlike the copyist, is capable of making something from nothing very closely approaches Kant's own association of the genius with sublime creation ex nihilo in paragraph 43 of *The Critique of Judgment*. The strong and numerous parallels between the Rousseauist legislator and the Kantian genius merit more thorough exploration in another context.

61. Rousseau, "[Sur le goût]," in *Oeuvres complètes*, tome 5, 482. Rousseau continues, once more anticipating Kant (this time on the difference between the categorical sublime and the "pathological" beautiful): "The beautiful has for its rule only our whims, our caprice . . . , [in it] we are guided only by what pleases us. Those who guide us are artists, powerful people, rich people, and what guides them in turn is their vanity."

62. For a similar position on the moral dubiousness of mimesis, see Kant, *Grounding for the Metaphysics of Morals*: "Worse service cannot be rendered morality than that an attempt be made to derive it from examples. . . . Whence have we the con-

cept of God as the highest good? Solely from the idea of moral perfection, which reason frames a priori and connects inseparably with the concept of a free will. *Imitation has no place at all in moral matters*. And examples serve only for encouragement... in setting aside their true original, which lies in... [a] genuine supreme principle of morality that must rest merely on pure reason, independently of all experience..." (20–21). It bears noting that a few lines later in this argument, Kant explicitly locates happiness and the inclinations (Rousseau's "passions") in the realm of "experience," of "unexceptionally empirical [elements]" (21). And, he adds later: "Everything empirical is not only quite unsuitable as a contribution to the principle of morality, but is even highly detrimental to the purity of morals. For the proper and inestimable worth of an absolutely good will consists precisely in the fact that the principle of action is free of all influences from contingent grounds, which only experience can furnish" (34).

63. Although Huet identifies the importance of this opposition in *Mourning Glory* (68), it was first brought to my attention by Claudine Kahan in her graduate seminar on the sublime at Yale University, 1996. My debt to Professor Kahan's illuminating literary and philosophical perspective, referenced in more general terms in the Acknowledgments, is especially great in this chapter.

64. It is thus only insofar as the Rousseauist lawgiver *fails* to live up to his theoretical ideal—fails to transcend representational and ontological difference—that I can agree with Michel Serres's comment on the "obvious" parallelism between *The Social Contract*'s legislator and its writer. See *Le Parasite* (Paris: Grasset, 1980), 160: "The author of *The Social Contract* is obviously the superior man, the wise man, he who is capable of transforming each person into a part of the grand whole. He is beyond the passions yet knows them intimately..., etc." With its emphasis on the private passions and differential tendencies displayed by the writer in *The Social Contract*, my analysis clearly runs counter to that of Serres.

65. For an illuminating discussion of the example as a peculiar entity suspended between the particular and the general, see Giorgio Agamben, *The Coming Community*, trans. Michael Hardt (Minneapolis: University of Minnesota Press, 1993), 8–9.

66. One of Rousseau's favorite British writers, Henry Fielding, summarizes this problem in the opening line of his 1742 novel, *Joseph Andrews* (New York: Penguin, 1971): "It is a trite but true observation, that examples work more forcibly on the mind than precepts..." (39).

67. Similarly, in *Scenarios of the Imaginary: Theorizing the French Enlightenment* (Ithaca: Cornell University Press, 1987), Josué Harari highlights the vexed interplay between theory and example in Rousseau's *Émile*. In his reading of this text, Harari aptly notes that the *philosophe*'s pedagogical "theory sustains itself *outside* of the examples" (50). In this way, Rousseau anticipates Kant's famous proposition in *The Critique of Pure Reason* that reason is the "faculty of deducing the particular from the general." However, in the passages analyzed here, the *philosophe*'s recourse to examples as the basis of general truths, instead of the other way around, demonstrates just how difficult it really is to effect a consistently abstract and generalized discursive stance.

68. It bears remarking that a similar opposition between revolutionary justice on the one hand and grace on the other resurfaces in Jules Michelet's quintessentially "Romantic-Jacobin" *Histoire de la Révolution française*, ed. Gérard Walter (Paris: Gallimard/Bibliothèque de la Pléiade, 1964). In Michelet's text, however, grace is

associated explicitly and entirely with the religious and monarchical institutions of the Old Regime and therefore with the *in*justice that prevailed before the Revolution.

69. From a Lacanian perspective, error and speech together compose the "truth" of the individual subject. As Lacan says in *Le Séminaire XI: Les Quatre Concepts fondamentaux de la psychanalyse,* ed. Jacques-Alain Miller (Paris: Seuil, 1973), the subject is an effect of speech—is realized only through speaking—which is why a Terrorist poetics, with its antisubjective bias, would naturally favor, for example, the sublime silence that Longinus identifies with Ajax or that Rousseau associates with the "prince or legislator." In a related vein, the Lacanian psychoanalytic model, following that of Freud, holds that the repressed truth of a subject's desires surfaces most clearly in his or her "errors," such as revealing slips of the tongue: "Impediment, failure, split . . . it is there that [we] seek the unconscious" (*Le Séminaire XI,* 25). Terror also opposes the articulation and proliferation of subjective desires, whence, perhaps, its pronounced antipathy to error. An extensive Lacanian analysis of the suppressions enacted by Terrorist discourse would be possible and indeed fruitful, but because the task of "psychoanalyzing the revolution" has already been undertaken by other scholars (notably the Freudian Jacques André, much cited in chapter 2, below), I have refrained from doing so in this book and have restricted myself instead to importing from Lacan a few illuminating concepts of particular relevance.

70. Louis Althusser, "Sur le *Contrat social* (les décalages)," *Cahiers pour l'analyse* 8: *L'Impensé de Jean-Jacques Rousseau* (1970): 5–42; cited and translated by de Man in *Blindness and Insight,* 138.

71. The generic designation "prose poem" is Rousseau's, though I would caution the reader whose expectations have been conditioned by Baudelaire's efforts in the genre that, in the case of Rousseau's text, the operative word is really *prose* and not *poem.* See "Premier Projet de Préface" to *Le Lévite d'Éphraïm,* in *Oeuvres complètes,* tome 2, 1205.

72. Rousseau, *Le Lévite d'Éphraïm,* in *Oeuvres complètes,* tome 2, 1205–23; see page 1206. All subsequent references to this work are designated *Lévite* and appear in parentheses in the body of the text. In the vast corpus of work devoted to Rousseau, I have encountered only two scholars who discuss *Le Lévite d'Éphraïm,* and one of them, Jean Starobinski, makes just a passing reference to this text. The other, Thomas Kavanagh, devotes to it an excellent chapter, "The Victim's Sacrifice," in *Writing the Truth: Authority and Desire in Rousseau* (Berkeley: University of California Press, 1987), 102–23, which postulates that "The *Lévite* speaks directly of what might be called 'the dark side' of the general will" (114). I am indebted to Professor Kavanagh for the insightful comments he made in response to a paper I delivered on *Le Lévite d'Éphraïm* at the Modern Language Association in December 1999.

73. I am grateful to Maurie Samuels for calling my attention to this aspect of the Levite tribe. Although the Levite starts out as a fallible human being besieged by desire, his short bildungsroman relates his transformation into a kind of self-transcending Rousseauist legislator who feels no human passions and who can thus mete out sublime justice.

74. See Carole Pateman, *The Sexual Contract* (Stanford: Stanford University Press, 1988). Pateman's central thesis has recently been disputed by Lori Jo Marso, *(Un)Manly Citizens: Jean-Jacques Rousseau's and Germaine de Staël's Subversive Women* (Baltimore: Johns Hopkins University Press, 1999), but Marso's strict focus on

Rousseau's novels and her concomitant failure to analyze *The Social Contract* or *Le Lévite d'Éphraïm* make her refutation of Pateman's "sexual contract" less compelling in the broader context of Rousseau's opus.

75. This translation of the *Lévite* relies heavily on the elegant rendering provided by Thomas Kavanagh in *Writing the Truth;* most notably, I have borrowed from him the lovely and alliterative "men of meekness."

76. For a discussion of the distinction between wife and concubine in Rousseau's story and in the original biblical narrative, see Kavanagh, *Writing the Truth,* 113.

77. On the close parallelism between the father and the head of state, see *The Social Contract:* "The family may... perhaps be seen as the first model of political societies: the head of state bears the image of the father, the people the image of his children..." (50).

78. While Kavanagh asserts in his analysis of this metaphor that "this community is a sham, an anticommunity leagued in common transgression... of the law of Israel" (*Writing the Truth,* 116), my contention here is that the Benjamite gang is, on the contrary, the monstrous double of the Israelite clan. For both require the same structural and actual sacrifice—that of a feminine other—in order to assert themselves as communities; in this crucial respect, they are the same.

79. Kavanagh, *Writing the Truth,* 121.

2. The Terror That Speaks

1. Although the Gregorian calendar was abandoned under the Terror in favor of a new system of designating and measuring time, I have chosen not to use the revolutionary calendar's dates in reference to the historical events discussed in this work. My goal is to enable readers unfamiliar with the revolutionary calendar to retain a clear sense of chronology.

2. Michelet, *Histoire de la Révolution française,* tome 2, 761. I provide my own translations of Michelet's language in this chapter because the standard English translation by Keith Botsford (Wynnewood: Kolokol Press, 1973) elides or significantly alters many of what I find to be his richest turns of phrase.

3. The reader should be aware from the outset that I alternate between the terms *Robespierrist* and *Montagnard* in describing the political allegiances of Robespierre, Saint-Just, and their close allies. The former term is self-explanatory; the latter describes the radical leftist delegates of the National Convention, who sat high up in the back of the assembly and therefore came to be known as the Mountain (la Montagne). By the middle of 1793, there was a growing rift among various members of the Montagne, notably between Robespierre's contingent and the even more militant "Ultra-revolutionary," or Hébertist, party led by Jacques-René Hébert and supported by the Parisian *sans-culottes*. Because of this rift, by the time of the Terror not all Montagnards can be said to have held properly Robespierrist points of view. Thus, although it is generally adequate to allude to Robespierre, Saint-Just, and their politics as Montagnard in nature, in instances where it is necessary to distinguish them from the Hébertists I take care to use the term *Robespierrist*.

4. On the "enormous influence exercised by Rousseau on Robespierre," and specifically on the latter's "in-depth familiarity with *The Social Contract*," see Claude Mazauric's introduction to *Écrits* (Paris: Messidor/Éditions sociales, 1989), 22–23.

While problematizing the facile historiographical narrative that posits Rousseau as the "cause" of the French Revolution (c'est la faute à Voltaire, c'est la faute à Rousseau), James Swenson's splendid book, *On Jean-Jacques Rousseau: Considered as One of the First Authors of the Revolution* (Stanford: Stanford University Press, 2000), does not actually contest the centrality of Rousseau in Robespierre's political thought.

5. One of Rousseau's most pronounced legacies to the Revolution, the republicans' adoption of transparency as a political and aesthetic stance, has also been discussed in Antoine de Baecque, *The Body Politic: Corporeal Metaphor in Revolutionary France 1770–1800*, trans. Charlotte Mandell (Stanford: Stanford University Press, 1997); Huet, *Mourning Glory;* and Thomas Crow, *Painters and Public Life in Eighteenth-Century Paris* (New Haven: Yale University Press, 1987).

6. Louis-Antoine Saint-Just, "Second discours sur le jugement de Louis XVI," in *Oeuvres complètes,* ed. Michèle Duval (Paris: Gérard Lebovici, 1984), 401. To avoid confusion with other sources for Saint-Just's writings, all subsequent references to this volume are designated "Duval" and appear in parentheses in the body of the text.

7. Louis-Antoine Saint-Just, "Sur les factions de l'étranger," in *Discours et rapports,* ed. Albert Soboul (Paris: Messidor/Éditions sociales, 1988), 154. All subsequent references to this volume are designated "Soboul" and appear in parentheses in the body of the text. Wherever possible, I refer not to older, more expansive collected works but to this edition—and to Mazauric's similar anthology of Robespierre's writings—because of the relatively widespread availability of the paperback Messidor editions.

8. On the Rousseauist general will as the ideological foundation of the first French republic, see Auguste Cochin, *Les Sociétés de Pensée et la Démocratie: Études d'histoire révolutionnaire* (1921; Paris: Éditions Copernic, 1978); François Furet, *Interpreting the French Revolution,* trans. Elborg Foster (Cambridge: Cambridge University Press, 1991), 73; and Marc-Éli Blanchard, *Saint-Just et Cie: La Révolution et les mots* (Paris: A.-G. Nizet, 1980), 53. See also note 4, above.

9. Maximilien Robespierre, "Sur la volonté générale," in *Oeuvres de Maximilien Robespierre,* ed. Laponneraye (Paris, 1840), tome 2, 694. All subsequent references to this volume are designated "Laponneraye II" and appear in parentheses in the body of the text.

10. In response to helpful prodding from Debarati Sanyal, I should make a brief remark about genre. While certain readers may suspect that the (orally delivered) speeches of the Montagnard leadership differ qualitatively from the (textually rendered) musings of Rousseau, and thus that the two bodies of work call for generically distinct forms of analysis, this apparent opposition is undermined by a few basic facts of the speeches' composition and transmission. First of all, although the Terrorist leaders' orations often appear to have the urgent and spontaneous quality of an ancient Roman harangue, these pronouncements—like those of Cicero and the Montagnards' other rhetorical models—were precisely, carefully crafted in advance for calculated effect. (For more on the importance of classical rhetoric during the Revolution, see chapter 3, note 30, below.) Robespierre in particular was notorious for submitting his speeches to a painstaking and laborious revision process before delivering them before his peers. Second, and perhaps more to the point, in order to dispel any charge of engaging in their proceedings behind closed doors (like the often secretive cabinets of the Old Regime), the *conventionnels* decreed that all their speeches should be made public: "Let us place the entire universe in

the confidence of our political secrets," Robespierre declared. Orations at the Convention and in the political clubs were thus recorded by journalists attending their sessions, and, in the case of longer or more significant speeches, published as separate pamphlets and disseminated throughout the republic. For this reason, I find it not only appropriate but important to treat the discourses of Robespierre and Saint-Just as written documents, which offer themselves up just as surely as Rousseau's meditations to fine-grained textual analysis. Any Derridean worth his or her salt, however, would deem even these qualifications unnecessary, in light of the deft deconstruction to which Derrida submits the traditional opposition between orality and writing (as promulgated by none other than Rousseau) in *Of Grammatology*, part 2: "Nature, Culture, Writing," 95–316.

11. As Camus eloquently observes in *The Rebel: An Essay on Man in Revolt*, trans. Anthony Bower (New York: Vintage Books/Random House, 1956): "Absolute virtue is impossible . . . and leads, with implacable logic, to the republic of the guillotine" (124) and to "the final acceptance of principles in silence and death" (128).

12. In *The Life and Opinions of Robespierre* (n.p., 1974), N. Hampson suggests that Robespierre's 1789 defense of one Dupond, unjustly imprisoned by a *lettre de cachet*, represented the young lawyer's definitive "conversion" to Rousseauist thought (35), by which Hampson presumably means a commitment to universal justice. The political function and significance of the *lettre de cachet*, under the Old Regime and during the Revolution, is discussed in chapter 3.

13. Maximilien Robespierre, "Sur la peine de mort," in *Oeuvres de Maximilien Robespierre*, ed. Laponneraye (Paris, 1840), tome 1, 157. All subsequent references to this volume are designated "Laponneraye I" and appear in parentheses in the body of the text.

14. On March 13, 1790, Robespierre requested before the Assembly that all prisoners still being detained because of *lettres de cachet* be liberated, no matter what their alleged crimes under the Old Regime. For, he asserted in terms that would soon become anathema to him, "it is better to forgive [faire grâce à] one hundred guilty men, than to punish a single innocent one" (Laponneraye I, 49). Here, in contrast to later texts, it is still possible to detect on Robespierre's thinking the impact of Rousseau's call for grace.

15. For his argument in favor of opening government jobs to all Frenchmen, no matter what their religion, see Robespierre, "Discours à la séance du 25 janvier 1790" (Laponneraye I, 43). For his advocacy of racial tolerance, see "Opinion de Robespierre sur la condition des hommes de couleur . . ." (Laponneraye I, 189–200). Finally, for his pronouncements about the necessity of an entirely free press, see Maximilien Robespierre, "Sur la liberté de la presse," in *Écrits*, ed. Mazauric, 81. All subsequent references to this volume are designated "Mazauric" and appear in parentheses in the body of the text. Wherever possible I refer to this abridged tome, rather than to older and more cumbersome collections of Robespierre's works (e.g., Laponneraye's, Bouloiseau's), because of the relatively widespread availability of Mazauric's edition.

16. See Maximilien Robespierre, "Sur le désarmement des suspects," in *Oeuvres de Maximilien Robespierre*, ed. Marc Bouloiseau, Georges Lefebvre, and Albert Soboul (Paris: Presses Universitaires de France, 1950), tome 8, 407. All subsequent references to this collection of Robespierre's works are designated "Bouloiseau" and appear in parentheses in the body of the text.

17. In another speech from 1791, on the subject of exactly which "interests" the new French Constitution should be designed to protect, Robespierre again came forward as a partisan of individual (as opposed to communitarian) advantage: "These interests are the primitive interests of man: his individual liberty, his pleasures [jouis-sances], the private interest that he attaches to the smallest piece of property..." (Mazauric 19). Nothing could be further, of course, from the systematic devaloriza-tion of individual interest that underpinned Robespierre's Terror.

18. Archives parlementaires de Paris, LXIII, 705. See also the revolutionary-era newspaper *Le Journal des débats et décrets,* no. 2 (April 19, 1793): "The success of a just revolution can demand the repression of a plot aided and abetted by the free-dom of the press" (322).

19. The evolution of Robespierre's approach to capital punishment, which I have of necessity treated in relatively schematic terms here, is traced in detail in Jacques Goulet, *Robespierre, la peine de mort et la Terreur* (Paris: Castor Astral, 1983).

20. See Arendt, *On Revolution,* 28, 37; and Christie McDonald, "Words of Change," in Sandy Petrey, ed., *The French Revolution 1789–1989: Two Hundred Years of Rethinking* (Lubbock: Texas Tech University Press, 1989), 33–34.

21. At the age of twenty-three, Saint-Just had written a fan letter of sorts to Robespierre—whose acquaintance he had not yet made—in the summer of 1790, calling him "the deputy not only of a province, but of the republic and of all hu-manity" and praising his effort single-handedly to "sustain our staggering nation against the tides of despotism and intrigue." See Maximilien Robespierre, *Corre-spondance de Maximilien et Augustin Robespierre,* ed. Georges Michon (Paris: Félix Alcan, 1926), 87–88. All subsequent references to this volume are designated "Michon" and appear in parentheses in the body of the text.

22. Thomas Carlyle, *The French Revolution: A History,* vol. 2 (New York: A. L. Burt Company, n.d.), 162.

23. On the mimetic relationship between Romantic historians of the Revolu-tion and the politicians about whom they write, see Linda Orr, *Headless History: Nineteenth-Century French Historiography of the Revolution* (Ithaca: Cornell Uni-versity Press, 1990).

24. As mentioned in note 3, above, the Montagnards derived their moniker from their habit of sitting high up in the rafters in the National Convention. The Girondins took their name from the southwestern region of France, la Gironde, from which three of their leading members hailed. They were also sometimes re-ferred to as Brissotins, after their influential comrade Jacques-Pierre Brissot.

25. For an account of the legal, constitutional, and even cultural problems raised by the proposal to try Louis XVI, see Michael Walzer, "The King and the Law," in Walzer, ed., *Regicide and Revolution: Speeches at the Trial of Louis XVI,* trans. Marian Rothstein (New York: Columbia University Press, 1992), 35–46.

26. Walzer, "The King and the Law," 61.

27. Cited by Camus, *The Rebel,* 127; translation modified.

28. Sigmund Freud, "Medusa's Head," in *Sexuality and the Psychology of Love,* ed. Philip Rieff (1963; New York: Touchstone/Simon and Schuster, 1997), 202.

29. Neil Hertz, "Medusa's Head: Male Hysteria under Political Pressure," in *The End of the Line: Essays on Psychoanalysis and the Sublime* (New York: Columbia Uni-versity Press, 1985), 161–93.

30. This discussion of the rhetorical question is informed by de Man's own question in *Allegories of Reading*: "What is the use of asking, I ask, when we cannot even authoritatively decide whether a question asks or doesn't ask?" (9–10).

31. For an excellent analysis of the systematic marginalization and devalorization of "the foreigner" in revolutionary discourse, see Sophie Wahnich, *L'Impossible Citoyen: L'Étranger dans le discours de la Révolution française* (Paris: Albin Michel, 1997); as well as Julia Kristeva, *Strangers to Ourselves* (New York: Columbia University Press, 1991), 148–67. The Girondins, incidentally, did not share the Montagnards' xenophobia; they prided themselves on a cosmopolitan vision of the rights of man, extending to foreign as well as French people, which later contributed to their demise at the hands of the rival party.

32. It bears noting that, just as *The Social Contract* retrospectively posits a mythical "instant" in which the original transition from natural to civil man took place, the revolutionary calendar also creates an originary moment in republican history *after the fact*: for the calendar is developed in Year II (October 1793), taking the declaration of the republic in September 1792 as its retroactive starting point. For further commentary on this *après coup* reconstruction of the past in the present, see Caroline Weber, "Freedom's Missed Moment," in Weber and Howard G. Lay, eds., *Yale French Studies* 101: *Fragments of Revolution* (spring 2002).

33. Jean-François Lyotard, *The Differend: Phrases in Dispute*, trans. Georges van den Abbeele (Minneapolis: University of Minnesota Press, 1988), 5.

34. Lyotard, *The Differend*, 27–28. I must confess that Lyotard does not explicitly qualify his paradigmatic animal-victims as trapped or domesticated. Nonetheless, because his schema rests on the idea that the animals find themselves in a situation where being understood by human beings actually has a bearing on their existence, I take this to mean that he is not referring to animals living in the wild.

35. As Blanchard notes in *Saint-Just et Cie*: "Soon [the king] is no longer a person. He is a *monster*. . . . The text is drawing a magic circle around an extraordinary being whose 'very name brings war down upon an agitated nation . . .'" (37).

36. The porcine iconography that cropped up around Louis XVI, particularly after the royal family's aborted flight to Varennes, is also discussed in de Baecque, *The Body Politic*, 63–75; and Lynn Hunt, *The Family Romance of the French Revolution* (Berkeley: University of California Press, 1992), 49–51.

37. Blanchard, *Saint-Just et Cie*.

38. Michelet, *Histoire de la Révolution française*, tome 2, 1278; my emphasis.

39. On this concept, see Slavoj Žižek, "You Only Die Twice," in *The Sublime Object of Ideology* (London: Verso, 1989), 131–50.

40. On the Robespierrists' frequent efforts to base their assertions on the authority of "the People," see François Furet, *Revolutionary France 1770–1880*, trans. Antonia Nevill (Oxford: Blackwell, 1992), 71–72; and Lynn Hunt, *Politics, Culture, and Class in the French Revolution* (Berkeley: University of California Press, 1984), 23.

41. Camus, *The Rebel*, 155; Marc-Éli Blanchard, "The French Revolution: A Political Line or a Language Circle," in Jacques Ehrmann, ed., *Yale French Studies* 39: *Literature and Revolution* (1967): 64.

42. Friedrich Nietzsche, *The Genealogy of Morals*, trans. Francis Golffing (New York: Doubleday/Anchor, 1956), 160. Christie McDonald makes essentially the same point in her suggestive article on the way language shaped the events of the Revolu-

tion in August 1789: "The need to name and rename as events unfolded (to rewrite history through names and naming) demonstrates to what extent rhetoric became a measure of mastery and control; and the changes of language . . . were no more pacific than the political changes that accompanied them." See McDonald, "Words of Change," 40.

43. As Gérald Sfez observes in his juxtaposition of political Terror in Machiavelli and Robespierre, "What really inspires stupor and admiration is a *gesture* . . . (like the killing of the pope). This Terror is silent." See Sfez, "Les Langues de la Terreur," in Catherine Kintzler and Hadi Rizk, eds., *La République et la Terreur* (Paris: Éditions Kimé, 1995), 150. This formulation is illuminating because it explicitly identifies action and silence as the two critical components of Terrorist (anti)discourse: the options likewise available to Rousseau's ideal political leader, who either does something or falls silent. On the subject of violence as the guarantor or foundation of revolutionary Terror, see also Colin Lucas, "Revolutionary Violence, the People and the Terror," Baker, Furet, and Lucas, eds., *The French Revolution and the Creation of Modern Political Culture*, vol. 4, 57–80.

44. Étienne Barry, *Essai sur la dénonciation politique* in *Discours prononcés les jours de décadi dans la section Guillaume Tell* (Paris: n.p., 1793), 60.

45. Cited by Jacques Godechot, *La Révolution française: Chronologie commentée* (Paris: Perrin, 1988), 125.

46. Jean de La Fontaine, "Le Chêne et le roseau," in *Les Fables* (Paris: Imprimerie nationale, 1985), 84.

47. Incidentally, as a further attack on monarchical genealogy, in 1793–1794 the Committee of Public Safety ordered the removal of twenty-one statues, representing the line of kings descending from the Tree of Jesse, from the western portal of Notre-Dame. These statues' heads, like that of Louis XVI, were promptly lopped off. For an interesting analysis of this episode, see Huet, *Mourning Glory*, 146–48.

48. More specifically, the Terror was first declared on September 5, 1793, and its mechanisms elaborated in a series of decrees passed in September and October of the same year, the centerpiece of which was the Law of Suspects, discussed below. On the "space of negation" opened up by the overthrow and execution of Louis XVI, see Carla Hesse, "The Law of Terror," in Wilda Anderson, ed., *MLN* 114, no. 4 (September 1999): 710. In this article, Hesse catalogs the numerous other decrees that were passed alongside the Law of Suspects to shore up republican unity (715). Although Hesse does not explore in depth the semiotic or discursive ramifications of these legal maneuvers, she rightly concludes that they represent a "move to abstraction" on the part of the Terrorist government (714).

49. The Hébertists' own "Ultra-revolutionary" ideas about political Terror (discursively and philosophically quite distinct from those of the Robespierrists) lie outside the scope of this study, although Béatrice Didier fruitfully analyzes the rhetoric of *Le Père Duchesne* in *Écrire la Révolution, 1789–1799* (Paris: Paris Universitaires de France, 1989), 103–20, as does Gérard Walter in *Hébert et le Père Duchesne* (Paris: Janin, 1946), chapter 12, "L'Esprit et la langue du *Père Duchesne*," 271–304. I discuss the Hébertists further in chapter 3, below. For the time being, I should simply note that the power wielded by Hébert and his followers, due largely to their association with the *sans-culottes* and the Paris Commune, to a great extent kept Robespierre and his henchmen in a position where they had to employ the forceful and violent means favored by their rivals. For better or for worse, the threat of being dis-

credited among the lower-class Parisian population, to whom the Hébertists catered, kept the Robespierrists honest—that is to say, militant—in their persecution of potential republican enemies.

50. Cited by Jacques André, *La Révolution fratricide: Un Essai psychoanalytique sur le lien social* (Paris: Presses Universitaires de France, 1993), 154 (no source provided). In the same work, André expands upon the significance of the hydra in Terrorist discourse: "The mythological figure of the hydra, to which the Revolution makes almost daily reference, is the perfect figure for the monstrosity of multiplicity and its incessant reproduction" (169).

51. Hans Robert Jauss, *Question and Answer: Forms of Dialogic Understanding*, trans. Michael Hayes (Minneapolis: University of Minnesota Press, 1989), 85. Significantly, his thoughts on the ideologically manipulative potential of "all-or-nothing" rhetorical questions are developed in a brief analysis of the abbé Sieyès's influential pamphlet of 1789, *Qu'est-ce que le tiers état?* (What is the third estate?), which, Jauss notes, "reaches its high point in this well-known sequence of questions: 'What is the third estate? Everything.—What has it been in the political order up until now? Nothing.—What does it want? To have a meaningful place in that order'" (85).

52. See André, *La Révolution fratricide*, 146: "To Be One or Not to Be."

53. Jacques Guilhaumou, "Fragments of a Discourse of Denunciation" (1789–1794), in Baker, Furet, and Lucas, eds., *The French Revolution and the Creation of Modern Political Culture*, vol. 4, 139–56.

54. Maurice Blanchot, "Everyday Speech," in *The Infinite Conversation*, trans. Susan Hanson (Minneapolis: University of Minnesota Press, 1993), 238–39. Without focusing specifically on the Law of Suspects, Lynn Hunt similarly describes the Revolution's annihilation of private life in "Révolution française et vie privée," in Philippe Ariès and Georges Duby, eds., *Histoire de vie privée*, vol. 4: *De la Révolution à la Grande Terreur* (Paris: Seuil, 1985), 21–51.

55. Blanchot, "Literature and the Right to Death," 319. On this subject, see also Saint-Just's avowed commitment to rooting out personal secrets and private thought in "On the Mode of Execution of the Decree against the Enemies of the Revolution": "Identify the secret movements of every heart; move beyond the intermediary ideas that separate you from the goal toward which you are striving" (Soboul 150). Here, as we find so often in the speeches of Saint-Just and Robespierre, the privileging of transparent, unmediated communication emerges as the flip side of the eradication of personal "intimacy."

56. "Décret de la Commune de Paris," October 10, 1793, cited by André, *La Révolution fratricide*, 155. For a cogent overview of the symbiotic relationship between the Paris Commune and the Montagne during the Terror, see Simon Schama, *Citizens: A Chronicle of the French Revolution* (New York: Vintage Books/Random House, 1989), 756–60.

57. See Prologue, note 25, above.

58. First conceived in 1790 and vigorously endorsed by Barère in 1793, the Convention's attempts to eliminate "non-French" languages and patois from the republic were, legislatively and philosophically, numerous, varied, and highly complex. For this reason and because they were not actively promoted by the two Montagnards under consideration here, I have elected not to address them in this chapter. I refer the interested reader to Michel de Certeau, Dominique Julia, and Jacques Revel, eds., *Une Politique de la langue: La Révolution française et les patois* (Paris: Gallimard, 1975).

59. As early as the fall of 1792, Robespierre uses such rhetoric to attack his opponents' merciful leanings: "Emotional sensitivity that feels almost exclusively for the enemies of liberty is highly suspect in my eyes" (Mazauric 195).

60. See chapter 1, note 6, on Rousseau's "prosopopoeia of Fabricius."

61. Quoted by J. M. Thompson, *Robespierre* (Oxford, 1939), 108.

62. Carlyle, *The French Revolution*, 331.

63. Stanley Loomis, *Paris in the Terror: June 1793–July 1794* (Philadelphia: Lippincott, 1964), 284.

64. The eroticized rhetoric of perversity that the Montagnards level against their enemies deserves further investigation. In one of his unfinished writings, Saint-Just directly opposes antirepublican depravity to republican morality when he maintains that "perversity and virtue play such great roles" in revolutionary politics (Duval 969). At the Festival of the Supreme Being, Robespierre contrasts perverted self-interest with selfless patriotism in similarly stark terms. Whereas the Supreme Being "silences," according to the Incorruptible, "the most imperious and the most tender passions before the sublime Love of the nation," its chief antagonist, evil, "belongs to the depraved man who oppresses his neighbors or allows them to be oppressed." This statement appears in Robespierre, *Discours au peuple réuni pour la fête de l'Être suprême*, pamphlet no. 355 (Paris: Imprimerie de la Commission d'instruction publique, 1794), 2. All subsequent references to this text are designated "Commission" and appear in parentheses in the body of the text.

65. See Jacques Lacan, "Kant avec Sade," in *Écrits*, tome 2 (Paris: Seuil, 1971), as well as Slavoj Žižek, "Kant with (or against) Sade," in *The Žižek Reader* (Oxford: Blackwell, 1999).

66. See Blanchard, *Saint Just et Cie:* "The definite but timid 'I' that wanted to be a 'one' has become 'we': at the same time the sum of all well-meaning patriots' 'I's and the integration of a common identity that destroys and recuperates to itself alone all individuals" (54).

67. Loomis, *Paris in the Terror*, 361.

68. See chapter 1, note 37, for more detail on Rousseau's formulation of this problem and for a reference to Keith M. Baker's excellent essay "Representation" on how it impacts the leaders of the Terror.

69. "It is this which has obliged the founders of nations throughout history to appeal to divine intervention and to attribute their own wisdom to the Gods" (*Contract* 87). What better way, in Blanchot's terms, to "usurp the appearance of the universal"?

70. For his first military mission, from October 17 to December 30, 1793, Saint-Just was stationed with French republican troops along the Rhine. Two more missions with troops in the north of France followed in 1794—one from January 22 to February 13, and another from April 29 to May 25—and for the last two weeks of June, the Committee of Public Safety charged him with overseeing "the armies of the Republic from the ocean to the Rhine." It is because of these frequent absences from the nation's capital that Saint-Just disappears somewhat from my account of the final months of the Robespierrists' reign. He did, however, return to Paris on June 29, 1794, to be guillotined with his colleagues a month later.

71. On the schism between Hébertist and Robespierrist Montagnards, see note 3, above.

72. In a more pragmatic sense, Robespierre's opposition to the Cult of Reason also stemmed from his fear that if his extremist opponents, Hébert and Chaumette, succeeded in controlling religious discourse in the new republic, then political dominance would soon follow. See Loomis, *Paris in the Terror*, 279–80.

73. Cited by F.-A. Aulard, *Le Culte de la Raison et le Culte de l'Être suprême* (Paris: Félix Alcan, 1892), 89.

74. Aulard, *Le Culte de la Raison*, 88–89; Picard's emphasis.

75. Mona Ozouf, *Festivals and the French Revolution*, trans. Alan Sheridan (Cambridge, Mass.: Harvard University Press, 1988), 164.

76. In *Mourning Glory*, Huet cites a telling ordinance passed by the Committee of Public Safety, at Robespierre's directive, on April 12, 1794: "On the facade of buildings formerly devoted to worship, in place of the inscription *Temple of Reason,* those words from the first article of the degree of the National Convention of 18 Floréal will be inscribed: 'The French People recognizes the existence of the Supreme Being and the immortality of the soul'" (49).

77. Cited by M. David, *Fraternité et la Révolution française* (Paris: Aubier, 1987), 187.

78. Huet, *Mourning Glory*, 43–47.

79. See Rousseau, *Lettre à d'Alembert* for the *philosophe*'s most famous and most radical idea for a public spectacle: "And what will be the objects of these spectacles? Nothing, if you please . . ." (233).

80. Jacques-Louis David, "Plan de la Fête à l'Être suprême" (Paris: Imprimerie nationale, 1794), 55.

81. In *Mourning Glory*, Huet summarizes: "The cult of images and the cult of women were thus replaced by a new religion and a new spectacle: a stage without actors, a theater without an audience, a God without representation" (47).

82. David, "Plan de la Fête à l'Être suprême," 52.

83. Cited by Aulard, *Le Culte de la Raison*, 287, and again by Huet, *Mourning Glory*, 40; Huet's translation and emphasis.

84. Jean-Joseph Goux, *Les Iconoclastes* (Paris: Seuil, 1978), 13, Goux's emphasis; cited and translated by Huet, *Mourning Glory*, 46.

85. Huet, *Mourning Glory*, 46.

86. Huet, *Mourning Glory*, 46–47. For more consideration of the French revolutionaries' use of Hercules as an antidote to standard, female allegorical figures, see de Baecque, *The Body Politic;* and Hunt, *The Family Romance of the French Revolution.*

87. See Hunt, *The Family Romance of the French Revolution.*

88. Cited by Chantal Thomas, "La Foutromanie révolutionnaire," in *Oeuvres anonymes du XVIIIᵉ siècle: L'Enfer de la Bibliothèque nationale,* tome 4 (Paris: Fayard, 1987), 271. For a more extensive treatment of the same subject, see also Chantal Thomas's book, *The Wicked Queen: The Origins of the Myth of Marie Antoinette* (New York: Zone Books, 1999).

89. On the uninterrupted menstruation that supposedly plagued Marie Antoinette during the final weeks of her life, see Thomas, *The Wicked Queen*, 129–30.

90. Cited by Aulard, *Le Culte de la Raison*, 90.

91. Ozouf, *Festivals and the French Revolution*, 129.

92. Camille Desmoulins discusses this incident, which occurred on March 4, 1794, in *Le Vieux Cordelier,* ed. Pierre Pachet (Paris: Belin, 1987). See chapter 3.

93. André, *La Révolution fratricide*, 130. On the Terror's consistent "efforts . . . to represent women as dangerous deviants," see also Schama, *Citizens*, 795–802.

94. See Olympe de Gouges, *Écrits politiques 1792–1793*, tome 2, ed. Olivier Blanc (Paris: Côté-Femmes, 1993).

95. David, "Plan de la Fête à l'Être suprême," 50.

96. This account of the celebration is given by Revolutionary Tribunal jurist Joachim Vilate, *Causes secrètes de la Révolution du 9 et 10 Thermidor* (Paris, n.d.), and cited by Marie-Louise Biver, *Fêtes révolutionnaires à Paris* (Paris: Presses Universitaires de France, 1979), 95; David's script for Robespierre's speech reads: "It [Atheism] returns to nothingness with the same rapidity as the conspirators struck down by the blade of the law" ("Plan de la Fête à l'Être suprême," 52)—language that quite clearly, with its insistence on instantaneous action and sublime destruction, recollects the rhetoric adopted by the Montagnards at Louis's trial.

97. On a more basic level, of course, Robespierre's destruction of an effigy constitutes yet another example of his aversion to representation. See Huet, *Mourning Glory*, 37.

98. See Marie-Joseph Chénier, "Hymne à l'Être suprême," printed in *Discours prononcés les jours de Décadi dans la section Guillaume Tell*, tome 3 (Paris: Massot, n.d.), 11–13. This poem is stunning in its use of exclusively masculine imagery to narrate the creation of the universe, and to praise the "father of nature, / he who creates and he who conserves," who is responsible for it all. Perhaps it is the "seed" with which the Supreme Being "sowed . . . the universe" that is figured visually by the "formidable discharge of artillery" in which the festival culminates.

99. Like the line about "an impure blood nourishing our fields," this line is taken from the French republican (and still national) anthem, "La Marseillaise." See my discussion of Figure 1.

100. David, "Plan de la Fête à l'Être suprême," 56.

101. See also Robespierre's 1793 proposal for a new draft of the Declaration of the Rights of Man and the Citizen, in which the rights in question are accorded explicitly and exclusively to men; for instance: "The men of all countries are brothers" (Mazauric 247); and "liberty is the power that belongs to man" (Mazauric 248). Women were explicitly excluded from this (and the final) version of the Declaration on the Rights of Man. For more on the complexities of women's status in revolutionary France—a vast topic unto itself—see, among others, Joan B. Landes, *Women and the Public Sphere in the Age of the French Revolution* (Ithaca: Cornell University Press, 1988); Sara Melzer and Leslie Rabine, eds., *Rebel Daughters* (Oxford: Oxford University Press, 1992); and Louise Laflandre-Linden, *1789–1793 les Femmes* (Paris: SPM, 1994), 13–19. Also of interest is Marie Duhet, ed., *Cahiers de doléances des femmes en 1789 et autres textes* (Paris: des femmes, 1981).

102. André, *La Révolution fratricide*, 192; André's emphasis.

103. See André, *La Révolution fratricide*, 191–231; and Hunt, *The Family Romance of the French Revolution*, 53–88.

104. Colette Soler, "The Curse on Sex," in *Sexuation: sic 3*, ed. Renata Salecl (Durham: Duke University Press, 2000), 47–48.

105. See André, *La Révolution fratricide*, 141.

106. In his analysis of Alejo Carpentier's novel *Siglo de las luces* (Mexico City: Compañía de ediciones, 1962) (*Explosion in a Cathedral*, trans. John Sturrock [Min-

neapolis: University of Minnesota Press, 2001]), itself a vivid illustration of the shortcomings and contradictions of the Jacobin Revolution, Ross Chambers has described this "male" intolerance for difference as "the 'virility' of a certain phallogocentric conception of power (the sublimity of an absolute)." Ross Chambers, *Room for Maneuver: Reading (the) Oppositional (in) Narrative* (Chicago: University of Chicago Press, 1991), 190. Influenced (like myself) by Huet's persuasive theorization of a "revolutionary sublime," Chambers draws many of the same conclusions as I do here about "the inevitable 'fall' into mediation" (190) that even the Revolution's most extreme, purportedly unmediated political strategies enact. But because his focus is largely on Carpentier's latter-day representation of the revolutionary period, I do not cite him at length in this chapter. However, Chambers's ideas about "oppositional" discourse and its double quality of both colluding with and subverting repressive power structures are crucial for—and surface more explicitly in—my readings of Desmoulins and Sade.

107. See Furet, *Revolutionary France 1770–1880*, 146.

108. Michelet, "Préface de 1869," in *Histoire de la Révolution française*.

109. Oddly enough, in his unfinished theoretical writings on governmental policy and reform, Saint-Just touches in passing on the alienating consequences, for even the most politically committed individual, of sacrificing oneself entirely on the altar of the general will. In the introduction to his *Fragments d'institutions républicaines*, the young Montagnard explains that he hopes his text will make future generations think of him with fondness and admiration, because "even the man who [is] obliged to isolate himself the most from others and from himself likes to feel close to future generations [and so] drops his anchor in the future and presses posterity—which is innocent of today's evils—to his bosom" (Duval 967). Saint-Just's description of himself as radically isolated "from others and from himself"—a position that proceeds necessarily from his and Robespierre's own insistence on eschewing the warm bonds of love and friendship for the abstract bonds of fraternity—imbues with some pathos the rigid revolutionary posture that he consistently attempted to adopt in his public discourses. What is more, his suggestion that such an isolated man might to some extent overcome his loneliness by "press[ing] posterity... to his bosom" through writing places a more life-affirming (and writerly!) spin on a political and philosophical position that I identify, as Huet so convincingly does, with a nihilistic (and antilinguistic) preoccupation with death. Because of the rambling and fragmentary nature of Saint-Just's *Institutions républicaines*, which furthermore was written in private and so never presented as official Terrorist policy, I have chosen not to examine the text in this chapter. Nevertheless, it is a fascinating work in its own right and as such warrants much further investigation.

110. See Blanchot, "Literature and the Right to Death": "When the blade falls on Saint-Just and Robespierre, in a sense it executes no one. Robespierre's virtue, Saint-Just's relentlessness, are simply their existences already suppressed, the anticipated presence of their deaths, the decision to allow freedom to assert itself completely in them and through its universality to negate the particular reality of their lives.... The Terrorists are those who desire absolute freedom and are fully conscious that this constitutes a desire for their own death, which they realize, and consequently they behave during their lifetimes not like people living among other people but like beings deprived of being, like... pure abstractions beyond history..." (319–20).

It is in this way that the Robespierrist Terror foreshadows the "death-based subjectivity" that Jonathan Strauss describes in *Subjects of Terror: Hegel, Nerval, and the Modern Self,* chapter 2, "Death-Based Subjectivity," 23–73. Marie-Hélène Huet's emphasis on the "will of the French Revolution" as a testament—a preoccupation with loss and with legacy—also supports this reading; see Huet, *Mourning Glory,* part 2: "Last Will and Testament," 97–179. Like my own and like Blanchot's, both of these analyses are indebted to Hegel's seminal discussion of the Terror in the *Phenomenology of Spirit,* 355–63, where the philosopher unforgettably remarks that "the sole work and deed of universal freedom is therefore *death,* a death too which has no inner significance or filling, for what is negated is the empty point of the absolutely free self" (360; Hegel's emphasis).

111. Peter Brooks's commentary on this question so eloquently designates the discontents that the Montagnards' Manichaean rhetoric was bound to elicit that I cannot resist citing it here: "*Que veulent ceux qui ne veulent ni vertu ni terreur?* What do they want indeed? Saint-Just uses the logic of melodrama, the exclusion of the middle ground. But somewhere between republican virtue and republican terror lies a denied space that clamors for attention, and satisfaction." See Peter Brooks, "Opening the Depths," in Petrey, ed., *The French Revolution 1789–1989,* 122. It is precisely such a denied space that my readings in this book (particularly in chapters 3 and 4) attempt to define; I am grateful to Brooks for his insightful counsel along these lines.

112. In *The Rebel,* Camus writes: "From the moment [the Convention] condemns him to the moment he stretches his neck to the knife, Saint-Just keeps silent. This long silence is more important than his death [itself] . . . [for] in the end, contemptuous both of tyranny and of a people who do not conform to Pure Reason, he resorts to silence himself. His principles cannot be brought into agreement with things as they are, because things are not as they should be. Principles alone are reliable, and mute" (129; translation modified).

113. In his recent biography *Robespierre* (London: Longman, 1999), John Hardman summarizes the two conflicting versions of the gunshot wound—self-inflicted or inflicted by the hostile *gendarme* Charles-André Merda—in the historiography of the Revolution. Hardman then goes on to say that he himself "prefer[s] the suicide explanation, and take[s] the increasingly belligerent measures discussed at the end by the Robespierrists as evidence not of confidence but of despair" (202). In a slightly different vein, Jean Thorel's *La Fin de Robespierre* (n.p., 1975) hypothesizes that there were in fact two bullets: that Merda shot the Incorruptible in his cell just as the prisoner was attempting to shoot himself. However, as Antoine de Baecque sagely points out in *Glory and Terror: Seven Deaths under the French Revolution,* trans. Charlotte Mendell (New York: Routledge, 2001), "scholars have been quarreling over this point for centuries" (145), and in the absence of definitive new evidence, I am content simply to observe that both murder and suicide conform to the death-bearing logic promulgated by Robespierre himself under the Terror.

114. Slavoj Žižek, *Tarrying with the Negative* (Durham: Duke University Press, 1993), 37.

115. Alain Badiou has devoted an excellent essay to this subject, entitled "Qu'est-ce qu'un Thermidorien?" in Kintzler and Rizk, eds., *La République et la Terreur,* 53–64.

116. Cited in Hardman, *Robespierre,* 196.

117. Carlyle, *The French Revolution,* 357.

3. The Bridle and the Spur

1. Maximilien Robespierre, in *Papiers inédits trouvés chez Robespierre, Saint-Just, Payan, etc., supprimés ou omis par Courtois* (Paris: Baudoin Frères, 1828), tome 3, 366. Without providing a source, Desmoulins's biographer Janssens quotes Charlotte Robespierre as having said that this passage referred explicitly to *Le Vieux Cordelier*. See Jacques Janssens's discussion of this posthumous note in *Camille Desmoulins: Le Premier Républicain de France* (Paris: Perrin, 1973), 590.

2. The problem of finances surfaces again and again in *Le Vieux Cordelier*, because Desmoulins was repeatedly criticized by his opponents, especially Saint-Just, for having married a woman from a wealthy family. This is probably why the author often reminds his readers that his publisher, Desenne, is receiving all of the proceeds from *Le Vieux Cordelier*: "It has to be the first time that an author asks his bookseller to keep the profits for himself, but truly it is in this case that La Fontaine would have been right to say: *Other people look for treasure, and I avoid it*" (*Vieux Cordelier* 40).

3. Camille Desmoulins, *Le Vieux Cordelier*, ed. Pierre Pachet (Paris: Belin, 1987), 40. All subsequent references to this volume are designated *Vieux Cordelier* and appear in parentheses in the body of the text.

4. Desmoulins's numerous journals prior to *Le Vieux Cordelier* included *La France libre*, *Les Révolutions de France et de Brabant*, and *La Tribune des patriotes*. Probably his best-known individual speeches were the incendiary "Discours de la Lanterne" and his "Opinion sur le jugement de Louis XVI"—the latter delivered in support of Saint-Just's and Robespierre's radical proposals. Also in an orthodox Robespierrist vein, he composed a tome entitled *Histoire des Brissotins: Fragment d'une histoire secrète de la Révolution*. This work, undertaken as part of the Montagnards' campaign against their Girondin rivals, most likely formed part of the larger "history of the Revolution" on which he claimed, in the first *Vieux Cordelier*, to have been working before resuming his journalistic exploits.

5. Alphonse de Lamartine, *Histoire des Girondins* (New York: F. Gaillardet, 1847), 324.

6. In response to Saint-Just's accusations that Desmoulins was "conspiring" against the republic, the journalist wrote: "Citizens, I 'conspired' for your liberty... on July 12, when, a pistol in my hand, I called the nation to arms and to freedom, and when I, first of all, put on the national cockade that you can no longer attach to your hats without remembering me" (*Vieux Cordelier* 73).

7. See, for example, Camille Desmoulins, *Les Révolutions de France et de Brabant*, in *Oeuvres*, ed. Albert Soboul (Munich: Kraus Reprint, 1980), tome 8, 82–85.

8. The Company of the Indies was France's colonial trading monopoly, which the revolutionary government slated for liquidation after the fall of the monarchy. The two Hébertists who oversaw the process, François Chabot and Claude Basire, took advantage of their position to speculate in the company's stock (which they extorted from its anxious former directors) and to skim considerable profits (which they neglected to register in the company's official records). Fabre participated in this dirty business by accepting bribes from Chabot and Basire and even by putting his signature to false documentation of the liquidation process. To make matters worse, before he was implicated in the scandal, Fabre volunteered to investigate it

on behalf of the Robespierrist government, thereby confirming the Montagnard leaders' worst fears about the surface reversibility of vice and virtue.

9. Cited by Jacques Janssens, *Camille Desmoulins*, 741. Janssens bases his narrative of Desmoulins's death largely on the eyewitness account of A.-V. Arnault, *Souvenirs d'un sexagénaire* (Paris, n.d.).

10. See Chambers, *Room for Maneuver*, chapter 4, "Graffiti on the Prison Wall: Writing under Dictation," 175–233.

11. Camille Desmoulins, *La Tribune des patriotes* (Paris: Société littéraire typographique, n.d.), 2.

12. Although Danton eventually became known as the leader of the Indulgents, his track record beforehand was, like Desmoulins's, more militant than lenient. One telling example is his response to the "September massacres" of 1792, when disgruntled mobs stormed the jails of the nation's capital in search of counterrevolutionaries and killed fourteen hundred prisoners in cold blood—an event that Danton reportedly dismissed as necessary to appease the people of Paris. More generally, as minister of justice he consistently advocated Terror as a means of securing the nation's stability, until some key military victories against France's external enemies led him to conclude that it was no longer necessary. At this point, Danton, Desmoulins, and their allies decided to undertake the cause of clemency. If I choose to focus on Desmoulins rather than Danton in this book, it is because the journalist's articulation of a politics of clemency is also, quite explicitly, a poetics of clemency, whereas Danton's self-proclaimed orientation, in old-school Montagnard style, tends more toward "action" than "writing."

13. As Ross Chambers remarks in *Room for Maneuver*, interpretation is always a function of the reader's desire—a problem that becomes particularly sticky in the case of "oppositional" discourse that ironizes a repressive ideology in order to critique it (177). Because the very nature of irony prevents it from being "definitively" taken as such, it runs the risk of being taken as a nonironic affirmation of that which it attempts to undercut. Like Sade, apropos of whom I address this difficult issue in chapter 4, the ambiguous and playful qualities of Desmoulins's texts invite multiple readings. At the very least—my own "desire" to read *Le Vieux Cordelier* in a certain way aside—this invitation to multiplicity undermines or challenges the Terrorist will to homogenize and stabilize meaning.

14. See Gilles Deleuze and Félix Guattari, *Kafka: Toward a Minor Literature* (Minneapolis: University of Minnesota Press, 1986).

15. As Schama notes in *Citizens*, Desmoulins's writings were "deliberately addressed to the revolutionary elite" (812). With their erudite allusions, complicated syntax, and elliptical style, Desmoulins pointedly distanced himself from the ersatz "popular" tone and content of Hébert's journal, *Le Père Duchesne*, which employed foul-mouthed vocabulary and sweeping innuendo to appeal to the Parisian *sans-culottes*. The paradox here is that while Desmoulins viewed Hébert as an enemy of genuinely free expression—the author of *Le Père Duchesne* was perfectly content to dismiss any and all of his opponents as "fuckers"—the language of *Le Vieux Cordelier* was (is) much less accessible to a wide readership.

16. See Jean-Paul Bertaud, "An Open File: The Press under the Terror," in Baker, Furet, and Lucas, eds., *The French Revolution and the Creation of Modern Political Culture*, vol. 4, 298–301.

17. See chapter 2, note 31.

18. See de Baecque, *The Body Politic*, 310–14; as well as Hunt, *The Family Romance of the French Revolution*, 84.

19. On Lacan's conceptualization of the relationship between error and the speech and desire of the individual subject, see chapter 1, note 69, above.

20. Although Desmoulins addresses questions of sexual difference much less than Robespierre or the Montagnard leaders, it is possible to read in his disparaging reference to his potential detractors' "little penholder" a crude evocation of female genitalia—placed in implicit opposition to his own obviously phallic and therefore virile "republican pen." If we adopt this interpretation, the conceit then becomes another adoption of the Terror's own rhetoric (in this case, its misogyny) against the Terror's principal aims, which in this case would be to silence Desmoulins's own controversial utterances.

21. Jacques Lacan, *Télévision* (Paris: Seuil, 1974), 9.

22. For a more detailed articulation of this view as applied to the writer himself, see Desmoulins, *La Tribune des patriotes:* "One cannot demand that a writer of periodicals always tell the truth, especially when he is writing about [current events in] his native land, in a manner more conjectural than historical. At the limit, all that one can fairly ask of him is good faith, or what we might call *relative truth,* since Candide himself, even when he is in error, says only what he thinks, and such candor is always an advantage…" (4).

23. Stéphane Mallarmé, "Mystery in Literature," in *Mallarmé: Selected Prose Poems, Essays, and Letters,* trans. Bradford Cook (Baltimore: Johns Hopkins University Press, 1956), 33; translation modified.

24. Rousseau's best-known use of this expression appears in the opening lines of his *Confessions,* in *Oeuvres complètes,* tome 1, 5: "I want to display to my peers a man in all the truth of nature, and this man will be myself. Myself alone [moi seul]."

25. See Janssens, *Camille Desmoulins,* 547.

26. The date of Robespierre's speech was November 21, 1793; Desmoulins published the second issue of *Le Vieux Cordelier* on December 10, 1793.

27. For more on the subtle rhetorical self-effacements effected (or affected) by Robespierre and Saint-Just, refer to chapter 2.

28. For the quoted phrase, see Michelet, *Histoire de la Révolution française,* 745.

29. Desmoulins cited in Janssens, *Camille Desmoulins,* 553.

30. On the French revolutionaries' appropriation of classical antiquity, see Harold T. Parker, *The Cult of Antiquity and the French Revolutionaries* (New York: Octagon Books, 1965); and Claude Mossé, *L'Antiquité dans la Révolution française* (Paris: Albin Michel, 1989). Parker is particularly interesting in that he provides a statistically based list of "books the revolutionaries read" (18–19); this list ranks Tacitus fourth of the republicans' top fifteen authors, above both Rousseau and Voltaire.

31. Karl Marx, *The Eighteenth Brumaire of Louis Bonaparte* (1963; New York: International Publishers, 1991), 15.

32. Camille Desmoulins, "Discours dans le procès de Louis XVI, sur la question de l'appel au peuple" in *Oeuvres,* ed. Soboul, tome 1, 481.

33. See Janssens, *Camille Desmoulins,* 561, for a detailed historical corroboration of this view.

34. In fact, the snippet of Tacitus's original Latin that Desmoulins includes in his footnote also prevents readers from seeing the term *counterrevolutionary* as a "literal translation." Here is the Latin as provided in *Le Vieux Cordelier: "Primus*

Augustus cognitionem de famoisis libellis specie legis ejus tractavit..." (51). It is almost as if Desmoulins truncates the original at precisely the point where one might have hoped to find a Latin version of *counterrevolutionary,* in order to make his pretension to a "literal translation" even more unreliable and outrageous.

35. "Décret de la Commune de Paris," October 10, 1793, cited by André, *Révolution fratricide,* 155.

36. Cited in Janssens, *Camille Desmoulins,* 561.

37. See Janssens, *Camille Desmoulins,* 561.

38. The profligacy for which Danton was known also, in financial terms at least, characterized Fabre d'Églantine. See Robespierre's character assessment—unpublished during his lifetime—of Fabre in *Papiers inédits trouvés chez Robespierre,...,* vol. 3, 347–49: "Just ask d'Églantine's friends; they will tell you that [even] the revenue from his plays was always devoured, so to speak, before the first performance... a fact that is closely related to this man's knavishness" (347). As mentioned in note 2, above, Desmoulins endeavored to protect himself from similar accusations of spendthrift by consistently reminding his readers that all the revenues generated by *Le Vieux Cordelier* went to his publisher, Desenne, not to himself.

39. See Sigmund Freud, *Beyond the Pleasure Principle,* trans. and ed. James Strachey (New York: Norton, 1961), for a conceptualization of death as the cessation of libidinal expenditure. From a Freudian perspective, the Montagnards' preoccupation with death and recourse to killing dovetails perfectly with their stated commitment to controlling or suppressing desire (libido). For Sade's critique of this repressed approach to death, see chapter 4.

40. Janssens, too, reads this passage as a reference to Dillon (*Camille Desmoulins,* 561).

41. The same goes for the description of the "suspect" military personage: "*Multa militari famà metum fecerat.*" Tacitus presents the general's heroic reputation *(famà),* not the general himself, as causing fear *(metum).*

42. Carlyle, for instance, describes Robespierre's face as a "poor seagreen," his personality "full of sincere cant, incorruptibility, virulence,... barren as the east wind!" (*The French Revolution,* 320).

43. On Robespierre's uniqueness in wearing a wig during the revolutionary period, see Madame de Staël, *Considérations sur la Révolution française* (Paris: Delaunay, Bossange and Masson, 1818), 140–41.

44. Carlyle, *The French Revolution,* 329.

45. Janssens, *Camille Desmoulins,* 560–61.

46. Louis Blanc, *Histoire de la Révolution française* (Paris: Pagnerre, Furne and Cie., 1864), 121.

47. Desmoulins actually alludes briefly to this "army of women" at the end of his third issue (*Vieux Cordelier* 57).

48. In June 1792, Lafayette had marched on Paris in an attempt to put a stop to the Revolution. When the coup failed, he fled to Austria, further confirming the general's reputation as a traitor (despite the fact that the Austrians themselves wasted no time in imprisoning him as a spy).

49. For a helpful overview of this complex issue, see Schama, *Citizens,* 693.

50. Jean-François Laharpe, a devout Catholic and adamant opponent of the Revolution, makes a strikingly similar argument a few years after Thermidor, in his

treatise *Du Fanatisme dans la langue révolutionnaire* (Paris: Marchands de Nouveautés, 1797).

51. See Desmoulins's portentous remark to Robespierre, made in 1790 and quoted in chapter 2: "You are faithful to your principles, however it may be with your friends."

52. Stéphane Mallarmé, *Igitur*, in *Oeuvres complètes*, ed. Henri Mondor and G. Jean Aubry (Paris: Gallimard/Bibliothèque de la Pléïade, 1945), 451.

53. My use of a contemporary phrase in this context is deliberate, insofar as it designates the rigidness and hypocrisy of the discursive norms that Desmoulins's journal works to contest. One useful summary of the origins and meanings of the term *politically correct* is Ruth Perry, "A Short History of the Term *Politically Correct*," in Patricia Aufderheide, ed., *Beyond P.C.: Toward a Politics of Understanding* (Saint Paul, Minn.: Graywolf, 1992), 72–73.

54. On the widespread allusion to and idealization of Greco-Roman republicanism in the revolutionary period, see note 30, above.

55. Niccolò Machiavelli, *The Prince*, ed. Christian Gauss and trans. Luigi Ricci (New York: Oxford University Press/Mentor Books, 1952), 90. For a detailed juxtaposition of Terror as conceived by Machiavelli and the Montagnards, see Sfez, "Les Langues de la Terreur," 129–59.

56. Machiavelli, *The Prince*, 89.

57. The remainder of this citation is interesting in the context of the psychosexual dynamics of the Terror, reviewed in chapter 2: "moderantism, which is to moderation what impotence is to chastity, and excess, which resembles energy no more than hydropsy resembles good health" (Mazauric 289). Robespierre's attack on moderantism becomes an imputation of sexual inadequacy ("impotence"), in contrast to the "chastity" and vitality ("energy") of the true republican.

58. For an economical account of Marat's trial by his sworn enemies, the Girondin *conventionnels*, in the spring of 1793, see Schama, *Citizens*, 716–19. For a similar treatment of his funeral, in which "the sacralization of Marat became a powerful tool of revolutionary propaganda," see Schama, *Citizens*, 742–45. As Schama points out (without referring forward to Desmoulins's attempt to draw an analogy between himself and the great martyr), "to identify with Marat rapidly became a testimony of revolutionary purity" (745). For an extremely detailed and perceptive analysis of the festivals organized surrounding (and artistic representations of) Marat's death, see T. J. Clark, *Farewell to an Idea: Episodes from a History of Modernity*, chapter 1, "Painting in the Year Two" (New Haven: Yale University Press, 1999), 15–53.

59. Robespierre cited in Janssens, *Camille Desmoulins*, 613.

60. Desmoulins cited in Janssens, *Camille Desmoulins*, 614.

61. Cited by Michelet, *Histoire de la Révolution française*, 700.

62. As with the phrase "myself alone," borrowed by Desmoulins from Rousseau's *Confessions*, "burning is not the same thing as responding" establishes a close parallel between the French journalist and the Swiss *philosophe*. This parallel, it should be noted, is ideally suited to Desmoulins's deterritorialization of Terrorist discourse, since it enables him to assume the mask of republican orthodoxy while also trotting out aspects of Rousseau's thought that the Terrorists themselves suppressed (specifically, the emphasis on discursive and political permissiveness).

63. Cited by Michelet, *Histoire de la Révolution française*, 701.

64. Michelet, *Histoire de la Révolutions française,* 757.

65. In his *Histoire de Robespierre,* Ernest Hamel posits a direct link between Desmoulins's writings and Fabre's arrest, a link whose nexus was the Incorruptible's paranoid fury: "What [Robespierre] reproached [Fabre] with the most was Fabre's having indoctrinated Camille Desmoulins and set him on the deplorable path where the author currently found himself" (359–60).

66. See Fabre d'Églantine, *Oeuvres politiques,* ed. Charles Vellay (Paris: Fasquelle, 1914), 173–74: "The regeneration of the French people [and] the establishment of the republic have led necessarily to the reform of the vulgar era. [After the fall of the monarchy,] we could no longer count the years when the kings oppressed us as a time when we were actually alive. The prejudices of the crown and the clergy, and the lies propagated by both, sullied every page of the calendar that we had been using." Quite clearly, this notion of a past purged of all royalist reminders echoes Robespierre's attempt at the king's trial to banish the monarch to a temporal and ontological zone noncoincident with that of revolutionary France: "Louis *was* king, and the republic *is* founded." See chapter 2.

67. See Michelet, *Histoire de la Révolution française,* 702; and Janssens, *Camille Desmoulins,* 619.

68. This figure would in fact become a reality just over a month later, on March 4, when a group of Hébertists, including the publisher Momoro, draped the tables of the Declaration of the Rights of Man in black crepe, the ritual that signified a revolutionary call to arms. The move was a protest against the constraints that Robespierre and company had been placing on free speech. Desmoulins refers to this very incident in his seventh, unpublished issue: "Is there anything as criminal and as threatening to liberty as this mortuary cloth that Momoro...had thrown atop the Declaration of the Rights of Man, this black veil...and the signal of the *tocsin*?" (*Vieux Cordelier* 128). As we shall see in our examination of this issue, however, the dueling narrative voices that Desmoulins adopts in the seventh issue make it difficult to take literally any of the pronouncements it contains and, in this case, to determine whether he truly sees Momoro's gesture as "criminal."

69. See Jean-Jacques Rousseau, "Fiction ou morceau allégorique sur la révélation," in *Oeuvres complètes,* tome 4, 1044–54.

70. "Nobody," Desmoulins notifies his readers, "has proven the necessity of revolutionary measures by stronger arguments than I have, even in my *Vieux Cordelier*—which people have not wanted to understand" (*Vieux Cordelier* 100).

71. Like the Jacobins, the "new" Cordeliers—Hébertists with strong ties to the Paris Commune—were a powerful political club during the Terror. Also like the Jacobins, they expelled Desmoulins on the basis of his proposed committee. Desmoulins had, however, been at odds with the majority of the Cordeliers for some time before his expulsion—as the title of his journal itself suggests.

72. Jacques Godechot, *La Révolution française* (Paris: Perrin, 1988), 316.

73. Interestingly enough, Longinus uses an uncannily similar conceit in his aesthetic treatise: "Sublime impulses are exposed to greater dangers when they are left to themselves without the ballast and stability of knowledge; they need the bridle as often as the spur" (*Hypsous* 101).

74. Pierre Pachet puts the matter succinctly in his introduction to Desmoulins's journal: "This repartition is quite obviously a ruse: everything that one speaker hesitates to say, the other expresses explicitly" (*Vieux Cordelier* 25). I regret that the

broader issue of dialogism, which has been famously treated by a range of thinkers (Bakhtin, Jauss, and many scholars of Rousseau and Diderot), cannot be treated here in the detail it demands.

75. Desmoulins used ellipses, not blanks, to disguise the identities of the people referenced in this issue.

76. On the collusion between public and private represented by the *lettre de cachet*, see Arlette Farge, *Le Désordre des familles: Lettres de cachet des Archives de la Bastille*, intro. Michel Foucault (Paris: Gallimard/Julliard, 1982), 15 and 347. My reading of the *lettre de cachet* is also indebted to the one that Lucienne Frappier-Mazur proposes in her work on Sade; I refer to her analysis of the Sadean conflation of public and private spheres in chapter 4.

77. On Barère's support for the abbé Grégoire's attempts to homogenize language in the republic by ridding the state of "non-French" languages and dialects, see chapter 2, note 58. For all his links to the Robespierrists in the early 1790s, Barère was also a shameless political opportunist and turned against them during Thermidor to save his own skin.

78. Like Barère, Momoro was soon to turn against Robespierre as well, protesting that the Incorruptible was preventing him from performing his duties as "the Premiere Publisher of Liberty." See note 67, above.

79. Lacan, *Télévision*, 9.

80. In Lacanian terms, this all-encompassing framework is of course the symbolic order or the "Big Other"—which, fortuitously, is one of the labels that Sade devises for Robespierre's Supreme Being in his critique of republican state religion. See chapter 4.

81. Desmoulins cited by Janssens, *Camille Desmoulins*, 9.

4. The Second Time as Farce

1. On Sade's political opportunism during the Terror, see Francine du Plessix Gray, *At Home with the Marquis de Sade* (New York: Simon and Schuster, 1998), 337–39.

2. Hilary Mantel, *A Place of Greater Safety* (New York: Henry Holt, 1992), 628–29.

3. Mantel, *A Place of Greater Safety*, 629.

4. Mantel, *A Place of Greater Safety*, 630.

5. For a detailed account of the accumulated "political faux pas" that Sade committed during the months leading up to his arrest as a counterrevolutionary, see du Plessix Gray, *At Home with the Marquis de Sade*, 342–43.

6. Mantel, *A Place of Greater Safety*, 629.

7. For a succinct overview of Sade's brush with death on 9 Thermidor and a helpful refutation of earlier scholars' erroneous statements on the subject, see Maurice Lever, *Sade: A Biography*, trans. Arthur Goldhammer (New York: Farrar, Straus, and Giroux, 1993), 465–68.

8. D.-A.-F. de Sade to Gaufridy, January 21, 1795, in *Correspondance*, ed. Alice M. Laborde, tome 24 (Geneva: Slatkine, 1995–1996), 25; Sade's emphasis.

9. After his arrest in December 1793, Sade was detained in numerous places before winding up in Picpus, which was less a jail than a *maison de santé*—a hospital where the wealthy could buy time away from the relatively efficient execution schedule in effect in the other prisons. First he was taken to the Madelonnettes, then to

the Conciergerie, and finally, thanks to the efforts of his devoted mistress Constance Quesnet, to Picpus. He was freed from there on October 15, 1794.

10. See note 33, below.

11. Sade's exemplary libertine Juliette, for instance, takes great pleasure in availing herself of the Old Regime's despotic practices: "Five or six ladies who in the past few months have thought to challenge my social position are presently lodged in the Bastille," she triumphantly informs her friend Noirceuil. See D.-A.-F. de Sade, *Juliette,* trans. Austryn Wainhouse (New York: Grove Press, 1968), 257. All subsequent references to this text are designated *Juliette* and appear in parentheses in the body of the chapter. Where necessary to my analysis, I modify Wainhouse's translation and include words and phrases from the corresponding French original: *Histoire de Juliette ou les prosperités du vice,* in D.-A.-F. de Sade, *Oeuvres complètes,* ed. Annie Le Brun and Jean-Jacques Pauvert, tomes 8 and 9 (Paris: Pauvert, 1986). Page numbers refer to the English edition.

12. Hegel likewise emphasizes the radical lack of passion that attended the Terrorists' deployment of the guillotine; in the *Phenomenology,* he describes its work as resulting in "the coldest and meanest of all deaths, with no more significance than cutting off a head of cabbage" (360). In this regard, Hegel's perspective resembles that of Sade. It seems to me that a sustained juxtaposition of these two thinkers' readings of the Terror would be extremely, if unexpectedly, illuminating—as against what is now the relatively commonplace association, via Lacan, of Sade with Kant.

13. D.-A.-F. de Sade, *Philosophy in the Bedroom,* in *Justine, Philosophy in the Bedroom, and Other Writings,* ed. and trans. Richard Seaver and Austryn Wainhouse (New York: Grove Press), 329. In instances where my analysis requires that I modify the English translation to reflect greater fidelity to the original, I include the relevant French words in brackets; at such moments the edition I am using is Sade, *La Philosophie dans le boudoir,* in *Oeuvres complètes,* tome 3. All subsequent references to Sade's novel (which I prefer to call the *Philosophy in the Boudoir*) are designated *Philosophy;* they appear in parentheses the body of the chapter. All page numbers refer to the English edition.

14. As Lucienne Frappier-Mazur observes in her masterful study, *Writing the Orgy: Power and Parody in Sade,* trans. Gillian C. Gill (Philadelphia: University of Pennsylvania Press, 1996), "beheadings are extremely rare" in Sade's prerevolutionary writing, probably "because this manner of execution is too swift to offer any satisfaction" to his libertine heroes (124–25). Frappier-Mazur refers to a guillotine execution scene at the end of *La Nouvelle Justine;* this and the one from *Juliette,* analyzed above, are the only two I have been able to locate in Sade's fiction.

15. See Chambers, *Room for Maneuver: Reading (the) Oppositional (in) Narrative.*

16. Chambers's emphasis on the reader's desire follows logically from the radical uncertainty inherent in irony itself. As de Man states in *Blindness and Insight,* "In [irony], the relationship between sign and meaning is discontinuous, involving an extraneous principle that determines the point and the manner at and in which the relationship is determined. . . . [In the ironic utterance,] the sign points to something that differs from its literal meaning and has for its function the thematization of this difference. But this important structural aspect . . . clearly lacks discriminatory precision" (209). In Chambers's schema, the desire of the text's interpreter fills in for the "extraneous principle" by which irony is determined. Linda Hutcheon describes the matter more concisely in *Irony's Edge: The Theory and Politics of Irony*

(New York: Routledge, 1994): "Irony isn't irony until it is interpreted as such. . . . Someone attributes irony; someone makes irony happen" (6).

17. See above all Maurice Blanchot, "The Main Impropriety," in Jacques Ehrmann, ed., *Yale French Studies* 39: *Literature and Revolution* (1967): 50–63. See also Paul Éluard, "Le Divin Marquis," *La Révolution surréaliste* 8 (December 1, 1926): 8–9; and Jules Janin, "Le Marquis de Sade," *Revue de Paris* (November 1834): 321. An important exception to this tendency surfaces in the work of Annie Le Brun, who likewise—although not in great detail—insists on Sade's oppositional stance with respect to the Terror. In her study *Sade: A Sudden Abyss,* trans. Camille Naish (San Francisco: City Lights Books, 1990), she criticizes Blanchot in particular for "prefer[ring] to emphasize the similarity between Saint-Just and Sade, rather than casting light upon the moral breach that divides them" (172). In *Coldness and Cruelty* (New York: Zone Books, 1991), Gilles Deleuze also insists on some important intellectual differences between Sade and Saint-Just and even briefly mentions the possibility that Sade's version of "republicanism" offers an ironic perspective on Saint-Just's political philosophy (77–79). Deleuze's analysis, however, centers almost exclusively on how the two men conceive of political institutions (a topic I do not address in this work) and therefore does not overlap much with my own reading of Sadean versus Montagnard politics.

18. Two of the most intelligent examples of this approach are: Marcel Hénaff, *Sade: The Invention of the Libertine Body,* trans. Xavier Callahan (Minneapolis: University of Minnesota Press, 1999), chapter 2, "Saying Everything, or the Encyclopedia of Excess," 55–83; and Philippe Sollers, *Sade dans le texte: L'Écriture et l'expérience des limites* (Paris: Seuil, 1968). In terms of "apolitical" readings, I should also mention Philippe Roger's superb *Sade: La Philosophie dans le pressoir* (Paris: Bernard Grasset, 1976), which argues persuasively against the detection of a "political credo" in Sade's texts (169–71). While I take Roger's point about the difficulty of determining consistent political tenets in the Sadean oeuvre, I should say that it is Roger himself who inspired me to read the libertine writer in conjunction with or against the grain of Terrorist discourse. Roger looks at Sadean language as an astute subversion of classical rhetoric and observes that "in declaring war on [such] rhetoric, he takes aim at the very mechanism of discourses of power" (190)—a perfect description, it seems to me, of Sade's enterprise in ironizing Robespierrist language.

19. Angela Carter, *The Sadeian Woman* (New York: Pantheon Books, 1978), 136.

20. Frappier-Mazur, *Writing the Orgy,* 160. Additionally, I have learned much from another scholar who stresses the ironic nature of Sade's republican writings: Lynn Hunt. In *The Family Romance of the French Revolution,* chapter 5, "Sade's Family Politics," 124–50, Hunt persuasively reads the *Philosophy in the Boudoir* and the political treatise at its center as an "almost always paradoxical, if not ironic . . . commentary on the revolutionary experience" (125). Nonetheless, my analysis differs from Hunt's in that her focused emphasis on the family dynamics of Sade's novel—which she sees as a parodic reworking of those promulgated by the Revolution—precludes consideration of a number of other ideological subversions that the text effects in direct response to the Terror.

21. Pierre Saint-Amand, *The Libertine's Progress: Seduction in the Eighteenth-Century French Novel,* trans. Jennifer Curtiss Gage (Providence: Brown University Press, 1994), 121. My reading also intersects with Saint-Amand's meditation on Sade's violent philosophical inversions (although Saint-Amand does not identify the

Terror as one of the author's intellectual targets). See *The Laws of Hostility*, chapter 5, "The Politics of Crime (Sade)," 129–48.

22. In fact, Sade frequently, if critically, stresses the persistence of desire in hermeneutics. In one letter describing the effects of prison life—with its protocol of coded exchanges and secret signals—on his view of language, he writes: "This system of signals and numbers [that prevailed] in the Bastille as in my latest place of detention, had the dangerous effect of habituating me to believing in phantoms that gratified my hope and in hypotheses that nourished it. This imprinted on my brain the sophistic character for which people often criticize me in my writings." In *Oeuvres complètes*, tome 12, 26.

23. More generally, on the suitability of the ironic mode to political critique, see Hutcheon, *Irony's Edge*, 4–6.

24. Sade, *La Nouvelle Justine ou les malheurs de la vertu*, in *Oeuvres complètes*, tome 7, 184. All subsequent references to this novel are designated *Justine* and appear in parentheses in the body of the chapter.

25. In this way, my perspective on the political implications of Sade's writing both resembles and parts company from that of Max Horkheimer and Theodor W. Adorno. In their *Dialectic of Enlightenment*, trans. John Cumming (1944; New York: Continuum, 1989), they assert that in *Juliette*, "private vice constitutes a predictive chronicle of the public virtues of the totalitarian era" (118). Varying this formula somewhat, I maintain that Sade's multifaceted conception of private vice parodies the public virtues of the Robespierrist era rather than predicting those of the twentieth century.

26. D.-A.-F. de Sade, *Sade contre l'Être suprême*, ed. Philippe Sollers (Paris: Gallimard, 1996). For Sollers's remarks on the provenance of this text, originally held to be apocryphal, as well as on the identity of the Rome-based "dear Cardinal" to whom it is addressed, see Sollers's "Avertissement de l'éditeur," 57–58. All subsequent page references to this work, designated *Contre*, appear in parentheses in the body of the text.

27. See for example Sade to the Committee of General Security, March 18, 1794, *Correspondance*, tome 23, 178. Benoît Jacquot's splendid new film *Sade* (2002) nicely captures the opportunism behind the ex-marquis's republican political activity.

28. Sade to the Committee of General Security, August 16, 1794, in *Correspondance*, tome 23, 211.

29. See, for instance, his *Voyage d'Italie*, the 1791 edition of *Justine*, and an early draft of *Aline et Valcour*, as well as selected passages of the *120 Journées de Sodome*, written while Sade was in the Bastille (and presumed lost by him after the prison was stormed).

30. On the indeterminate, potentially parodic nature of these writings, see Frappier-Mazur, *Writing the Orgy*, 123.

31. See du Plessix Gray, *At Home with the Marquis de Sade*, 339; as well as Lever, *Sade*, 462.

32. This is the speech in which Robespierre, as if to concede that his Supreme Being represents a reversal of the de-Christianizing course his government has been following up until this point, cites Voltaire's famous quip: "If God did not exist, we would have to invent him" (Mazauric 285).

33. In June 1772, Sade and his valet fed bonbons laced with Spanish fly to four prostitutes in a Marseilles brothel. Although the plaintiffs eventually withdrew their

charges, in September the two men were found guilty of "poisoning and sodomy," crimes punishable by death; the public burning of their effigies symbolized their "civic death" in anticipation of actual executions, which Sade, at least, evaded by escaping to Italy. See Lever, *Sade,* chapter 10, "The Marseilles Affair," 195–216.

34. In this respect Sade's critique of the Revolution anticipates that of Edgar Quinet, who writes in *La Révolution* (Paris: Belin, 1987): "[The Jacobins] want their acts of violence, their iniquities, and their ferocity to be adored as sacred. Let us put an end to this sanguine mysticism" (505).

35. D.-A.-F. de Sade, "Avis aux propriétaires et principaux locataires des Maisons siutées dans l'arrondissement de la Section," August 1, 1793, in *Correspondance,* tome 23, 97.

36. The story is that Sade resigned as section president in August 1793 after being unable to approve a measure he himself describes in a letter as "a horror, an inhumanity." When presented with this thoroughly upsetting proposal, whatever it was, Sade actually fainted and woke up spitting blood—a surprising and interesting detail given his monstrous image. In *At Home with Marquis de Sade,* du Plessix Gray hypothesizes that the event that triggered Sade's breakdown and subsequent resignation was a request that he recommend capital punishment for one of the section's "counterrevolutionaries" (335). While this explanation certainly fits with Sade's own disapproving remarks about the death penalty, discussed further below, there is no documented evidence to support this particular construction of his "horror." See Gilbert Lely, *Vie du Marquis de Sade* (Paris: Pauvert/Garnier Frères, 1982), 480, for a reprint of Sade's own account of the episode. In any case, like his declaration of atheism, Sade's resignation as president most likely constituted another one of the political missteps that led to his arrest as well as to the section members' unwillingness to save their former president.

37. See Le Brun for a similar remark on the import of Sade's attack on republican religion in *Yet Another Effort:* "In the course of this implacable text, Sade proves that the new republicans are indeed using the same machine . . . transformed into an instrument of domination. Thus the war machine of atheism ends up producing the Supreme Being; . . . and the machine of revolutionary rhetoric ends up producing the guillotine" (158).

38. On this dynamic, see Jacques-Alain Miller, "Context and Concepts," in Richard Feldstein, Bruce Fink, and Maire Jaanus, eds., *Reading Seminar XI: Lacan's Four Fundamental Concepts of Psychoanalysis* (Albany: State University of New York Press, 1995), 10. See also chapter 1, note 69, on the paradoxical Freudian/Lacanian notion that the "truth" of the subject reveals itself precisely in the subject's so-called errors, in the inversions or subversions of his or her conscious intent.

39. Hénaff, for example, asserts: "For Sade, the only sexual pleasure is the sexual pleasure of the head . . ." (*Sade,* 68). On the importance of the imagination in Sadean libertinage, see Hubert Damisch, "Écriture sans mesures," *Tel Quel* 28 (1967): 54–56; and Harari, *Scenarios of the Imaginary,* chapters 5 and 6, 133–93.

40. This is one of Blanchot's insights in "The Main Impropriety": "[The libertine intellect possesses] an infinite power of negation [that] in turn expresses and rescinds, by means of a circular experience, the notions of man and of nature, finally to affirm man in his entirety" (58).

41. As conceptualized by Freud in *Jokes and Their Relation to the Unconscious,* ed. and trans. James Strachey (New York: W. W. Norton, 1960), humor involves a

suspension of the reality principle in favor of the pleasure principle. Structurally speaking, humor is thus a differential phenomenon in that it opens up a gap between reality and pleasure, or rather it "unblocks" libidinal forces that the reality principle has been attempting to inhibit for its own countervailing purposes.

42. Indeed, when using Hénaff's terminology I should specify that the crux of his argument consists in *opposing* the lyric—feeling, sentimental, subjective—body to the "libertine body" he posits as Sade's great invention. Although Hénaff carries it out beautifully, this reading fails to miss the crucial historical and cultural point of reference for the Sadean libertine body, which ironically and precisely mimics the body of the citizen living in a Terrorist society. See Hénaff, *Sade,* chapter 1, "The Overthrow of the Lyric Body," 17–54.

43. See Hunt, *The Family Romance of the French Revolution,* 122–23, and "Male Virtue and Republican Motherhood," in Baker, Furet, and Lucas, eds., *The French Revolution and the Creation of Modern Political Culture,* vol. 4, 195–208. See also chapter 2.

44. See Hénaff, *Sade,* 40. Hénaff is referring here to the noticeably one-dimensional psychological profile of Sade's characters. For these creatures, there is no depth, no internal conflict, only unflagging commitment to "vices" or (in the case of Sade's heroes' victims) "virtues." This psychological flatness could itself be read as an ironic appropriation of Terrorist thought, which demands that the subject's individualistic leanings and characteristics dissolve into the abstract generality of an *état sans réserve.*

45. On Sade's dislike of "the sinister David" in particular and of the "bad taste" of revolutionary artists in general, see *Contre,* 63, 69, 73, 79, and 96–97. Desmoulins, incidentally, loathed David as well; see *Le Vieux Cordelier* 119 for his own sharp political and aesthetic attack on the painter-propagandist.

46. For the original passage, see Voltaire, "De l'horrible danger de la lecture" (1765), in *Mélanges,* ed. Jacques van den Heuvel (Paris: Gallimard, 1962), 713.

47. The rest of this quotation is interesting insofar as it associates philosophy explicitly with the kind of private withdrawal *(réserve)* that *The Social Contract* and the Terror forbade. As opposed to the private and independent intellectual activity that is philosophy, "everything should now be festival, gathering, collective hymn, group entertainment.... A mere withdrawal [une simple réserve] would seem sacrilegious" (*Contre* 83–84).

48. On the freedom of the press during the Revolution and the Terror, see Bertaud, "An Open File."

49. The hypocrisy of Robespierre's recourse to a Supreme Being is what Philippe Sollers leaves out of the equation when he remarks in *Sade dans le temps* that "the revolutionary project, ... in aiming to be first and foremost a social project, in making liberty and equality principles by which men should be governed, reiterates—in what we might call a horizontal fashion—the transcendental fallacy (the Cults of Reason and of the Supreme Being are imitations)" (374).

50. See Slavoj Žižek's discussion of the "totalizing" effects of the master-signifier (also referred to by Lacanians as the phallus) in *For they know not what they do* (London: Verso, 1991), 23.

51. Jacques Lacan, "L'Amour et le signifiant," in *Le Séminaire XX: Encore,* ed. Jacques-Alain Miller (Paris: Seuil, 1975).

52. Hegel, *Phenomenology of Spirit*, 358: "The *beyond* of this its [individual consciousness's] actual existence hovers over the corpse of the vanished independence of real being, merely as the exhalation of a stale gas, of the vacuous *Être suprême*."

53. Needless to say, this is a rather unorthodox notion from a Marxist perspective, despite Sade's uncannily prescient proclamation about having nothing to lose but his chains.

54. For one of Sade's more sustained warnings against religious principles pretending to "universality," see *Juliette*, 372–78. Here, as in the works examined in this chapter, Sade challenges the universal nature of religion by pitting it against the irrepressible and inevitable particularity of the passions: "Is there a single religion which can withstand the fire of the passions? And are not the passions ... preferable to religions ... ?" (*Juliette* 378).

55. Georg Lukács, *The Theory of the Novel*, trans. Anna Bostock. (1971; Cambridge: MIT Press, 1987), 92. Perhaps even more to the point, Deleuze describes Sadean irony as a subversion of the classical (Platonic) "process of thought whereby the law is made to depend on an infinitely superior Good" (83); the mock-worship of a Being-Supreme-in-Nastiness espoused by libertines such as Dolmancé and Juliette, discussed below, represents precisely such a subversion.

56. See the exchange between Eugénie and Dolmancé that immediately follows the reading of the pamphlet (*Philosophy* 339–40).

57. On this massive program to overwrite virtually every facet of prerevolutionary life, see Serge Bianchi, *La Révolution culturelle de l'An II* (Paris: Aubier Montaigne, 1982).

58. See, for instance, Saint-Just at Louis's trial: "Between the people and its enemies, there remains nothing in common but the blade. Those who cannot be governed by justice must be governed by the blade" (Soboul 118). On the implications of this figure and its link to the "right to death," see Michel Foucault, *The History of Sexuality: An Introduction*, vol. 1, trans. Robert Hurley (1978; New York: Vintage Books/Random House, 1990), 144.

59. Pierre Klossowski, *Sade My Neighbor*, trans. Alphonso Lingis (Evanston: Northwestern University Press, 1991), 91.

60. See Žižek, *For they know not what they do*, 10–11, for a lucid discussion of the Hegelian "dialectic of the topsy-turvy world [verkehrte Welt]" that informs my reading here.

61. See Hunt, *The Family Romance of the French Revolution*, 140, 125. Because, as mentioned in note 20 above, Hunt's focus does not exactly overlap with mine, I do not refer much to her reading in my analysis of the *Philosophy in the Boudoir*. From a broader methodological standpoint, however, her admirable unpacking of the Sadean republic's paradoxical and parodic aspects has strongly influenced my approach to the text.

62. "The one constant to all Sade's monstrous orgies," Angela Carter notes, "is that the whip hand is always the hand with the real political power and the victim is the person who has little or no power at all" (*The Sadeian Woman*, 24). Similarly, in his essay "Sade," which prefaces the English edition of *Philosophy in the Bedroom*, 37–72, Maurice Blanchot observes: "Virtue in Sade's world—Virtue which is tenacious, humble, continually wretched and oppressed but never convinced of its errors—suddenly declares in a most reasonable manner: Your principles presuppose

power. If my happiness consists in never taking into account the interests of others, in exploiting every opportunity to hurt or injure them, there will perforce come a day when the interests of others will likewise consist in doing me harm; in the name of what shall I then protest?" (41). Needless to say, the structural instability of libertine "freedom" is also the instability of Robespierre's Terror, which dictates that he and Saint-Just themselves must die once they lose the power to enforce their "principles."

63. Claude Lefort, "Sade: The Boudoir and the City," in *Writing: The Political Test*, trans. David Ames Curtis (Durham: Duke University Press, 2000), 70.

64. This reading runs counter to that of Béatrice Didier in *Écrire la Révolution 1789–1799*, which posits Augustin's exclusion as an "aristocratic proposal" that betrays Sade's fundamentally profeudalist politics (28–29).

65. See Caroline Weber, "Madame de Mistival's Differend: Animality and Alterity in Sade's *Philosophie dans le boudoir*," *Utah Foreign Language Review* (1997): 49–61, and "The Sexist Sublime in Sade and Lyotard," in *Philosophy and Literature* (forthcoming).

66. See chapter 2, notes 33 and 34, above.

67. In *Sade dans le temps*, Philippe Sollers suggests a similar reading of the name of Saint-Fond, the despotic French minister in Sade's *Juliette*. "Fond," however, means "bottom" or "depth," whereas "Ange," which means "angel," is to my mind much closer to "Just" in its overdetermined emphasis on virtuous conduct.

68. Libertines should avail themselves of "menials," according to the by-laws of the secret society to which Sade's Juliette belongs, because "such souls . . . are plentiful; moreover, they can be changed like skirts" (*Juliette* 432).

69. See also Hénaff on saying "all" as "the Master's exclusive claim" (*Sade,* 65).

70. The masculinization of Sade's female libertines and the ultimate authority held by men in his libertine communities have been much remarked upon elsewhere. See, for example, Deleuze on how in the case of female libertines, "their actions, the pleasures they enjoy together, and their common projects are all in imitation of man; man is the spectator and presiding genius to whom all their activities are dedicated" (*Coldness and Cruelty,* 59).

71. See Jacques Lacan, "La Signification du phallus," in *Écrits*, tome 2, 103–18. It should be noted that Lacan does not equate the phallus with discursive totality ipso facto; on the contrary, he posits the phallus as the central, organizing principle of lack around which everything else, symbolically speaking, takes shape as "All." In this sense Lacan's conception of the phallus resembles the Terrorist notion of "saying everything," which constitutes totality through exclusion, transcendence through limitation, and so on.

72. Carter, *The Sadeian Woman,* 5. Carter also points out that the penis/vagina opposition, which corresponds to a mastery/slavery relationship, has less to do with the "official gender" (24) of Sade's characters than with their libertine convictions (which signify phallic strength) or lack thereof (which betray "feminine" weakness).

73. Because Sade's "hatred of the maternal function" (Carter, *The Sadeian Woman*) has been the focus of so much scholarly discussion (see Gilles Deleuze, *Coldness and Cruelty;* Lucienne Frappier-Mazur, *Writing the Orgy;* Lynn Hunt, *Family Romance and the French Revolution;* and Jacques Lacan, "Kant avec Sade"), I will not elaborate upon it here. In the context, however, of Sade's remarks to Bernis about the Terror's horrendous program of "decreation," the devalorization of maternity in the *Philosophy in the Boudoir* and *Yet Another Effort* is of specific political import.

Conversely, the novel's attack on maternity could be read as a disparagement of the Robespierrists' insistent promotion of maternity (for instance, at the Festival of the Supreme Being) as a woman's foremost joy and obligation.

74. Lacan, "Kant avec Sade," 148.

75. Carter, *The Sadeian Woman*, 78.

76. For a thorough if perhaps insufficiently dialecticized study of how Justine is narratologically and ontologically silenced throughout *La Nouvelle Justine*, see Caroline Weber, "The Limits of 'Saying Everything,'" Ph.D. dissertation, Yale University, 1998, 134–59.

77. For the complicity of this stance with that of bourgeois individuality and instrumentality, see Horkheimer and Adorno, Excursus II, "Juliette or Enlightenment and Morality," in *Dialectic of Enlightenment*, 81–119.

78. Before *La Nouvelle Justine* (1797), Sade made Justine's sad-sack story the basis of the novella *Les Infortunes de la vertu* (1788) and the novel *Justine, ou les malheurs de la vertu* (1791).

79. Le Brun, *Sade*, 201, 202.

80. On this distinction, see Gérard Genette, *Figures III* (Paris: Seuil, 1972), 183–224.

81. See Le Brun, *Sade*, 195. This qualifier appears in the novel's last paragraph, a brief third-person narration relating the death of the heroine, "unique in her kind" (*Juliette* 1193).

82. See, for example, *Juliette* 431n, 489n, and 491n.

83. "Woman has one innate virtue. It is whorishness. . . . Woe unto her whom a thoughtless and stupid virtuousness ever keeps prisoner of dull prejudices; a victim of her opinions and of the chilly esteem she hopes for, almost always in vain, from men, she'll have lived dry and joyless and shall die unregretted" (*Juliette* 492). For better or worse, this harangue presages quite accurately the fate with which Justine, for her dogged disavowal of sexual pleasure, is ultimately rewarded.

84. For more general remarks on the "censorship of sentiment/sensitivity [sensibilité]" in Sade, see Klossowski, *Sade My Neighbor*, 22.

85. See *Juliette* 418 and 418n.

86. On the "quilting point" *(point de caption)* as the genesis of the ideological Ego-Ideal, see Lacan, *Le Séminaire III*, 293–305; and Žižek, *For they know not what they do*, 7–60.

87. See Žižek, *For they know not what they do*, 17–18. Given the novel's narrative structure, in which an omniscient narrating "I" looks back on the blunders of her past, one could even make a convincing argument that Juliette's original encounters with people accusing her of sentimental weakness become retroactively posited, by the *erzählendes Ich*, as the explanation for the falling out between Saint-Fond and the *erlebendes Ich*. Such a retroactive positing of meaning is in complete conformity with the logic of the "quilting point," which always functions to make sense *after the fact* of what was otherwise a series of entirely contingent phenomena. On the future anteriority of ideological quilting, see Jacques Lacan's discussion of *Athalie* in his *Séminaire III;* as well as Weber, "Freedom's Missed Moment."

88. See note 67, above.

89. See chapter 1, note 69.

90. On the iconography of Marianne in the First Republic of France, see de Baecque, *The Body Politic*, 320–23.

Epilogue: The Revolution Eats Its Children

1. Pierre Vergniaud, "Discours à la Convention nationale," printed in *Le Moniteur universel* 75, March 16, 1793, 702. I am grateful to Ib Johansen for helping me to locate this speech, much referenced but often erroneously attributed to Danton.

2. See Hénaff, *Sade*, on Hegel's presentation of "the figure of Chronos, where instants are negated for the benefit of a transcendent, totalizing time" (123).

3. For a more general (Hegelian) articulation of the relationship between the particular and the general, see Žižek, *For they know not what they do*, chapter 1, "On the One," 7–60.

4. Marx, *The Eighteenth Brumaire*, 15.

5. For an overview of antitotalitarian critiques of "politically correct" language, see Werner Sollors, "The Multiculturalism Debate," in Wendy F. Katkin, Ned Landsman, and Andrea Tyree, eds., *Beyond Pluralism: The Conception of Groups and Group Identities* (Urbana: University of Illinois Press, 1998), 83–84.

6. A fact not often remarked upon by deconstruction's critics is that de Man himself rigorously labored to undo the apparent antinomy between history and literature, between referential truth and figural language. See above all the essays in his collections, *The Resistance to Theory*, foreword by Wlad Godzich (Minneapolis: University of Minnesota Press, 1986), and *Aesthetic Ideology*, ed. Andrzej Warminski (Minneapolis: University of Minnesota Press, 1996). See also Ernesto Laclau, "The Politics of Rhetoric," in Tom Cohen, Barbara Cohen, J. Hillis Miller, and Andrzej Warminski, eds., *Material Events: Paul de Man and the Afterlife of Theory* (Minneapolis: University of Minnesota Press, 2001), 229–53. In *For they know not what they do*, Slavoj Žižek lucidly summarizes the issue when he asserts that "deconstructive" efforts like de Man's do not, as is commonly charged, merely lump history and rhetoric into one amorphous *il n'y a pas de hors-texte* mess, but rather work to demonstrate that "the establishment of truth as something which is prior to and independent of 'secondary' rhetorical effects and figures is [itself] *founded upon a radical rhetorical gesture*" (33–34; Žižek's emphasis).

7. In a related vein, see Tom Cohen, *Ideology and Inscription: "Cultural Studies" after Benjamin, de Man, and Bakhtin* (Cambridge: Cambridge University Press, 1998).

8. See Ernesto Laclau and Chantal Mouffe, *Hegemony and Socialist Strategy: Toward a Radical Democratic Politics* (London: Verso, 1985). This work in its entirety is compelling for its suggestion that "society does not exist"—that social and political interactions are necessarily shot through with antagonisms between and among incompatible subjective perspectives. In making this argument, Laclau and Mouffe cite the similar findings of Claude Lefort in *L'Invention démocratique* (1981; Paris: Fayard, 1994), which asserts the structural inability of an ideology of "unity . . . to erase social division" (172).

9. See Laclau and Mouffe, *Hegemony and Socialist Strategy:* "Every attempt to establish a definitive suture [i.e., an eradication of intersubjective differences] and to deny the radically open character of the social . . . leads to what Lefort designates as 'totalitarianism,' that is to say, to a logic of construction of the political which consists of establishing a point of departure from which society can be perfectly mastered and known . . . , [of] attempt[ing] to reimpose an absolute center and to re-establish the closure that will restore 'unity'" (187–88).

10. In *Hegemony and Socialist Strategy,* Laclau and Mouffe call for "a form of politics which is founded not upon dogmatic postulation of any 'essence of the social,' but, on the contrary, on [an] affirmation of the contingency and ambiguity of every 'essence,' and on the constitutive character of antagonism" (193); this political model would be "an 'order' which exists only as a partial limiting of disorder" (193). Similarly, for his part Lefort imagines "the experience of a society that cannot be seized, that cannot be mastered, in which the people will be sovereign, of course, but will not cease to call its own identity into question—in which identity itself will remain latent. I repeat: the experience of a society that cannot be seized, [which] elicits a discourse of multiplicity" (*L'Invention démocratique,* 173).

Selected Bibliography

Principal Primary Sources

Desmoulins, Camille. *Oeuvres*. Ed. Albert Soboul. 10 vols. Munich: Kraus Reprint, 1980.

————. *La Tribune des patriotes*. Paris: Société littéraire typographique, n.d.

————. *Le Vieux Cordelier*. Ed. Pierre Pachet. Paris: Belin, 1987.

Robespierre, Maximilien. *Correspondance de Maximilien et Augustin Robespierre*. Ed. Georges Michon. Paris: Félix Alcan, 1926.

————. *Discours au peuple réuni pour la fête de l'Être suprême*. Pamphlet no. 355. Paris: Imprimerie de la Commission d'instruction publique, 1794.

————. *Écrits*. Ed. Claude Mazauric. Paris: Messidor/Éditions sociales, 1989.

————. *Oeuvres de Maximilien Robespierre*. 2 vols. Ed. Laponneraye. Paris, 1840.

————. *Oeuvres de Maximilien Robespierre*. Ed. Marc Bouloiseau, Georges Lefebvre, and Albert Soboul. Paris: Presses Universitaires de France, 1950.

————. *Papiers inédits trouvés chez Robespierre, Saint-Just, Payan, . . . , supprimés ou omis par Courtois*. 3 vols. Paris: Baudoin Frères, 1828.

Rousseau, Jean-Jacques. *The Basic Political Writings*. Ed. and trans. Donald A. Cress. Indianapolis: Hackett Publishing, 1987.

————. *A Discourse on Inequality*. Trans. Maurice Cranston. London: Penguin, 1984.

————. *An Essay on the Origin of Languages*. Trans. John H. Moran. Chicago: University of Chicago Press, 1966.

————. *Lettre à d'Alembert*. Paris: Garnier-Flammarion, 1967.

————. *Oeuvres complètes*. Ed. Bernard Gagnebin and Marcel Raymond. 5 vols. Paris: Gallimard/Bibliothèque la Pléïade, 1964–1995.

————. *The Social Contract*. Trans. Maurice Cranston. London: Penguin, 1968.

Sade, Donatien-Alphonse-François, Marquis de. *Correspondance*. Ed. Alice M. Laborde. 27 vols. Geneva: Slatkine, 1995–1996.

————. *Juliette*. Trans. Austryn Wainhouse. New York: Grove Press, 1968.

————. *Justine, Philosophy in the Bedroom, and Other Writings.* Trans. Richard Seaver and Austryn Wainhouse. New York: Grove Press, 1965.

————. *Oeuvres complètes.* Ed. Annie Le Brun and Jean-Jacques Pauvert. 15 vols. Paris: Pauvert, 1986–1987.

————. *Sade contre l'Être suprême.* Ed. Philippe Sollers. Paris: Gallimard, 1996.

Saint-Just, Louis-Antoine. *Discours et rapports.* Ed. Albert Soboul. Paris: Messidor/ Éditions sociales, 1988.

————. *Oeuvres complètes.* Ed. Michèle Duval. Paris: Gérard Lebovici, 1984.

Critical Works and Other Sources

Agamben, Giorgio. *The Coming Community.* Trans. Michael Hardt. Minneapolis: University of Minnesota Press, 1993.

Althusser, Louis. "Sur le *Contrat social* (les décalages)." *Cahiers pour l'analyse* 8: *L'Impensé de Jean-Jacques Rousseau* (1970): 5–42.

André, Jacques. *La Révolution fratricide: Un Essai psychanalytique sur le lien social.* Paris: Presses Universitaires de France, 1993.

Arendt, Hannah. *On Revolution.* 1963. London: Penguin, 1990.

Ariès, Philippe, and Georges Duby, eds. *Histoire de vie privée.* 4 vols. Paris: Seuil, 1985.

Aulard, F.-A. *Le Culte de la Raison et le Culte de l'Être suprême.* Paris: Félix Alcan, 1892.

Baczko, Bronislaw. "The Terror before the Terror?" In Keith M. Baker, F. François Furet, and Colin Lucas, eds., *The French Revolution and the Creation of Modern Political Culture,* vol. 4, *The Terror,* 19–38. London: Pergamon Press, 1987.

Badiou, Alain. "Qu'est-ce qu'un Thermidorien?" In Catherine Kintzler and Hadi Rizk, eds., *La République et la Terreur,* 53–64. Paris: Éditions Kimé, 1995.

Baecque, Antoine de. *The Body Politic: Corporeal Metaphor in Revolutionary France 1770–1800.* Trans. Charlotte Mandell. Stanford: Stanford University Press, 1993.

————. *Glory and Terror: Seven Deaths under the Reign of Terror.* Trans. Charlotte Mandell. New York: Routledge, 2001.

Baker, Keith Michael. "On the Problem of the Ideological Origins of the French Revolution." In Dominick LaCapra and Steven Kaplan, eds., *Modern European Intellectual History,* 197–219. Ithaca: Cornell University Press, 1982.

————. "Representation." In Keith M. Baker, François Furet, and Colin Lucas, eds., *The French Revolution and the Creation of Modern Political Culture,* vol. 1, *The Political Culture of the Old Regime,* 469–92. London: Pergamon Press, 1987.

Baker, Keith Michael, François Furet, and Colin Lucas, eds. *The French Revolution and the Creation of Modern Political Culture,* 4 vols. London: Pergamon Press, 1987.

Barry, Étienne. *Essai sur la dénonciation politique in Discours prononcés les jours de décadi dans la section Guillaume Tell.* Paris: n.p., 1793.

Barthes, Roland. "Literature and Signification: Answers to a Questionnaire in *Tel Quel.*" In *Critical Essays,* trans. Richard Howard, 261–79. Evanston: Northwestern University Press, 1972.

Benveniste, Émile. *Problems in General Linguistics.* Trans. Mary Meek. Coral Gables: University of Miami Press, 1971.

Bertaud, Jean-Paul. "An Open File: The Press under the Terror." In Keith M. Baker, François Furet, and Colin Lucas, eds. *The French Revolution and the Creation of Modern Political Culture*, vol. 4, *The Terror*, 297–308. London: Pergamon Press, 1987.

Bianchi, Serge. *La Révolution culturelle de l'An II*. Paris: Aubier Montaigne, 1982.

Biver, Marie-Louise. *Fêtes révolutionnaires à Paris*. Paris: Presses Universitaires de France, 1979.

Blanc, Louis. *Histoire de la Révolution française*. Paris: Pagnerre, Furne et Cie., 1864.

Blanchard, Marc-Éli. "The French Revolution: A Political Line or a Language Circle." *Yale French Studies* 39: *Literature and Revolution*, ed. Jacques Ehrmann (1967): 64–78.

———. *Saint-Just et Cie: La Révolution et les mots*. Paris: A.-G. Nizet, 1980.

Blanchot, Maurice. "Everyday Speech." In *The Infinite Conversation*, 238–45. Trans. Susan Hanson. Minneapolis: University of Minnesota Press, 1993.

———. "Literature and the Right to Death." In *The Work of Fire*, 300–344. Trans. Charlotte Mandell. Stanford: Stanford University Press, 1995.

———."The Main Impropriety." *Yale French Studies* 39: *Literature and Revolution*, ed. Jacques Ehrmann (1967): 50–63.

Blum, Carol. *Rousseau and the Republic of Virtue: The Language of Politics in the French Revolution*. Ithaca: Cornell University Press, 1986.

Brooks, Peter. "Opening the Depths." In Sandy Petrey, ed., *The French Revolution 1789–1989: Two Hundred Years of Rethinking*, 113–42. Lubbock: Texas Tech University Press, 1989.

Camus, Albert. *The Rebel: An Essay on Man in Revolt*. Trans. Anthony Bower. New York: Vintage Books/Random House, 1956.

Carlyle, Thomas. *The French Revolution*. 2 vols. New York: A. L. Burt Co., n.d.

Carter, Angela. *The Sadeian Woman*. New York: Pantheon, 1978.

Certeau, Michel de, Dominique Julia, and Jacques Revel, eds. *Une Politique de la langue: La Révolution française et les patois*. Paris: Gallimard, 1975.

Chambers, Ross. *Room for Maneuver: Reading (the) Oppositional (in) Narrative*. Chicago: University of Chicago Press, 1991.

Clark, T. J. *Farewell to an Idea: Episodes from a History of Modernism*. New Haven: Yale University Press, 1999.

Cochin, Auguste. *Les Sociétés de Pensée et la Démocratie: Études d'histoire révolutionnaire*. 1921; Paris: Éditions Copernic, 1978.

Cohen, Tom, Barbara Cohen, J. Hillis Miller, and Andrzej Warminski, eds. *Material Events: Paul de Man and the Afterlife of Theory*. Minneapolis: University of Minnesota Press, 2001.

Crow, Thomas. *Painters and Public Life in Eighteenth-Century Paris*. New Haven: Yale University Press, 1987.

Darnton, Robert. *The Forbidden Best-Sellers of Pre-Revolutionary France*. New York: W. W. Norton, 1996.

David, Jacques-Louis. "Plan de la Fête à l'Être suprême." Paris: Imprimerie nationale, 1794.

d'Églantine, Fabre. *Oeuvres politiques*. Ed. Charles Vellay. Paris: Fasquelle, 1914.

Deleuze, Gilles. *Coldness and Cruelty*. New York: Zone Books, 1991.

Deleuze, Gilles, and Félix Guattari. *Kafka: Toward a Minor Literature*. Minneapolis: University of Minnesota Press, 1986.

de Man, Paul. *Aesthetic Ideology*. Ed. Andrzej Warminski. Minneapolis: University of Minnesota Press, 1996.

————. *Allegories of Reading: Figural Language in Rousseau, Nietzsche, Rilke and Proust.* New Haven: Yale University Press, 1979.

————. *Blindness and Insight.* Minneapolis: University of Minnesota Press, 1983.

————. *The Resistance to Theory.* Foreword by Wlad Godzich. Minneapolis: University of Minnesota Press, 1986.

Derrida, Jacques. "Differance." In *Margins of Philosophy,* 1–28. Trans. Alan Bass. Chicago: University of Chicago Press, 1982.

————. *Dissemination.* Trans. Barbara Johnson. Chicago: University of Chicago Press, 1981.

————. *Of Grammatology.* Trans. Gayatri Spivak. Baltimore: Johns Hopkins University Press, 1974.

Didier, Béatrice. *Écrire la Révolution, 1789–1799.* Paris: Presses Universitaires de France, 1989.

Duhet, Marie, ed. *Cahiers de doléances des femmes en 1789 et autres textes.* Paris: des femmes, 1981.

du Plessix Gray, Francine. *At Home with the Marquis de Sade.* New York: Simon and Schuster, 1998.

Ehrmann, Jacques, ed. *Yale French Studies* 39: *Literature and Revolution* (1967).

Escoubas, Éliane. "Kant or the Simplicity of the Sublime." In Jeffrey Librett, ed. and trans., *Of the Sublime: Presence in Question,* 55–70. Albany: State University of New York Press, 1993.

Farge, Arlette. *Le Désordre des familles: Lettres de cachet des Archives de la Bastille.* Intro. Michel Foucault. Paris: Gallimard/Julliard, 1982.

Foucault, Michel. *The History of Sexuality: An Introduction,* vol. 1. Trans. Robert Hurley. 1978; New York: Vintage Books/Random House, 1990.

————. *The Order of Things: An Archaeology of the Human Sciences; A Translation of "Les Mots et les choses."* New York: Random House/Vintage Books, 1973.

Frappier-Mazur, Lucienne. *Writing the Orgy: Power and Parody in Sade.* Trans. Gillian C. Gill. Philadelphia: University of Pennsylvania Press, 1996.

Freud, Sigmund. *Beyond the Pleasure Principle.* Trans. and ed. James Strachey. New York: W. W. Norton, 1961.

————. *Civilization and its Discontents.* Trans. and ed. James Strachey. New York: W. W. Norton, 1961.

————. *Jokes and Their Relation to the Unconscious.* Trans. and ed. James Strachey. New York: W. W. Norton, 1960.

————. "Medusa's Head." In *Sexuality and the Psychology of Love,* 202–3. Ed. Philip Rieff. 1963; New York: Touchstone/Simon and Schuster, 1997.

————. *New Introductory Lectures on Psychoanalysis.* Trans. and ed. James Strachey. New York: W. W. Norton, 1933.

Furet, François. *Interpreting the French Revolution.* Trans. Elborg Foster. Cambridge: Cambridge University Press, 1981.

————. *Revolutionary France 1770–1880.* Trans. Antonia Nevill. Oxford: Blackwell, 1992.

Genette, Gérard. *Figures III.* Paris: Seuil, 1972.

Godechot, Jacques. *La Révolution française.* Paris: Perrin, 1988.

Gouges, Olympe de. *Écrits politiques.* Ed. Olivier Blanc. 2 vols. Paris: Côté-Femmes, 1993.

Goulet, Jacques. *Robespierre, la peine de mort et la Terreur.* Paris: Castor Astral, 1983.

Goux, Jean-Joseph. *Les Iconoclastes*. Paris: Seuil, 1978.

Guilhaumou, Jacques. "Fragments of a Discourse of Denunciation (1789–1794)." In Keith M. Baker, François Furet, and Colin Lucas, eds., *The French Revolution and the Creation of Modern Political Culture*, vol. 4, *The Terror*, 139–56. London: Pergamon Press, 1987.

Habermas, Jürgen. *Communication and the Evolution of Society*. Trans. Thomas McCarthy. Boston: Beacon Hill Press, 1979.

Harari, Josué V. *Scenarios of the Imaginary: Theorizing the French Enlightenment*. Ithaca: Cornell University Press, 1987.

Hardman, John. *Robespierre*. London: Longman, 1999.

Hegel, Georg W. F. *Phenomenology of Spirit*. Trans. A. V. Miller. Oxford: Oxford University Press, 1977.

Heidegger, Martin. *Being and Time: A Translation of "Sein und Zeit."* Trans. Joan Stambaugh. Albany: State University of New York Press, 1996.

Hénaff, Marcel. *Sade: The Invention of the Libertine Body*. Trans. Xavier Callahan. Minneapolis: University of Minnesota Press, 1999.

Hertz, Neil. "Medusa's Head: Male Hysteria under Political Pressure." In *The End of the Line: Essays on Psychoanalysis and the Sublime*, 161–93. New York: Columbia University Press, 1985.

Hesse, Carla. "The Law of the Terror." *MLN*, ed. Wilda Anderson, 114, no. 4 (September 1999): 702–18.

Hoffmann, Paul. *Théories et modèles de la liberté au XVIIIe siècle*. Paris: Presses Universitaires de France, 1996.

Horkheimer, Max, and Theodor W. Adorno. *Dialectic of Enlightenment*. Trans. John Cumming. 1944; New York: Continuum, 1989.

Huet, Marie-Hélène. *Mourning Glory: The Will of the French Revolution*. Philadelphia: University of Pennsylvania Press, 1997.

Hunt, Lynn. *The Family Romance of the French Revolution*. Berkeley: University of California Press, 1992.

———. "Male Virtue and Republican Motherhood." In Keith M. Baker, François Furet, and Colin Lucas, eds., *The French Revolution and the Creation of Modern Political Culture*, vol. 4, *The Terror*, 195–208. London: Pergamon Press, 1987.

———. *Politics, Culture, and Class in the French Revolution*. Berkeley: University of California Press, 1984.

———. "Révolution française et vie privée." In Philippe Ariès and Georges Duby, eds., *Histoire de vie privée*, vol. 4, *De la Révolution à la Grande Terreur*, 21–51. Paris: Seuil, 1985.

Hutcheon, Linda. *Irony's Edge: The Theory and Politics of Irony*. New York: Routledge, 1994.

Jakobson, Roman. *Fundamentals of Language*. Paris: Mouton, 1971.

Janssens, Jacques. *Camille Desmoulins: Le Premier Républicain de France*. Paris: Perrin, 1973.

Jauss, Hans Robert. *Question and Answer: Forms of Dialogic Understanding*. Trans. Michael Hayes. Minneapolis: University of Minnesota Press, 1989.

Jenny, Laurent. *La Terreur et les signes: Poétiques de rupture*. Paris: Gallimard, 1982.

Kant, Immanuel. *The Critique of Judgment*. Trans. James Creed Meredith. Oxford: Clarendon Press, 1991.

———. *Grounding for the Metaphysics of Morals*. Trans. James W. Ellington. 1928; Indianapolis: Hackett, 1991.

Kavanagh, Thomas. *Writing the Truth: Authority and Desire in Rousseau*. Berkeley: University of California Press, 1987.

Kelly, Christopher. "Taking Readers as They Are: Rousseau's Turn from Discourses to Novels." *Eighteenth Century Studies* 33, no. 1 (1999): 85–102.

Kintzler, Catherine, and Hadi Rizk, eds. *La République et la Terreur*. Paris: Éditions Kimé, 1995.

Klossowski, Pierre. *Sade My Neighbor*. Trans. Alphonso Lingis. Evanston: Northwestern University Press, 1991.

Kristeva, Julia. *Strangers to Ourselves*. New York: Columbia University Press, 1991.

Lacan, Jacques. *Écrits*. 2 vols. Paris: Seuil, 1966 and 1971.

———. *Le Séminaire III: Les Psychoses*. Ed. Jacques-Alain Miller. Paris: Seuil, 1981.

———. *Le Séminaire XI: Les Quatre Concepts fondamentaux de la psychanalyse*. Ed. Jacques-Alain Miller. Paris: Seuil, 1973.

———. *Le Séminaire XX: Encore*. Ed. Jacques-Alain Miller. Paris: Seuil, 1975.

———. *Télévision*. Paris: Seuil, 1974.

LaCapra, Dominick, and Steven L. Kaplan, eds. *Modern European Intellectual History*. Ithaca: Cornell University Press, 1982.

Laclau, Ernesto. "The Politics of Rhetoric." In Tom Cohen et al., eds., *Material Events: Paul de Man and the Afterlife of Theory*, 229–53. Minneapolis: University of Minnesota Press, 2001.

Laclau, Ernesto, and Chantal Mouffe. *Hegemony and Socialist Strategy: Toward a Radical Democratic Politics*. London: Verso, 1985.

Lacoue-Labarthe, Philippe. "Sublime Truth." In Jeffrey Librett, ed. and trans., *Of the Sublime: Presence in Question*, 71–108. Albany: State University of New York Press, 1993.

Laflandre-Linden, Louise. *1789–1793 Les Femmes*. Paris: SPM, 1994.

La Fontaine, Jean de. *Les Fables*. Paris: Imprimerie nationale, 1985.

Laharpe, François de. *Du fanatisme dans la langue révolutionnaire*. Paris: Marchand de nouveautés, 1797.

Lamartine, Alphonse de. *Histoire des Girondins*. New York: F. Gaillardet, 1847.

Landes, Joan B. *Women and the Public Sphere in the Age of the French Revolution*. Ithaca: Cornell University Press, 1988.

Le Brun, Annie. *Sade: A Sudden Abyss*. Trans. Camille Naish. San Francisco: City Lights Books, 1990.

Lefort, Claude. *L'Invention démocratique*. 1981; Paris: Fayard, 1994.

———. "Sade: The Boudoir and the City." In *Writing: The Political Test*, 67–84. Trans. David Ames Curtis. Durham: Duke University Press, 2000.

Lely, Gilbert. *Vie du Marquis de Sade*. Paris: Pauvert/Garnier Frères, 1982.

Lever, Maurice. *Sade: A Biography*. Trans. Arthur Goldhammer. New York: Farrar, Straus and Giroux, 1993.

Librett, Jeffrey S., ed. and trans. *Of the Sublime: Presence in Question*. Albany: State University of New York Press, 1993.

Locke, John. *Second Treatise of Government*. Ed. Thomas P. Peardon. 1952; New York: Macmillan, 1987.

Longinus. *Of the Sublime*. In *Classical Literary Criticism*. London: Penguin, 1965.

Loomis, Stanley. *Paris in the Terror: June 1793–July 1794.* Philadelphia: Lippincott, 1964.

Lucas, Colin. "Revolutionary Violence, the People and the Terror." In Keith M. Baker, François Furet, and Colin Lucas, eds., *The French Revolution and the Creation of Modern Political Culture,* vol. 4, *The Terror,* 57–80. London: Pergamon Press, 1987.

Lukács, Georg. *The Theory of the Novel.* Trans. Anna Bostock. 1971; Cambridge, Mass.: MIT Press, 1987.

Lyotard, Jean-François. *The Differend: Phrases in Dispute.* Trans. Georges van den Abbeele. Minneapolis: University of Minnesota Press, 1988.

McDonald, Christie. *The Dialogue of Writing: Essays in Eighteenth-Century French Literature.* Waterloo, Ontario: Wilfrid Laurier University Press, 1984.

———. "Words of Change." In Sandy Petrey, ed., *The French Revolution 1789–1989: Two Hundred Years of Rethinking,* 33–46. Lubbock: Texas Tech University Press, 1989.

Machiavelli, Niccolò. *The Prince.* Ed. Christian Gauss and trans. Luigi Ricci. New York: Oxford University Press/Mentor Books, 1952.

Mallarmé, Stéphane. *Oeuvres complètes.* Ed. Henri Mondor and G. Jean Aubry. Paris: Gallimard/Bibliothèque de la Pléiade, 1945 (Published in translation as *Selected Prose Poems, Essays, and Letters.* Trans. Bradford Cook. Baltimore: Johns Hopkins University Press, 1956).

Mantel, Hilary. *A Place of Greater Safety.* New York: Henry Holt, 1992.

Marin, Louis. "On the Sublime, Infinity, *Je ne sais quoi.*" In Denis Hollier, ed., *A New History of French Literature,* 340–45. Cambridge, Mass.: Harvard University Press, 1989.

Marso, Lori Jo. *(Un)Manly Citizens: Jean-Jacques Rousseau's and Germaine de Staël's Subversive Women.* Baltimore: Johns Hopkins University Press, 1999.

Marx, Karl. *The Eighteenth Brumaire of Louis Bonaparte.* 1963; New York: International Publishers, 1991.

Melzer, Sara, and Leslie Rabine, eds. *Rebel Daughters.* Oxford: Oxford University Press, 1992.

Michelet, Jules. *Histoire de la Révolution française.* Ed. Gérard Walter. Paris: Gallimard/Bibliothèque de la Pléiade, 1964 (Published in translation as *History of the French Revolution.* Trans. Keith Botsford. Wynnewood: Kolokol Press, 1973).

Miller, Jacques-Alain. "Context and Concepts." In Richard Feldstein, Bruce Fink, and Maire Jaanus, eds., *Reading Seminar XI: Lacan's Four Fundamental Concepts of Psychoanalysis,* 3–18. Albany: State University of New York Press, 1995.

Nietzsche, Friedrich. *The Birth of Tragedy and the Genealogy of Morals.* Trans. Francis Golffing. New York: Doubleday/Anchor, 1956.

———. "On Truth and Lie in an Extra-Moral Sense." In *The Portable Nietzsche,* 42–47. Ed. and trans. Walter Kaufmann. 1954; London: Penguin, 1976.

Orr, Linda. *Headless History: Nineteenth-Century French Historiography of the Revolution.* Ithaca: Cornell University Press, 1990.

Ozouf, Mona. *Festivals and the French Revolution.* Trans. Alan Sheridan. Cambridge, Mass.: Harvard University Press, 1988.

Pateman, Carole. *The Sexual Contract.* Stanford: Stanford University Press, 1988.

Perry, Ruth. "A Short History of the Term *Politically Correct.*" In Patricia Aufderheide, ed., *Beyond P.C.: Toward a Politics of Understanding,* 71–79. Saint Paul, Minn.: Graywolf, 1992.

Petrey, Sandy, ed. *The French Revolution 1789–1989: Two Hundred Years of Rethinking*. Lubbock: Texas Tech University Press, 1989.

Quinet, Edgar. *La Révolution*. Paris: Belin, 1987.

Roger, Philippe. *Sade: La Philosophie dans le pressoir*. Paris: Bernard Grasset, 1976.

Saint-Amand, Pierre. *The Laws of Hostility: Politics, Violence, and the Enlightenment*. Trans. Jennifer Curtiss Gage. Minneapolis: University of Minnesota Press, 1996.

———. *The Libertine's Progress: Seduction in the Eighteenth-Century French Novel*. Trans. Jennifer Curtiss Gage. Providence: Brown University Press, 1994.

Schama, Simon, *Citizens: A Chronice of the French Revolution*. New York: Vintage Books/Random House, 1989.

Serres, Michel. *Le Parasite*. Paris: Grasset, 1980.

Sfez, Gérald. "Les Langues de la terreur." In Catherine Kintzler and Hadi Rizk, eds., *La République et la Terreur*, 129–59. Paris: Éditions Kimé, 1995.

Soler, Colette. "The Curse on Sex." In Renata Salecl, ed., *Sexuation: sic 3*, 39–53. Durham: Duke University Press, 2000.

Sollers, Philippe. *Sade dans le temps*. In D.-A.-F. de Sade, *Sade contre l'Être suprême*. Ed. Philippe Sollers. Paris: Gallimard, 1996.

———. *Sade dans le texte: L'Écriture et l'expérience des limites*. Paris: Seuil, 1968.

Sollors, Werner. "The Multiculturalism Debate." In Wendy Katkin, Ned Landsman, and Andrea Tyree, eds., *Beyond Pluralism: The Conception of Groups and Group Identities*, 63–104. Urbana: University of Illinois Press, 1998.

Staël, Germaine de. *Considérations sur la Révolution française*. 3 vols. Paris: Delaunay, Bossange et Masson, 1818.

Starobinski, Jean. *1789: Les Emblèmes de la raison*. Paris: Flammarion, 1973.

———. *Le Remède dans le mal*. Paris: Gallimard, 1989.

———. *Transparency and Obstruction*. Trans. Arthur Goldhammer. Chicago: University of Chicago Press, 1988.

Strauss, Jonathan. *Subjects of Terror: Hegel, Nerval, and the Modern Self*. Stanford: Stanford University Press, 1998.

Swenson, James. *On Jean-Jacques Rousseau Considered as one of the First Authors of the French Revolution*. Stanford: Stanford University Press, 2000.

Thomas, Chantal. "La Foutromanie révolutionnaire." In *Oeuvres anonymes du XVIIIᵉ siècle, L'Enfer de la Bibliothèque nationale*, tome 4, 267–80. Paris: Fayard, 1987.

———. *The Wicked Queen: The Origins of the Myth of Marie Antoinette*. New York: Zone Books, 1999.

Thompson, J. M. *Robespierre*. Oxford, 1939.

Tocqueville, Alexis de. *The Old Regime and the French Revolution*. Trans. Stuart Gilbert. Garden City: Doubleday, 1955.

Velkley, Richard L. *Freedom and the End of Reason: On the Moral Foundation of Kant's Critical Philosophy*. Chicago: University of Chicago Press, 1989.

Voltaire. *Mélanges*. Ed. Jacques van den Heuvel. Paris: Gallimard, 1962.

Walter, Gérard. *Hébert et le Père Duchesne*. Paris: Janin, 1946.

Walzer, Michael, ed. *Regicide and Revolution: Speeches at the Trial of Louis XVI*. Trans. Marian Rothstein. New York: Columbia University Press, 1992.

Weber, Caroline. "Freedom's Missed Moment." *Yale French Studies 101: Fragments of Revolution*, ed. Caroline Weber and Howard G. Lay (Spring 2002).

————. "Madame de Mistival's Differend: Animality and Alterity in Sade's *Philosophie dans le boudoir.*" *Utah Foreign Language Review* (1997): 49–61.

————. "The Sexist Sublime in Sade and Lyotard." In *Philosophy and Literature.* Forthcoming.

Žižek, Slavoj. *Did Somebody Say Totalitarianism? Five Interpretations in the (Mis)Use of a Nation.* London: Verso, 2001.

————. *Enjoy Your Symptom!* New York: Routledge, 1992.

————. *For they know not what they do.* London: Verso, 1991.

————. *The Sublime Object of Ideology.* London: Verso, 1989.

————. *Tarrying with the Negative.* Durham: Duke University Press, 1993.

————. *The Žižek Reader.* Ed. Elizabeth Wright and Edmond Wright. London: Blackwell, 1999.

Index

Caroline Weber is assistant professor of Romance languages at the University of Pennsylvania. She has published articles on eighteenth-century French fiction, drama, and political theory. She is coeditor, with Howard G. Lay, of *Fragments of Revolution,* a special issue of *Yale French Studies.*